words of encouragement
Patricia

The White Umbrella

Patricia Elliott

Funding assistance
received from
the Canada Council and
the Saskatchewan Arts Board

The White Umbrella
Published by Post Books
The Post Publishing Public Company Limited
136 Na Rangong Rd., Klong Toey
Bangkok 10110, Thailand
Tel: (662) 240-3700 ext. 1691-2
Fax : (662) 671-9698
postbooks@bangkokpost.co.th
www.bangkokpost.net/postbooks

Text © 1999 Patricia Elliott
Maps © 1999 The Post Publishing Public Company Limited

Cover design by Watchara Ritmahan
Maps by Sataporn Kawewong

First published in Thailand in November 1999
Printed in Thailand by Allied Printers
The Post Publishing Public Company Limited

Set in: Avant Garde, Macha and Helvetica

National Library of Thailand Cataloging-in-Publication Data
Elliott, Patricia.
The White Umbrella. — Bangkok: Post Books, 1999.
404 p. 1. Shan (Asian people). — Burma. 2 Burma — History.
I. Title. 959.1
ISBN:974-202-046-9

All rights reserved. No part of this book
may be reproduced or transmitted in any form
or by any means, electronic or mechanical,
including photographing, recording or
by any information storage or
retrieval system without written permission from the publisher,
except for the inclusion of brief quotations in a review.

To Shan people everywhere

and

Don and Ringo J., too

Table of Contents

6
Map of Burma
People... Pronunciation Guide...
Chronology of Major Events... Acknowledgements...
Prologue by Bertil Lintner...

One
22
Map of Northern Shan States... Illustrations...
A Bride's Journey... Conquest...
The Palace... The Prince's Last Child...
The Three Sisters... Change... The Contract...
Sold... A New Life...
Mahadevi...

Two
102
Map of Southern Shan States... Illustrations...
The Crater in the Paddy Field...
The Invasion... The Lake... The New Masters...
The Undesired Pawn... The Emperor's Birthday Present...
No More Jaggery... Aftermath...
Farewell Shan State...

Three
174
Map of Rangoon... Illustrations...
Evil Beginnings... The President-Elect...

"We Are Free"... First Lady...
Mortars and Leeches... The Painted Train...
A Prayer for Deliverance...
Great Expectations... Back to Golden Valley...
The Cocoon...

Four
254
Route of Sao's Escape... Illustrations...
Member of Parliament... An Invitation... Two Emperors...
The Big Split... "Let Us Wash Our City with Our Sweat"...
The Caretaker... Welcome to the Underground...
Season of Rain... Night of Guns... Home...
The Funeral... The Warning...
The Flight...

Five
340
Map of the Golden Triangle... Illustrations...
The Shan State Army... Survival of the Fittest...
Voices in the Wilderness... The Last Adventure...
Bitter Melon...

378
Epilogue...
Author's Notes...
List of Sources...

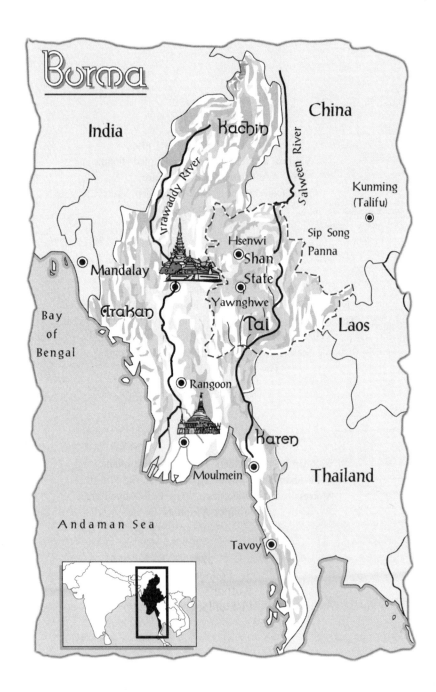

People

Hsenwi Palace
    Sao Hearn Hkam (Sao)   Princess of Hsenwi
    Khunsang Ton-huung   Sao's father
    Nang Hkam Zeng   Sao's mother
    Prince Hom Hpa   Heir to the throne
    Royal Mother   Prince Hom Hpa's mother
    Mary Josephine   Sao's classmate/relative
    Louise   "
    Princess Van Thip   "
    Saw Ohn   Sao's nephew

Yawnghwe Palace
    Prince Shwe Thaike   Sao's husband
    Tiger   Sao's son
    Tzang   "
    Tzang-On   "
    Ying Sita   Sao's daughter
    Myee   Sao's son
    Harn   "
    Leun   Sao's daughter
    Htilar   Sao's adopted daughter
    Daw Nyunt May   Eldest co-wife
    Daw Mya Win   Youngest co-wife
    Hseng   Co-wife's son
    Haymar   Co-wife's daughter
    Stanley   Co-wife's son
    Prince Sai   Heir to the throne
    Pat   The Heir's wife
    Hseng-Phu   Yawnghwe Chief Minister
    Ko Latt   "

The politicians
Aung San	"Father of Independence"
U Nu	Post-war prime minister
Ne Win	Burma Army commander
Ba Maw	Pre-war prime minister/head of state during Japanese occupation
U Saw	Pre-war prime minister/assassin

Colonial and occupation governments
Major Yates	Participant in British conquest
Lt. Daly	"
Superintendent Hildebrand	"
Chief Commissioner Croswaite	"
Reginald Dorman-Smith	Pre-war governor
Hubert Rance	Post-war governor
Mutaguchi Renya	Japanese 15th Army commander after March 1943
Lord Louis Mountbatten	Allied Southeast Asia commander/Viceroy of India
Philip Fogarty	Shan State Resident

Insurgents and warlords
Chang Shi-fu, alias Khun Sa	Kokang rebel with ties to the opium trade
Khun Kya Nu	An SSIA/SSA leader
Lo Hsin Han	Kokang Home Guard captain
Li Mi	An early leader of the Chinese rebel soldiers in exile (Kuomintang—KMT)
Li Wen Huan (Old Li)	A later KMT leader
Captain Naw Seng	Kachin leader, later with Communist Party of Burma
Olive Yang	Kokang leader
Jimmy Yang	"

Pronunciation guide

Aung San	ong sawn
Aung San Suu Kyi	ong sawn soo chee
Hearn Hkam	huh'rn kam
Hsenwi	sen-wee
Kengtung	cheng-toong
kyat	ch'yat
Maymyo	may-myoh
Myosa	m'yoh za
Ne Win	ney win
Sao	sow
Saopha	sow-pah
Shwe Thaike	shwey tike
Tai	dtie
Taunggyi	tong-ji
Thai	tie (an aspirated *t*, as in *Tom*)
Tzang	t'sawhng
U Nu	oo noo
Yawnghwe	yawng-hway

A note about names

Tai names are usually preceded by an honorific of some kind: for example, "sai" for a young man, "nang" for a young lady, "sao" for a prince or princess. Sao is often followed by a further designation, such as "Sao-nang" (young princess) or "Sao-mae" (princess-mother). The Burmese honorifics "U", for uncle, and "daw", for older woman, are also used. For clarity's sake, I have restricted use of the simple appellation "sao" to the main character and used equivalent English language titles for others. Some names and identities of people living in Burma today have been changed.

Patricia Elliott

Chronology of Major Events

1885	Britain overthrows the King of Mandalay. Burma claimed as a province of British Indian Empire.
1887	The princes of the Shan Plateau submit to British rule.
1915	Sao Hearn Hkam, a princess of the Shan State of Hsenwi, is born.
1930	Rebellion against British rule in Burma, led by Saya San.
1931	Saya San captured and executed for treason. Growth of nationalist movement in Burma. The Shan princes travel to London for talks about potential Burmese independence.
1937	Sao is given in marriage to Prince Shwe Thaike of Yawnghwe.
1938	Sao recognised as Mahadevi—or Chief Queen—of Yawnghwe.
1942	Japan conquers Burma. Japanese forces occupy Yawnghwe Palace.
1945	Japan withdraws. Britain returns to negotiate independence.
1947	The Panglong Agreement—the foundation of the Union of Burma—is signed. Burmese leader Aung San is assassinated.
1948	Burmese independence. Sao's husband becomes President of Burma. Mutiny by Karen separatists and communist hard-liners within the army.
1949	Chinese revolution. Defeated nationalist forces—the KMT—take refuge in Shan State.
1956	Sao Hearn Hkam became an MP. U Nu elected Prime Minister.
1958	Burma Army commander General Ne Win takes control of parliament.
1960	Ne Win steps down. Democratic elections return U Nu to power.
1961	Prince Shwe Thaike leads constitutional reforms talks.
1962	General Ne Win's second coup. Prince Shwe Thaike dies in jail.
1963	Sao escapes to Thailand.
1964	Foundation of the SSA resistance force, with Sao as Chair and her son Tzang as a top military leader.
1969	Height of American and Chinese involvement in the Golden Triangle. Growth of the opium trade and client armies. Sao leaves for Canada.
1973	Failed SSA attempt to gain U.S. support in exchange for destroying opium. The SSA begins accepting communist support instead.
1976	Sao's son Tzang pushed out of the SSA by pro-communists.
1984	Shan resistance forces fall under the control of opium warlord Khun Sa.
1988	Democratic uprising in Burma.

Acknowledgements

Sao Hearn Hkam—or Sao Yawnghwe, as she is known in Canada—aided me with unfailing patience and kindness during the course of researching this book. The same goes for her sons, Tiger Yawnghwe, Dr. Chao-Tzang Yawnghwe and Harn Yawnghwe, who assisted greatly with details and background information.

Although I am indebted to all the sources listed in the bibliography and more, some deserve special mention, such as Dr. Yawnghwe's early book, *The Shan of Burma: Memoirs of a Shan Exile* (Singapore, 1987), a wealth of scholarly detail augmented by vivid personal recollections.

The old colonialists left voluminous writings behind. Sir Charles Crosthwaite, Clarence Hendershot, John Nisbet and Sir James George Scott all wrote about the British incursion into Shan State in great detail. Their works are listed in the bibliography. Maurice Collis' *Lords of the Sunset: A Tour in the Shan States* (London, 1938) provides an excellent travelogue of the landscapes and personalities of the late 1930s, including descriptions of the British Residency in Taunggyi, the Kengtung trial, a royal funeral and other aspects of Shan life which I drew on to describe this period.

My favourite colonial source, though, was *A Burmese Loneliness: A Tale of Travel in Burma, the Southern Shan States and Kengtung* (Calcutta, 1918). The author, Captain C.M. Enriquez of the 21st Punjabs, begins with the words, "These pages are born of Solitude." Then he plunges into 266 pages of detail about life in Shan State, telling us about people, temples, landscapes, old folk wisdom, the flowers and birds of the forest (named in English, Burmese and Tai), song lyrics, his discovery of Buddhist thought and a general wealth of information of which I was the glad inheritor. Thankfully it was written in another age, for such a work would never be published today—too quirky, too obscure, too dense in detail, the bean-counters would say.

The Tai people have also been active recorders of this time period and earlier, particularly through their detailed local chronicles. Sao's brother, Sao Yape Hpa, wrote an English translation of the Hsenwi Chronicle, which goes back to the earliest creation of the Tai kingdoms. Her son Tiger has also done a great deal of work in recent years recording the early Tai leaders. Others have concentrated on telling the Tai side of the colonial conquest. Sao Saimong Mongrai's *The Shan States and the British Annexation* (Ithaca, 1965) is one of the better-known documents in this regard.

Readers of Louis Allen's superb book Burma: *The Longest War 1941-45* (London, 1984) will recognise the story of Lt.-Gen. Mutaguchi Renya and other details of wartime Burma. Allen, a wartime intelligence officer, fluent Japanese speaker and prodigious researcher, was one of the few equipped to tell the story from both sides. The result is a terribly moving account of that time. Sadly, Dr. Allen is no longer with us, but his book stands as the best one can read about wartime Burma.

Dr. Allen's book helped my writing come alive with detail, as did an oral account recorded by U Khin, *U Hla Pe's Narrative of the Japanese Occupation of Burma* (Ithaca, 1961), the Karen veteran General Smith Dun's *Memoirs of the Four-Foot Colonel* (Ithaca, 1980), Dr. Ba Maw's remembrances, *Breakthrough in Burma* (New Haven, 1968), and U Nu's *Burma Under the Japanese: Pictures and Portraits* (London, 1954).

The modern period is traditionally covered by scholars and observers such as Hugh Tinker, Frank N. Trager, J.S. Furnivall and Joseph Silverstein. But there are plenty of lesser-known, more lively sources published by journalists, insurgents and dissidents who keep the grassroots memories alive. Rebels on the border regularly produce pamphlets and mimeographed books about their history. One which I picked up in my travels, *Historical Facts About Shan State* (1986) was particularly interesting for its details about the Panglong Agreement, including a blow-by-blow description of the discussions leading up to its signing. With plain, tattered covers and thin pages, such publications are a real find. I hope the Tai people continue producing them.

Alfred W. McCoy's *The Politics of Heroin in Southeast Asia* (New York, 1972) is considered a ground-breaker in the fascinating field of narco-politics. With enduring popularity, it has recently been published in an updated edition, *The Politics of Heroin: CIA Complicity in the Global Drug Trade* (Brooklyn, 1991).

Journalist Bertil Lintner has done a great deal to gather stories from people on the border and inside Burma. His travels have taken him all over the hill country and he continues his quest to understand Burma's complex history and personalities, and to bring the story to the public eye. Lintner's books *Land of Jade: A Journey Through Insurgent Burma* (Edinburgh, 1990) and *Outrage: Burma's Struggle for Democracy* (Hong Kong, 1989) are well worth obtaining copies of if readers wish to discover more about Burma's ongoing struggles for freedom and democracy.

Finally, I am indebted to the lively and courageous coverage of the *Bangkok Post* and its earlier sister publication, the *Bangkok World*. Some of the reporters who have done a stellar job tracking the Golden Triangle since the 1970s include: Anussorn Thavisin, Banyat Tasaneeyavey, Kamthorn Sermkasem, Pichai Khunseng, Sanit Chittsunat, Philip Knightly, Anthony M. Paul, Thaung Myine, Theh Chongkhadikij, John Everingham, Zaw Win, Subin Kheunkaew and Nusara Thaitawat.

Patricia Elliott
Canada

Prologue

On March 1, 1962, a visiting Chinese ballet troupe staged a performance in Burma's capital, Rangoon. It attracted a large audience, among whom could be seen General Ne Win, then Commander-in-Chief of the country's armed forces. The show went on until late at night. When it was over, Ne Win shook hands with the leading Chinese ballerina, and then quietly left. The audience thought that he was also going home to sleep after watching the show.

Meanwhile, Burma's democratically-elected prime minister, U Nu, had been meeting leaders from the Shan, Karenni (Kayah) and some of the country's other ethnic minorities. Secessionist elements within the Karen minority and smaller groups of Karennis, Pa-Os and Mons, plus communist insurgents, had been up in arms virtually since Burma's independence in 1948. They had been followed by smaller bands of Shans in 1958 and Kachins in 1961, and now there were rumours of an impending rebellion all over the sensitive frontier areas.

To address the crisis, U Nu had convened a seminar in Rangoon, where the minority leaders, led by Sao Shwe Thaike, the Saopha, or prince, of the Shan State of Yawnghwe, had submitted a proposal to amend the limited federalism provided by the constitution of the time. Such reforms were considered necessary to placate the increasingly restless non-Burman nationalities of the Union, who comprised some 40 per cent of the total population.

Modern-day Burma is a country of many nationalities and diverse geographic regions, and even the name of the country has been questioned by many. When the Dohbama Asiayone, the most militant Burman movement during the colonial era, was established in the 1930s, there was a debate among the young nationalists as to what name should be used for the country: the formal, old royal term "Myanma" or the more colloquial "Bama", which the British had corrupted into "Burma" and made the official name of their colony.

According to A Brief History of the Dohbama Asiayone, an official publication published in Rangoon in 1976, the nationalists agreed Myanmar "meant only the part of the country where the Burmans lived", while Bama (Burma) encompassed all the nationalities. Half a century later, in 1989, Burma's new military rulers decided that the opposite was true and renamed the country "Myanmar". A similar confusion exists in English, where some scholars maintain that "Burman" refers to the majority people who inhabit the plains whereas the term "Burmese" covers the language of the Burmans, as well as the citizens of that country, including the minorities. All these contradictions reflect the inescapable fact which many historians are still reluctant to acknowledge: there is no term in any language which covers both the Burmans, comprising 60 per cent of the population, and the minority peoples, as no such entity existed before the arrival of the British in the 19th Century.

According to the 1931 census, the last proper census ever taken in Burma and the frontier states, the Shans were the largest minority ethnic group, comprising seven per cent of the population. Early migrants from southern China, they are more closely related to the Thais and Laotians than to other ethnic groups in Burma. The word "Shan" is actually a corruption of "Siam", the old name for Thailand, and is a name given to them by the Burmans. The Shans call themselves "Dtai" (sometimes spelled "Tai" or, across the border in south-western China, "Dai"). In *The White Umbrella*, the author has chosen "Tai", the designation popularly used among people in the geographic area she writes about, the high plateau of north-eastern present-day Burma. There the Shans settled in valleys between ridges on both sides of the Salween River and established an abundance of principalities, varying in size and importance. The smallest, Namtok, measured thirty-five square kilometres and was inhabited only by a few hundred peasants scattered in two or three tiny villages, while the largest, Kengtung, encompassed 32,000 square kilometres—roughly the size of Belgium—and had a population of several hundred thousand.

The Shans today are found on all sides of the borders in Burma, Thailand, Laos, China and even in north-western Vietnam. There are also pockets of Shans in northern and southern Kachin State. In addition, there are two northern Shan states in north-western Burma outside the boundaries of modern-day Shan State: Singkaling Hkamti and Hsawnghsup (corrupted in Burmese to "Thaungdut").

Official Burmese sources usually accuse the British of having conducted "divide and rule" tactics by deliberately isolating the minorities from mainstream Burmese politics. While that may be true, it is also correct to say that the various hill peoples in Burma's periphery have throughout history tended to perceive the Burmese as untrustworthy arch-enemies. Although both Burma and China engaged in frequent military clashes with the fiercely independent Shan princes, neither was able to achieve effective conquest of their princely states. Only the 19th Century British conquest of Burma and its surrounding territories brought those hostilities to an end. Within colonial Burma, however, the Shan States were administered separately from Burma Proper, with recognition given to the rule of the traditional Saophas.

The Shan States' decision to join Burma and ask for independence from Britain was taken at a conference of minority representatives in February 1947. In the Shan town of Panglong, the Burmese nationalist leader Aung San and twenty-three ethnic representatives signed the Panglong Agreement, the key document in post-war relations between the frontier peoples and Rangoon. Among other points, the document promised full internal autonomy for frontier states, and the right to secede from the Union after a ten-year trial period.

On paper, everything was ready for the declaration of Burma's independence from Britain, scheduled for January 4, 1948. But on July 19, 1947 a tragic, unexpected event occurred: Aung San was assassinated, along with other state leaders, among them Sao Sam Htun, the Shan Saopha of Mong Pawn.

The prospects for a peaceful union were poor. The country's infrastructure had been destroyed in World War II, and its inner circle of competent leadership was murdered. Immediately following independence, Karen secessionists and communist rebels took up arms. Then, in 1950, nationalist Chinese Kuomingtang (KMT) forces crossed into Shan State and established a reign of terror in the hills. To counter the KMT, the Burma Army marched into Shan State, using heavy-handed tactics which created resentment and fear among the Shan populace. Squeezed between two forces perceived as foreign, a strong nationalist movement developed which flowered into armed rebellion. The first Shan rebel army, the Noom Suk Harn, was established in 1958, and the first battle was fought in 1959, at Tangyan, in the north.

It was while these violent activities were going on in the remote frontier areas that Sao Shwe Thaike and the other constitutional leaders of the minority peoples instituted their movement to preserve the Union by strengthening its federal character. As leader of the federal movement, Sao Shwe Thaike commanded considerable respect from not only the minorities, but also the Burman majority. Having served as Burma's first president from 1948 to 1952, he was no separatist, but wanted a fair deal for the minorities to avoid a large-scale civil war. The ethnic seminar in Rangoon was a step in the process.

The armed forces had other plans, however, and in the early hours of March 2, 1962, troops moved in to take over strategic positions in the capital. At about two o'clock in the morning, Prime Minister U Nu was arrested. Five other ministers, the Chief Justice, and over thirty Shan and Karenni leaders were also taken into custody.

There was no bloodshed in Rangoon, apart from a shoot-out at Sao Shwe Thaike's house on Kokine Road. His seventeen-year-old son Sai Myee was gunned down by the raiding soldiers when Sao Shwe Thaike "resisted arrest", as the official report said.

On the following day the federal 1947 constitution was abolished and the bicameral parliament dissolved. Burma's fourteen-year experiment with federalism and parliamentary democracy was over. In its place, Ne Win and an inner circle of military officers, the so-called Revolutionary Council, ruled by decree. Wielding more power over the state machinery than anyone had since the last monarch was deposed by the British in 1885, they forced a new ideology called the "Burmese Way to Socialism" on the country.

The students, always at the forefront of any protest movement in Burma, were the first to demonstrate openly against the military take-over. Sai Tzang, a son of the incarcerated ethnic leader Sao Shwe Thaike, witnessed the protests at the University of Rangoon on July 7. He remembers it was a cool, balmy evening. The students were in high spirits until they noticed soldiers being deployed along University Avenue, armed with newly-issued West German G-3 assault rifles.

Soon a small Fiat arrived and three officers stepped out to confer with their colleagues in charge of the troops facing the campus. The students booed and whistled. After a short while, the Fiat drove away. One of the remaining officers turned around to face the students, raised his arms and waved them above his head in a circular motion three times.

"We looked at each other, wondering what it all meant," Sai Tzang recalls. "Our questions were answered immediately and violently by gunfire."

Officially, 15 were killed and 27 wounded. But both neutral observers and students who were present during the shooting say the university looked like a slaughterhouse, where not 15 but hundreds of potential leaders of society in many fields lay sprawled in death. The man in charge of the operation was Sein Lwin, one of Ne Win's closest lieutenants, and the orders to kill came directly from the strongman himself.

The army had clearly wanted to show just who was in charge but the massacre on the campus prompted hundreds of students to join the underground. Sai Tzang, being Shan, went to the guerrillas of his ethnic group in the north-east, where the insurgency flared anew. Anger rose even further when the authorities informed Sao Shwe Thaike's family that "the president has expired in jail". Another popular Shan leader, Sao Kya Hseng, the Saopha of Hsipaw, also disappeared after the coup and was last seen in a military camp in western Shan State. Relations between the ethnic minorities and the central authorities in Rangoon were never to be the same again. The civil war that U Nu's ethnic seminar had been convened to prevent was now a reality.

Then, at the end of 1963, Sao Shwe Thaike's widow, the Mahadevi of Yawnghwe, Sao Hearn Hkam, miraculously managed to escape from Rangoon with her youngest surviving son and two daughters. The escape, through Karen State to Mae Sot in Thailand, was planned by a group of sympathetic Rangoon-based politicians and aided by a senior Shan monk and a young medical student, Sai Nyan Win (later known as Hseng Harn). Ne Win's Military Intelligence Service (MIS) heard of the escape a few days after they had slipped out of Rangoon, and search teams were promptly dispatched in pursuit. But all that they could lay their hands on was an unknown woman travelling with three children near the border town of Myawaddy. The real Mahadevi—who is the subject of *The White Umbrella*—had already crossed the border to Thailand.

The Mahadevi's escape was something of a coup, and on March 25, 1964 representatives of several Shan rebel groups met in Chiang Mai to form the unified Shan State Army (SSA) with the Mahadevi of Yawnghwe as its paramount leader. Under her leadership, and assisted by her son Sai Tzang, the SSA grew to become one of Burma's strongest and best-organised rebel armies, and perhaps the only rebel army in the Shan area that was genuinely fighting for an ideal; the Shan hills were also the home of numerous private forces that were involved in the local opium trade. The Shan states form part of the Golden Triangle, the world's most important source of opium and its derivative, heroin.

In the beginning, the hopes of the young Shan nationalists were high. But as the years went by, the strength of the Burmese army grew, war weariness set in, and many Shans preferred to settle in northern Thailand. Even the Mahadevi eventually left for Canada in 1969, but her son, Sai Tzang, remained behind in the jungle, where he became better known under his noms de guerre, Sao Hso Wai and Khun Loum Hpa. But he also left for Chiang Mai in the mid-1970s as factional infighting was tearing the movement apart. This book describes those crucial years in detail and the role the Mahadevi and her family played, and continue to play from exile in North America and Europe.

Their activism was recharged when a new era in Burma's modern history began in 1988. That year, millions of people all over Burma took to the streets to demand an end to military rule and a restoration of the democracy they had enjoyed prior to the 1962 coup. The demonstrations were crushed with unbelievable brutality. Thousands of young people were mowed down by the army's machine guns as Ne Win's henchmen stepped in to reassert power.

Yet another brutal phase in Burma's modern history followed, but this time, there emerged a national leader who the army could not crush: Aung San Suu Kyi, the daughter of the country's independence hero, Aung San. She emerged not only as the most prominent advocate of democracy for Burma but also perhaps as the only Burmese politician who the minorities felt they could trust. After all, her father had signed the Panglong Agreement, and the violation of that accord was the main reason why the country's ethnic minorities resorted to armed struggle.

Even so, the minorities felt that they needed to look after their own interests as well. The mass movement of 1988-89 saw the birth of the National League for Democracy (NLD), Aung San Suu Kyi's party. The Shans, however, set up their own Shan National League for Democracy (SNLD), which was loosely allied with the NLD but still different. When the country went to the polls in May 1990, as the army had promised when it reasserted power in September 1988, the NLD captured 392 of the 485 parliamentary seats. The SNLD swept Shan State. With twenty-three seats, it became the second-biggest party in the parliament.

Seeing the power and popular support of parties such as the NLD and the SNLD, the army reacted in its own inimitable way: it ignored the outcome of the election, refused to convene the elected parliament and began to arrest the winners of the election. Today scores of elected MPs are still in jail, have fled the country, or have been forced to resign. Several have died under torture in prison. For some reason, Burma's junta seems to distrust the Shan more than any other nationality in the country, perhaps because the military believes they are more prone to be secessionist because they are so fundamentally different from the others.

Whatever the reason, the outcome is an unprecedented reign of terror in Shan State which has seen the forced relocation of hundreds of thousands of peasants into strategic hamlets where the army believes that they can be more easily "controlled". Hundreds of thousands of other Shans have escaped to Thailand, where they work as farm hands, construction workers or on fishing boats. "Ethnic cleansing" is a strong and often misused phrase, but there is no other way to describe what is happening in Shan State today.

But the hope for a better future has not been extinguished, and both the NLD and the SNLD continue to operate, albeit under extremely difficult conditions. In the long run, however, it seems impossible that the Burmese military can maintain its increasingly anachronistic style of government, and its brutal repression of its own people. The fall of Indonesian strongman Suharto in May 1998 also demonstrates that no dictatorship can last forever.

When change comes to Burma, its old leaders and heroes will surely be remembered. The Mahadevi of Yawnghwe and her family, who revitalised the Shan movement and gave it a clear political direction, are bound to be among them.

Bertil Lintner
Bangkok

One

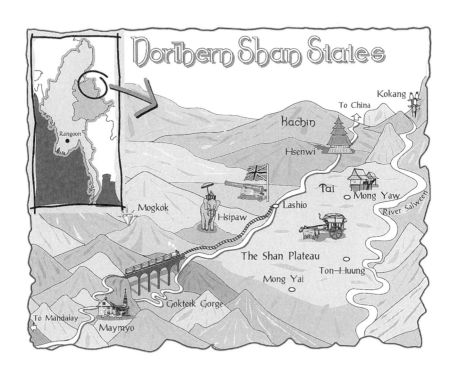

Sao Hearn Hkam in her wedding dress.

Sao's brother,
Prince Hom Hpa.

Sao (left) and one of her sisters, seated on a traditional divan.

Sao and young friends at the Prince of Hsipaw's funeral in 1928. Sao is kneeling (right) between two small girls. Her sister Mary Josephine is in the same row on the left. Next to Mary Josephine is Princess Van Thip of Kengtung.

(Above) Inside the old palace's Great Hall of Audience.

(Right) The old Hsenwi Palace.

(Below left) Today's St. Agnes' Convent. (Don Jedlic)
(Below right) The New Haw at Hsenwi.

Paung Daw U Temple.
(Don Jedlic)

(Left) The Nat throne, inside the Great Hall of Audience. (Don Jedlic)

(Above) A worshipper placing gold leaf on the Five Images. (Don Jedlic)

A Kalaw street, with typical colonial-era houses. (Don Jedlic)

A Bride's Journey

When Sao was old and living alone in a windswept Canadian prairie city she began to recall her childhood in images so vivid that they left her sleepless. Awake, she seldom bothered rising from her bed, knowing the small rooms of her apartment contained little to occupy her mind.

She lived in a senior citizens' high-rise that, although well-populated, was nothing like the earthy, busy little town of her childhood. Each apartment was its own autonomous little unit, windows facing either the street or the garden being the only variance. Sao's apartment contained books of English history and a tiny cluttered kitchen still heavy with the aroma of curry and sauce if she hadn't eaten in the cafeteria that day. Most times she cooked her own meals—she, who couldn't even boil rice until she was in her forties. Lying in darkness, the thought made her smile. She felt no bitterness over the loss of servants and cooks who carried her meals on silver platters long ago, only an aching, empty wonderment as to their fate. Where did they all go after the coup d'état? Such answerless questions kept her awake, too, not just the memories.

In a closet next to the entrance were a few albums crammed with old family photographs. She seldom looked at them anymore, didn't need to. The pictures, carried out of Burma by friends and relatives over the years, were fixed in her mind. Inside small scalloped-edged squares were her mother, her uncles, cousins, nephews, sisters, herself as a young girl. Sao never considered herself beautiful like her sisters were. Her face was a little too broad and plump, she thought, her nose not quite delicate enough. She lacked the classic beauty of a royal princess. But that is what she was: a princess of the Shan States of Burma.

There was one image that she liked well enough to hang on her living room wall, a hand-coloured studio portrait of herself in her wedding attire of gold Mandalay silk with pearl accents. In fact, the picture was taken at a London studio some years after her wedding, so the smile was more open and confident than it might have been on her actual wedding day, which she remembered as perhaps the most miserable moment of her life.

The delicately coloured photo hung above a formal family portrait of herself and the children. The girls wore western-style dresses and bobbed hair. The boys were dressed in the traditional tunics, broad pants and turbans of their people, tiny images of their father, the first president of newly-independent Burma.

If she left her bed, what else would she find in the little apartment that was her home now? She had a television set which at the press of a button could be made to chatter endlessly about scandalous murder trials, Hollywood movies and, occasionally, news from the frozen city outside her window, Edmonton. On a nearby book shelf she kept a Buddha image and pots for burning incense, an antidote to the futile, earthly desires that wavered on the TV screen. The Buddha statuette was 800 years old and made of black stone taken from the Mekong delta. It was a gift from the abbot of the Marble Temple in Bangkok, Thailand. She'd come to Thailand as a refugee from neighbouring Burma, after losing power, wealth, husband and son in one night of gunfire. When the abbot gave her the statuette, she was about to lose control of her rebel army, too.

These should have been the thoughts that invaded her sleep: the mistakes, rivalries, and disappointments of a lifetime of political struggle. Instead, the images that jolted her awake were simple things that seemed to have no connection to great events.

She remembered, for example, the garden at Hsenwi Palace, where she was born. It wasn't like the neat collection of hardy flowers tended by her elderly neighbours outside the Edmonton highrise, a garden that spent most of its days under the snow-pack. No, the garden of her childhood was a wild, exotic place full of mangoes and orchids, at its best during the May showers. After a good soaking, fat red worms appeared on the garden path. As a child, Sao was terrified of those worms.

So strange, she thought now, because nothing else in life scared her.

Even when she fled to the border years later, she wasn't frightened. She always thought someone would help her, that things would turn out okay. Maybe she remembered her childhood fear and how her favourite cousin used to lift her onto his shoulders, high above the red worms, so high that she could reach up to the trees and pluck down pomegranates. That's how it was in the Shan States—people took care of each other, and if you were hungry, you only had to reach into a tree.

Everything was lost now. The palace was burnt down, and where were all her cousins? Dead or scattered to the four corners of the earth. You can never guess a man's fate.

Now, a woman's fate was an easier matter. Sao could recite a woman's destiny in a few words: the aristocratic Hsenwi women married well and had children. When they died, all the townspeople and villagers came to their funerals to pay respect.

How, then, did she end up alone in this cold northern town? The world changed, and women's destinies became complicated, too, not like in her mother's time.

She often thought about her mother. After all, her whole life had been spent trying to avoid her mother's fate—a minor wife in a remote feudal palace. From an early age, Sao chose challenges, fought obstacles, reached out to the world. In contrast, her mother, when she was young, could not even have placed her home village on a map.

A century later and several oceans and continents away, Sao could close her eyes in the darkened apartment and see in one sweeping vision the whole of her mother's horizon: the Yaw River valley in the Shan highlands, in what is today north-eastern Burma, nestled in the mountainous heart of Southeast Asia.

The Yaw valley, Sao remembered from childhood visits, had abundant water and several scattered villages set in feathery bamboo groves. Each village specialised in a particular trade or craft and was prosperous in its own fashion. The main village, called Mong Yaw, sat at the edge of a grassy plain where cattle and oxen grazed.

Nang Hkam Zeng—Sao's mother—lived in the valley until 1890, the year she turned fifteen. She knew every tree and house. Each morning she gazed across the grassy plain and watched the sun rise over Loisak, a high limestone peak some two-and-a-half miles distant.

At Loisak's foot was a settlement of a few Chinese traders and some Paluang mountain folk who grew tea and opium poppies. The Paluang pickled the tea leaves and mixed them into sour, invigorating salads. The poppy pods they scraped with little curved knives, then formed the sap into gummy bricks. The Chinese traders took the bricks to Mong Yaw's market, where they sold for eight or ten rupees a viss (about three-and-a-half pounds). The locals bought only a little, for their aches and pains. If the harvest was good, the traders packed the excess onto mules and carried it away to southern China.

Beyond Loisak, the Salween River rushed from north to south through steep gorges and tangled rain forest, effectively cutting the highlands in half on its 1,740-mile journey from the Tibetan Himalayas to the Andaman Sea. The Salween was too rough to navigate, and only a few pole-raft ferries plied the quieter spots. Nang Hkam Zeng heard that fearsome head-hunters called the Wild Wa roamed the other side of the roaring river. There were other peoples about, too: the Lisu, the Kachins, the Akha, the Lahu. In the surrounding peaks, which rose as high as 9,000 feet, they grew tea and slashed and burned small vegetable plots out of the jungle. Altogether, more than twenty distinct ethnic groups shared her homeland.

Nang Hkam Zeng's people occupied the flat rice-plains between the mountain ridges, in well-settled, self-sufficient villages. The most populous ethnic group, they called themselves Tai.

Mong Yaw, her home village, had several hundred bamboo and thatch homes raised on thick stilts above the damp. At the bottom of each house's ladder-like stairs was a large mud-plastered thatch basket for storing rice grown in the nearby paddy fields. Each family had a little garden, too, for growing chillies, onions and other zesty treats. Meat and pungent fish paste they bought at the local bazaar, held every five days.

Good Buddhists, every one, the villagers lit incense sticks in the morning and paid homage to the Lord Buddha and to the local spirits, called Nats. Then they drove their buffalo to the fields, where man, woman and beast worked side by side to prepare the ancient, fertile soil for planting.

The farmers lived by the seasons, planting in the rains of July and harvesting in the cool, bright weather of November. They had water-wheels and bamboo irrigation works to aid their task. Toiling under fierce high-altitude sunshine, they shaded their heads with loose-wrapped turbans and conical bamboo hats. Their clothes were made of simple homespun cotton, suited for country life. The men wore baggy trousers caught at the waist with a broad sash and Chinese-style collarless jackets with a row of cotton buttons down the middle. The women wore short jackets which buttoned at the side, called an aingyi, and wrapped themselves waist to ankle with colourful sarong-like swatches of cloth. Bent over the wet paddy, they hiked their dresses to their knees.

The storytellers said Nang Hkam Zeng's people were descended from the brothers Khun Lu and Khun Lai, who climbed down from heaven on a ladder made of gold or iron, depending on who was telling the story. Nang Hkam Zeng also heard their ancestors were born in the distant mountains of Mongolia more than 5,000 years ago, and that is why they had light golden skin and were taller than the other peoples who lived in the mountains.

The Tai, Sao's mother learned from an early age, were more than simple tribespeople. Their history was glorious, their culture intricate and sophisticated.

In monasteries scattered throughout the valley, the monks kept chronicles that told of past kings and princes, written in curling script on dried palm leaves.

The original Tai of Mongolia, the local scholars believed, were gradually pushed southward by successive Chinese emperors until finally they arrived in Yunnan—Land of the Southern Cloud—and there established their first kingdom in 629 AD. It was called Nan-chao, "the Southern Lords". It was written that whenever the Nan-chao king went out from his palace, a large retinue preceded him, carrying billowing standards, feathered fans, and a parasol of iridescent kingfisher's feathers. He raised a stout-walled capital, Talifu, on the banks of a wide, placid lake.

The kingdom's jewel was a broad valley of paddy fields completely encircled by sub-tropical mountains. It was called Sip Song Panna, the Twelve Districts. Centuries later, Nang Hkam Zeng's neighbours still spoke of Talifu as their Camelot, and the rice-heavy fields of Sip Song Panna as their Shangri-La.

In the early days of Nan-chao, some Tai princes ventured beyond the emerald fields of Sip Song Panna, carrying five seals of the king over the southernmost mountains of his domain. On the other side, they discovered a lofty, luxuriant tableland of some 62,500 square miles. Undulating mountain ranges ribbonned southward; between their peaks nestled broad, fertile valleys. The average elevation was about 3,000 feet, making for a pleasantly cool climate. Sheltered by mountains, watered by fresh streams, each valley was governed by local headmen. Through alliances with the headmen, the Tai adventurers created a second kingdom.

It was a fortunate development. After Kublai Khan's soldiers stormed Talifu's walls on January 7, 1253, the Khan's southward sweep was soon brought up short by the jagged mountains. Safe behind the peaks flourished the second, more southerly, Tai kingdom. By now it was greater than the first, stretching west to India's Assam, east to Thailand's Chiang Mai, north to Sip Song Panna, and south to the Burmese delta and the Gulf of Martaban. The Tai people spread themselves even further, into modern-day Thailand, Laos and Cambodia. They took on characteristics of their own, but always looked back on the highland people as Tai-long—"the Great Tai"—their founding culture.

To hold the far-flung empire together, the Tai kings made use of the indigenous structure of valley-states. For each valley, the king appointed a prince called a Saopha, or Celestial Ruler, who was guided by a Council of Ministers. At the township level, the Saopha in turn appointed a Myosa—an "Eater of the Town"— to collect taxes and oversee local affairs. Below the townships were Village Circles consisting of several individual villages and administered by various grades of headmen.

The internal system worked well—it was external problems which brought about the empire's demise. The Tai kings faced constant pressure from neighbouring Chinese and Burmese empires. Skirmishes, invasions and full-scale wars followed in steady succession. After 1554, the kingdom dwindled. The last Tai king died throneless in 1604.

He left his Saophas behind, princes without a king. Reluctantly, the Saophas began to pay tribute to the King of Mandalay, who lived in a sprawling red-walled fortress on the north Burma plain. The people of the plains were called Burmese. They originally came from Tibet, it was thought, and they shared little in common with the Tai. The two groups couldn't understand each other's languages, they had separate histories and cultural practices, and they worshipped differently, the Burmese being more strict in their Buddhism.

Despite the tribute, the Mandalay rulers gained no real influence over the mountainous frontier, which encircled the dusty plains like a horseshoe. The Saophas continued to rule over their valley princedoms with all the authority accorded to Celestial Lords—beings who occupied a higher plane of existence than ordinary mortals.

Their rule continued unchanged through the centuries, so that by the time Sao's mother came into the world, there was still a Saopha on the state throne and a township Myosa to watch over Mong Yaw valley. The local Myosa, in fact, was her own grandfather. His house was slightly larger and grander than an ordinary village home, with a little extra space for meetings and for receiving visitors.

Nang Hkam Zeng's grandfather kept the valley well-organised. Each year in June or July, he called village meetings to assess the amount of tax to be paid in rice by each household, set according to the year's harvest after taking into account any extenuating circumstances. A certain number of exemptions were allowed for poor households and people with no supporting family members. Village headmen carried out the actual collection, retaining ten per cent for local improvements, such as upgrading homes and market areas.

The remainder went to the state capital, Hsenwi. Twice a year, Nang Hkam Zeng's grandfather travelled to the palace to pay obeisance to the Saopha on behalf of the villagers, as had been done through the generations for more than a thousand years.

There were 49 like townships within the state. In return for loyalty and taxes, their feudal overlord was expected to support monasteries, schools and road-building, and to protect the farmers from bandits and invading armies.

Although a celestial being, the Saopha still depended on his township officials and village headmen for his power. The title Saopha was only semi-hereditary. If a man could take the throne—

by birth, by guile or, failing that, by force—he had the right to name an heir and attempt to establish a dynasty. But an uncooperative council of ministers—which included prominent Myosas—could easily thwart such ambitions.

Alliances were required, and such alliances were best cemented through marriage. The Great Saopha of North Hsenwi State —to whom Nang Hkam Zeng's grandfather paid obeisance—knew this well. He himself came to the throne through his marriages to all four daughters of a rebellious general. He built a palace with four apartments, and ever after kept four wives. When a wife died, she was swiftly replaced, usually with an important local official's daughter or niece.

Many years later, Sao's mother told her about the day the palace officials came to Mong Yaw village. Her mother was just five or six years old at the time. The strange grown-ups examined her eyes, nose and hair, and then they called for her astrological charts and conferenced for a long time in Grandfather's house. Later she was presented with a tight-fitting silk court dress, or thamein, and a matching aingyi jacket with five detachable jewel buttons to fasten it shut. It was rather fancy for a little girl.

So attired, Sao's mother became Nang Hkam Zeng, Lady Golden Jewel, a future wife of the Great Saopha of Hsenwi.

Ten years later, at age fifteen, Sao's mother was called to the palace. The trip would take her fifty miles around a mountain spur, first west to Lashio, then north-east toward Hsenwi town. Only a few days' travel, but a world away from her quiet valley.

The year was 1890. At dawn she fastened her aingyi with the five jewel buttons, and then touched her head three times to the floor before her parents, a gesture of deepest respect called the kadaw.

March was a popular month for travelling. The weather was dry and clear, there was little work to do in the fields, and the two swampy stretches between Mong Yaw and the main road at Lashio town were passable. It was common for a young lady of good standing to travel in a bullock cart shaded by a canopy of woven bamboo strips. The prince provided two officers in fancy dress to accompany the cart. There was no ceremony. Despite her silk aingyi and jewelled buttons, Nang Hkam Zeng was still a commoner, just another village girl sent to serve her husband.

To survive the jolts of a bullock cart ride one had to sit just so: in the centre, swaying lightly to the cart's movements, outstretched hands resting on the cart's high sides. This was likely her parents' last image of her, as she rode west across the broad valley floor toward a steep ridge some four miles distant.

From atop the ridge Nang Hkam Zeng could see her village, now just a line of dark green trees. Who knows what was in her heart? She must have heard the bazaar-talk about her husband: that he had the blood of the feared Wild Wa in his veins, that he even murdered a man in a fight for a girl.

The Great Saopha of Hsenwi was well-known for his exploits, being a former salt trader who rose from obscurity to help overthrow a disliked, over-taxing prince. He went by the name Khunsang Ton-huung, in homage to his humble beginnings as a headman's son in the little butcher's village of Ton-huung, near the Salween River. Some people called him a rogue and a bandit, but he was popular. One of his first acts as Saopha was to declare that he and his heirs would pay taxes, like ordinary people.

He'd not had much luck during his reign, though. The man he overthrew fled to Mandalay fortress for protection. The Mandalay king, knowing a bird in the hand was worth two in the bush, helped the refugee prince raise an army against Khunsang Ton-huung. He devised to incite other Saophas against the upstart salt trader, too. The constant warfare left Hsenwi state impoverished and easy prey for other invaders.

Nang Hkam Zeng heard her husband now paid tribute to the men called the Khula Khao, the White Indians, who came from beyond the ocean. She'd never seen the foreigners with her own eyes. They belonged to the world beyond Mong Yaw valley, a world that came closer with every bump of her wooden cart.

Distance was measured in bullock-stops, one bullock-stop equalling the eight-mile stretches an animal could go without stopping to rest. It was three bullock-stops to the crossroads at Lashio, where the White Indians settled.

After a heavy stretch of jungle, the trail switch-backed down and up the steep banks of the Yaw river, then disappeared into a swampy quagmire. Her husband's men laid tall grass across the swamp, making a passable bridge. Crossing a broad plateau,

Nang Hkam Zeng saw the trampled grasses of a military encampment, evidence of Khunsang Ton-huung's wars.

Further on, the cart passed a few villages and a foreign-inspired experimental farm. It was a strange-looking place, with rows of seedlings marked by little signs. Nang Hkam Zeng wondered, what could the White Indians teach the Tai about farming?

When they came upon Lashio, there wasn't much to see. Once a sizeable Shan town, all of its 1,000 houses were burnt down during the Saopha's wars. The white men had taken over the ashes and made it an administrative centre. In the near distance she saw a few new structures clinging to a bump of a hill. The foreigner's flag, the Union Jack, waved over top the buildings.

Past Lashio, Nang Hkam Zeng's cart turned north on the Hsenwi Track, about the only thing that passed for a road in that area. A jostling line of mule trains stretched into the dust-shrouded distance. Hsenwi lay a further twenty-five miles down the trail. Beyond was China.

The road was a wonder. Great piles of hides and cigar leaves, dripping containers of honey and varnish, jangling brass and copper bowls, stacks of straw hats bobbed around her bullock cart. Heavy loads of salt, baskets of oranges, candles, betel nuts, salt fish and tobacco, followed the trail to China. From the other direction came Chinese tea, silk, and ginger.

Mule trains tangled when they passed one another, causing the muleteers to holler and swat at their animals to separate them. Nang Hkam Zeng watched the scene with amusement. Although no one knew it yet, the trade route would soon prove itself to be both a blessing and a curse, coveted by foreigners and pursued by competing powers. Already the British administrators in Lashio had a name for it: they called it the Golden Road to Cathay.

To Nang Hkam Zeng, it remained the road to Hsenwi palace—in her young life, a destination no less significant.

Conquest

In the first month of Nang Hkam Zeng's marriage, her husband travelled south to meet the British at Fort Stedman on the eastern shore of Inle Lake, in the southern principality of Yawnghwe. He travelled in slow procession, accompanied by his ministers of state, umbrella bearers, royal guards, horse grooms, pages, cooks and court musicians. At the same time, Sir Charles Crosthwaite, Chief Commissioner for Burma, set out on roads under heavy construction, on a two-week journey from the edge of the plains up into the hilly Frontier Areas, as the British called their newest territory.

In fact, Britain's journey into Nang Hkam Zeng's homeland had begun many years earlier, when 18th Century merchants of the British East India Company noticed great teak timbers floating in the mouth of the Salween River. Teak was a tall, dense tropical hardwood with an unusual property: when iron and steel fittings were embedded in its timbers, the wood's natural oils protected them from rust and corrosion. It was the perfect material for building the ships Britain needed to contain the rival French empire.

Lured by timber, the British gradually expanded their trading posts and settlements throughout the 1800s, finally annexing southern Burma as a part of British India in 1858. They faced a powerful check to further expansion, though. Two hundred and thirty-seven miles north, the King of the Ava Dynasty sat in his massive Mandalay fortress-palace, protected by soaring watchtowers, a moat and walls so thick a team of elephants could walk on them.

Stalemated, the British lost ground. France meantime expanded through Indochina, swallowing up what are today Vietnam and Cambodia. The French colonies were successful. Healthy revenues were raised through the issuance of permits to local opium traders. There was no shortage of buyers for the product: Britain's opium wars with China had created a large market of addicts in that country. For the Europeans, opium was more than a cheaply-sold market good: it was a powerful tool of state used to bankrupt enemies, pull down trade barriers and buy the loyalty of local armies.

With Indochina under their control, France turned toward Mandalay.

King Thibaw, the Mandalay ruler, made the mistake of sending a mission to Europe to explore a trade agreement with the French. The British responded immediately: they mustered troops and marched north across the hot Burma plain toward his fortress.

The King, it turned out, was a paper tiger. Despite its moat and watchtowers, Mandalay Palace fell on November 28, 1885, almost without a fight. The British commander found King Thibaw seated in a summer house in the palace garden.

The last ruler of the Ava dynasty walked down the stairs of the Hall of Audience and through the Red Gate. It was his first time outside the palace walls during his seven-year reign. Outside, two bullock carts waited to carry him and what remained of his entourage to a river steamer and exile in India.

A few days later, the royal white elephant, a symbol of regal power, died of colic and was dragged away unceremoniously through the streets by British soldiers. Then the soldiers moved into the palace and renamed it Fort Dufferin.

On December 31, 1885, Lord Rudolph Churchill, Secretary of State for India, concluded in a despatch: "The arrogance and barbarity of the native court, the oppression of British subjects, the hindrance to British commerce, the intrigues of foreign nations, are forever terminated in Upper Burma." Inside Fort Dufferin, Britain's soldiers pulled apart Thibaw's twenty-six-foot-high gilt throne and sent it down river after the king, to become a museum curiosity in Calcutta.

With Mandalay easily defeated, the British turned their attention to a high wall of mountains just forty miles east, which they remembered as the source of the teak-wood that floated down the Salween River. The Burmese informed them the people of that land were called "Syam", which sounded a little like "Siam" to English ears. Eventually they rendered the word into "Shan", and named the land of the Tai "the Shan States".

One English officer of the time noted that the people preferred to call themselves Tai, but concluded: "We call them Shan, and so they will remain, whatever they may say." The act of naming was an act of power.

In May 1886, the Shan States were declared part of British India. The following year, two columns were mustered and sent forth to declare British law. One column went south; the other turned north toward the territory of Khunsang Ton-huung, Prince of Hsenwi. The northern column, led by Major Yates, consisted of two guns, fifty rifles of the Royal Munster Fusiliers, one hundred rifles of the Bombay Army, and seventy-five native and British mounted infantry.

In late 1887, they set out across the dusty Mandalay plain toward the sheer face of the Shan plateau. From the foot of the plateau, the soldiers followed a narrow switchback up through sweet-smelling pines. With every step the air became more cool and clear. They made their camp at the top of the ridge, on the easternmost border of the Shan States. It was a pleasant setting. Light evening frosts were followed by days of pleasant sunshine, far removed from the dust, heat and noise of lowland Mandalay.

Leaving their camp in late December, the soldiers set out across a broad sweep of open savannah and rolling hills. Thirty-four miles north-east, they came upon a spectacular gorge. Its rock walls plunged 2,000 feet to a fast-moving stream. At one end, where the stream roared into a cavern, there was a natural stone bridge marked by a small monument that commemorated two local headmen who cleared the trail "so as to make it passable for men and laden oxen".

After crossing the dizzying span, the column pressed forward through rolling tablelands. The trail took them past irrigated fields of peas, beans, okra and rice. Wild apples, pears and other fruits grew freely on the hillsides. Gradually the road descended to lowland forests. Towering stands of teak, ironwood and other hardwoods rose above the canopy. Trails branched north of the main road into the folding hills, where it was said gold, silver and lead were mined.

Despite the apparent plenitude, a strange, unnatural quiet blanketed the land. Fields were abandoned, houses empty. No one save the soldiers themselves moved on the trail. Nearing Hsenwi, the column passed burnt-out villages and abandoned military camps, scenes of a land at war with itself.

Just outside of Tawng Peng village, a sniper fired on the column, killing two mules and wounding a driver. An ominous silence descended as the men gingerly made their way past needle-sharp bamboo stakes to the edge of Hsenwi town.

While the soldiers encamped, Yate's civil officer, Lieutenant Daly, took a few men and continued on into what was left of the town, looking for the "chief".

It seemed that the someone had already done the job for them: Hsenwi State was in ruins, torn apart by warring neighbours allied to the former King of Mandalay.

The soldiers set up a tent near the palace, at the time a simple building distinguished from its neighbours only by the fact that it was still standing. Seated at a camp table, the Lieutenant drafted a written request to meet with the "chief" of the "tribe", Khunsang Ton-huung.

At first, Khunsang Ton-huung stalled for time. He sent a message back, stating he had already surrendered to the Chinese. It was plausible. The Chinese, wishing to check the advancing colonialists, were also making overtures to the Tai princes.

The British obviously didn't believe him, or didn't care. Instead of leaving, they settled in for a wait.

On the second day, a steady stream of Tai and Kachin country folk passed by the army tents. Despite the town's horrific state, the local bazaar stuck to its once-every-five-days schedule. The foreign soldiers toured the stalls, and were surprised to see shoes from China and cloth from Manchester among the vegetables and straw hats.

Meanwhile, Khunsang Ton-huung sat in his palace, mulling his options. His men had a few flintlocks and Brown Besses, a poor match against new machine guns and case shot. Perhaps, he thought, he could put the British weapons to work on his side, against his enemies. In that sense, the column's arrival was rather opportune. On the third day, he picked his way through the ruins to Daly's rough canvas shelter.

There was no time for ceremony. Khunsang Ton-huung agreed to follow the British column to nearby Mong Yai, where they would meet up with the southern column, also accompanied by a contingent of princes. The journey took them south through deserted villages, past dilapidated market sheds, over broken-down bamboo footbridges. On March 1 they passed three white pagodas. Beyond were the remains of a town, and, beyond that, a loose grouping of camps. The southern column had already arrived, led by Colonel Edward Stedman and a civilian colonial official, A.H. Hildebrand.

Among the crowd was the son of Khunsang Ton-huung's deposed enemy, come to press his father's claim to the Hsenwi throne. He offered the British an annual tribute of 15,000 Indian rupees, or 2,610 pounds sterling, no small sum at the time.

Khunsang Ton-huung offered 500 rupees, not a penny more. Lucky for him, the British preferred the cut of his jib. When Hildebrand's deputy, J. George Scott, sized up the two competitors, he observed that Khunsang Ton-huung was "conspicuously tall and muscular", while his rival's son was "a colourless sort of youth". Thus, although Khunsang had no blood tie to the throne and offered the lower tribute, the British gave his claim full consideration.

To settle the matter of Hsenwi state once and for all, Hildebrand ordered the assembled Saophas, fifty village headmen, and assorted monks and elders to meet in a pavilion constructed especially for the occasion. Khunsang Ton-huung waited three days for their decision. In the end, he won Hsenwi palace and a territory of 6,300 square miles and 135,000 inhabitants. His annual tribute, payable to the colonial government in Rangoon, was set at 2,000 rupees. He accepted the terms.

His enemy received a smaller but wealthier southern slice consisting of 2,200 square miles and the town of Mong Yai—and he was stuck with his initial offer of 15,000 rupees tribute.

The British stayed a few more days before breaking camp. They found it was "great fun" watching the "chiefs" interact. Scott wrote in a private letter: "At first they all camped separately, scattered about over the wide paddy stubbles round about here, but now they are beginning to gather closer together, and some of them are actually quite chummy. When we have a football match, or when the band plays, they all gather round and even the most standoffish are bound to meet. Khunsang Ton-huung has already wheeled into line a bit...The chiefs will want civilising before they are fit for ladies' society, all except a few."

The British interlopers were flush with a sense of benevolent accomplishment. For the first time in many years, the warring Shan leaders had met and made democratic decisions as a group. Scott and Hildebrand could congratulate themselves. A long-standing feud had been decided peacefully, evidence of the "civilising" factor of British rule. They didn't foresee that the new "chums" would quickly develop a united front for freedom from colonial rule.

As Superintendent, in March the following year, 1888, Hildebrand toured the north and presented each Saopha with a Writ of Authority, or Sanad. The terms were simple: Britain would not interfere with local rule. The Saophas were free to levy taxes, dispense justice, and nominate an heir "for the approval of the Government". Together, the traditional princes would govern 1.3 million people and 62,500 square miles, an area slightly larger than England and Wales combined. In return, the forests, minerals and other natural resources belonged to the Crown. The princes would faithfully pay tribute to the new colonial government in Rangoon, as they had once paid tribute to the Kings of Mandalay.

No one could call the arrangement fair. To the Saophas it was the price of peace, with a promise of local autonomy.

All of them agreed to abide by the state borders set out in their Sanads. The factional warring ceased, allowing the princes to introduce new crops, build schools, establish medical dispensaries and repair roads.

The British were busy, too. They strung 4,000 miles of telegraph line, took over the jade, silver and ruby mines, brought the teak forests under the rule of the Forest Department, and recruited 3,000 men into a "native army", the Shan levy.

It took three years for Britain's top man in Burma, Chief Commissioner Crosthwaite, to find time in his schedule to make the arrangement official. It was this meeting which brought Khunsang Ton-huung of Hsenwi to Fort Stedman—named after the leader of the southern column—for a grand durbar.

The setting could not have been more beautiful. Inle Lake, long, narrow and wrapped in mist, lay between smoke-blue mountains. A guard of honour of the Shan levy waited near the shore with all the princes of the Shan States.

Dressed in their best silk tunics and flowing trousers, the Tai rulers were an impressive sight. They numbered thirty-three, of varying grades of nobility. A few princes were accompanied by a full contingent of courtiers. These were the Great Saophas, or Saopha-longs, from the largest and wealthiest states: Hsenwi and Hsipaw in the north, Kengtung in the east, and Yawnghwe and Mong Nai in the south. Also among the crowd were about fifty lesser noblemen, including Myosas and village circle chiefs.

Their host, the Great Saopha of Yawnghwe, had one of the largest courts in the land: 174 guards and sentries, eight clerks, four elephant keepers, four horse-grooms, three Myosas, three ministers, twelve umbrella bearers, two revenue officers, four deputy ministers, a judicial clerk, a collector of fines, one finance officer, one interior man, one jailer, and a flock of stewards and pages. His court employed sixty boatmen, too, who poled a golden barge in the shape of a hintha, a mythical bird.

The prince lent his Hintha barge to Superintendent Hildebrand, to help him make an impression on his Rangoon superior. The Superintendent's grand entry caused a rather long delay but, finally, the assembly heard the sound of approaching gongs and cymbals as the fantastic barge broke through the morning mist and glided toward shore, Hildebrand aboard.

The assembly then proceeded toward a temporary bamboo hall raised on the parade grounds of Fort Stedman. Inside, Chief Commissioner Crosthwaite greeted the princes one by one. He reminded them of the importance of paying their tributes, which financed the British garrisons in Shan State "for their benefit". Then he invited each to swear allegiance to Queen-Empress Victoria.

However distasteful the task, Khunsang Ton-huung was a practical man. Under the British peace, he had built a palace with four apartments. A new bride, the Myosa of Mong Yaw's grand-daughter, awaited him. He had a chance to establish a dynasty in peace, and to improve conditions for his people. When his turn came, he stepped forward and made his oath.

The Palace

Nang Hkam Zeng's journeys were never so grand as her husband's. She was only a female who must bump her way toward Hsenwi in the back of an oxcart. Past a turn in the road several hours beyond Lashio, she came to a broad rice plain stretching to a wall of mountains. The Namtu River wound out of the hills like a turquoise ribbon. At the foot of the mountains sat Hsenwi town.

Most princely capitals were tiny places, built mainly to serve the palace. Hsenwi was no exception. Its entrance was marked by a wooden bridge and riverside market-ground. A tall Chinese-style pagoda on a small hill overlooked a single street of houses and the royal palace.

The palace was called Hsenwi Haw. A Haw was the name given to any four walls and a roof that sheltered royalty, even if the arrangement was only temporary. A makeshift bamboo shack could be a Haw. Hsenwi Haw was a real teak palace, though, built in the style of the Mandalay kings, a graceful single-storey structure consisting of several connected buildings. There were the four apartments for the four wives, a treasury, council rooms and rooms for worship. The Haw's centrepiece, the Great Hall of Audience, had an impressive staircase and was topped by a tall pya-thet, a multi-tiered spire of tapering roofs.

The entire sprawling hardwood construction was raised on thick teak pillars set in an earthen mound, surrounded by a ring of outbuildings: servants' quarters, officials' houses, four cookhouses (one for each apartment), stables and gardens. Without her escort, Nang Hkam Zeng would soon have been lost. The palace complex contained as many buildings as Hsenwi town itself.

There are no living witnesses to tell us who greeted Nang Hkam Zeng when she arrived at Hsenwi Haw, or of how she settled into her apartment. In any case, what would onlookers know? If she felt sorrow, joy, or fear, it wouldn't show. Girl-children became women overnight in those days. She had no need of the illusions of men, who rode in golden boats, signed treaties and created their own destinies. We can only imagine her tiny figure moving resolutely, calmly, into the shadows of darkly polished teak.

The palace, Nang Hkam Zeng soon discovered, was a byzantine, boisterous, inner world. In addition to the household staff and the prince's retainers, there were three co-wives and their children, and several children of deceased wives. Altogether the women and children numbered about forty. They shared their apartments with "upstairs girls", distant relatives who acted as nannies or ladies-in-waiting in return for shelter and sweetmeat money.

The daily routine was simple enough. Every morning Nang Hkam Zeng meditated at a private altar in her apartment. After that, she oversaw the apartment's kitchen boys and girls, and helped watch the royal children. Once in five days she browsed through the riverside market, where bolts of English cotton, silver betel boxes, Buddha images, and oil-paper umbrellas were for sale. On Saturdays the wives trooped off to one or more local temples to give offerings and pay respect to images of Lord Buddha.

Religious observances and festivals, or poys, marked the passage of time. Beginning in July, they observed the Buddhist Lent. The days were spent in quiet contemplation, commemorating the time the Lord Buddha descended to earth from the heavenly abode of celestial beings to teach his mother about the Eightfold Path to Nirvana. No one was allowed to marry, build a new home or engage in celebrations until the moon turned full in late September or early October.

At the end of Lent, the townspeople set out candles in paper lotus flowers for the Festival of Lights. Thousands descended on Hsenwi town during the festival. In the evenings, the royal wives and their children paraded by torch-light to the monasteries in the hillsides. There were four monasteries under palace sponsorship, and countless pagodas and temples in the surrounding hills. In pleasant open-air resthouses called salas, the adults listened to stories of the Buddha's life and took turns reading the scriptures aloud. Outside, orange-robed novices lit fire-balloons that rose high into the moonlit sky.

After the religious observances, the prince's men opened two tall white umbrellas in the Hall of Audience, signifying that the twice-yearly Ceremony of Obeisance, or Kadaw Poy, was in session. The Great Saopha took his place on a gold divan between the umbrellas. The Chief Minister had a cushion facing the throne; behind him, all the Myosas and village heads of Hsenwi state knelt on the shining teak floor.

From her apartment Nang Hkam Zeng could hear their rhythmic, sing-song speeches and oaths of loyalty echo through the cavernous hall all day long, as one by one the officials crawled forward to the feet of their Celestial Lord to perform the kadaw, touching their heads to the shining floor, palms pressed together, prayer-like. They presented pyramid-shaped offerings of fruit, rice, flowers and banana leaves, artfully arranged on pedestalled silver and gold platters. Through all of this the Great Saopha sat motionless like a carved god, not a man but an object of veneration.

The festive atmosphere continued until the next full moon, when the monks received their requisites for the coming year. Under a phalanx of umbrellas they climbed the staircase to the Great Hall of Audience to receive new robes and alms bowls from the prince. When night fell and the moon rose, there were more fire-balloons and torch-light parades.

Then in April, the white umbrellas were opened again for the Tai New Year and the second Obeisance Ceremony, a less solemn affair than the first. April marked the height of the hot season, when the sun had no mercy for humans or their Celestial Lords. After the sing-song speeches ended and the Great Saopha finally stirred and gave his blessing to the assembly, the noblemen erupted in a single joyful shout and dashed like schoolchildren into the blinding sunlight. Just outside the door, the townspeople waited with buckets of scented water. At the sight of the emerging, blinking nobles they rushed forward and, in a moment of total pandemonium from which everyone emerged soaking wet, the Water-Splashing Festival began.

Over the next several hours the fun spread throughout the town, led by a winding procession of oxcarts bearing great urns of water. Drummers beat the long-drums and groups of men joined in dances, while others whirled in the fantastic costumes of mythic birds and beasts. As the sun sank into the paddy fields, sparkling arches of water danced over the dusty street. Laughing people chased one another down with buckets, ladles, anything that held water, until all the townspeople were well and truly cleansed for the new year.

There was also an annual gambling festival held once a year to raise income for the state. Gaming masters bid for the right to open stalls, then for a full seven days dared passers-by to try their luck. Everyone, even the royal ladies, bought a ticket on the Thirty-Six Animals Lottery, the most popular game. The lottery manager dropped misleading hints about which animal figure was hidden in a locked box hanging from a bamboo pole, revealed nightly.

On poy nights, Burmese theatre companies put on plays under the stars. The performances featured a beautiful lady singer flanked by two comics who made fun of her while she sang.

Offstage, the Burmese entertainers didn't mix well with their Tai hosts: the strange climate and food made them ill, and they seemed more prone to gambling-sickness and drunkenness than the locals. People looked down on the actors, but they enjoyed the shows. The royal wives were given front-row seats. It was said a prince of Kengtung fell in love with the slender nape of a neck at just such a play. He proposed marriage without seeing the woman's face, which was covered in pock-marks.

It might have been true, or it might have been one of the stories told to break the tedium of daily life. At the festival's end the hidden lottery animal was revealed for the last time, winning tickets paid out, gambling stalls dismantled, and the ladies returned to the Haw, where they had few duties beyond the bearing of children.

Even this was done with ceremony, in temporary pavilions in the palace garden. As the years passed, Nang Hkam Zeng entered the pavilion several times. Four of her children survived. She soon learned that the task of producing heirs was fraught with danger and disappointment. Those that lived through childhood fevers might later fall victim to court intrigues. And increasingly, these intrigues were being manipulated by the White Indians who settled in Lashio town.

From her apartment window, Nang Hkam Zeng saw the British officials who came and went through the gates of Hsenwi Haw. Their visits were few, but there was no escaping the creeping impact of these strange beings.

In 1900, the colonial government hired American engineers to span Gokteik Gorge. Near the natural stone bridge, they created an iron viaduct nearly half a mile long and 850 feet high, the largest in the world.

The mines also underwent expanded development. A centuries-old mine near Lashio, the Namtu-Badwin, was taken over by the British-owned Burma Corporation. Employing new mining techniques, they soon transformed the site into the world's leading lead and silver mine. Indian, Gurkha and Chinese workers were given the resulting jobs, not locals.

Far away in the land of the Queen-Empress, treaties were signed that changed the shape of the Tai world. The Shan States of Yunnan—the original Tai homeland—went to China. China in turn gave up a portion of the Tai territory to France's Laotian colony. At the same time, Britain obtained from China a wild, mountainous territory called Kokang, sandwiched between the Salween River and the new Chinese border. Kokang's Chinese-speaking Myosa was brought under the administration of the Hsenwi prince.

The Kokangese proved adept at the opium trade, which was placed under a new license system developed by the British. The restrictive licenses resulted in a flourishing black market. The more illegal opium became, the more profitable it was. A brick of opium that sold for 65 rupees in the Shan markets went for 200 rupees in China. When Old Yang, the Kokang Myosa, came to the Haw for the twice-yearly obeisance ceremonies, he seemed cocky and flush with new wealth.

Nang Hkam Zeng's husband and the other Tai princes continued to use British forces to settle local disputes and uprisings. At one point, in 1892, the northern Kachins laid siege to Hsenwi town. The Kachins were close hill-cousins to the Tai; in fact, they'd played a significant role in helping Khunsang Ton-huung gain the throne. But now they were angry with the prince.

George Scott, the top official in Lashio, was angry, too. His assessment of the Hsenwi prince had changed since their first meeting at Mong Yai. Now he called the prince "evil tempered", and blamed him for the revolt, saying he treated his Kachin subjects too harshly.

In fact, the Kachins revolted partly because they thought Khunsang Ton-huung was paying too much tribute to Britain: the annual remittance had risen to 10,000 rupees, nearly eight per cent of the state's revenues.

At Hsenwi Haw, Nang Hkam Zeng and the royal ladies waited in fear until a small British force arrived from Lashio to disperse the rebels. Despite their complaints about Khunsang Ton-huung, the British still aided the prince because there remained a lot to accomplish in the Shan States, notably the opening of a land route to China. Maintaining peace was paramount to success.

While helping bolster the Hsenwi throne, the British became a great annoyance to the prince. They were always pressuring, needling, inspecting, or, in their words, "wheeling him into line". They wanted the Great Saopha's sons to attend school in Rangoon "where they would be properly trained and cared for".

The Tai Saophas would have none of this old trick. In the old days, the Mandalay kings demanded the same. They kept the sons as hostages, trained them in Burmese culture and language, and then sent them against their fathers.

In 1902 the British compromised by setting up a special school in Shan territory. It was opened in Taunggyi, a burgeoning little British town on a hilltop near Inle Lake, settled after the original lakeside Fort Stedman location proved itself too swampy and hot for Englishmen. Taunggyi was named colonial capital of the Shan States. There was already an English club and a main street of sorts, and a British headmaster for the new Shan Chiefs School.

Khunsang Ton-huung accepted the compromise location with a compromise of his own. He sent only a minor son, not one likely to inherit the throne, to the foreigner's school.

One day in early 1915 this minor son, called Prince Hom Hpa—Prince Ruling-the-Sky—was startled and flustered when the headmaster called him into his office. He could tell by the headmaster's rising inflection that a question was being asked, just like when the teacher asked "Is the cat black?" or "Are you a bad boy?"

This was too complicated, though: something about his father.

Flummoxed, Prince Hom Hpa whispered, "No." At least it was an answer.

The headmaster looked confused. He leaned forward, then suddenly asked something understandable: "Are you sorry?"

Now Prince Hom Hpa said with greater confidence, "No!"

Finally a translator was called for and the minor prince learned that his father Khunsang Ton-huung, the Great Saopha of Hsenwi, was dead.

There was a lot more the headmaster could have told the young man that day. It was written in the Sanad, his father's Writ of Authority: an heir could be nominated "for the approval of the Government."

Well, the British didn't approve of the Great Saopha's eldest son, so they exiled him to Rangoon.

Then they realised that if the second in line took the throne, jealousies and rebellion might arise; they exiled him as well, to an isolated northern gem-mining centre called Mogkok.

There would be no ruling Prince in Hsenwi for now, they decided. In the meantime, the minor son in their care, young Prince Hom Hpa, should practice his English and learn something about British government. Their plans for the boy's future remained unspoken.

With no Great Saopha on the throne, life entered a new phase at Hsenwi Haw. A few months after the Saopha's death, Nang Hkam Zeng made her way to the birthing pavilion, no doubt grateful that this would be her final duty to her late husband. The child, a girl, was born on May 27, 1915, in the time of gentle rains called the mango showers. It was said to be the season of hope.

Within moments the Chief Minister and the court astrologers arrived to record the event on a palm leaf, which would serve as a lifelong reference for astrological readings. Then they debated the appropriate name for a child born on this day. They settled on Sao Hearn Hkam—Princess Gold House.

The Prince's Last Child

It was the child Sao Hearn Hkam's luck to grow up in a time of unprecedented freedom for the women of Hsenwi Haw. Without a ruling prince to serve, her mother and the co-wives made a vegetable garden near the road. The widows enjoyed the hot sun on their necks and the smell of fresh-turned soil. Their skin grew brown and wrinkled, and they laughed more often. With a stable of fat ponies to choose from, Sao's mother went riding in the hills every morning. She became a skilled horsewoman.

Affairs of state were left to others, although a Mahadevi, as a chief wife was called, or a Royal Mother to the Heir could run a state as well as any man. In fact the largest Shan state, Kengtung, was ruled by a woman, Princess Thip Htila, who came to power under the favour of the British. When she was still a young, unknown princess, Thip Htila slipped into a British army encampment under cover of darkness and warned them of an impending attack by her own people.

"I perceived that the Shans must have some overlord, and I liked the English better than the French," she explained later. Now she acted as Regent to the heir, a thin, delicate boy of thirteen.

In Hsenwi, though, there was neither regent nor Mahadevi. For some reason, Khunsang Ton-huung never bothered to elevate one wife above the others.

In the absence of a ruler, the palace's Council of Ministers carried on their administration under the watchful eye of the British. One of their tasks was to recruit soldiers for far-away battles.

In the summer of 1917, when Sao Hearn Hkam was just two years old, a handful of Tai fighters sailed away to Mesopotamia. Among them was her future husband. He wasn't much of a marriage prospect then, earning just fourteen shillings a day as a private in the 85th Burma Rifles. For this poor pay he crossed the Tigris and assaulted Turkish trenches while bullets and shrapnel filled the desert air like buzzing insects. Burma's material contribution to the war effort was substantial: fifty-three steamers, forty-three launchers, twenty flats, sixty cargo boats, four dredgers, as well as cash amounting to 2.75 crores (crose: 10 million Indian rupees, Burma's currency then) in war loans, twenty-nine lakhs (one lakh equals one million rupees) to the sick and wounded, and 18.5 lakhs to other war charities. Burma was a rich country, everyone knew; despite the war they exported 1.7 million tons of rice that year.

The British were grateful for the assistance, so much so that they were publicly more inclined toward granting a greater measure of independence, once the crisis was passed. The Burmese were "true brothers and partners with us in our great inheritance of Empire," one British official commented.

But all these grand events existed in the outside world, far beyond the care of young Sao Hearn Hkam. The girl's understanding of the world around her was contained in the fleeting images and memories that run through a child's mind without beginning, ending or context.

Once she went on a trip. She remembered being at Maymyo railway station, at the edge of the Shan plateau. Second Brother was there to meet them. He'd travelled down from Mogkok, where the British had sent him before Sao was born. In his arms he carried a small boy, a little older than Sao.

"Your nephew," her mother said.

Jewels dangled from the little boy's hat, the legendary rubies, emeralds and sapphires of Mogkok. Sao reached out from her mother's arms to touch the bright objects. Second Brother laughed and gave her two rupees. Such riches! She didn't know what to do with them, so she gave them to her mother.

Next, they were in Rangoon, in the house of Eldest Brother. Her brother wasn't there, though. They had come for his funeral. When she got back to Hsenwi, Sao remembered nothing of the funeral. She only remembered looking from the window of Eldest Brother's house and seeing the golden spire of Shwedagon Pagoda, the holiest shrine in Burma. It was unimaginably tall and covered in shining gold plate, topped by a hti, a gold umbrella fringed with dangling jewels. They looked like the jewels on the little boy's hat. Again she reached out her hand, blinking up into the blue sky, but these jewels were far too high and remote for her touch.

These fleeting memories were all Sao would ever know of her two exiled half-brothers until many years later, when Second Brother returned to Hsenwi Haw old and bent, a different man.

She never wondered why these two brothers went away any more than she wondered why the sun rose and set in the sky, or why there were foreigners living in the Shan States. The only foreigner she took note of was the local Assistant Resident, Mr. Gaudoin.

Mr. Gaudoin and his wife kept a small bungalow in town, where he was trying valiantly to introduce a new type of well. He dug and dug, but his wells came up dry. So strange, the townspeople thought, because there was water everywhere in the Shan States. His other passion was weaving, which he felt would provide a steady income for the people if they used his modern hand-loom. The local weavers shrugged their shoulders, knowing there was no sense in competing against cheap English cloth.

To maintain good relations, though, the young princesses of the Haw attended his weaving classes. They enjoyed their visits to the Gaudoins' bright little bungalow, where they drank tea and chatted, feeling free and sophisticated.

Then one day Mr. Gaudoin disappeared, and so did one of Sao's elder sisters, Princess Seng-U. The news spread that she and Mr. Gaudoin had run away to Yunnan. No one condemned the princess. She had fair skin and deep-set eyes like a European, so it must have been her fate to marry one. But the royal women felt sorry for Mrs. Gaudoin, who died in childbirth while her husband and the princess eloped. The child survived and was adopted by Seng-U when the couple returned to the Shan States.

Sao wondered if Mr. Gaudoin would be in trouble with his bosses, but she heard he had done a good deed while in Yunnan —he helped bring a rebellious Saopha to heel—and was forgiven for running away. Later, he was promoted and moved to Maymyo. Sometimes they saw him tramping up and down the country roads in his magistrate's robes.

Sao shrugged off the incident—an adult matter—and got on with her games. For children, life at Hsenwi Haw was nothing short of paradise. The Haw was set on thick teak pillars, which created a shady underworld kingdom. On hot days boys and girls together ran from pillar to pillar, playing tag and hide-and-seek. They held contests to see who could count the pillars; no one got further than 200 before losing track.

There was no distinguishing which child belonged to which mother, who was royal and who was not, although the retainers' children gained some extra respect because they were more resourceful, knowing such things as how to get honey from the forest.

The Haw was full of smooth mats, perfect for sliding down the grassy ramparts. The children called this game "train". To them, trains were as natural to the Shan States as bullock carts and mule caravans. Sometimes they played train until the sun set over the paddy fields and the mothers called them in for supper. By this time, the passage from the main entrance to the apartments was dark as night and full of imagined ghosts. They ran down the hallway in a pack, shrieking, laughing, and scaring each other half to death.

When the market came to town every five days, Sao always begged her nanny to take her.

"You'll get in the habit," the nanny warned, before relenting.

Then they would set off together down the dusty street toward the turquoise river. In the market there was an ancient woman who sold stacks of dried fruits salted with chillies. Her breasts hung to her waist and were as flat as the chilli-fruit. When Sao asked the old lady to raise her jacket so she could get a better look, the woman just laughed and said, "All these things I'm not going to take away when I die. I'm going to leave them to you." Many years and hard times passed before Sao noticed her own body was ageing and she finally understood the fruit-vendor's words.

When she was four, Sao travelled by Shan pony across the rugged countryside to Mong Yaw village, where her grandmother still lived. They rode in a large group—her mother, her immediate brothers and sisters, and their personal attendants—singing and telling stories all the way. There were wild apricots and orchids along the trail, and green mountains that went up and up around them like the sides of a monk's alms-bowl.

The best part of the journey was when they crossed the Yaw River and followed the trail into the jungle. A different world from the rice plains of Hsenwi closed in tight around them in a tangle of dripping vegetation. Sao had no fear. To the Tai, the jungle was a place of refuge and plenty, full of ripe fruits and blooming flowers.

The following year, 1920, Sao went to the Burmese school in Hsenwi town, where she met Burmese children for the first time. The school had been established by the British, who wanted everyone to flow into the same melting pot so there would be peace in the land and they could continue their road-building and tree-cutting. Sao was never able to manage the long, looping vowels of the Burmese. She closed her mouth hard at the ends of words, the way the Tai do. In school she learned about the Burmese emperors, the King in England, and the old Queen-Empress Victoria, who was dead now. Outside of school her mother taught her to read Tai script and her favourite nephew, Saw Ohn, took her walking among the tombs of her forefathers. Khunsang Ton-huung's tomb was surrounded by white flowers with golden centres. Once it was broken into by graverobbers, but there were no jewels inside for them to steal.

Saw Ohn teased Sao: "I call you auntie, but I'm older than you. Ask anyone."

Sao supposed it was true. She had plenty of older sisters and half-sisters, and some of them had children before she was born. Ultimately, it was simple: they were all one family. Years later, when Saw Ohn became the President's aide-de-camp and she was the First Lady of Burma, he still teased her about being older. For now, though, they were just children, exploring together the crumbling brick foundations of Old Hsenwi. Their elders told them that once 10,000 princes and Myosas gathered here to swear their loyalty to the Tai king.

If only the English could read the palm-leaf chronicles, what things they could learn! But they never bothered, never saw Sao and her people as anything more than a primitive Burmese "tribe". When the Crown Prince of England visited Burma he only went as far as Mandalay, where he was treated to a Tai dance performance and a selection of handicrafts.

"I bought several things, little crude lacquer bowls and a woman's headdress that will make a wonderful cushion," his travelling companion, the future Earl Mountbatten of Burma, wrote in his diary.

The Tai upper class, on the other hand, were ready to learn everything they could about Britain. After some initial reluctance, the Saophas decided that a British education was the fastest route to understanding the new power in Burma. The first to reach this conclusion was the Prince of Hsipaw, a large state south-west of Hsenwi. He sent his heir off on foot across the western-most Arakan mountains to India for schooling. From there the boy found a place at Oxford and sailed away to England in 1890.

Three years later, the Great Saopha of Hsipaw visited England himself, where he saw the soldiers of the world parade past Queen Victoria, some with skin like the night sky, others with skin as pale as the moon. He was impressed, and concluded then and there that his decision was correct; the next ruler of Hsipaw would know this world empire from the inside out. Returning home he encouraged the other Saophas to take advantage of Britain's education system.

Thus, after three years of struggling with the Burmese language, Sao and her next-eldest sister, Princess Seng-Sanda, were sent away to convent school in Maymyo to learn English. They travelled by cart as far as Lashio, where they boarded a train that carried them west across a broad plain dotted with high limestone hills, each one topped with a shining pagoda. The train chugged through Namtu valley and Hsipaw State then rumbled across the trembling Gokteik Gorge Viaduct toward Maymyo. Sao was only eight years old, but she wasn't afraid or lonely on the journey. Even though her life seemed quite ordinary to her, she was a princess of Hsenwi. A contingent of bodyguards watched over her all the way to Maymyo. Such children cannot imagine danger.

The Three Sisters

Maymyo sprouted from the campsite where the British troops rested before beginning their conquest of the Shan States. Named for a British officer, Colonel May, the town gained rapid fame among the colonialists as a pleasant refuge and desirable army posting. The Tai wondered at the choice of townsites: it was a scenic spot washed by cool breezes and pine needle scent, but there were no paddy fields or irrigation canals. Such places were suitable only for rough mountain tribes who practised hai farming, the most basic form of shifting hill-field cultivation. But then the British didn't come as farmers, everyone knew. Throughout the Shan States they chose high, rocky places from which to rule.

Daily, trainloads of pianos, silver tea services and bulky furniture crawled up from the Mandalay plain and disgorged their contents on the railway platform, causing knots of Englishwomen to squeal at the crushing of hat boxes and the overturning of fine china. The wives of Sikh and Gurkha soldiers waited anxiously for trunkfuls of saris. Crates of bibles and bandages were deposited at the feet of American Baptists, who operated schools and hospitals in remote valleys. Maymyo was a jumping-off point for a great cultural spread engulfing the Shan States.

Outside the station, horsedrawn gharies—covered taxis imported from India—waited under the clock tower for the new arrivals. They departed one by one down Station Road with a clatter of hooves on cobblestones, toward the tall pines that ringed the town and shaded its country mansions. There were a few especially large buildings hidden in the suburban forest, including Candacraig, the bachelor's chummery for the Bombay Burmah Trading Company, which held the teak forestry concession.

St. Joseph's convent school was bigger than Candacraig but there was a homey, cottage-like feel to the place. Its buildings were clad in sun-warmed rosy-coloured bricks.

The nuns were French but taught lessons in English. In contrast to the English ladies at the train station, they arrived with few possessions and few thoughts of home, a trait which Sao admired. They pulled the children to their bosoms and called them by English names. In her dormitory, Sao practised the unfamiliar sound of the name she'd been assigned: "Agnes", so disagreeable-sounding. Her sister became "Mary Josephine". They adjusted to the new names. In the children's eyes, the confident Europeans were their teachers and elders. Their decisions were paramount.

Sao was enrolled in the third standard. Being young, she quickly absorbed the English language. She studied history, maths, hygiene, and Burmese geography. The students also learned hymns but never thought about their meaning—they were just songs.

The rhythm of Sao's life slowly conformed to the Christian calendar. They went home for Christmas and stayed in class right through the hot season, although the weather seldom got very uncomfortable in Maymyo. Instead of Hsenwi's Water-Splashing Festival, she attended Easter Mass in the church; there was a purple bed with a canopy over it for the cross of Jesus. Catholicism, she decided, was not much fun but the pageantry of the Church was captivating in its own way. It was something new anyway: she practised walking backwards so she could strew flower petals at the feet of the priest when he carried the Sacrament. There were no dramatic conversions to Christianity among the students, though. To the Buddhist mind, religion was something achieved through long years of study and introspection. Sao regarded Catholic thought as just another subject in a curriculum that was capturing her mind. She loved learning, especially reading and writing, and was not yet aware that the pro-education philosophy of the Saophas was extended to girls in only a limited fashion.

In the second year of Sao's studies, the girls and women of Hsenwi Haw were once again pulled into the orbit of a ruling male. Prince Hom Hpa—the young man who ten years earlier couldn't understand that his father was dead—returned suddenly into their lives, now a handsome soldier with thick bristly hair and a quick grin. The British educated him, trained him in their army and then favoured him with the Hsenwi throne.

Among the old wives, Prince Hom Hpa's mother gained instant status. She was the Royal Mother now, a tiny old thing who fancied herself a great matchmaker. She lived in the middle apartment, and all the children paid her special respect.

There were other changes in the household: the new prince married a woman from Hsipaw and made her his Mahadevi. A whole new set of family members arrived with the Mahadevi, and a new 'sister' joined Sao and Mary Josephine at school. Lady Mya Zeng was a stunningly beautiful girl, brought to the household by the Mahadevi as a future marriage prospect for one of Sao's nephews. The Mahadevi had named the girl herself: Mya Zeng meant "Emerald". When she arrived at the convent school, though, the nuns renamed her Louise.

At school, Sao, Mary Josephine and Louise became known as the Three Sisters. They were a privileged trio, to be sure, although their elder brother had trouble gaining them any special treatment from the nuns. The prince's dominion ended at the convent gates. When he objected to the girls' attendance at mass, the nuns merely smiled beatifically and said, "Oh, but all the children attend mass, and if we leave them behind they'll be alone in the dormitory."

The children were free to ramble when not at class, though. There were no worries about robbers and kidnappers back then. They often pooled their rupees and hired a ghary to take them into town. There they feasted on strawberries and poked through the central market. Sometimes they picnicked at the Botanical Gardens, where the Europeans had planted rare saplings around a pretty little lake.

In Maymyo, the three sisters were just anonymous school girls in identical navy pinafores and bobbed haircuts. But when they returned to Hsenwi Haw during school holidays, social divisions became more clear. Louise has a way of being irritatingly faultless once she exchanged her school uniform for a dainty jacket and sarong. Under the Mahadevi's loving tutelage, she could comb her hair just so, blending her school-girl bob into a switch of false hair according to the traditional style. She teased Sao and Mary Josephine, who always had strands falling here and there. She also had a way of causing the two blood sisters to fight each other, until the day they formed a pact against her. Class snobbery that Sao had never felt as a young girl now began to rise in her heart. Louise was not royal. She was not a princess, and would never have the title Sao spoken as her name. She was just "Nang Louise", Lady Louise, and she was far too bossy for her station. Sao began to treat the girl with cool politeness. She stopped including Louise in the fun with her blood sisters.

One year, Sao came home for school break to find the old Haw silent and empty. Her brother the prince had built a new Haw in the style of an English country manor. It sat on a hill near town, outshining the best colonial mansions in Maymyo. A guard at the gate presented arms when she arrived.

It was a beautiful mansion, encircled by a colonnaded veranda. Inside, a wide foyer opened into a sitting room with sofas and a piano. A carpeted staircase led to the upstairs bedrooms, which were outfitted with the latest European-style beds and dressers. Most intriguing, there was a garage and a new car, the first her family had ever owned.

What was missing from the scene was Sao's mother. Nang Hkam Zeng had remarried and moved into a simple house in the town rather than enter the world of electric lights and English.

Sao accepted everything as it was. She neither missed the Old Haw, nor considered living with her mother. She was a royal princess and therefore belonged to the household of the ruling prince, the new Great Saopha of Hsenwi.

Prince Hom Hpa's rule was more restricted than his father's, though. As a province of British India, Burma had just five seats in the 145-member Indian legislature. In 1922, the Shan princes had most of their powers stripped away with the creation of the Federated Shan States. The Federation was administered by the

Federated Shan Chiefs Council, whose executive consisted of British officials. The princes were just members, reduced to carrying out the very basics of local administration under colonial rule.

Within this system the British tried to control aspects of the larger picture, in particular the burgeoning opium trade. Burma was slowly moving from being a net importer of opium to a producer, and the Americans were raising the rafters in the League of Nations over the issue. In 1924, American federal narcotics officials estimated there were 200,000 addicts in the U.S., 94 per cent of whom were using a new synthetic opium-based product called heroin. In 1925, the Geneva Convention imposed regulations on heroin exports. The British officials, however, lacked the local know-how and family connections to exercise effective control over the opium fields of the eastern Shan States. Still, they refused to trust the Saophas to regulate the trade. They were convinced that their ledgers and rule books and civil servants could do the job.

In 1928, when Sao was about to turn thirteen, she and her sisters were given leave from school to attend an important state funeral in neighbouring Hsipaw. It was a festive, well-attended affair. The dead man was the prince whose father sent him marching over the Arakan mountains for schooling, before the turn of the century. So educated, he became a progressive, respected member of the Chief's Council.

During the seven days his body lay in state, families high and low camped out on the palace grounds. Sao's elder brother introduced her to Hsipaw's next Great Saopha, who had carried on the Hsipaw family tradition and obtained a degree from Oxford University. Prince Ohn Kya was a thoroughly modern, forward-thinking young man. Like Sao's brother, he was fired with the idea of turning the Shan States into a self-governing nation. For now, though, the scene was given over to ancient traditions. There were food and games until the seventh night, when a line of chanting orange-robed monks accompanied the prince's bier—a colourful construction with a seven-tiered spire—to the funeral pyre.

The dead man's bed of kindling was lit by gun-powder rockets guided to the pyre with ropes. It was a fantastic spectacle.

Next morning, the monks gathered the ashes and bits of bone into a decorative urn for interment in a small shrine-like tomb.

For the journey, the Hsipaw prince's last earthly remains were lifted to the back of an elephant, shaded by the white umbrella of regal authority. Sao was awed by the splendid display, so different from the solemn services of Christianity. Only the richest princes kept elephants, she knew, because an elephant could eat an entire banana tree in one day.

The ex-Great Saopha of Hsipaw had several elephants to lead the procession to his tomb. Behind the beasts walked his ministers, the palace guard, his twenty-four widows, his heir, the noble families, the townspeople and the villagers. High up in a tree, two travelling Japanese photographers recorded the event, amusing everyone with their limb-clinging antics. There was no wailing or crying, because a good man travels to a higher plane after death. To mourn openly would be tantamount to admitting he was not a good man.

Perhaps it was a matter of cementing a political alliance, or maybe, like the Prince of Kengtung, Prince Ohn Kya of Hsipaw glimpsed a lovely nape at his father's funeral. Shortly after the funeral, news travelled to Hsenwi Haw that he had set his sights on Sao's fifteen-year-old sister and schoolmate, Mary Josephine.

The family was horrified. The hopeful bridegroom already had a chief wife.

"She'll have no better status than a serving girl," the ageing Royal Mother declared.

Sao's brother agreed, but what was the solution? After all, his own Mahadevi came from Hsipaw—Prince Ohn Kya was her brother. He couldn't afford to insult a man who was at once his brother-in-law, his neighbour, and his political ally.

That year, the three sisters were kept sequestered at the palace while a decision was worked out. Sao had been looking forward the fifth standard, but now she sat at home, wondering what the French nuns were doing. She pictured the convent in the cool mid-winter morning light, a light frost on the lawn and the smell of woodsmoke rising from the kitchen building.

Finally, her brother announced his decision: all three sisters would be sent far away. In time, the Hsipaw prince would spy another girl and forget about Mary Josephine. The new arrangements for their education had already been made.

Thus in 1929, the three sisters boarded a private train carriage for Kalaw, a British hill station in the southern state of Yawnghwe.

As there was no direct rail line, the girls followed a long C-shaped route that took them west to Mandalay, then 189 miles south through the heart of the Burma plain before doubling back into the southern Shan hills. Leaving Shan State, once again Sao saw the pine-forested hills of Maymyo, but this time she could only crane her neck out the train window and watch her former classmates disappear into the crowd on the railway platform. Then the train wheezed its way down from the hills to Mandalay as night fell. Sao was asleep long before they reached old King Thibaw's sprawling city on the northern plains.

The next morning she wakened to a landscape that seemed impossibly flat and severe. The Shan plateau was just a thin blue streak on the eastern horizon. All day they chugged south through the flat and dusty plain, past palm-encircled little villages and paddy fields, the distant line of hills still shimmering on the eastern horizon. The bodyguards slid the windows up, and a fine soot from the engine fire settled on Sao's arms. The train swayed and its wheels clattered lightly. When night fell, Sao slept soundly, awakening when the whistle sounded the approach of Thazi station.

Although it was still dark, the mountains seemed nearer. She could feel their coolness. They turned east toward the sun's hidden glow, passing through cactus and scrub brush until suddenly the track rose through the thickening forests of the southern Shan hills.

By lunchtime, the train was still crawling and switchbacking upward past rushing streams and tall stands of teak. Finally, the rail line flattened a little and a few villages and farms came into view. Bamboo groves rose on either side of the heaving locomotive. They came upon Kalaw suddenly, a picturesque mountain town nestled in a bowl of green peaks.

The train hissed to a stop, steam bellowing from the engine car. A clutch of vendors rushed the platform with baskets of oily pinewood; Kalaw's firewood was highly regarded in the Shan States. Its sweet scent filled the mountain air like incense. Gurkha soldiers loved this place because the wood-smells and the chilly mountains reminded them of their homeland, Nepal. From the station platform, Sao saw the Gurkhas' timbered houses marching up the hillsides. It looked just like a Himalayan town in a picture-book. The highest house of all, though, was made of brick. It belonged to the British official in charge of the hill station. There was nowhere you could go in Kalaw without looking up and seeing the sprawling mansion, which overlooked the whole town, the cricket pitch, the country club, and the new golf course.

The convent school was just off the golf course road, behind an iron gate. "St. Agnes's", the sign said, an echo of Sao's English name. At first sight, she was disappointed. St. Agnes's lacked the charm of her old school. It was a neat, modern-looking collection of unadorned timber buildings, clustered around a bare courtyard with a young trees. Perhaps the courtyard reminded the nuns of home—they were Italian.

Sao, Mary Josephine and Louise settled into their new surroundings as best they could. Many of the students were Anglo-Burmese. "We are King George's daughters," they said to Sao and her sisters, as if a drop of British blood was greater than the purest Tai blood in the world. The ancient social rankings of the Shan States meant nothing to them, or to the Italian nuns.

On Sundays, the girls crossed the road and passed through the large arching doors of Christ the King Church. At the entrance they dipped their fingers in Holy Water, kept in a large, pearly clam shell. Although the interior was homely, decorated with locally-carved stations of the cross, it looked very grand to the students. Father Lissoni led the Mass under a ceiling of tiny gold stars painted on a blue sky. He was a strange-looking creature, with sad eyes and a bushy forked beard. Above his head, Jesus floated on a plaster cloud, radiating gold streamers. Pews creaked, the hymnals smelled of wet ink and sunlight tumbled through the tall windows.

The girls sang Come Holy Ghost as they were trained, but every now and then someone echoed a line in a high, comical voice. The nuns could never look quickly enough to find out who the jokers were and, by the end of the song, their wimpled faces were red with frustration. Sao didn't mind teasing the nuns a little, but not out of spite. She felt they were good old things, who never acted homesick and only thought about doing good for their God. She didn't mind being just an ordinary schoolgirl in their eyes. To the nuns there was no high and low, only good students and bad. Sao was a good student and never a source of serious trouble. The worst she did during her stay at Kalaw was to participate in the latest spiritual fad from Europe, a seance. Holding hands in a darkened dormitory room, Sao and her classmates tried to stifle their screams and laughter as they listened for the spirit's knock. In the end, the only soul they raised was a scolding Italian nun.

One day the students went on a field trip to Inle Lake. They took the train west, descending sharply to a broad valley, where the town of Heho sat next to a wide market ground for trading buffalo. Then they climbed up and over a second hump of mountains to Yawnghwe valley, a marshy plain resting between tall blue ridges.

From the station, a fleet of pony-carts took them south seven miles along the valley floor to Yawnghwe town, set between the marshes and Inle Lake. At the edge of town was Yawnghwe Haw, where the local prince and his wives lived. It seemed old and imposing, not at all like the bright new Haw in Hsenwi.

In fact, the whole town seemed pressed into stillness by the hot, marshy air and Sao was glad when they finally reached a weedy canal that led to Inle Lake. In a softly rocking boat she closed her eyes and dreamed. Next year she would be fifteen, near marriageable age, but husbands didn't interest Sao. In a few more years she would be eligible for university. What should she study? The shadow of Yawnghwe Haw passed from her mind. She opened her eyes and saw the wide blue expanse of Inle Lake just ahead.

Change

For the Tai New Year of April, 1930, Sao and her sisters slipped some rupees to the school cooks for a few extra treats from the market. That was the extent of their celebrations. To their foreign teachers, it was just another day.

The astrologers, though, regarded this particular New Year as very important. The stars pointed toward a time of great change.

As if to punctuate the predictions, in the early hours of May 6 an earthquake struck southern Burma. The news was slow to filter into Kalaw. At first, Sao heard only a handful of people were killed and some buildings in Rangoon damaged. As the days passed, the students filled the dining hall with excited chatter. Bits of information, heard through relatives and travellers—there was no radio at the convent—began to gel into a dramatic story. At the quake's epicentre at Pegu, just 48 miles from Rangoon, pagodas that had stood for thousands of years were dust. The death count rose into the thousands. It was a major disaster.

Thankfully, the Shan states were far removed from the epicentre. The students felt little real connection to the tragedy which continued to unfold in the lowlands.

In the rural south, where farmers had already undergone enough unsettling change in the past decades, the impact was far greater. A deepening sense of unease about the future took hold. The old kings of Burma could be cruel to the common people, but at least they maintained a sense of order, people thought. Everyone had their place in society, and land passed from one generation to the next. These days, Indian moneylenders known as chettyars were gobbling up farmland while local economies collapsed in the wake of new roads that pressed deeper into the countryside, bearing a tide of cheap imports. Such were the conditions the British Indian Empire brought to the poorest of Burma—not the well-appointed convent schools and private train carriages that Sao and her sisters enjoyed.

For the subsistence farmer, life was sliding out of control and no one could guess what might happen next. Rumours flew and some villagers began gathering swords and building a few home-made shotguns. One by one, the bravest travelled south to Tharawaddy district, seeking the jungle sanctuary of a former Buddhist monk and herbalist whom they called Saya San, meaning Teacher San. Teacher San talked about the excesses and corruption of the new world and about the need to rebuild a virtuous society. Then on October 28 at 11:33 p.m.—an auspicious moment chosen by astrologers—a white umbrella was raised over Teacher San's head and he was proclaimed the Thupanaka Galon Raja, the new King.

The Burmese countryside erupted in the sudden, violent storm of a classic agrarian uprising. As British troops advanced, Teacher San's followers held amulets and chanted incantations. They pointed their fingers at soldiers, expecting them to fall.

Through all of this, the nuns at the Kalaw convent carried on their lessons as if nothing were happening. If they worried the rebellion would spread to the Shan States, they never let on. The students continued their lessons and after-school games, oblivious. But every now and then Sao felt the earth quiver beneath her feet. Aftershocks and small quakes continued to rock Burma, as if the land were trying to shake off the tragic and violent battles.

Far away, the British troops pressed on, undeterred by tremors and unharmed by magic, determined to capture the self-proclaimed king who dared challenge the colonial government's power. Within a year the southern Tharawaddy stronghold was broken and Teacher San was arrested and charged with seditious treason. He was executed on November 28, 1931.

That same year, Sao's brother, the Prince of Hsenwi, travelled to London in an attempt to secure the future of the Shan States. He was joined by three other young, educated princes from Yawnghwe, Mong Mit and Hsipaw. They represented the new, progressive leadership of the future. Prior to their journey abroad, the men spent hours speculating among themselves what might happen to their states if Burma someday became independent of Britain.

It's only a matter of time, they thought. True, the British troops sent Teacher San to the Blessed Realm, but that was an easy matter. Ideas were much harder to kill.

At the University of Rangoon, students shook their heads at the folly of Saya San's peasant rebellion. Why revive old kings and old magic? Through home-grown groups which sprang up under the umbrella of the General Council of Burmese Associations, they talked about new ideas drifting in from European campuses.

In coffee houses from Paris to Saigon, students were engaged in a debate about nationhood, a fresh concept. What was the modern nation-state, how did it apply to colonial possessions?

Over milky tea and oily pastries in the University Avenue teashops, Rangoon students joined the discussion. They agreed the people of Burma constituted a nation no matter how you defined it. The Burmese had no government of their own, though, and they called the Englishman "Thakin", meaning Master. A few of the students began calling each other "Thakin". It sounded right—weren't they, not the English, the rightful masters of their country?

The younger princes of the Shan States, including Sao's brother, watched these developments with some concern. The nationalist movement raised some prickly questions. If Burma was a nation, what were the Shan States? More importantly, who would decide? Well before the Thakins had achieved any prominence, the young Shan princes began planning for a time of greater Burmese independence.

When they arrived in London for a Special Roundtable Conference, the prince and his friends argued for separate recognition as a protectorate—not a colony and not a piece of Burma. They noted that Britiain had made individual treaties with the Saophas and that their states were administered more or less independently from Burma, through the Shan Federation's Council of Chiefs. In the event of greater independence, British officials should negotiate separate terms for the Shan States, rather than lumping them in with their long-time adversaries, the Burmese.

Such arguments were beyond British understanding. The British couldn't conceive of their colony as an amalgamation of separate territories, or of the frontier peoples as anything more than backward "hill tribes". The less cohesive, more borderless traditional forms of social organisation were hard to grasp. They believed a country was a single chunk of definable territory, and that all the land they'd conquered in the late 1800s was "Burma". They had no desire to carve off a slice of the prosperous colony, for whatever reason. Prince Hom Hpa's mission failed.

Returning to Hsenwi Haw in bad temper, he was immediately immersed in the never-ending daily complications of managing a growing family. He and his Mahadevi had adopted a son and a daughter, and now the boy was pining to go to school in England. His wife supported the idea. A degree from Oxford was tradition among the men of her Hsipaw family.

The old Royal Mother had plenty to say, too. She informed the prince that an appropriate match had been found for Mary Josephine: the prince's Chief Minister. We must start thinking about the other girls, too, she reminded him. There were only so many school fees one household could support, especially if the prince's heir was going to study abroad. Wasn't it time for the girls to close their books and come home? After all, they weren't going England.

It was all too much for Prince Hom Hpa: he made a few swift decisions before turning his attention to more important matters of state.

At the beginning of 1932, Sao made a new friend at Kalaw, another royal princess. Princess Van Thip of Kengtung transferred from St. Michael's Anglican School in Maymyo. When she arrived at the Kalaw convent, Sao felt an immediate bond. The Kengtung girl carried the delicate shoulders and porcelain complexion of her powerful family, members of the Hkun branch of the Tai family, but her feisty spirit belied her China-doll looks. She laughed frequently, spoke English fluently, and was as lively and head strong as her famous Auntie, the retired Regent of Kengtung—the woman who warned the British troops, ruled a state, and once grazed her ponies on the Governor's lawn in Rangoon.

Princess Van Thip introduced Sao and her sisters to Joan, the Kengtung excise commissioner's daughter. On Saturdays, the small gang went hiking through cool bamboo groves in the peaks above town. They explored caves and waterfalls, and exchanged dreams of the future. They vowed to pass the tenth standard matriculation exams and meet each other at university.

Sao was sixteen years old and looking forward to writing her exams for the seventh standard when the devastating news arrived from Hsenwi: Mary Josephine must return home for her wedding, and Sao and Louise must come home, too.

There was one more completely unexpected piece of information for the sisters: their beautiful and spirited Kengtung friend, Princess Van Thip, was also called to Hsenwi Haw, to become a minor wife to the prince.

Sao was more upset by the news of Princess Van Thip's fate than was the bride herself. The Kengtung princess merely shrugged and said she didn't mind marrying Sao's brother, even though her bride groom already had a wife and two children and was much older than she. Perhaps she had known all along that this was her future.

Sao, on the other hand, couldn't accept the sudden turn of events. Back home, she pleaded with her brother to at least let her stay in school long enough to write the seventh standard exam. Prince Hom Hpa didn't see the point. Sao had been a top student, always placing first in her class.

"I know you'd pass, so why bother?" he asked.

The prince argued that the girls knew enough to get along in society. They could do housework and tell the kitchen boys how to prepare an English dinner table. It was more than enough to ensure high status in a marriage.

Marriage! The word made Sao's head spin. Suddenly she saw her future: a loveless bondage to one of her brother's toadies. Her husband would bow and scrape, and she and he would follow Prince Hom Hpa's orders for the rest of their days.

"I will never marry a man who depends on you for a living," she vowed. It was the start of a long-running argument, which she planned to win through sheer stubbornness.

As the years passed, the offspring of various Myosas were suggested as grooms. To each one she sniffed, "Oh, him—my brother's servant."

One day her exasperated brother handed her a piece of paper. On it was written, "I will marry the man who does not rely on Prince Hom Hpa for a living." There was a space for her to sign her name. Sao considered the ageing ministers of state who trooped in and out of her brother's office, and their sons. She didn't want to marry any of them. In fact, she didn't want to marry, period.

She signed her name, Sao Hearn Hkam. The agreement provided a safe way to end the constant fighting. After all, everyone who was anyone relied on her brother for a living.

The Contract

Without school, Sao spent long days reading books, going to market, enjoying the festivals and greeting Hsenwi Haw's constant stream of callers. When the Ceremony of Obeisance was held, all the nobles and their families came to town. Old Yang from Kokang brought a weedy collection of children with him, including a fierce, thick-legged little girl with close-cropped hair called Olive.

"Watch out for that one," the townspeople joked. "She carries a revolver in her school-bag."

Everyone knew that the Yang family was growing rich from opium. Everyone knew, too, that they lacked an opium-grower's licence. Sao's brother had a licence, but the palace's crop was small; sales were restricted to a few British medical firms. Locally, special shops sold to licensed addicts and to a few old Kachin and Paluang folk who liked a little opium mixed with their tobacco.

The black-market trade was something else altogether. Its tentacles wormed across the globe. Other countries complained, especially the United States. Pressured by the League of Nations, the British sent teams of police into the hills to cut down poppies.

A few illicit fields in rural Hsenwi were burned. The results were promising at first: the 1936 Shan State crop was just eight tons, down from thirty-seven tons a decade earlier. But beyond the policeman's reach, remote pockets of opium production were more difficult to stamp out. Kokang state was one such pocket. There were few other goods the local people could produce profitably in competition with cheap imports. Old Yang used his China connections to assist the trade, in return for a tax on profits. It was good business. In Kokang's main town, Tashwehtang, he built a stone mansion with a tiled roof, encircled by stout walls set with broken glass and a heavy wooden gate. But he still had to kneel to Sao's brother on Obeisance days.

Sometimes the local British officials came to the Ceremony of Obeisance, too, but unlike Old Yang they never knelt or presented offerings. Instead, they observed from a row of chairs placed on a low platform on the prince's right. They came into the hall standing as tall as the Saopha and, even worse, they kept their shoes on within the sacred premises. Prince Hom Hpa didn't mind, though. Accepting different customs was the sign of an educated, cosmopolitan mind. He didn't want the British to think him old-fashioned.

Because the road to China went right through Hsenwi, plenty of touring foreigners stopped by the palace for lunch or tea. Princess Van Thip, Sao's schoolmate-cum-sister-in-law, entertained them graciously in the parlour of Hsenwi Haw. The prince married her for just such a task. She projected an air of modernity. His first wife, the Mahadevi, had often proudly told the household about her trips to England as a child. But when English-speakers called, she lingered in the background with the maids, eclipsed by the prince's new, educated wife.

The young Princess Van Thip quickly tired of life in Hsenwi, however. It was a sleepy backwater compared to her home in Kengtung, the largest and richest of all the Shan States, a 20,000-square-mile triangle of land wedged between the borders Thailand, Laos and China. The capital was a walled and moated city on an open plain surrounded by forbidding mountains. Its buildings were richly carved with peacocks and lions.

Like Kokang, Kengtung was east of the Salween, in prime poppy-growing territory. The Kengtung Saopha refused to accept

British opium restrictions, arguing that without poppy revenues he wouldn't be able to pay his annual tribute of 30,000 rupees to the colonial government.

Left alone for the time being, the renegade state flourished. The Kengtung Saopha's splendid Indian-style palace eclipsed the Yang family's stone mansion, or any other building in the Shan States for that matter.

No wonder, then, that Princess Van Thip grew bored with Hsenwi's single dusty street and little riverside market. To ease her homesickness she brought some young relatives to live with her, including an amusing young man who teased Sao endlessly. But when the school year began, all the boys went off to learn, leaving Sao behind.

Sao missed school but, unlike Princess Van Thip, she was never bored with life around Hsewni Haw. The royal princesses had a tennis court, well-bred saddle horses, and a car and driver at their disposal. The riding trails took them to the forest, where they visited the family's elephant, a gift from Kengtung. The beast was stabled outside town because there was nowhere to keep an elephant at the modern Haw.

Sometimes the family motored to the neighbouring state, Hsipaw. At the local Saopha's mansion they spent sumptuous afternoons around a concrete swimming pool set in a rose garden. Other times they visited Mong Yai where, in marked contrast, the local Saopha lived in a dark old teak palace with nine kowtowing wives. It was like stepping back in time. Her brother's adopted son and daughter came from Mong Yai's ever-expanding brood of royal offspring.

The days passed gently. Sao was only dimly aware that beyond her family's hilly enclave the Great Depression was overtaking the globe. Fortunately, the Shan States were still largely self-sufficient. The natural richness of the land protected people from want, even after the international rice market tumbled. In lowland Burma, where the farmers' work was tied to export markets, production slowed and prices rose locally almost as fast they fell internationally. But in Hsenwi, people just ate the rice they grew in their own fields. They suffered neither glut nor want.

At the Haw, persons familiar and new drifted through the sitting room and settled on the velvet sofas under the chandeliers. Sao's brother had gained a reputation as an up-and-comer in political affairs.

He and his friends discussed conditions which pointed toward greater self-rule. First, a world-wide drop in commodity prices meant the colonies no longer made a rich return for London. Second, the rivalry with France had faded. Third, Britain was under pressure to fulfil promises of self-determination made when colonial troops were needed for the Great War. London was ready to loosen the reins, the parlour pundits guessed, but not completely: a second war might break out, placing a premium on colonial resources again.

Sao added little to the discussions. After the usual introductory small-talk, she settled back in her chair and left the adults to their debates. She smiled and listened to the words swirl around her as lazily as the ceiling fans above.

One day there was a new face in the parlour, a slightly corpulent, middle-aged Tai man with the stiff posture of an army officer. Sao needed no introduction. Although they'd never met, she knew him by reputation: Prince Shwe Thaike of Yawnghwe was a leading Saopha. She remembered how imposing his palace looked when she passed by it during her school field trip to Inle Lake.

According to local lore, he'd inherited the place unexpectedly from his uncle, the man who leant Superintendent Hildebrand his golden barge in the shape of a Hintha back in 1890. Under British rule, Yawnghwe state entered a period of political decline. Before the invasion, the late Saopha's power was derived from close ties to Mandalay palace; he was an adopted son of King Thibaw, and he kept one of Thibaw's wives and a son at Yawnghwe Haw. When Thibaw fell, the Saopha became embroiled in an ultimately useless succession war, which the British played to the hilt as an opportunity to divide and rule. They supported the Yawnghwe Saopha against his enemies, even knighted him, but they took plenty of concessions in the bargain.

Perched in hill-top Taunggyi, just ten miles away, the British regime overshadowed Yawnghwe valley. Then one day in 1917, on the shore of a small lake at the foot of the hill, a farmer found an albino crow. He brought the crow to the Haw, where it was recognised as a pure soul reborn in animal form to guide and protect the state. The bird's captor was rewarded with a life-long appointment as Keeper of the Crow.

The Great Saopha decided to recapture some faded glory. When his Haw burnt to the ground, he viewed the fire as a rebirth. He hired local artisans to raise a magnificent palace on the town's northern boundary. The new Haw mixed tradition with modernity. Instead of being raised on wooden pillars, its foundation was a main floor of sturdy red brick. On top of the brick base sat three traditional ceremonial halls constructed of injin, the most ancient and stately of the Shan hardwoods, seasoned and stripped of sapwood. In the garden his workmen raised a special pavilion for the white crow.

The palace took years to build and the Saopha died before its crowning glory was complete: a seven-tiered spire, the symbol of highest royalty, made in honour of his ties to the old Mandalay court.

One other important task was left undone: he never named an heir. Without an heir, the British appointed one of their own officials to administer the state until the palace's Council of Ministers provided an agreeable nomination.

In 1927, the Council announced that the childless Saopha had died with the name of a young British-trained army officer on his lips. He was one of several minor nephews, an unknown among the Tai but well-known in the ranks of the colonial forces, being Burman Officer-in-Charge of the Northeast Frontier. At the British Residency in Taunggyi, his nomination was met with immediate and enthusiastic approval.

To his complete surprise, thirty-three-year-old Prince Shwe Thaike found himself inherited of his uncle's populous court, the unfinished Haw, and some 1,300 square miles of territory. He had neither expected nor desired anything more than an army career. But in 1929, after six months' special training, he left his army post and moved into the traditional-style Haw by Inle Lake.

Seven years later, he radiated the self-assured, slightly overfed image of middle-aged success. On the cusp of forty years, he was senior among the progressive Shan princes, and just hitting his political stride nationally.

When Sao entered the parlour that afternoon, he was deep in conversation with Prince Hom Hpa's mother, a cup of tea balanced on one round knee. He looked up at her rather myopically through thick eye-glasses. There were introductions, a polite exchange of hellos, and then he turned his square army-officer shoulders back toward the Royal Mother. He knew the old lady's brother from his army days. Sao sank into her chair and listened while the two swapped family stories.

After a while her brother appeared and the two men retired to the veranda for cigars and, Sao supposed, more serious conversation. There was much to talk about. London had just handed down the Government of Burma Act. Under the Act, Burma would no longer be ruled as an Indian province, but would become a separate entity. Britain would appoint a Secretary of State for Burma, advised by a partially-elected local legislature. The Act's drafters hoped it would appease those who reminded Britain of her wartime promises of greater independence.

Prince Shwe Thaike of Yawnghwe was one of the colonial soldiers who spent his youth dodging bullets for the Empire, so he no doubt took special interest in the Act. This was the pay-back, although its provisions for home rule were badly watered down and the Shan States were paid scant attention.

At least, this is what Sao assumed the discussion might entail.

When the meeting was over, her brother called her into his office. He stood by his desk, a piece of paper in his hand. She recognised it instantly. He laid it down on the desk and she saw in one glance her own childish signature, impulsively penned five years earlier to end an argument. Above her name sat the words, "I will marry the man who does not rely on Prince Hom Hpa for a living."

She couldn't believe he still had it. Her brother's voice echoed across a great distance, as if suddenly her ears were stuffed with silk and she was falling backwards into nothingness. Prince Shwe Thaike, the Great Saopha of Yawnghwe, ruled one of the wealthiest, most powerful princedoms in the Shan States. He depended on no one for his living, least of all her brother. The wedding was set for June 1937. She was the bride.

Sold

Sao had one year to stop the marriage. She cried not once during this time, but she did engage her brother in some furious arguments. The intended bridegroom was twenty years her senior. He was already twice a widower, had one living wife, and had grown-up children. Sao herself would turn twenty in May, an old maid by others' standards but still young by her own. The thought of marrying this middle-aged friend of her brother was revolting and terrifying. She wondered what she did in a previous life to deserve such a fate. To complicate matters, a young relation from Kengtung —the same lad who used to tease her during school breaks— unexpectedly declared his love for her. She begged her brother to let her marry the younger man, who in fact would have been a very agreeable match from the family's perspective. But it was too late. Promises had been made, arrangements set.

Soon the whole state was gossiping about the young Princess of Hsenwi's distress. Some joked that she threw herself down the staircase but was saved by the luxurious carpet. Word spread to Yawnghwe State, but Prince Shwe Thaike refused to back down.

How could he? His bride-choice was tangled up in the strange history of his inheritance. On taking the throne, Prince Shwe Thaike married two sisters from Yawnghwe. A third wife, a young Maymyo aristocrat he'd met while soldiering, lived in a compound in town—the other wives didn't want her in the palace. The Maymyo wife died young, leaving a son who later died, too, in his teens. Then the two sisters died as well; tuberculosis was suspected. They left three children behind.

With three wives dead, a rumour spread: the women died because they were not royal enough to live under the seven-tiered spire raised over the Haw by the Prince's late uncle.

When the Prince married a third sister from the same family of locals, the mutterings grew darker. Nothing good would come of this low-born nephew and his common wives living beneath a symbol of highest royalty, the people opined.

Prince Shwe Thaike was not a superstitious man, but he was politically astute. To win over his subjects, he must marry a true princess. The one he'd found, though, was proving to be a royal pain. She didn't try to run away or create scandal, but her behaviour was no less exasperating. She simply faced her family down with one unbending phrase: "I don't want to marry him."

The Yawnghwe Saopha could see the marriage agreement unravelling. He considered taking the matter to the British courts. The British had plenty of laws: breech of verbal contract might apply. The magistrate in Taunggyi advised him, however, that the princess was of age to make her own decisions.

At this point he might have wondered himself if there was some way to back out. An unwilling, headstrong wife spelt nothing but trouble. By now, though, the whole state was waiting to see who would win the battle.

Sao's refusal was shamelessly public. Luckily for Prince Shwe Thaike, however, there were other distractions to keep the pundits and bazaar-talkers occupied. 1936 was a year of political unrest, as Burma prepared for its transformation from a province of India to its own country under the British Crown.

The leaders of the unrest were the students at Rangoon University. No longer a faceless bunch, they called themselves Thakins, Masters, the respectful term used to address Englishmen.

The alternative, they said, was to be a Kyun, a slave. The Thakin movement's leader was Aung San, charismatic editor of the *Oway*, the student newspaper. He adopted traditional dress, and when he and his followers clacked through the streets on their wooden sandals, labourers and vendors nodded approval. It was the first tiny thread binding ordinary people to the new world of politics. The *Oway* produced great reams of broadsheet decrying the new Government Act, under which Burma would still be subject, ultimately, to colonial control. Aung San was expelled from campus for his ink-stained efforts.

In Aung San's defence, a second student leader emerged, a sad-eyed little elf of a man who called himself Thakin Nu, "Master Tender".

Fired by dreams of becoming a great playwright, Thakin Nu left his impoverished delta farm village for an education in Rangoon. He studied hard, graduated, took work as a lawyer in a provincial town, married a rich local girl, and then, dissatisfied with obscurity, returned to university and easily fell into Aung San's orbit. To earn money, he tutored students and translated the works of others: the *Communist Manifesto* and Dale Carnegie's *How to Win Friends and Influence People*. In his mind, left-wing economic theories were stirred into the same pot as a salesman's advice. The combination served him well; he became president of the Students' Union and Aung San's unofficial second-in-command.

Aung San's expulsion from campus left Thakin Nu briefly adrift. He realised it was up to him to fill Aung San's place. He was willing to try. He led his fellow students to the gates of the Governor's mansion, where they burned the Union Jack. Leading the chants, Thakin Nu felt suddenly emboldened, as good a leader as any.

When the elections were held, a handful of Thakins decided to run. They won four seats.

There was no clear majority in the new House of Representatives when it convened in April, 1937. A scholarly college lecturer named Dr. Ba Maw led a coalition comprised mainly of members of Sinyetha, the Poor Man's Party. True to the party's name, several upcountry members could barely scrape together enough rupees for train fare to Rangoon. One of their first acts was to vote themselves a salary of 225 pounds sterling. The four young opposition Thakin members declared they would not accept a single pence of the MP's salary. The Thakins were determined to be selfless, incorruptible, a new breed of leader. They attacked the new constitution with great vigour, declaring it a sham democracy under the thumb of the London-appointed Secretary of State.

As it turned out, Britain did not even appoint a separate secretary for Burma, but instead rolled the position into the India portfolio. The promised separation from India existed on paper only. Nothing had changed. In protest, the Thakins burned the Government Act outside the parliament building.

If Sao had gone to university, as she had dreamed, she would have had a front row seat for these exciting events. Instead, she lived in her own private despair, a prisoner of Hsenwi Haw. At night she gazed out her bedroom window over the rooftops of the town. She thought about her elder sister, the one who ran away to Yunnan with Mr. Gaudoin. In those days there was no ruling prince to stop her. Sao's situation was quite different. Her brother had taken to monitoring her mail and her movements. There was no way she could make it past the guard at the Haw gates, and if she did, where would she go? The town beneath her window looked lonely and deserted. She knew no one would help her.

When the mango showers of May ended and the coming monsoon clouded the south-western skies, villagers from throughout the state began arriving for the wedding. The mansion on the hill became a scene of anxious activity as arrangements were made for the guests' accommodation and entertainment.

A beautiful court dress of gold silk with pearl accents arrived from Mandalay. Through all of this, Sao voiced not one opinion or suggestion.

It has nothing to do with me, she told herself.

On the chosen day, her maid wound the glittering Mandalay cloth around Sao's hips, fastened the jacket's dainty jewel buttons, placed a drape of gold cloth across one shoulder, and swept her hair into a luxuriant ebony mass captured in place by a brilliant diamond solitaire pin and matching diamond comb.

Outside, the bridal procession waited to escort her down to the old Haw in the town.

It has nothing to do with me, Sao said again.

It was not a big wedding as such weddings go, and the ceremony was unusual in that it was held indoors instead of in an open-air pavilion, as was more common. Inside the Great Hall of Audience, in the musty darkness of ancient wood, Sao knelt beside her groom, the Prince of Yawnghwe. She remembered her childhood games beneath the hall, racing from pillar to pillar, hair flying, knees dirty, free and happy as the wind, laughing between shadow and sunlight. Then suddenly she was a grown woman and her brother took her hand and bound it to the groom's with a silk scarf. She felt a trickle of ceremonial water on their outstretched wrists.

It was over. She was married. Head lowered, she followed her husband outside into the dull, humid glare.

He and his attendants led the procession, happily accepting the guests' well-wishes. Sao walked behind unsmiling, a demeanour accepted with great approval: it showed the correct attitude of a demure Tai bride. In a dream she heard the sound of jokes and laughter float down the procession line, her brother's voice rising above the others. According to custom, his men had stretched a gold chain across their path. Her brother demanded a toll. With much jocularity, the groomsmen handed over a token sum and the chain was raised. Her brother stood back with his characteristic grin and the procession moved forward. The transaction was complete.

Sao and her husband left Hsenwi a few days after the wedding, travelling by car down a rough seasonal road that cut 125 miles through the centre of the Shan states, roughly paralleling the River Salween's journey to the southern jungles. The driver struggled mightily with the road, grinding gears and swiping at the dusty windscreen with a rag. They were followed by an entourage of similarly-challenged vehicles which carried the Prince's wedding attendants and other officials of the Yawnghwe court, as well as the couple's wedding gifts, mostly silverware and blankets. Of her own belongings, Sao packed only a few dresses and some jewellery.

She was miserable, but her spirit knew only survival. She pushed the emotions down and passed the long journey chatting lightly with her new husband as if he were a polite acquaintance. They travelled slowly, stopping at villages where people were gathered to greet the Prince and his new bride. Receiving their respectful salutations, Sao felt like she'd suddenly been transformed into an old married lady.

After three days, they came to the main highway at Loilem and turned west toward Taunggyi, where twin cathedral spires rose against a green crest of mountain and new bungalows nestled like steps in the hillside, climbing from rutted streets to a shining white pagoda. Red and white poinsettia and pink cassia bloomed everywhere, easing the colonial capital's rough, half-built frontier character.

Descending Taunggyi hill they followed three tight hairpins before Yawnghwe valley was revealed briefly through the trees. The pale shape of White Crow Lake, where the albino crow was discovered long ago, lay stretched across a checkerboard of paddy fields. A stand of tall Flame-of-the-Forest trees lined its banks, scarlet blooms raised skyward on silver limbs. With another turn in the road, the view disappeared and they continued their descent through forest until they reached the valley floor and the crossroads to Yawnghwe town. Turning south they passed by paddy fields on their right, ploughed and ready for seedlings. On the left, water buffalo raised their snouts from reedy ditches, horns curving back to glistening shoulders, ears flapping lazily, their work done until the November harvest.

Gradually the fields gave way to a broad marsh that marked the entrance to the town. The road curved around a squat white pagoda that was still under scaffolding. Every Saopha must commission pagodas and temples to gain merit; although Prince Shwe Thaike would be hard pressed to better his predecessor's fantastic creations, this was a start.

Skirting the town's quiet streets, Sao remembered her school field trip—the sultry marshy air, the odour of wetlands beyond the coconut groves, and the cold imposing bulk of Yawnghwe palace. Nothing had changed. The driver steered the car along a long loop of road to the palace's eastern entrance, where guards saluted crisply and then hurried to pull the gate shut behind them.

On that first day, the Prince led her on a brief tour of the palace. The main floor, brick-walled, was given over to offices. Below the offices were an iron-barred basement treasury and a storage area for ceremonial litters, elephant howdahs, and other dusty family heirlooms. A narrow staircase led to a second-level terrace where the upstairs servants' quarters and three great wooden halls were set: the Inner Hall for private family worship and meditation; the Middle Hall, where the Prince gave his formal instructions to his ministers of state; and the Great Hall of Audience, where the Ceremony of Obeisance was held. Four large apartments were attached to the main building, each with a door opening out onto the stone terrace. Sao knew one must be the home of the Prince's other living wife, who was nowhere to be seen.

From the terrace Sao looked out on the palace grounds: four tennis courts, an orchid garden, flowering paduak and tamarind trees, stables, a parking garage, a cookhouse, the unmarried servants' quarters and two pleasantly furnished courtyards placed north and south. Although the albino crow was long dead, its pavilion still stood near the southern courtyard. It was said black crows never perched on its roof, out of respect. Near the northeastern corner of the Haw was a shrine containing thirty-eight Buddha images and beyond it, by the eastern gate, sat a large, plainly-built spirit house. Prince Shwe Thaike explained that this was where the town Nat, or guardian spirit, resided. Its house was built in the square Burmese style because the Nat came from Burma. The spirit came to Yawnghwe in ancient days, guarding an early Saopha who had escaped from the Mandalay court. Pursued by the King's men, the Nat turned the fleeing Saopha invisible whenever the soldiers came near.

The townspeople came freely to Yawnghwe Haw to pay homage to their Nat and, in dry years, to collect water from the palace, the Prince explained. Sao listened and looked, saying nothing. She noticed a line of servants hurrying her few possessions and wedding gifts from the driveway into the bowels of the palace. Somehow she knew she would never see the gifts—glimpsed only briefly at the end of the ceremony—again.

She was being swallowed up, just like her mother.

When they come to the Great Hall of Audience Sao imagined herself entering a dark, claustrophobic cavern. Instead she was surprised to find the room was spare and bright, of immense size with rows of arching lead glass windows that pulled in the dull pre-monsoon light and scattered it beautifully across the hardwood. She followed gilded pillars to a low platform set against the western wall, where the Hall's only decorative items were placed: a tall gilded dais for the palace Nat—a different creature from the town Nat who lived outside—and her husband's royal divan, facing east and flanked by folded white umbrellas.

At this moment Sao had much to consider. That which ensnared her—blood, social standing and a seven-tiered spire—must now be made to work in her favour. For the first time since the wedding she looked her husband square in the face. He had thick dark eyebrows and plump lips, like a well-fed child's. Behind the spectacles, his eyes looked weak. She found she was not the least bit afraid of him.

"I will sit on that throne beside you," she said to him slowly and clearly, so there would be no mistaking her words. "I didn't come here to be your concubine."

A New Life

Perhaps because Lent was soon upon them, Sao formed the early impression that the Yawnghwe folk were more quiet and pious than their northern cousins. Between the town centre and the main canal was a strip of Buddhist land containing temples, monasteries, a novices' examination hall built by her husband, and the tombs of past Saophas. The streets were shaded by banyan trees with heart-shaped leaves, of the kind the Buddha sat under to gain enlightenment.

Every Saturday Sao visited one or two of the temples, followed by a servant who carried her offerings. On weekdays, accompanied by a royal guard, she walked Yawnghwe's few streets under an oil-paper umbrella, wandering past the tall wooden houses of her husband's ministers and high officials. Except for a few small shops, the town's major function was to serve the palace. At the town's southern end, simple dirt footpaths meandered between thatch-roofed houses, leading to fields of tall sugarcane.

Noting the bodyguard and her fine clothes, the townspeople treated her with respect, but not unduly so. She chatted easily with those who spoke English or Tai, although many did not. Nearly half of her husband's subjects were the descendants of thirty-six families transplanted in 1379 from Tavoy, on Burma's southernmost archipelago, to help populate the marshy Yawnghwe princedom. How they fared the uprooting is a tale untold, but they did adapt, survive and become their own people, known as the Intha. From one generation to the next the Intha fished the shallow water of Inle Lake and paid homage to twenty-seven successive Saophas.

There were other strange people who came walking from the high hills beyond Inle Lake, including Paduang women who stretched their necks long with encircling brass rings. They moved with slow grace, heads bent forward like deer, legs and arms circled with brass as well; at times their faces visibly bore the pain of their beauty.

On her walks, Sao liked to visit the Indian merchant's shop because Pa-O tobacco farmers from the southern part of the state often stopped there. The Pa-O dressed alike in black cottons and had the ruddy, weather-beaten features of men of the land. They were cousins to the Karen people, whose large territory stretched along the jungled border with Thailand. The shop-keeper served them tea and entertained them for hours, making plenty of sales in the bargain. The Pa-O called the shop-keeper Mr. Nine Paise because, they joked, everything in his shop cost nine paise, just one paise short of a rupee.

Returning to the Haw from these small journeys, there was little for Sao to do but read and watch the falling rain. Her closest companions were books about politics, history and the world beyond. She became quite an expert in English history.

Her new family was hardly as complex and boisterous as the Hsenwi bunch; there was no gang of young people to befriend. The closest to her in age was the Heir-Apparent, a son of the Prince's deceased first wife, but he was off studying engineering at King's College in Canterbury, England. His younger brother, Prince Hseng, was preparing to join him abroad in September. That left just one child at the Haw, Sanda, a little daughter of the Prince's still-living but never-seen other wife. The other wife had obviously been sent away for the time being.

Sao and the Prince lived together in the Middle Apartment. With the other wife in exile, she could almost imagine being part of a normal couple instead of a polygamous royal marriage. She couldn't know happiness, but at least the Prince was kind to her.

The apartment had a few modern touches, namely electric lights and a western-style spring bed. At night the whole household went to bed when the Prince did because it was he who called for the generator to be shut down. Sao felt stranded when the lights flickered and died and the generator's hum faded to silence. Sex she could stand, because what else could you do, she reasoned— it was a big Haw and there was no one to save her.

In September the rains passed and she discovered she was pregnant. She thought nothing, just absorbed the knowledge.

The fields beyond Yawnghwe Haw ripened to gold. In October, she and the Prince drove up the hill to Taunggyi for a sitting of the Shan Council. The frontier capital's population had grown to a few thousand people and its fruit trees had matured, so that now their branches hung heavy with pears and apples. There were now two streets of Indian and Chinese shops, at the end of which sat the British Residency, a palatial brick building with two wings, a centre-block, three fireplaces and a grand entry hall.

An ageing Indian servant met them at the gate and led them to a large cheerful room, where cocktails were served. The windows, open to the breeze, overlooked an English garden of sweet-peas, asters and roses.

"I live in an earthly paradise!" boomed Philip Fogarty, British Resident for the Shan States, when he greeted the assembled Saophas and their wives.

As president of the Shan Council, Fogarty would host several parties that week and have ample opportunity to repeat his sentiment. It was not the first time Sao heard the British mention the Shan hills and paradise in the same breath and she knew it was heartfelt, not empty flattery. From Taunggyi to Maymyo, in cosy bungalows and gracious mansions, the British officials discovered a world of crisp mountain air, dazzling sunshine and blossoming trees. Far removed from the bureaucracy in Rangoon, even further removed from the dismal cold of their homeland, they were revitalised.

That evening, the talk around Fogarty's dining table quickly settled on a sensational murder that had recently occurred in Kengtung state. By now all the Saophas and their ladies knew the details by heart: on the last day of Lent, the Kengtung Saopha enjoyed a dance performance at his Hall of Justice and then at 8:30 p.m. walked in formal procession to his Haw for dinner, accompanied by his family and the court musicians.

"How slowly the music plays, like a dead march," he said to his sister, just moments before a bearded man dressed in black pushed forward with a pistol in each hand. The palace guard continued to present arms, like toy soldiers, while Kengtung's Great Saopha thudded to his knees and the murderer slipped away.

A few months later a bookish twenty-year-old gave himself up to police and confessed all, accusing the Saopha's half-brother of luring him into the plot. The two men were tried before a British judge at the courthouse in Taunggyi.

By February 1938, the public was riveted by an unfolding tale of opium, power, jealousy, and the fallout of British attempts to control the Kengtung throne and the drug trade. The half-brother involved was none other than the stubborn fellow who refused to give up the opium trade in 1936, saying he could not pay the colonial tribute without it, a stand which ultimately led the British to depose him.

At first the deposed Saopha tried to defeat his replacement with magic spells. When that strategy failed, he recruited his cousin's son to carry out the assassination. In his confession, the young lad said he gulped three fingers of whisky for courage, pressed a fake beard to his face and then went forth into the night to shoot the new Kengtung prince. At the trial's end the older man was convicted to life in prison while his young protégé was allowed passage to exile in Thailand. Proud Kengtung State, the largest in the land, with its moated city and sprawling palace, was given over to a British regent.

The events in Kengtung were a fatal mixture of poppies and politics that presaged the region's tragic future. At the time, though, the public failed to realise just how powerful a crop opium was becoming. Instead they pointed to the practice of polygamy as the seed of Kengtung's undoing.

There can never be orderly secession in a household of half-brothers and rival wives, people said. Sao agreed strongly with this point and didn't mind telling people so, arguing that feudal marriage had no business in the governance of a modern state.

She kept away from the courtroom crowds, though, because she saw no entertainment in watching a man stand trial under the British. Later in February, her husband took leave of Yawnghwe Haw and travelled north to act as pallbearer at a state funeral in Mong Mit, a remote but influential princedom. The deceased was the retired ruler of the state; some years earlier he had relinquished power to his son, one of the four "young progressives" among the Tai princes. The son had a degree from Cambridge, five Bloodhounds, a Great Dane and an English wife. Under his direction, the funeral was a mixture of old and new: elephants led the march to the funeral pyre, an Italian catering firm supplied the food.

During meals, the attending princes had ample time to discuss events of the world, including gathering conflicts in Europe and China. The previous July there had been a serious incident in China, where Japan's Imperial Army was slowly spreading across the north from their base in Manchuria. Just nine miles from the Chinese emperor's Beijing capital, Japanese soldiers were tasked with guarding Marco Polo bridge. There had been tension, but no open warfare as yet. Then one warm July night the Japanese officer in charge of Marco Polo bridge, startled by moving shapes in the darkness, fired the first shot against Chinese troops, touching off a rapidly-widening conflict.

On their journey to the Mong Mit funeral, some of the guests saw long lines of conscripts—17,000 of them altogether, they'd heard—travelling north. The men were ordered to metal the road from Lashio to the Chinese border by June. The road was to be used for transporting relief supplies to Chinese troops battling the Japanese occupiers. It was the same route Sao's mother followed as a young bride, the Golden Road to Cathay that sparked a jealous rivalry between empires and led to the annexation of the Shan States. Having never reached its full potential as a trade corridor to China, the trail was now being shaped to a new purpose by the world powers. It was about to be reborn as a fiercely-contested pawn of war called the Burma Road.

The conscripts carried on their work through the hottest months of the year, toiling under a blazing sun and a sky that remained endlessly blue and clear day after day. The same relentless sky reached all the way to Yawnghwe, where Sao entered the final stages of her pregnancy while the temperature climbed. Luckily, the high elevation of the Shan plateau brought cooling night breezes to temper the steamy heat of day. She craved tomatoes, even though the doctors and midwives warned her that eating tomatoes in pregnancy caused itchiness in old age. As her body grew, her appetite diminished until finally all she wanted was glutinous rice and boiled fish.

She experienced none of the nervousness that was her due as a first-time mother. Her every need was taken care of, she knew, so she felt nothing, neither fear nor anticipation. She merely waited. From inside her apartment, she listened to heavy machetes splitting bamboo in the garden, as workmen raised her birthing pavilion.

When she finally entered the pavilion everything was ready: an airy retreat with a comfortable bed and bath, and nurses to keep a twenty-four-hour vigil. Together, they awaited the first pains.

During her confinement, people from all around the state gathered to celebrate the birth and the Tai new year. Gradually they filled up the pavilion's reception hall. By the time Sao entered labour, the crowd had overflowed into the garden.

On April 15 the doctor arrived for the final contractions and delivered her of a healthy baby boy.

As it was the custom to wait until the child was named and formally presented in public, the celebrants outside the birthing pavilion passed the next several days drinking tea, feasting, visiting, and playing cards late into the night. When Sao and the baby slept, the nurses hurried outside to shush the throng.

Sao and the Prince chose the name themselves. They called him Prince Hso Khan Hpa, Tiger Clawing at the Sky, Tiger for short. On the seventh day, Prince Tiger was introduced to the people. The birth, the great crowds and the atmosphere of high occasion might have overwhelmed some women, but not Sao. Surrounded by respect and good will, she could feel her social position rising and, with it, her determination to rule Yawnghwe at her husband's side.

Mahadevi

At the end of the Buddhist Lent of 1938, it was announced that persons attending the Ceremony of Obeisance would pay homage to the Very Just King of Great Lineage of Yawnghwe State Who is Full of Dignity and the Arbiter of Life, Prince Shwe Thaike, and his Mahadevi, the Lady of the Seal, Princess Hearn Hkam.

Sao was neither consulted nor forewarned of her elevated status, but it hardly mattered. As she promised herself and her husband, she took her place beside him in the Great Hall on a silk-pillowed divan between the white umbrellas, where she sat wrapped motionless in stiff glittering silk, legs tucked elegantly beneath her, hair upswept and pinned with shining jewels. Her shoulders sloped gracefully, pale hands rested in her lap, and her face—soft chin, wide dark eyes, cheeks the translucent rose gold of the upper class—was absolutely still and calm. Beside her, Prince Shwe Thaike sat in satin turban and tunic, a second glowing object of veneration. Before her knelt the ministers, Myosas and all the village headmen, bathed in the light of the hall's arched lead-glass windows.

All morning the officials crept forward and touched their heads to the polished floor before their Great Saopha and Mahadevi. The title Mahadevi was borrowed from the classical Pali language, maha meaning great and devi meaning a princess whose soul resided at a higher level than ordinary mortals. More than just having her position raised in marriage, Sao had entered a higher plane of existence, one reserved for Celestial Rulers, the god-kings and goddess-queens of the Shan States.

Afterwards, the supplicants took their lunch and the remote, bejewelled Mahadevi was restored as an entertaining hostess who told jokes, poked fun, took a stand in discussions, and challenged the ministers and Myosas to accept her as an educated, strong-minded woman. She smiled radiantly, revealing a tiny, charming gap between her front teeth. If anything was amiss in her life, no one could tell.

The year Sao became Mahadevi of Yawnghwe, the Prince's other wife moved back to the Haw and took up residence in the south apartment, next to Sao and the Prince. She was about Sao's age, a tall woman with strong, elegant features. Sao felt no jealousy, but neither was she particularly friendly toward the woman. She noticed Daw Nyunt May's relationship with the Prince was wholly different from her own. The woman lived in service to her husband, and he abused her for it. If she answered back, he shouted at her with a soldier's curses.

It must have been a lonely life. Daw Nyunt May had watched one sister after another die off under the Prince's roof. She had no children of her own, and so happily shared Tiger's care with his nursemaids and attendants. Sao stubbornly began to isolate herself from such domesticity.

That's why the Prince married me, she thought. He was bored with his old-fashioned wife.

Sao herself said whatever she liked to her husband. Her fearless wit left him either speechless or amused. The Prince's friends laughed and said, "See what you get when you marry a modern girl!"

One day, Daw Nyunt May's youngest sister came to the Haw. Still school-aged, she performed the kadaw at Prince Shwe Thaike's feet. After, she didn't go home but moved into the south apartment with her sister. Her name was Nang Mya Win. She swore she would never formally marry the Saopha, but she didn't refuse his attentions. Perhaps it was the only life she could imagine. Her parents raised their girls to be wives in the palace.

Sao was sickened and deeply embarrassed by her husband's open acceptance of the girl. He paid for her schooling, like a father or uncle might, but everyone in the state acknowledged her as a minor wife. Sao had spoken out publicly on many occasions about the need to end such feudal arrangements.

"I am for one husband, one wife," she used to say to whomever was listening.

That was when she was indeed the only wife at Yawnghwe Haw. Now there were three. She accepted Nang Mya Win and treated her as a daughter, but never publicly referred to her as a co-wife. It was too humiliating.

At least among the women she held the highest rank and sat on the throne as Mahadevi. She had a place in the running of the state, too. If she walked into her husband's office, the ministers had to pay her respect and include her in the discussions. She listened to them talk about budgets and public works, slowly gathering knowledge. It was better than staying in her room, reading.

The state earned about 380,000 rupees a year through taxes and forestry concessions, she learned. From that sum, 130,000 was forwarded to the Federated Shan States' common pool. The remainder paid for public salaries, local administration, jails, police and courthouses. To prepare for the fiscal year, the Prince and his revenue officers boated out to the family retreat, a graceful little palace on an artificial island in the middle of Inle Lake. They called it "Bo Te", the Officer's House, a place surrounded by quiet, satin-like water.

The lake palace was all part of the comforts of a Shan royal family's life. In addition to state expenditures, a ten per cent allowance was afforded to the Great Saopha for personal expenses, an amount strictly supervised by the British Resident to ensure there was no mixing of state and personal spending. Every year, the Prince presented his household books to British accountants, showing what amounts were spent to entertain state guests, to support monasteries and monks and to maintain his palace, staff and household.

Although everything was above-board and accounted for, there was no denying the royal family lived in conditions so far above their subjects that it was like comparing heaven and earth. What farmer could afford more than one wife, a stable of riding horses, a garage full of cars? The villagers tilled the land in simple cotton clothes, and paid their taxes honestly because to under-report a harvest spelled bad luck for the next year. From their meagre earnings they were expected on various occasions to present gifts of gold, silver, cloth and food to their betters, and some local officials no doubt took advantage of this. The farmers followed the centuries-old social order because it was the only life they knew, and because the Prince was their benefactor who cared for them in times of trial and paid for their simple milestones of life, be it a new house, a boy's ordination ceremony or a wedding celebration. The day was coming when young men would challenge this way of life, but not yet.

In his role as benefactor, Prince Shwe Thaike used part of his personal allowance to provide for the education of poor students. He sent several of the more promising ones to university. He was also passionate about promoting westernised health care, although it was not an easy job. The idea of a hospital—a single building filled with the sick and dying—was beyond the experience of people who were used to being cared for at home, and who hoped to die under their own roof. The Prince kept strict watch on his subjects, badgering those who missed check-ups and immunisations. It was Sao's duty to convince the hold-outs that ghosts didn't stay to haunt the hospital, but went home when the body died.

Sao also occasionally accompanied her husband to Rangoon. There was a good unsurfaced road to the capital now, but they preferred to travel by train, a slower journey but less dusty and cramped. It took two days. When they arrived, their schedule typically included state dinners and meetings at Government House, the official residence of the Governor of Burma. It was a palatial three-storey Victorian mansion set in a beautifully-tended garden on an ample square of land that stretched all the way from Ahlone Road to the corner of Windsor and Prome. Disembarking from a chauffeured limousine at the mansion's grand doors, they were greeted by a nine-gun salute, an honour prescribed in the Prince's Writ of Authority.

Government House was not the only building of note. Under the colonialists, Rangoon had become Southeast Asia's foremost city. The new buildings south of the railway station were exceedingly elegant: the Court House, the Port Commissioners' Building, Grindlay's Bank, the Bank of Hong Kong and Shanghai, the Bank of India. Colonnaded and corniced, the gleaming white facade of the Strand Hotel faced the Rangoon River, where steamers crowded the jetties. From here, the country's major exports made their way down the river to the sea. Burma was the world's top rice exporter. There was oil, too, carried by pipeline 376 miles from the Yengangyuang fields of north-central Burma, Britain's largest far eastern oil discovery.

In contrast to the edifices of bureaucracy and finance, the country's parliament building was a small two-storey building with an unadorned pyramid-shaped tile roof, as plain-looking as an army mess hall. Nearly invisible from Maha Bandoola Street, it sat behind the gate of the Quadrangle, a square of land surrounded by three wings of the massive Secretariat Building.

Within the Secretariat's endless corridors, Britain's Chief Secretary presided over ten secretaries, three joint secretaries, five deputy secretaries, nine under-secretaries, five assistant secretaries, seven registrars, and a host of support staff of the Indian civil service. They lived by the Secretariat Code, a huge volume crammed with correction slips and addendums. Their windows overlooked the tiny parliament building, a fitting architectural arrangement. The Secretariat was the source of the country's true governance, not parliament.

Not far from the Secretariat was City Hall and Sule Pagoda. Squat and bulbous, the pagoda sat at the hub of several busy streets, the widest being Sule Pagoda Road. From morning till past sunset, the spicy-sweet smell of Indian curries and the garlicky steam of Chinese noodles drifted onto the road. The restaurants defined Rangoon's cosmopolitan nature for, above all, this was a city of immigrants: 250,000 Indians and 40,000 Chinese together outnumbered the 160,000 Burmese, who were mostly landless labourers.

The British influence skirted Sule Pagoda and travelled like a vein north, following the flame trees of Prome Road past the Governor's mansion, the Good Shepherd Convent and Girl's School, the exclusive Pegu Club. Haunts of the wealthy clustered around the city's two picturesque lakes—the swimming and boating club on Royal Lake, and the yacht club on Victoria Lake, which the locals knew as Inya Lake. Between the lakes was Golden Valley, a suburb of well-built mansions and bungalows. Just east of Golden Valley, imported thoroughbreds thundered around the Race Course's grass oval. In a satellite town beyond the city's northern limit was Mingaladon International, one of the most modern airports in Asia.

Rangoon was impressive, but Sao didn't enjoy her visits. She hated the city's heat; even the water tasted too warm. At get-togethers, conversation was limited to a bewildering tangle of political gossip; the Burmese parliament had become a nest of corruption, intrigue and racial tension. Trying to follow all the charges and counter-charges in the newspaper made her head ache.

There were still people with good intentions, however. Seeing little hope in their quarrelling elder countrymen, young and idealistic parliamentarians looked abroad for inspiration. Some met with Indian communist party officials who told them about a world where all men were equals. Others looked to Japan, a strong Asian country that had resisted imperialism.

Sao regarded the whole lot of Burmese politicians and activists as a dubious bunch. The less time her husband spent in Rangoon, the better for the Shan states, she thought.

At luncheons and receptions she met the leaders of the new establishment, comprised of a few respected elder politicians and a handful of influential Burmese who had homes in Golden Valley. Pundits nicknamed them the Golden Valley Party. She and her husband developed a friendly acquaintance with the new prime minister, Dr. Ba Maw. The former professor wore round, heavy-rimmed spectacles on a square, slightly western-looking face: it was said he was part-Armenian. He exuded a steady and dignified intelligence. Although he came from the world of academe and Prince Shwe Thaike from the military, the two men were cut from the same cloth: British-educated, well-travelled and well-read. They enjoyed each other's conversation.

Every now and then, the Burmese prime minister returned the visits. He liked Shan State, especially during the festivals. Yawnghwe's major poy was in March. The Saopha issued gambling licenses and hired theatre troops to entertain the crowds. The proceeds from the gambling licenses went to assist the poor, a gesture Sao thought generous. She couldn't understand why some newspaper editorials criticised the practice. Even Ba Maw complained when he saw two Burmese being held in the stocks in the middle of the poy grounds.

"They're drunk and causing trouble," explained the Saopha. "If you want to take them in your car back to Rangoon, fine, I'll set them free." The PM let the matter drop.

Sao found the exchange amusing. Naturally her husband's police should have the power to use the stocks: was he not the Celestial Lord of his state, the Benefactor and the Arbiter?

In addition to political and administrative functions, the royal family of Yawnghwe played a strong religious role in the life of the valley. At the full moon of late September or early October, the Prince crossed Inle Lake on a ceremonial barge, accompanied by a flotilla of musicians and celebrants. The royal ladies and their children travelled in separate paddle-boats, enjoying the procession's slow and majestic progress, for this was a holy occasion not suitable for roaring boat-motors. At Inle's southernmost shore they disembarked and climbed a wide marble staircase to one of the most famous temples in the Shan states.

Inside the temple were five small images of great antiquity and history, two of the Buddha and three of his disciples. In ancient times the images were given to the King of Burma by an old crone of the Shan states, but when the King tried to carry them away to Burma nothing but bad luck befell him, so he cast them away.

It was an old story that everyone knew well, and no one doubted it when Prince Shwe Thaike's predecessor said he had rediscovered the five statues many centuries later, lying half-buried at the base of a tree. They were simple little figures, just a few inches high, with large noses and lotus-leaf caps, formed in the attitude of Paung Daw U, or Buddha-in-the-Lotus-Pond. To house the ancient images, the former Saopha built his most fanciful legacy, Paung Daw U Temple. He laid the temple's elevated courtyard with imported Italian marble so that pilgrims could gaze on Inle Lake with stone-cooled feet.

Thereafter, it was the Saopha's annual duty to carry the images by golden barge to all the little fishing villages on the lake so that the people could gain merit by rubbing small squares of gold leaf—purchased for a few paise—onto the images. After several years, the images looked like five shining pear-shaped gold lumps. Their lake journey continued to the next full moon, ending at a special pavilion on Yawnghwe town's strip of Buddhist land, where for several days the people prayed and celebrated, while the monks climbed the Dragon Stairs to Yawnghwe Haw to receive their new robes and alms bowls for the year.

More than religious symbols, the five gold-covered statues were symbols of national pride, for these were the very images that refused to leave the Shan States in the hands of a Burman. In fact, Sao's husband took his name from the sacred images. Shwe Thaike meant Arriving Gold, for he was born on the day the images arrived in Yawnghwe. They were a potent discovery in the hands of a ruler, and their care was a most important royal responsibility.

Like most Shan citizens, Sao thought the five images told an important lesson about the essential separateness of Burma and the Shan States. As a woman, she couldn't touch the sacred images, but she entrusted her offerings to Prince Shwe Thaike and prayed that he would heed the lesson of the images and lead their country well in the days to come. As for her, she had her own duties to fulfil as Mahadevi, including the birth of another child. On April 26, 1939, once again at the height of the hot season, Sao brought into the world another little boy whom they named Prince Hso Lern Hpa—Moon Tiger Crossing the Sky. The doctor looked worried; he detected a heart murmur in the tiny chest. He could only guess that it was a hole in the heart, a condition that might improve with time if the boy avoided strenuous activities.

The child looked fine, though. They nicknamed him Tzang, meaning Elephant, a wise and patient animal. Sao felt her life was moving into the stately pattern of womanhood. A new year, a new baby. But the outside world was giving birth to new things too, labouring toward its own painful delivery of events. Sao never imagined what lay ahead. No one did.

Two

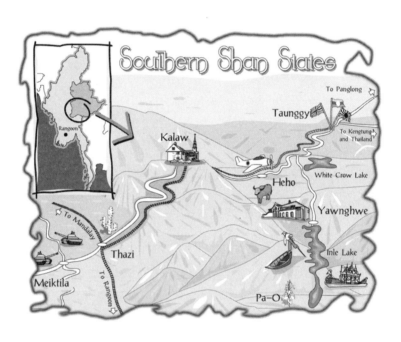

Sao's husband, Prince Shwe Thaike of Yawnghwe.

Prince Shwe Thaike with daughter Ying Sita and son Myee.

Tzang, Tiger and Daw Daw Bu, the comptroller's wife who entertained them with her stories.

(Above) Sao and the children. From left to right: Ying, Harn, Tiger, Sao, Tzang, Myee. Seated on floor: Leun and Haymar. (Asia Photo Studio)

(Left) Myee at Yawnghwe Haw.

Myee's ordination ceremony at Yawnghwe Haw.

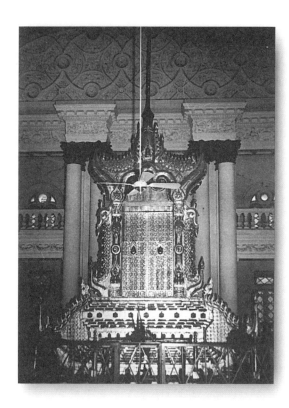

King Thibaw's Throne, in the Marble Hall of the President's House. (Mya Photo Syndicate)

A ceremonial barge. (Don Jedlic)

(Right) Monks descending the Dragon Stairs after receiving their yearly requisites.

(Below) Yawnghwe Haw: The Great Hall of Audience and the Dragon Stairs. (Don Jedlic)

An Intha village on Inle Lake. (Don Jedlic)

A Shan market. (Don Jedlic)

The Crater in the Paddy Field

Although Sao hoped her husband would lead the Tai people to independence, it turned out that Prince Shwe Thaike was destined instead to serve once again in a foreign uniform. Throughout 1938 and 1939, Germany spread across the continent of Europe, engulfing Poland, Austria and parts of Czechoslovakia. German Jews struggled to emigrate to safe lands. There was talk in Rangoon of annexing a portion of the Shan States for their resettlement. When Edmund de Rothschild visited the family's Inle Lake retreat, Prince Shwe Thaike volunteered a portion of Yawnghwe State for the would-be emigrants. Whether out of fear of raising anti-foreigner sentiment or because of the world-wide complacency toward the plight of the Jews, the offer was forgotten. Locally, British officials were more focused on manoeuvring the different parties within Burma's governing coalition. In March, the nationalist-leaning Prime Minister Dr. Ba Maw was replaced by U Pu, a strong supporter of the British Empire.

This led the scholarly Ba Maw to join his Poor Man's Party with the young Thakins, who had just set up the Communist Party of

Burma with help from the Communist Party of India. The first Communist secretary-general was the expelled student newspaper editor, Aung San, who had since joined the staff of the *New Burma* newspaper.

At the same time, the Thakins undertook secret discussions with Japanese agents. The agents whispered promises of self-rule if the young men agreed to help Japan liberate Burma, indeed all of Southeast Asia, from the colonial masters. It was exciting, clandestine stuff. Suddenly independence seemed achievable, not just a dream. The Indian communists provided a platform and Japan had a real military, not just placards and slogans. Had not Japan seized Chinese ports, sending foreigners into flight? And now they pressured the British to close the Burma Road and its supply pipeline to southern China. In addition to a strong army, Japan had already signed a pact with Germany. It mattered not to the young Communist Party members that the pact was anti-Soviet, only that it was made with Britain's foe. They told one another that events were leading toward a mighty clash of east and west, from which a new Burma would rise.

Fuelled by youthful ambition, the Thakins couldn't see that one small country placed between two great world powers had a limited future, nor could they yet imagine the death and destruction that must arise from such a terrible conflict. They didn't have the eyes of Lieutenant-General Mutaguchi Renya, the young Japanese officer who fired the first shot at Marco Polo bridge. When his commander arrived on tour from Tokyo, Mutaguchi begged the man to send him to the front in atonement for the savage war he'd created. At the time, everyone expected the main front-line would be the Sino-Soviet border, but already Japan's eyes were turning south toward the soft, resource-rich underbelly of colonial Asia.

On September 3, following Germany's invasion of Poland, Britain declared war and once again mustered its colonial forces. Within a few days of receiving his recall, Sao's husband donned his officer's uniform and left the palace for the barracks at Taunggyi.

He was given two assignments: first, help raise a territorial force and, second, periodically travel the border areas to gather intelligence on the local situation. The first matter was easy. Most of the princely states were wealthy and willing to contribute toward the force. They raised 60,000 pounds sterling for the war effort. The

Saophas also had the power to press conscripts into action, although there were plenty of volunteers—mostly hill-dwelling Chins and Kachins—who were happy for the chance to earn a soldier's pay.

As for his second assignment—intelligence-gathering—Prince Shwe Thaike had no trouble arranging casual visits to various relatives and acquaintances in far-flung areas. Sometimes Sao went along, stopping in Hsenwi to visit her family. The Prince told her what he told the British: the border people and their cousins in Thailand were not likely to put up much of a fight in the event of a Japanese invasion. Still, an invasion seemed so remote a possibility—a successful invasion even more remote—that when he delivered his intelligence reports to Taunggyi, they were merely noted and filed.

Sao never understood her husband's confidences to be anything more than personal observation, or his trips in the countryside to be anything more than pleasant holidays. She didn't learn he was actively engaged in intelligence work until some years later. His soldiering seemed a respected profession, nothing more, and war was something to listen to on the wireless in the long tropical night, with a cool drink under the ceiling fan.

Life carried on lazily in the years before the invasion. Another child was born the following hot season, in April 1940. They formally named him Prince Hso Lao Hpa, Star Tiger in the Sky, and nicknamed him Tzang-On, Little Elephant, after his older brother Tzang.

Daw Nyunt May took over most of the mothering. She tucked the children in at night. Sao didn't mind. She loved the children and their funny, stumbling antics, but there was a certain formality to their relationship, an emotional distance. Part of it had to do with her high position and part of it, perhaps, with her self-imposed social isolation from the other wives and from the household staff, who were all related to the Prince. While others played with the children, Sao busied herself in the office or stayed in her apartment. She enjoyed her children in her own way, from a distance. She was never one for strong emotions, she reflected, not a harsh person but just, well, cool-hearted, she supposed.

Her eldest boy, Tiger, was now a sturdy little fellow who tagged around after his half-sister Sanda. They conscripted the royal guards into endless games, because no village children dared enter the fenced and gated palace. Even the Great Saopha got down on his hands and knees sometimes to play horsy-back. He was anxious to instil some democratic, modern values in his sons. He instructed his children to call the servants "auntie" or "uncle", in the respectful manner due to elders. Once, when Tzang was a little older, the Prince overheard him tell his nursemaid, "I am a prince, so you have to do as I say." Summoned before his parents, the boy received a blistering lecture.

"Don't ever get on such a high horse again," thundered his father. "You are nothing. You're just a child."

Prince Shwe Thaike remained deeply influenced by his life in the army barracks. Born just a minor prince, he wasn't raised as royalty. Instead he learned a soldier's disdain for the soft life. He believed in discipline and hard knocks and noses-to-the-grindstone. But instilling these ideals was a great challenge under the circumstances: when Tiger had his hair cut, a personal attendant stood by to catch the holy locks before they touched the floor. It was all part of the daily life of a young god-king raised to embody the traditions of an ancient society that teetered on the edge of disaster and decline.

And what events foretold of catastrophes to come? During his border tours, Prince Shwe Thaike noted Japanese shop-keepers, fishermen and foresters seemed to pop up out of nowhere these days.

In Rangoon, a simple Japanese monk collected alms door-to-door, making contacts and arranging meetings. He introduced the Thakins to a Japanese newspaper correspondent, Minami Masayo, who, unknown to the young rebels, was secretly Colonel Suzuki Keiji of the Imperial Japanese Headquarters.

The colonial government finally began to grow nervous. With the Defence of Burma Act they outlawed the Thakin movement. Even the refined and erudite Dr. Ba Maw ended up sharing a jail cell with the young fellows he'd invited into his coalition. Among the detainees was the round-faced Thakin Nu, who led the student strike in defence of Aung San. He was taken to a romantically grim and spartan cell inside the walls of old Mandalay palace. A great place to write a novel, he decided.

Meanwhile, his charismatic friend Aung San stowed away aboard a Norwegian rice freighter bound for Amoy on the south China coast. He was just twenty-four years old. In Amoy, a Japanese agent stumbled upon him, wasting from dysentery in a cheap guesthouse. The agent spirited him to Tokyo, where he was greeted by his old Rangoon journalist contact, Minami Masayo, now revealed as Colonel Suzuki. The colonel was a dashing figure with a thick, upturned mustachio and carefully oiled and parted hair. He promised to bring thirty good men out of Burma for special military training under Aung San's command.

Wheels were turning, fates being constructed with untold consequences. In September, the Three-Power Pact between Germany, Italy and Japan was realised; Germany promised all of Southeast Asia to Japan. That same month Burma's new prime minister, U Pu, lost his government to a scrappy, disreputable fellow named U Saw. U Saw was so openly corrupt and blunt that he gained the admiration of Burma's Governor, Reginald Dorman-Smith, who preferred an honest crook to a dishonest saint.

In August 1941, on a battleship in the grey choppy waters off the coast of Newfoundland, Canada, British Prime Minister Churchill and U.S. President Roosevelt formed an alliance on the basis of certain principals, including the promise of freedom and self-government for all colonial countries. In Rangoon, Governor Dorman-Smith had already come round to the idea that the Burmese parliament deserved greater independence. He'd had no luck convincing the British Cabinet of this, though, even after the Atlantic Charter was signed and announced.

The people of colonial Asia took the Charter to heart and awaited a promise of freedom as the reward for defending European interests in the region. It was Dorman-Smith who suggested U Saw fly directly to London to discuss the matter.

One October afternoon, worshippers at Shwedagon Pagoda were startled by the roar of the PM's private plane as it buzzed low three times around the golden spire before sailing off into the wide blue sky, carrying U Saw and his Secretary of the Defence Council toward unexpected misadventure.

The London meeting was a bust: Churchill could barely contain his irritation over being asked to discuss constitutional matters in the midst of war. Bitterly, U Saw charted his return journey via the United States and the Pacific, but nearing the Hawaiian Islands his plane suddenly veered and turned back. From the aeroplane window he saw tall plumes of black smoke rising from Pearl Harbour. It was December 8, 1941, the morning after the Japanese attack, and there would be no continuing onward. The whole world was at war.

If U Saw had set out just two days earlier he might have returned safely to Rangoon and ended the whole unfortunate adventure with a glass of whisky at Government House. As it was, his plane was re-routed via Lisbon, where he made the grave mistake of calling on the Japanese Ambassador.

He never made it home: at a refuelling stop in Haifa on the Palestinian coast, the British arrested him for treason. His Secretary was allowed to continue on without him. U Saw was transferred to a British jail in Uganda.

Within a few days, the people of Burma learned that their prime minister was in a foreign jail and, even more humiliating, that Britain had declared Burma to be at war with Japan without bothering to consult the Burmese parliament. For the duration of the war, U Saw would languish in his cell, growing increasingly bitter until the day came for him to explode on the Rangoon political scene like an angry human bomb, changing the course of Burmese history and the future of the Shan states forever.

Shortly after the imposed declaration of war, Sao travelled home to Hsenwi for an extended visit while her husband made his rounds of the north country. Hsenwi Haw was still the gracious, welcoming country manor of her teenage years, and the old gang of sisters and cousins was lively as ever.

Everyone had heard about a bomb that had landed on Shan territory near the Chinese border; a motorcade was soon organised and the adventuresome, Sao included, set out to see this strange wonder. They followed the freshly surfaced Burma Road to Kutkai, a little military post and hill station, then travelled eight hours across a lonely red-earth plain set with jagged black hills. That evening they stayed at Muse, a bustling valley town on the Shweli River, which separated the Shan States from China.

Early next morning, Sao and her friends drove twenty-five miles along the Shweli Valley floor, past bamboo groves and Chinese-style stone houses until they reached the northernmost point of the Shan States, the border town of Namkham. It was a pleasant and exotic resting place, prosperous, fertile and crowded with colourful hill tribe peoples. At the edge of town was the famous teaching hospital of American missionary Gordon Seagrave. Crisply-uniformed Kachin nurses bustled between pretty stone buildings.

The doctor sometimes visited Hsenwi Haw. He seemed a friendly, dedicated man, although Sao had heard other missionaries gripe about his high-profile doctoring. It shocked her to learn that jealousies and posturing existed in the religious world, just as in any parliament or palace.

After gaining directions to the bomb site, Sao and her friends set off on foot toward a series of sharply-folded hills. It was an exhausting hike, climbing, descending, climbing, descending, but spirits were high and there were plenty of people on the trail, all of them trudging toward the bomb site like tourists on holiday. When they finally arrived, there wasn't much to see, just a wide, shallow depression in a paddy field. Sao felt a little let down, having expected destruction unimaginable from this, the very first modern bomb to land on their country. Instead she was met by a crowd of onlookers and picnickers, each one carrying a small tingle of excitement at the thought that dramatic events were happening on their very doorstep, just beyond China's blue hills.

The Invasion

It happened so quickly. Along the long border separating Thailand and Burma's frontier states stretched tumbled folds of jade-green mountains, criss-crossed with smugglers' paths and brimming with the resources of survival—small game, wild fruit, clean water and firewood. To the British mind, though, the jungle hills were impenetrable. To enter them meant certain death from malaria and starvation. To send an army over the land border, with supply trucks, armoured vehicles, heavy artillery—impossible.

But when Japan's 15th Army marched toward the border of Burma's southern archipelago, they didn't encounter such logistical problems. The Japanese soldiers used mules and bicycles, not heavy trucks. They carried few supplies, observing what the monkeys ate to determine which foods were safe and nutritious. This was not to say the way was easy: on the high, narrow trails a misstep meant sliding into the twisted roots and vines of the jungle floor below, with no way back up. They walked single-file, a thin line of soldiers stretching from peak to peak. During the day the temperature soared until every man was gasping and shaking sweat from his eyes. At night they froze, having only thin mustard-coloured jackets between their damp skin and the cold, high-altitude air.

Sometimes the men were cheered by the drone of bombers passing high overhead toward Rangoon, where Britain's big Blenheim transport planes sat on the runway of ultra-modern Mingaladon Airport like fat ducks in a pond. It was the third week of January 1942, and the attack on Burma had begun in earnest. A little more than one month into open warfare, the Allied navy already lay wasted in the Java Sea, Malaysia had fallen and French Indochina and Thailand had capitulated.

A fifth column marched in with the Imperial Army, thanks to Aung San's successful escape to Japan. True to his word, the mysterious Col. Suzuki smuggled a group of Aung San's friends out of Burma and gave them a year's special training on Hainan Island off the south China coast. They became known as the Thirty Comrades and, in the spirit of the moment, Col. Suzuki himself took a Burmese nom de guerre, Bo Mogyo—Officer Thunderbolt. He was their father figure, an accomplished soldier with a romantically thick mustache. Before leaving for the front, Suzuki and the Burmese youths mixed drops of their own blood into a pot of liquor and drank to brotherhood and Burma's freedom.

Thailand capitulated, offering the right-of-way. Arriving in Bangkok on December 31, 1941, Aung San immediately began recruiting young men from the border towns for his fifth-column Burma Independence Army (BIA). He was aided by a rumour that Officer Thunderbolt was a long-lost Burmese prince come to free their country from Britain. As the BIA infiltrated across the border, eager recruits joined their ranks. The formerly skinny, sick student Aung San became a major-general with 300 men.

A tough, handsome fellow named Ne Win was his second-in-command, and leader of his own column. At thirty-one, Ne Win was a little older than the other Thirty Comrades. He dropped out of school in the 1930s and became a postal employee, which provided him a working-man cachet among the students. His features were chiselled, his body muscular, his eyebrows rakishly arched. He looked like a movie poster come to life, the idealised Asian man. He was also a skilled practitioner of the ancient magic of yedaya chay, sometimes enacting bizarre rituals to bring about their opposite effect. For example, he believed that shooting his own reflection in a mirror would postpone death. He also had a personal number of power, nine, to be conquered and controlled through measures like taking action on the ninth day of the month, or on days which added up to nine. The Thirty Comrades were not a superstitious lot, but they were nonetheless impressed by Ne Win's arcane knowledge.

There were other lessons to learn. Together, Ne Win and Aung San mastered the cruel art of war. They crossed the border at Myawaddy, overtook Moulmein on the southern coast, then headed north toward Rangoon. At Tavoy, Aung San was said to have crucified an uncooperative village headman on a football goal post and then bayoneted him to death.

The students felt rough and invincible. Their enemy was completely unprepared for a land invasion.

It was Britain's constitutional duty to protect Burma but it was too late. The Burma Defence Force consisted of just 472 Burmans and 3,197 Kachins, Chins and Karens; Britain had been reluctant to arm the locals for service inside their own country. At the River Salween two British divisions, under strength and ill-equipped for close-in jungle warfare, put up a brief, unsuccessful stand, while overhead a few RAF pilots tried in vain to site the invaders through the forest canopy.

With Burma's southern airfields captured, the Japanese invaders chased the Salween defenders before them toward Rangoon, a city suddenly panic-stricken. Britain's prisoners were transferred north, her subjects alerted for imminent flight. The evacuation order came on February 18, 1942.

Once Rangoon was captured, two more Japanese divisions—the 56th and the 18th—arrived at the jetty near the Strand Hotel. Their goal was to drive a wedge between British troops in the south and Chinese troops guarding the Burma Road in the north under the American general, Joseph "Vinegar Joe" Stilwell.

Japan's 56th Infantry headed into Karen territory, just south of Yawnghwe. The Karen put up a fierce rearguard defence while the British scrambled to evacuate the region. The Karen were Britain's most loyal supporters in the region. Their ties went back to the earliest years of colonialism, when the first American and European missionaries made their way into the southern hills. The majority of Karen were monotheists who accepted the Christian Bible as the Karen's own Book of Knowledge, which, according to legend, was carried away west by a prince of ancient times, thus depriving the Karen people of religious instruction for many generations. Christianity was their own religion re-discovered, they theorised, and the foreigners were their brothers who had learned from the Book and then faithfully returned it. For this reason, and because the Japanese were marching through their home territory, the Karen fought harder and longer than anyone else. But finally they, too, had to turn and run, leaving the road open north through Yawnghwe state to Taunggyi.

Meanwhile, Japan's 18th Infantry under Lieutenant-General Mutaguchi Renya closed in on Taunggyi from the west. He led his men with special ardour, for he was the man who fired the first shot at Marco Polo bridge and then, astounded by the implications, begged his superiors to send him to the front. Feeling personally responsible for all that happened since, he believed the invasion of Burma was his opportunity to help end the war. He told himself that if they could just cut off the Burma Road supply line and capture the country's oilfields, Japan had a chance to live in peace. With sufficient oil they could become an island once more, without need of further territories.

As the invaders bore down on the quiet, sheltered valley of Inle Lake, young strangers with hard, glittering eyes and daggers in their belts appeared on the streets of Yawnghwe town. It was hard to tell if they were looters or "BIA men", as Aung San's soldiers were called. The market closed because no farmer wanted to leave his home undefended. Sao instructed her head cook, Uncle Ong, to send rice, salt fish and oil to Kalaw for the old nuns at St. Agnes's. At night she heard the occasional crack of gunfire—jumpy farmers, looters, who knew?

Then, in the twilight between retreat and invasion, Sao's youngest boy, Tzang-On, caught fever. For several days his soul fluttered feebly between this realm and the next. Hearing the news, Prince Shwe Thaike took a brief leave from the barracks, but when he arrived at Yawnghwe Haw, Tzang-On's funeral was already in progress. Sao said little about her grief. Ever after, when people asked her about the boy she would shake her head and look away, saying only, "He died—what can you do?"

Somehow it seemed natural that in those days both life and death were compressed together in brief, dramatic moments. On

February 4, shortly after Tzang-On's death, Sao gave birth to a daughter. She gave her a beautiful name: Princess Ying Sita Naw Seng Lao, Lady Jewelled Star Shooting Up From the Sea. Ying Sita, as they called her, came into the world heralded by the far-off crump of artillery fire and falling bombs. The old traditions of birth and celebration had fallen away. For the royal children, the new family ritual consisted of middle-of-the-night awakenings and being cradled through the magic darkness to an underground shelter in the garden.

Sao couldn't forget the bomb depression she saw near the Chinese border, how innocuous it seemed. Now these craters were appearing all over Burma like broken blisters. In Mandalay jail, inside Fort Dufferin, the Burmese politician-cum-novelist Thakin Nu listened for bombs, too, but had nowhere to run. The British transferred an additional 1,500 prisoners from besieged Rangoon, swelling their numbers to 3,000. It was hot, overcrowded and unsanitary, but there was a swell of shared excitement among the inmates. On February 19, Thakin Nu heard the first Japanese bombs fall just two miles away. As their jailers ran for cover, the prisoners laughed and danced in the open, waving their shirts in the air like flags.

Thakin Nu tried to stop them, told them to take cover, but the prisoners just laughed. Didn't this strange, sad-looking writer understand that Officer Thunderbolt, the long-lost prince, was coming to rescue them?

Meanwhile in Taunggyi, Prince Shwe Thaike's Shan battalions were sent to ferret fifth column BIA men out of the countryside, while the Prince struggled to complete plans to supply British troops with food. He asked local farmers to bring their produce to Yawnghwe Haw every five days but, even as the final arrangements fell into place, the British began melting away. The civil servants, officers' wives and other civilians made their exits one by one, taking seats on the last transport planes that arched out daily over the Bay of Bengal toward India, lifting the colonialists up and away from their "earthly paradise" forever. Prince Shwe Thaike was offered a place, but he refused. These were his hills, so why would he leave? On March 7, the last Blenheim thundered into the air from Prome, on the river flood plain between Rangoon and Mandalay, carrying two women, three children and a dog.

The Prince's Shan soldiers saw the British carrying heavy chests away with them. People said they were full of silver. Unpaid for two months, the men seethed at the rumour. Some defected, adding to the number of armed looters in the area.

On April 22, it seemed Taunggyi was lost to Mutaguchi's 18th Division. Two days later, though, Vinegar Joe arrived with his Chinese soldiers. Their lorries lumbered around town and then headed north to save the Burma Road. The effort was futile. On April 30, at one minute to midnight, the road was lost. Mutaguchi chased the Chinese forces into Yunnan, while Vinegar Joe Stilwell fled west toward India with a small party of Chinese and British officers, some journalists, and the Kachin nurses from Dr. Seagrave's hospital. The battle for the Burma Road was, he said, "a hell of a beating."

The next morning, the last of the Europeans left Kalaw, having heard the Japanese were on the road just miles away. Four officers, two sergeants, twenty Indian orderlies and cooks, and two Englishwomen—the widow of a colonel and her young niece—packed themselves into two cars and two trucks and headed north, hoping to reach China. They left behind their last colonial work, a half-built airstrip at Heho, on the flat, dry valley floor that served as the area's buffalo market. Finding the crossing to China cut off, they turned east. The Japanese caught up to them at the Myitkyina airfield just as their rescue plane, a Dakota, prepared to take-off. Many died in the strafing and bomb attack, including the young niece. Her aunt turned back toward Kalaw on foot while the remaining survivors set out on the long trek to India.

The stream of overland escapees dwindled with the miles. Surviving evacuees faced a thousand-mile journey through the Naga Hills to Imphal, a British-held base just inside India's Bengal State. The steep trail was strewn with rotting corpses, victims of cholera, exhaustion and injuries.

The country they left behind was unrecognisable. An angry black smudge of dust and smoke hung over Mandalay. The oilfield at Yenangyaung was aflame, set alight by retreating soldiers. In Rangoon, the papers of colonial bureaucracy—work orders, civil lists, appointments—fluttered down empty, ruined streets. And high on Taunggyi hill in the Shan states, a Japanese plane roared low, leaving only echoing silence in its wake. Outside the barracks hall, Prince Shwe Thaike stood alone and uncertain, suddenly demobilised, no longer a soldier of the British empire, staring up into a strange white blizzard of leaflets falling from the sky. The papers curled down softly, fluttered on the parade ground and entangled themselves in the poinsettias. Each one bore the same message, as deadly to the Prince as any bomb: Those who collaborated with the British will be beheaded. It was the morning of May 2, 1942 and all of Yawnghwe Valley lay wrapped in mist. There was nothing for him to do but return home, gather his family, and melt into the land.

The Lake

A few days later Sao found herself speeding down the long canal that led to Inle Lake, lulled by the sound of the boat's small engine. The children were nestled in the arms of nursemaids, housegirls and co-wives, heads nodding, eyes drifting. Her husband and a few of his officials and staff occupied a second boat. It was early, barely light outside. A buffalo, horns draped with water hyacinths, raised his head lazily from the water as the boats passed by. On a small footbridge a line of monks was momentarily frozen in the mist. Buffalo must eat, monks must still receive their morning alms, life went on even though it seemed the world had turned inside out.

It must be just how people felt when the King of Mandalay was overthrown so suddenly, Sao thought. With his fortress and his moat and his elephants the Great King was invincible one day, gone the next, like a grain of rice in a river. Just like the British. But the old Shan hills remained and when the royal family's boats glided out onto Inle Lake it was as wide and blue as ever, blending perfectly with mountains and sky so that all the shapes of the world fell away and Sao felt like she was drifting through ether.

A line of carefully-placed bamboo poles marked a southward path through shallow, weedy waters. The graceful, familiar shadow of Bo Te, the lake retreat, appeared and then sank back into the mist. Sao had no fixed sense of her destination. Inle Lake was fourteen miles long. She guessed they would travel for some distance yet.

The boatmen followed the bamboo markers to a distant shore that, when they finally drew near, proved to be another of the lake's illusions, not a shore at all but an entrance to the floating gardens of the Intha people.

The gardens were mats of rushes, reeds and cattail stems spread with aquatic plants and a layer of black silt from the lake's eastern shore, then planted with vegetables and flowers grown for temple offerings—lately purple asters, imported from Britain, had become popular. Each garden was anchored by a thin bamboo stake. They were almost constantly being enlarged, sunk or moved by their owners. The result was a shifting land-and-water-scape that could never be mapped or remembered by strangers, a perfect hiding place.

Their new home remained fairly comfortable during the pre-monsoon heat, even at midday. It was not a large house by royal standards, but roomy enough, double-storeyed and set on thick stilt legs above the water. Sao gave little thought to the former occupants—probably the local headman and his family. Obviously an advance party told them to move because their house was needed by the Celestial Lord and Lady, and so they did, as was their duty.

The older children thought it an adventure, like a pony ride in the hills. At meals everyone sat together picnic-style on the wooden floor. Sometimes Sao was hit by a feeling of unreality. Was this a holiday, or was this war? Were they really refugees now?

Occasionally the roar and shadow of an aeroplane passed over them, but most days Inle Lake remained wrapped in languid silence. In the evenings the family watched the first monsoon clouds gather in the west. In seasons past Sao waited on the rains with happy anticipation, but now the darkened skies and climbing humidity gave her a feeling of restless dislocation, broken only when the Chief Minister's boat bumped against the house's ladder-like stairs, bringing daily news from the outside.

Chief Minister Seng Hpu was one of Sao's only blood relatives at the Yawnghwe court, a cousin. He was a young man rather than the wizened elder one might expect, quick to act and quick to gather news. On May 8, he informed them that the Japanese victory was complete.

The Japanese soldiers arrived in Taunggyi looking ragged and hungry but so far posed no direct threat to the population, he told them. They seemed capable of living off the land in ways the British could never manage. There were disturbing rumours, though: in other parts of Shan State, it was said, the soldiers desecrated temples, even slaughtered cattle on temple grounds. The Japanese also had the disturbing habit of slapping people's faces when angered. Even some Burmese supporters were beaten and abused when they went to greet the victorious Imperial Army. In their propaganda the Japanese had emphasised that they were fellow Buddhists. They didn't act like Buddhists, though. Soldiers who slapped faces obviously had no respect for the soul of life which, for humans and animals alike, resided in the area of the head. Such people were capable of great brutality.

Sao and her husband had a more pressing concern, though: Aung San's Burma Independence Army had settled a division in Kalaw and was now ranging deep into Shan territory. The royal couple listened with alarm to reports of atrocities in the villages: rapes, lootings and executions. While the Japanese talked about co-prosperity, their Burmese counterparts carried on the ancient racial battle between plain and hills.

Lt.-Gen. Mutaguchi garrisoned a tank brigade in Taunggyi. In the morning the Japanese soldiers marched onto the parade ground, still littered with the leaflets that sent Prince Shwe Thaike into exile. They were just ten miles from Inle Lake, where the Prince and his family remained in hiding.

The Japanese soldiers were elated. From the hell of war they had stepped into a world of lightness and quiet peace. The long vista of Yawnghwe valley stretched before them. Everything seemed on a slightly larger scale than their native Japan, from the school buildings and public offices of the town to the wide, flat paddy fields in the valley.

Their orders were to set up a temporary local administration, utilising the Shan "chiefs". But where were these chiefs?

Japanese intelligence provided photographs of the Prince of Hsipaw's funeral procession, showing his splendid elephants and umbrella bearers. The pictures were taken by two Japanese photographers who hung from tree-limbs fourteen years ago to the amusement of the passing funeral procession, including school-aged Sao, Louise and Mary Josephine.

In Taunggyi, though, there was no evidence of a palace or elephants. Every day, the Japanese soldiers asked the people, "Who is the ruler of this place?"

The people shrugged their shoulders and answered, "If you don't know, you won't know."

These exchanges were of course reported to Sao and her husband in their lakeside exile. Sao was delighted by the taciturn, noncommittal response of the Tai people, who traditionally divulged little to strangers. The workings of the Shan states would remain a mystery to the Japanese for some time, she realised, for who could guess that the princes ruled from such tiny villages as Yawnghwe? Her own single-streeted home town, Hsenwi, wasn't even depicted on most foreign maps.

The Burmese soldiers were another matter, though. They knew the lay of the land. Sao and her husband discussed the tricky situation like equals. In the past year, on his brief leaves home from the army, Prince Shwe Thaike had learned to listen to Sao's sharply-worded assessments. Although her ideas were often quite incautious, the Prince appreciated his wife's unclouded view of the world. Caring little for diplomacy and power politics, she usually cut straight to the heart of the matter.

Together they laid out the main scenario: Yawnghwe lay directly between two armies, the Japanese Imperial Army in Taunggyi and their fifth-column Burma Independence Army in Kalaw. With no prince in the palace, the entire state was up for grabs. Sao turned the picture this way and that, but the answer always came up the same: the Japanese must be made to understand that the Shan States did not belong automatically to Burma. They had to learn to deal with the princes. It was the only way to save the Shan States from being engulfed by neighbouring Burma, Sao and her husband agreed. And there was only one way to accomplish such a thing: they had to return to Yawnghwe Haw.

Hearing the decision, the Prince's Chief Minister reminded him that the Japanese promised to cut off collaberators' heads. But he agreed with the Prince that they had to do something. They couldn't remain in hiding while the state was taken over by others. The arrangements for departure were swiftly made. Within a few days, the royal family returned to the palace without pomp. The cook Uncle Ong bustled about the cookhouse, happily preparing a welcome meal. His curries must be just so, he knew. The markets had not re-opened and his supplies were rapidly diminishing. The days of food shortages would soon be upon them.

It was nearly September. Looking out from her apartment window at the Great Hall of Audience, Sao realised the Tai New Year had come and gone without a Ceremony of Obeisance, and that no preparations had been made for the five sacred images' annual tour of Inle Lake. All the centuries-old traditions and rhythms of life were stripped away. She wondered, how must the people be managing?

Within a few weeks she had her answer. As word spread through the state of the Great Saopha's return, the village headmen made their way to the palace one by one. Their faces were lined and dusty, their eyes dark with worry. Seated before Sao and the Prince in their rough cotton clothes, they told stories of being forced to draw carts for the Japanese. Frightened and angry, they wanted the Prince and the Mahadevi to intervene.

"How can I look into this?" the Prince asked. "Me, I've never even seen a Japanese. What can I do?"

Sao felt hollow, helpless. They could not intervene unless they made contact with the Japanese commander in Taunggyi, but how could they make contact under threat of execution? As far as they knew, the promise of the leaflet that fell from the sky still stood: if the Japanese were aware of Prince Shwe Thaike's British army connections, he was a dead man. To comfort the villagers and send them on their way, though, the Great Saopha said, "I'll see what I can do."

Finally one morning the news arrived that the Japanese were waiting at the pagoda on the road into town. The Chief Minister recruited a friend to go meet them. Sao and the Prince waited nervously in the main-floor office. When the man returned, it was with a promise that there would be no beheadings.

Sao was forced to wait alone while her husband climbed into his jeep and disappeared through the eastern gate to meet his fate—their fate, really, for if there was bloodshed it would not stop at one man.

A calmness settled over her. She was willing to accept whatever happened next. Her husband's last words were: "We have to be friendly to them. There's no British Army anymore. They've all gone—nobody's left."

Prince Shwe Thaike survived his encounter at the pagoda, but at a price. The tank commander decided to station four members of the Kempei, the Japanese state security forces, at Yawnghwe Haw, along with about thirty foot soldiers. The Kempei would work out of the main floor offices while the family was given leave to continue occupying the second storey.

It was a frightening prospect: the Kempei were known for intelligence-gathering, arbitrary arrests and extreme brutality. How long could the family keep Prince Shwe Thaike's British army past a secret?

On the day the Kempei and soldiers arrived, the women and children gathered upstairs in a room directly above the main office. Tiger had to be restrained because he spotted the phonograph and wanted to play his favourite record, *God Save the King*. Shushing the boy, the wives strained to hear what was happening below them. They heard exclamations of delight when Uncle Ong served up jaggery, brown palm sugar, from his depleted stores. The Japanese seemed overly excited about the simple treat, which was hardly worthy of serving to guests.

They must be famished, the women agreed.

Beyond this initial commotion, it was difficult to tell what was happening. The voices of the men floated up, but the stilted, accented English of the Japanese and the low, fluent responses of Prince Shwe Thaike were a muddle.

Lying on his stomach, Tiger peered through a small hole in the floor. He saw men in yellow coats with tall black boots and long swords that hung from their belts almost to the floor. He had a tiny stick clutched in his fist, so just for fun he broke off a bit of the end and shoved it through the hole to see if it would hit one of the men. He missed and tried again. Suddenly his mother scooped him up, scolding him in a hushed voice. He could not understand why everyone was so angry and tense this day.

The tension never completely dissipated, even after weeks and months of living with the Japanese. Sao learned to deflect serious conversation with quick retorts and jokes. The Kempei officers teased her that everything was poorer in the Shan states than in Japan, that the eggs were smaller, the gardeners lazier.

"Japan egg very, very big. Japan garden too beautiful!", they crowed.

Still, they seemed impressed by the simplest fare. Khao lam, fragrant sticky rice roasted in a length of bamboo over a wood fire, was treated as a delicacy.

Good food was scarce. When the Japanese arrived, the farmers stopped bringing their produce to Yawnghwe Haw. The soldiers had to buy in the market like everyone else, although the pickings were slim. The cook kept the Kempei happy with more jaggery and khao lam roasted with a little minced pork.

Sao never learned to distinguish one Kempei from the other, or to call them by their names. They were all the same to her, little uniformed men with round spectacles. When they lifted their glasses together, the Japanese said, "Kan pei, Burma" and the Chief Minister replied, in his typically daring fashion, "Kan pei—cheers! Shan States."

A running battle with Tiger and the phonograph developed. He was obsessed with playing *God Save the King*. The royal ladies discussed breaking the record but decided it would be a waste, and that it would only send Tiger into a tantrum. Instead, knowing the boy couldn't read yet, they hid it in a stack of other records. Somehow, though, Tiger knew how to pick it out of the bunch. Whenever the ladies' backs were turned, the record went on the phonograph. It was an old-fashioned machine with no volume control. Whether or not the Japanese heard the song drifting down while they worked, or whether they even recognised the tune, nobody knew. At least they never mentioned it. It was impossible to guess what the Kempei knew about the Yawnghwe family, and what thoughts turned behind their round, spectacled faces. They took photographs of all the family members without explaining why, and kept track of their daily movements.

Sao longed to visit her relatives, or even to enjoy a picnic in the countryside. They were captives in their own palace. It hardly mattered, she conceded. Even if they were free, the roads weren't safe for travel. The respite from war was brief. By September the

Allies were already fighting back. They battled on land in the far west, while from the air their bombers struck Rangoon, Prome and Mandalay.

That same month, the "Conqueror of Burma", 15th Army Commander Lieutenant-General Iida Shojiro called his divisional commanders to a meeting in Taunggyi. He wanted to discuss the idea of next invading India. Mutaguchi, who was in charge of the Shan States, was doubtful about the plan and said so: it would be a great folly to chase the tiger into his den. By now, Mutaguchi was a respected protégé destined for advancement. Lt.-Gen. Iida listened carefully to his opinion. After the meeting, the invasion idea was dropped.

Mutaguchi returned to the north country, where most of his troops were stationed. The relaxing hill station, Maymyo, adapted itself to the new rulers. The old British army cantonment and red-brick mansions now rang with Japanese voices. A geisha house was established, the Inn of Brightness. The inn served sushi and sake, delicacies difficult to find even in Japan.

In November, Mutaguchi received his formal instructions for the administration of the Shan states. Military Administration Order #3 re. the Shan States read: "Especially in administering the Territories under the control of the Shan chiefs, the existing system, for the time being, shall be utilised."

The order went on to caution against interference in minor local affairs, followed by an encouragement to win popular support. Mutaguchi was to set up a state administrative office "concerning resource exploitation, education, postal services...and the selection of chiefs."

The order concluded: "Regarding the rule of chiefs, presuppose there will be reforms in the future."

Order paper in hand, the Japanese officer filled his days with administrative details. The yen was brought into circulation and Japanese schools were organised. Whenever he stopped thinking about his daily tasks, though, the same image floated through his mind: the balmy July night, the dark shapes near Marco Polo bridge, the surprising crack of gunfire from his own rifle. He thought that when they captured Burma's oil and cut off the Burma Road, he would be free of this vision, absolved of personally giving life to the Pacific War. Instead, the war carried on. Britain's Royal Air Force

(RAF) bedevilled them from bases in India. As long as the air attacks continued, the great peace Mutaguchi desired—for himself and for Japan—would never be realised.

If India were conquered, there would be no more Allied air bases to worry about.

He tried to push the idea from his head. An India campaign would be protracted, brutal and perhaps unwinnable, he told himself.

In this manner, the seed of an idea germinated and entwined itself in his daily thoughts like a gripping jungle vine. Mutaguchi's mental torture was both grandiose and self-inflicted. He wrote in his diary: "I started off the Marco Polo Incident, which broadened into the China Incident, and then expanded into the Great East Asia War. If I push into India now, by my own efforts, and can exercise a decisive influence on the Great East Asia War, I, who was the remote cause of the outbreak of this great war, will have justified myself in the eyes of the nation." Thus, even before Japan established a new government in Rangoon, the foundation for its undoing was already laid.

The New Masters

Prince Shwe Thaike was called to Rangoon several times during the first year of Japanese occupation. Sao was glad she didn't need to accompany him. The road was difficult and dangerous. Bridges were destroyed, there were bomb craters everywhere and there was always the chance RAF bombers would buzz the highway. When he and the other Saophas finally arrived in the city they were subjected to long lectures about the glories of Japan and the Greater East Asia Co-Prosperity Sphere.

The city was no longer genteel and welcoming. Messy heaps of doorknobs, plumbing and other fittings lay by the railway station, stripped from the colonial mansions by thieves and sold to wartime contractors. Those mansions which escaped destruction were taken over by Japanese. More than a thousand Japanese employees were brought in to run the military administration. The leftover houses went to a new class of Burmese officers and businessmen, who were able to rise into societal echelons formerly occupied by Englishmen and Indians.

The Indian civil servants and merchants had mostly disappeared from Rangoon's offices and shops. Nearly half of the country's one million-strong Indian population joined the long exodus out of Burma. Their leave-taking was bedevilled by bureaucracy and conflicting orders from the British masters. Only those who could show proper inoculation certificates made it onto the last planes and boats escaping Rangoon. The remainder were ordered to stand fast or were herded into northern refugee camps only to be bombed by the Japanese, until finally the last British defences broke and they were free to escape on foot across the mountains. The number of Indian casualties on the three-week journey to India was never recorded.

Many of Rangoon's other denizens, the landless Burmese labourers, dissolved into the countryside or were conscripted into "civil units," put to work sharpening bamboo stakes, fighting fires and clearing land for airstrips. Some of the women became mistresses to the Japanese. They rode about the city in cars and pedicabs, draped in jewels and silk. Bearers followed them through the central market near the railway station, carrying packing crates of currency notes. Inflation had risen drastically: a restaurant meal cost 10,000 rupees and a bottle of Carew's gin was 2,000. There was easy money to be made in Rangoon, though, and the restaurants were full of war profiteers.

Prince Shwe Thaike and the other Saophas spent their time in meetings with the Japanese commanders. They gained little and lost a great deal in the discussions. At least they successfully convinced the Japanese to dismantle Aung San's rapacious Burma Independence Army. Aung San himself was concerned about the BIA's unruly soldiers, and didn't stand in the way when they were replaced by a new force, the Burma Defence Army, under tighter Rangoon control.

What the Saophas lost were the states of Kengtung and Mong Pan, given by Japan to Thailand in thanks for allowing the right-of-way to Japanese troops during the invasion. There was some talk of opening the remainder of the Shan states to large-scale Japanese immigration.

Always the Prince returned to Yawnghwe Haw looking tired and dispirited. The palace itself was starting to look something like a refugee camp. Throughout the year, various Burmese officials arrived for a "holiday". They settled into huts among the garden's tamarind trees, afraid of returning to Rangoon. Among them were

Burma's Chief Justice and his wife, who became a good companion for Sao. Together the two women giggled behind the backs of the Kempei, especially when Prince Shwe Thaike assaulted the Japanese guests with veiled sarcasm.

One day a Kempei demanded, "Yawnghwe Saopha, why are you so proud?"

"Under the British I was nothing. You Japanese have made me a king," Prince Shwe Thaike replied.

Sao and the Chief Justice's wife burst into laughter. The Kempei appeared to take no notice, maintaining a satisfied expression. In Tai, the Prince said, "Ladies, ladies! Don't laugh! He might slap your faces."

It soon became apparent why the Japanese stationed their Kempei police in Yawnghwe. They were busy setting up a youth organisation to challenge the Saopha's power. Most of the recruits were young students who were educated in Rangoon on the Saopha's allowance. At university they learned to see the backwardness of feudalism and the yawning social gap between the Saopha and the people. Under the Japanese they now had an organisation, the East Asia Youth League, to help them redefine society.

One day a Kempei officer approached Sao and her husband with a list of Youth League members. Subtly taunting the Great Saopha, the officer inquired about the character of each fellow. For each name Sao's husband answered weakly, "A good student" or "A fine chap." Now it was the Kempei's turn to laugh

"Tell me what's so funny," Sao intervened sweetly. "I want to laugh, too."

The officer dabbed his eyes and caught his breath. "All of your 'good fellows' come to us and ask us to arrest the Saopha and cut off his head," he answered.

Of course Sao and her husband both knew this all too well, but what could they do? They still saw themselves as the paternal rulers; the students were their subjects who must be protected. It was better to look foolish and give the boys good recommendations.

Inwardly, though, Sao was furious with the youngsters. How could they be so ungrateful, these youths who would be ignorant farmers without the Saopha's education allowance?

They think themselves clever but they can't see the Japanese masters pulling their strings, she fumed. She secretly wished for a showdown. It came sooner than anyone expected. A few days later, a prominent Youth League member invited all the town elders to a dinner in the town. When the invitation arrived at Yawnghwe Haw, it was decided to send the Chief Minister. He set off for town fearlessly: no one at the palace felt seriously threatened by such pompous young fellows. But when hours passed and night fell without the Minister's return, Sao and her husband grew truly worried. Had the Minister lost his head? Then they heard the far-off sound of shouting from the direction of town.

Prince Shwe Thaike ordered the lights doused and sent a guard to find out what was happening. At this point, he might have wondered if Sao's cousin was a good choice for Chief Minister; hotheadedness seemed to run in her family. As for Sao, she sat in her darkened sitting room, thinking. If a mob is coming, let them come! She was tired of the silence, the constant capitulation. Then suddenly the generator hummed, the electric lights buzzed to life, and she heard the Minister's muffled voice below. A few moments later the Prince appeared, his wide shoulders stiff with displeasure, his face a mask of controlled anger.

"You'd better tell your relation to control himself," he said abruptly and then stomped from the apartment.

Immediately Sao sent a page to fetch the Minister. Within a few moments he entered the sitting room, clothes rumpled, eyes shining. Without knowing the details, she began: "Before I say another word, congratulations! I guess you've taught those young chaps a lesson. Now tell me what happened."

The Chief Minister grinned and spilled out his story: "Oh, they were abusing us for everything, madam—us, the Saopha, the state officers, everyone." When someone stood up and made a speech in favour of the Burmese, it was too much for her cousin.

"I gave him a big blow, such a blow!" he reported, sighing at the glory of the moment. "Then all the other officers hit whoever was next to him." The scuffle ended up outside on the road, and the students ran off into the night.

Sao tried to look stern and disapproving. "You must control yourself better," she said, as instructed. But she had already offered her congratulations, so the words meant nothing.

Sao wondered what her husband's motivation was in giving her the job of speaking to the Minister. He knew she supported such acts of rebellion. The Prince, on the other hand, strove to avoid trouble and keep communications open with the Japanese. He felt it was the only way to maintain some dignity and safety for his people.

Some weeks after the ill-fated dinner, the Japanese called for conscripts to clear land for the Heho airstrip, a job left half-done by the British. Yawnghwe's Youth League members were expected to provide most of the labour; they were young and healthy and should be willing to contribute to co-prosperity. When the youths refused, it was up to the Prince to do what he could to avoid bringing the wrath of the occupiers down on the people.

As enticement to report to the airfield, he ended up paying the youths a wage from his dwindling household budget. They took the money but felt no gratitude, for what was the Great Saopha but a feudal lord who slept on a golden bed while they must work? And did not the Mahadevi recently refuse to give clothing to the poor?

The latter story was true, although it was much different from Sao's perspective. She felt she had nothing to give, only some stiff ceremonial silk brocades that were no good to anyone in these times, including herself. Her everyday clothes—just a few cotton jackets and sarongs—were worn thin. She realised that they were growing poor. Although they lived in a palace, it was filled only with useless things, dresses that would never be worn and gilt divans that would never be sat upon.

At the end of July, 1943, the Burmese Chief Justice and his wife left their hut in the palace garden. All of Burma's former officials were ordered to return to their old positions, under the new "independent" government in Rangoon. Sao was sorry to see them go. Well, we're all just props in a play to be moved here and there, she thought. No one believed there would be any justice to administer under the Japanese, who used temples as latrines and forced elders to draw carts like animals.

Burma and the Shan States were rapidly turning into a vast labour camp before the royal family's eyes, but they were frozen, powerless. There was no word to describe their relationship with the occupiers: neither collaborators nor resisters, neither prisoners nor free.

On August 1, she and the Prince listened to the independence ceremonies on the Kempei's radio, their faces set in the unrevealing masks of survival. Sao was relieved her husband wasn't called to Rangoon for their sham ceremony. Travel was growing more dangerous every day. In Rangoon, they celebrated the day's cloudy sky, because clouds kept the RAF bombers away.

Through the radio's crackle, she heard the voice of their old friend, Dr. Ba Maw. The former prime minister had been adopted by the young Thakins because he shared a jail cell with them in the last days of British rule. He was the closest thing they had to an elder statesman. Aung San gave him the title Adipadi, the nearest Burmese translation of Fuhrer, and made him head of state. He would ceremoniously preside over a new government led by a perfectly-balanced triumvirate: the gentle poet, Thakin Nu, the fierce military man, Ne Win, and the charismatic political leader, Aung San.

Ba Maw's first act as Adipadi was to read out a declaration of war against Britain and the United States. "Now that independence has come to us out of this war, we must defend it in war," he said. Did he really believe Japan could deliver Burma to freedom, or had he merely constructed his own careful mask? On the radio, his voice sounded like a stranger's to Sao, blurred by static, revealing nothing. She listened for some hope that the nightmare of war would soon end, but heard none.

The Undesired Pawn

The slogan of Japanese-occupied Burma was "One Blood, One Voice, One Leader". The very idea made Dr. Ba Maw's heart sing. Every morning he donned his Dhamma Cap, a fez-like silk hat that he himself designed as a symbol of Burmese nationalism. The cap sat stiff and neat above his rugged features and large, round eyes, transforming his slightly westernised features into something new and strong, wholly Asian: the Adipadi of Burma.

However, when he flew to Tokyo in November, 1943, he traded in his Burmese dress for an elaborate Prussian-style uniform and jackboots. At the Diet Building, he took his place at a horseshoe-shaped table, alongside the representatives of Manchuria, Occupied China, Thailand and the Philippines. Looking around the table, the Burmese head of state was deeply moved. It was the first time Asians had ever met as leaders of their own countries. When his turn came to speak, he was nearly overcome with emotion.

"It is impossible to exaggerate the feelings which are born out of an occasion like this," Ba Maw began. "For years in Burma

I dreamed my Asiatic dreams. My Asiatic blood has always called out to other Asiatics."

"This is not the time to think with our minds, this is the time to think with our blood."

Ba Maw's belief in Burma's deliverance was heartfelt; it was tied into his own personal deliverance from the hands of the British. After the British arrested him, he was shunted from one location to the next under a hail of bombs until finally he escaped from a small provincial jail in the northern gem mining town of Mogkok, free at last.

As for his Asiatic blood, it had been rising for years and now it filled his every sense, blotting out his years at Cambridge and Bordeaux, his exotic part-Armenian ancestry, his life as a colonial premier. That he attended the coronation of King George VI, once a mark of status, no longer mattered. He had become a child of Burmese roots. He remembered that his father had been a court official at Mandalay palace, before the palace became Fort Dufferin.

In homage to his thin links to Burma's royal heritage, one day Ba Maw took some soil from Swebo—home city of King Alaungpaya, founder of the last dynasty of Burmese rulers —and used it to plant a tree on the shore of Rangoon's Royal Lake. After that he added a new title to his name: in addition to Adipadi, he became Mingyi, the Great King.

Ba Maw the Great King was full of ideas for enlightened rule. Japan gave Burma the basics: a state bank and a national army. Now was the time to create new organisations upon which to build a great civilisation: a strength and sports movement, a literature and translation committee, and a Sangha's organisation to develop religious thought and unite the various monastic orders under one Sangha, or monks' organisation.

But Ba Maw's enlightened civilisation stalled, for the Japanese overlords had other priorities as long as the military situation remained urgent. For one thing, they had an insatiable appetite for forced labour.

Instead of recruiting athletes and scholars for the glory of Burma, Ba Maw was given the task of raising 30,000 labourers to help clear the way for a rail line being laid from Bangkok to Burma. At the time it was just another important public work—it was not until after the war that the track became infamous as the Death Railway, a 300 mile-long graveyard for 100,000 Asian and 16,000 Allied prisoners of war. During its construction, though, Dr. Ba Maw thought only about defending his beloved Burma from foreign armies.

The Adipadi couldn't help but notice that many of the young Thakin politicians didn't seem as enthusiastic as he. In fact, they were increasingly closed-mouthed in the presence of their Japanese advisors. Although Ba Maw didn't know it, some had even tried to make contact with the Allies through Britain's Karen supporters. The Thakins were coming around to the mournful realisation that they had paid far too high a price for little or no political power. The Japanese generals were running the show and Burma was reduced to a tiny plot of territory from which to blockade southern China.

The Allies thought no better of Burma's national aspirations than the Japanese did. The British established bases at Imphal and Kohima on the Bengali-Burma border and there they sat, neither advancing nor retreating. When Churchill turned his mind to Burma, he imagined horrible jungles, clinging vines, tigers and wildmen—no place to fight a war with good English lads. His trepidation was not unjustified: in the first years of war, hill fighting had cost Britain 288,000 men to sickness alone. And if Burma were liberated, what then? Those young fellows in Rangoon wouldn't favour a return to British rule, the British prime minister guessed.

The American view was summed up in a memo from a U.S. political advisor to General Stilwell: "Domestically, our Government lays itself open to public criticism—'why should American boys die to recreate the colonial empires of the British and their Dutch and French satellites?'"

Nonetheless, the United States favoured a Burma campaign to open the corridor to China's nationalist troops, who were soldiers of a free republic. The Americans had established a U.S. bomber force inside China, the Flying Tigers of Kunming, which they supplied by dangerous high-altitude flights over a southern spur of the Himalayas they called the Hump. They wanted a road to replace the risky air route.

"By concentrating our Asiatic efforts on operations in and from China we keep to a minimum our involvement in colonial imperialism. We engage in a cause which is popular with Asiatics and the American public," Stilwell's advisor concluded.

A bit of an impasse developed between the two allied powers. The Americans wanted to build a new 500 mile-long road from India to China, routed through Burma's mountainous frontier. This required the recapture of northern Burma. The British would rather take southern Burma so they could at least get Rangoon back—who wanted all that northern wilderness? Neither power cared much about the country in between.

Throughout 1943, the future of Burma was lobbed back and forth in a series of Allied conferences. At an August meeting in Quebec City's stately Hotel Frontenac, the Combined Chiefs of Staff agreed that the strategy for Japan's defeat would be "to carry out operations for the capture of Upper Burma in order to improve the air route and establish overland communications with China. Target date: mid-February 1944."

Louis Mountbatten, promoted by Churchill as a "young and vigorous mind", was given command over the Southeast Asian theatre, with the American general, Vinegar Joe Stilwell, as his deputy commander. By September the Americans were busy building their new land route to China, which they call the Ledo Road. Immediately they stumbled upon the problem of having no acceptable currency with which to pay local labourers, and just as quickly they discover the enduring value of opium. Small cheesecloth-wrapped "pay" packets were kept in a safe, infinitely more compact than bales of useless Indian rupees. Altogether, the American forces distributed about twenty kilos of opium a month to porters, informers and workers, setting a pattern for future adventures in Southeast Asia that would last into modern times, the Vietnam War and beyond.

By November, support for the land route was beginning to slip. When Mountbatten, Stilwell, Churchill, Roosevelt and China's Generalissimo Chiang Kai-shek met in Cairo that month, the British participants were unenthusiastic about the Burma effort, perhaps influenced by the knowledge that Roosevelt and Chiang Kai-shek had already agreed in private talks on the need to end colonial rule in Asia. At the next conference, held in Tehran just two days following the close of the Cairo conference, Roosevelt, Churchill and Stalin decided to push back the Burma campaign in favour of European concerns.

By the time 1944 arrived, it appeared Burma's role was set: an unused, undesired pawn between the great superpowers.

In fact, such a fate would have been merciful compared to what was to come.

Mutaguchi's dream of death continued to haunt him. In the past year he'd risen through the ranks to the point where he now had real influence. On March 18, 1943 he took command of the 15th Army, stepping into the boots of his former superior, Lt.-Gen. Iida. He made his headquarters in Maymyo, the old colonial hill station with the new geisha house.

One month into his new posting, on May 17, Mutaguchi received an important visitor, Vice-Chief of General Staff for the Southern Army, Major-General Inada. Inada helped oversee the entire Southeast Asian theatre, but Mutaguchi had another, more personal, connection to the man.

"Do you remember when you were on a tour of inspection in Manchuria in 1939?" Mutaguchi asked the Major-General when they met.

When the Major-General showed no sign of recognition, Mutaguchi continued on in a rush: "I was Chief of Staff of the 4th Army then and I felt deeply the responsibility of having, as regimental commander, fired the first shot at the Marco Polo Bridge two years before. I begged you to use me somewhere I could die for my country."

"I feel now exactly as I did then. Let me go to Bengal! Let me die there!"

Silence. The Major-General blinked slowly, looked stunned. Then he cleared his throat and spoke: "It would no doubt satisfy you to go to Imphal and die there. But Japan might be overthrown in the process."

End of discussion. Mutaguchi was left utterly disappointed but still unable to let go of his mounting obsession. He got the idea of taking the British stronghold at Imphal in time for Emperor Hirohito's birthday, April 29, 1944. It was too maddening: he himself spoke against the invasion early in the war, and how swiftly everyone decided to take his advice! Now his own divisional commanders beneath him resisted his change of heart.

After the Major-General left, Mutaguchi turned to the new Burma Area Commander, General Kawabe Masakazu. The Commander would understand, Mutaguchi hoped, because he was there when it all began at Marco Polo Bridge. In fact he was Mutaguchi's immediate superior on the fateful night.

To Mutaguchi's great joy, the Commander agreed to take the idea to Tokyo on his next trip. Then Mutaguchi turned to his divisional commanders, generals and chiefs of staff, gradually wearing them down with his incessant lobbying.

Some war games in preparation for the proposed invasion were organised but they descended into a squabble over who was in charge and what the objectives were. Then suddenly, on January 7, 1944, against all odds, word arrived from Tokyo: go ahead with the invasion of India. Commander Kawabe had fulfilled his promise and turned the right ears. Mutaguchi was ecstatic. The emperor's birthday was four months away. He would give him India.

This time, instead of a Burmese fifth column, they would be accompanied by an Indian National Army, similarly intent on liberating their homeland from Britain. Their leader was an ex-mayor of Calcutta, Subhas Chandra Bose. Together they would sweep over the Arakan mountains like a monsoon rain, a reprise of 1942. What Mutaguchi never considered was that this time the British might not retreat.

The Emperor's Birthday Present

At Yawnghwe Haw, Sao heard the bombs at dawn, loud concussions which grew a little closer every morning. The Japanese offered few clues as to what was happening beyond their valley. All this was hidden from her: that in January, 1944, the Chinese began a successful campaign in northern Burma; that in February, a mysterious British-led brigade called the Chindits set out across 450 miles of mountain and jungle, blowing up bridges and cutting railway lines along the way; that on March 20, RAF pilots skip-bombed the great red walls surrounding Mandalay Palace, breaching them in twenty places.

Thus, by the time Lt.-Gen. Mutaguchi launched his invasion of India, Japan was already on the defensive in Burma. What had changed? In Europe, the Allies had gained the upper hand, although Germany still refused to fall. The Soviets had begun their initial advance, retaking the southern Ukraine in March. The Americans were slowly recapturing the central Pacific.

When Canadian pilots arrived to bolster bases in Calcutta and Sri Lanka, the Allies gained vastly superior air power in the Southeast Asian theatre. After studying the art of jungle warfare, they lost their fear of the high mountain passes between Bengal and Burma. More importantly, under Mountbatten's Southeast Asia Command, U.S. and British forces had reached a compromise on the matter of Burma—the Americans would concentrate on the Burma Road, while British forces planned for the recapture of Rangoon and the south. Prime Minister Churchill foresaw that Rangoon had the potential to set the stage for more important conquests, namely the recapture of Singapore, an essential commercial hub on the southern tip of Malaysia. Singapore was "the only prize that will restore British prestige in the region", he told the Chiefs of Staff. For this, not for Rangoon itself, he would support an advance into Burma.

On March 12, Mutaguchi's dream became reality as 155,000 troops marched on Allied bases at Kohima and Imphal. Bose's Indian National Army brought up the rear, crying, "To Delhi! To Delhi!" They carried bales of currency freshly designed and printed for liberated India.

But crossing the Naga Hills to the Imphal plateau, the Japanese forces faced unexpected resistance. At Kohima they found themselves engaged in a deafening close-range tank battle near a tennis court, just down the hill from the District Commissioner's bungalow. During a sixteen-day siege, even the hospital's wounded took up arms, until additional British, Indian and African troops arrived to relieve them.

The Emperor's birthday came and went without an inch of Indian territory secured. The Allied forces seemed more organised and fierce than ever before. Japanese casualties were rising. Allied soldiers slipped behind the Japanese lines and took the key northern city of Mytikina on June 2. Three days later, Mutaguchi met with Commander Kawabe. In his heart he knew they must retreat, but he couldn't form the words. He prayed that his discouraged silence would be understood by the Burma Area Commander. It was not. They fought on, losing one battle after another. By the end of June, the India invasion had collapsed completely.

The dream became a nightmare.

In a driving monsoon rain over 13,000 dead Japanese were counted on the Imphal battlefield. Some 65,000 additional Japanese troops later died of disease, hunger and wounds. The jungle paths became a long hellish trail of dying men and abandoned weapons.

Back in Maymyo, Mutaguchi stopped visiting the Inn of Brightness. He saw strange, terrifying creatures crawling on the floor near his bed at night, but when he called for his guards the creatures disappeared. Mornings were spent at a shrine of his own making, comprised of four saplings planted in the four directions. Mutaguchi's strange prayers—to what god, no one knew—went unheard.

Now the bombing of Burma began in earnest. The fury of the Allied air campaign was incomprehensible. RAF Liberators filled the sky, unloading anti-personnel bombs and attacking 5,000 miles of road with big 500- and 1,000-pound bombs. No country had ever before experienced such a constant, total rain of death. The Allies would not stop until every bridge, road, storehouse, and airstrip was destroyed completely, until every man-made structure of note in the entire country was a pile of smoking rubble.

While Burma crumpled under the heavy thud of bombs, Yawnghwe was spared the worst. Two or three bombs landed in the town-site, but there were only a few injuries and no deaths. Between early-morning trips to the garden bomb shelter, life carried on at Yawnghwe Haw in its strange, make-do fashion over the next few months.

The palace ladies attended Japanese language lessons, except for Sao. "My brother paid a lot of money for me to learn English, so I'd better keep it up," she laughed, as if it were a joke. The Kempei officers shrugged and let it go. Tiger, meanwhile, went to the town's public school. In days gone by he would have started off in convent school, then graduated to the Shan Chief's School in Taunggyi. Such a privileged education was now impossible, even for a son of the Great Saopha of Yawnghwe; these days, no one would send a child beyond the relative safety of home. Prince Shwe Thaike could comfort himself that public school would contribute to the boy's "democratisation", although the concept of democracy was even a worse joke now than it was in the days of British colonialism.

As for Tiger, he tried hard to fit in with his village classmates. But even children can sense the gulf between high and low-born. The other students hesitated to approach him. At home he played happily with his five-year-old brother Tzang, his elder half-sister Sanda, and the toddler, Ying Sita.

In April, the family celebrated his sixth birthday. They all had lunch together and then the Prince took him to the stable, where he presented Tiger with his own favourite white mare. The family had nothing else to give.

There was a new addition to the family: Nang Mya Win, the youngest co-wife, gave birth to a girl, Haymar, whom Sao adopted as her own. She called both the teenaged new mother and her child 'daughter' because, as Mahadevi, she was mother to them all. It would be years before Haymar would understand who her biological mother was. Sao became pregnant, too; the child was expected the following April. The situation caused no jealousies between the women. In such times, simple survival was the only thing worth fretting about.

The markets were open but nearly every scrap of food was bought up by the Japanese soldiers. There was hardly a potato left to eat. Although rice still grew in the fields near Yawnghwe Haw, farmers were no longer able to get the crop to the mills. When the Japanese complained about the unhusked rice provided to their soldiers, the Prince's Chief Minister snapped back, "Well, we are all eating the same thing." Sao was grateful for whatever reached their table because there were rumours of desperate starvation in Burma, and of women committing suicide from shame because they had no clothes to wear.

In one sense, the constant bombardment was a blessing, for her husband's dangerous trips to Rangoon were curtailed by the mounting military crisis. The Burmese capital was on constant alert. Wailing sirens filled Dr. Ba Maw's ears as he doggedly pursued his dream of a new, revitalised Burma. In his office in the former colonial Government House, Burma's Head of State seldom spared a thought for his old friend, the Prince of Yawnghwe. There was too much going on in Rangoon, too much danger in the air—and not just from falling bombs.

One day in mid-1944, the young rebel Aung San strode into the Adipadi's office. "We must try to end this war somehow. People are suffering needlessly," he announced bluntly.

"But this is war," replied Ba Maw, "and we cannot stop it as we like. How do you think we could do it?"

Aung San shrugged his epauletted shoulders and looked away. Both men knew the unspoken answer: earlier, Aung San's loyal protege Thakin Nu had already led a small delegation into this very room and told Ba Maw that they intended to go over to the

Allies. Aung San's faint shrug, a shimmering of gold fringe and coloured bars, was the punctuation mark at the end of a decision already written. The young men who made Ba Maw the Great Leader and Great King of Burma were about to bail out, leaving the Adipadi's world reeling, a last futile thought now blurting to his lips: "What about our independence and honour?"

Aung San regarded the elder statesman levelly. Truth and treason were the same thing now and there was no need to fear either, for Japan had surely lost the war.

"This independence we now have is only a name. It is only the Japanese version of home rule," the younger man said as he rose to leave.

Dr. Ba Maw was left to ponder the future of his country in a new light. In the months to come, a veil was lifted from his eyes. In the north, 100,000 Chinese troops advanced on the coveted Burma Road. From the west, the Allies crossed the Chindwin River, building the world's longest bridge in the process, a 1,154-foot-long Bailey Bridge. Then they moved toward the Irrawaddy, the great river that flowed through the heart of Burma and Rangoon itself.

Lt.-Gen. Mutaguchi, the architect of the failed India invasion, made a brief appearance in Rangoon before being recalled without ceremony to Tokyo. They never saw him again.

Late in 1944, Ba Maw noticed that the Japanese were busy mining and fortifying Shwedagon Pagoda, the soaring gold spire that symbolised Rangoon. The Japanese would make a final stand there even if it meant emptying the full fury of war on Burma's most important place of worship. What did they care? What did the Allies care? Burma's history, dreams and ambitions meant nothing in the showdown between global empires.

As a precondition for making a radio broadcast to bolster the peoples' spirit, Ba Maw asked Japan's Prime Minister to spare Rangoon from a destructive street-by-street defence. The PM agreed and Ba Maw made the address, clinging to one last thread of trust with the Japanese "liberators".

On April 30, 1945, the ashes of 40,000 Japanese soldiers, contained in thirty-seven large chests, were loaded onto a wooden boat and sent down the Rangoon River to the sea. The dead warriors were among the last to leave the graceful old capital, now the littered, crumbling home of looters and refugees.

That same day in Yawnghwe, Sao gave birth. It was a boy, sweet and uncomplaining. They called him Prince Hso Hom Hpa, Tiger Ruling the Sky, and nicknamed him Myee, Bear. Even as a little baby, he was a charming fellow. Everyone fell in love with him.

The new baby was a gentle distraction from the maelstrom that was advancing toward the Shan hills. They could hear the noise of battle daily now. Recently, the Japanese army headquarters had been moved from Maymyo to a forest villa just east of the railway junction at Thazi, only forty-eight miles from Yawnghwe. From here, the Japanese managed to launch a counter-attack on British forces holed up in Meiktila, not far from the western edge of the Shan plateau.

In days past, Meiktila was known as a place of healing: the air rising from its twin lakes was medicinal and the bark and leaves of its trees were used to treat everything from skin rashes to tuberculosis. Now, the screams of dying soldiers and the thunder of heavy artillery filled the air. The British were better armed and positioned than their attackers. They inflicted 2,500 casualties on the Japanese, compared to just 300 British casualties.

While the siege of Meiktila raged, the remnants of Mutaguchi's once-mighty 15th Army fled south from Mandalay into the Shan States. Passing through Shan villages, the soldiers took carts, cooking utensils, rice and bullocks, for they had nothing. With staring eyes and tattered uniforms, they moved like ghosts. They had by now lost count of colleagues dead; 3,000 corpses lined the trail of retreat.

In a last-ditch effort to aid the war effort, the Japanese soldiers stationed at Yawnghwe Haw went round to the houses of the town's small Indian community. They commandeered anything of value, including dowries, to aid Bose's Indian National Army. But when they returned to Yawnghwe Haw, they realised there was no use for the booty. The impossible had already happened. Japan's India invasion was a defeat. They locked the jewels and gold bangles in the basement treasury.

One week after the birth of Myee, leaflets rained down from the sky. This time the fluttering sheets of paper announced the surrender of Germany. On the same day, the Kempei disappeared from Yawnghwe Haw. From the back balcony of the South Apartment little Tiger watched the yellow-uniformed men lead his father's horses away. Thankfully, the grooms had hidden his white mare in the town.

The commander of a tank division headquartered in Taunggyi supervised the departure. Just as the British had done three years earlier, he invited Prince Shwe Thaike to join the retreat.

"Oh, I'm not so brave as you. I wouldn't be able to commit hara-kiri," responded the Great Saopha.

Accepting these words at face value, the commander told the Yawnghwe Prince that one hundred men would come the next day to guard the palace. The following day, word arrived that the number would be reduced to ten men. When no men appeared and there was no further communication, Sao and her husband realised that the long occupation of Yawnghwe Haw was over.

A few days later an incendiary bomb crashed into the south courtyard, instantly turning a decorative arch into two dust-wreathed pillars. Luckily the palace's Nat-spirit was on guard, for how else could one explain why the bomb did not detonate? Instead it just lay there in its own rubble in the pale morning light like some strange fish from the shallows of Inle Lake. In the rising light a wary circle of royal guards formed around the bomb, awaiting further orders. Their leader, the Chief Officer of the Golden Spear, had few options. None of them had the skill to disarm this deadly fish-from-the-sky. It was clear to all what the order would be: take the thing and throw it in the lake before it blows. The guards had already consigned their fates to the Nat, who had protected them thus far.

Curious onlookers gathered at the southern gate to watch the drama unfold. There was something missing from the scene, though. Where were the little princesses and princelings, straining from their nursemaids' arms to get a closer look? And should not the Mahadevi be on the terrace, raining down suggestions in her cool voice? For that matter, where was the Celestial Lord himself? That which the guards already knew dawned slowly on the townspeople—the royal family had disappeared again.

No More Jaggery

On May 16, 1945, Aung San arrived in Meiktila wearing full Japanese dress regalia. It wasn't the most appropriate outfit for a meeting with Field Marshal Sir William Slim, but it was the only formal suit of clothes he owned. He told Slim that he would aid the British, but his true goal was independence.

"You only come to us because you see we are winning!" Slim scoffed.

The old Aung San might have stormed off to burn the Union Jack for this insult to Burmese pride. The new Aung San merely answered coolly, "It wouldn't do much good coming to you if you weren't winning, would it?"

Slim was impressed. The Burmese student radical had matured into a calm, pragmatic politician capable of delivering 10,000 men to the Allied cause. Aung San's men had already risen against the Japanese, reportedly killing several officers. His star-clad banner flew everywhere along the road to Rangoon. Slim discerned that Aung San was a practical man, someone Supreme Commander Mountbatten could deal with when Burma was returned to Britain. There might be an election for some sort of local body when conditions stabilised, in which case the young Burmese leader would be useful.

But these were future concerns: the country wasn't yet fully recaptured. They still had the southward march to Rangoon ahead of them, and an eastward push along the road to Taunggyi to clean up the last pockets of resistance. More than 7,000 Japanese soldiers were fleeing to Thailand through the southern Shan states.

On June 9, the Allies took Kalaw without a fight. But Japanese forces remained east of Heho and there were 75-millimetre guns stationed on the outskirts of Taunggyi. Through the rest of June and July, the Allied soldiers sustained heavy fire as they inched their way forward, taking a village here, a hilltop there.

It rained nearly every evening now. At night there was thunder and in the morning, the concussion of falling bombs. The Allied planes flew directly over Inle Lake toward their targets on Taunggyi hill, their black shadows gliding over the lake's unrippled surface. Fishermen looked up, then returned to their work. Amid all that was happening there were still rice in the fields and nets in the water. Sao felt safe among the calm, unhurried villagers who were her neighbours now.

Once again the family was living in a simple lakeshore home. It was large enough to accommodate them all, with a small yard and a gated bamboo fence. The children enjoyed their freedom outside the confines of Yawnghwe Haw. Tiger and Tzang chased each other through the green paddy fields. The Great Saopha took them out in a boat for swimming lessons. Tiger eagerly jumped into the cool water while, Tzang, being younger, was afraid. His father threw him overboard, thinking, Well, not all lessons can be easy. In this way, Tzang learned to swim, too.

Within a short time the family's presence in the village was well known. Twice, lone American airmen arrived at the house. No one knew how they came because there were still plenty of Japanese around. Both times, Sao and her husband served tea and exchanged pleasantries, nothing special. For the children it seemed all very hush-hush and exciting: they were told to go take their naps and say nothing about the visitors. The children couldn't remember the British days, so these tall, white-skinned men were greatly intriguing. The strangers wore green uniforms instead of yellow, and they had blue eyes. They left the children chocolate bars—such a strange and wonderful taste—and comic books full of funny pictures of Hitler.

There were others who came to see the Saopha, including a delegation of Indians led by the shopkeeper Mr. Nine Paise. The Indians knew that their gold and jewels, taken to support the India invasion, still lay in the treasury of Yawnghwe Haw. They wanted the jewellery back now, explained Mr. Nine Paise.

The large crowd made Prince Shwe Thaike anxious. "The Japanese are still just a few miles away in Taunggyi. Do you want to get us all killed?" he pleaded.

The Indians refused to budge until the Saopha's anger rose. He told them: "Go now. I will post a guard at the gate, and any one of you who comes into this yard will be shot dead."

Sao said nothing during the exchange, but she was growing tired of this life of fearful inaction. Although the Japanese had all but lost the war, the Prince seemed powerless to do anything for the people.

The next group of supplicants were farmers who told the Prince that fleeing Japanese soldiers were looting their meagre possessions, even taking the doors and windows from their homes. A few of the farmers had rifles. Abandoned weapons were easy to find. They wanted to know if they could kill the soldiers. Listening from the next room, Sao heard her husband hesitate then say, "Well, if they act like robbers, then they are robbers and you may treat them as such."

This was not good enough for the men. "Does this mean we can kill them?" they pressed the Great Saopha, to which he answered vaguely: "I don't give orders to kill. I'm just saying what is." Sao couldn't keep silent. She stuck her head around the doorway and said, "Kill them. Kill them all. Nobody orders you to do it. I said it, that's all."

From that moment forward, the roles were drawn between Sao and her husband: she would say what he could not. She had become a leader in her own right, tougher and more populist than her cautious husband.

The war did not so much end in Yawnghwe valley as it slipped away gradually, day by day. The royal family had brought a radio with them to the lakeside house and for the first time in many years they could pick up Allied broadcasts and follow events in the Pacific region. News came from farther afield too: they heard about the United Nations Charter and wondered if this finally meant freedom for colonial peoples. They didn't hear about the terrible destruction of two Japanese cities—this information was at first reserved for generals and high-ranking politicians.

On August 14, far away in the rural south, the gentle writer-politician-now-refugee Thakin Nu whispered the story of Hiroshima and Nagasaki into his wife's ear. Later he would claim this was the only political secret he ever told her. The next day, August 15, 1945, the Emperor of Japan surrendered.

Rather than elation, Sao felt sorrow. So many lives lost, and for nothing. Men, oh, they are such great heroes, she thought bitterly. Even now that it was all over they continued to die. Some Japanese soldiers killed themselves. Others, not believing the surrender, continued their flight toward Thailand, drowning in neck-deep mud with their mothers' names on their lips. On August 19, Subhas Chandra Bose died in a plane crash.

A few Japanese soldiers arrived at the house asking to surrender to the Saopha, but Prince Shwe Thaike wanted no responsibility for the defeated men. The radio said that Supreme Commander Mountbatten was waiting in Rangoon to receive the Japanese surrender; the Prince told the soldiers he would provide them with a guide to take them to the capital.

"It's not our war. If you want to surrender, surrender to the British," he said.

The soldiers departed on a small boat with their guide, carrying jaggery sweets to sustain them on the journey. That was the last the Yawnghwe family saw of the Japanese invaders.

The Japanese left 185,149 dead in Burma. The British and Commonwealth forces, which included Canadians, Africans, Indians and Burmans, lost 14,326 men. An estimated 7,500 Chinese lay dead along the Burma Road. The number of civilians killed by bombs, disease and starvation was uncounted.

The country itself was utterly destroyed, having sustained more firepower than anywhere else in Asia save Japan itself. Entire towns and cities were gone. There was not a bridge left standing. Oilworks, mines, trains and ships were destroyed. The country's machinery and scientific equipment disappeared with the retreating army. Mandalay, the great city of the northern plain, was almost completely flattened: there was hardly a house left. A Japanese division had made a last stand inside old Mandalay palace; the great red walls now rose battered and broken from a hellish landscape. All that was contained within those walls—the gardens, pavilions and great halls of the last kings—was gone, never to be rebuilt.

When Sao and her family returned to Yawnghwe Haw, one of the Prince's first acts was to hold a meeting with the Indian community. He laid out their gold bangles and jewels and said gruffly: "Each man claim his property, and if anyone squabbles over a piece, I will keep it to myself." The surprised Indians took their jewellery back and relations between the two races were restored.

Next, the Great Saopha held a feast for his ministers and secretaries. They sat in a circle on bamboo mats while the kitchen boys carried in steaming trays of rice and red, oily curries. When the sweets arrived, three secretaries in turn protested, "No Jaggery!" The diners threw back their heads, amazed that they could laugh again.

Aftermath

Two months later, Sao took the children north to Hsenwi with the jeep and driver. By now there was some semblance of order in the country. Conscripts were pressed into clearing roads, just as they'd done for the Japanese. The jeep passed some members of the East Africa Corps marching down the road; the children could hardly tear their eyes away from the strange black-skinned men. Tzang thought their smiles shone like the moon.

The children were less impressed by the scene in Hsenwi town because they never knew how it looked before.

Sao took them to a small rise near the centre of town where broken timbers were being dragged away. She thought of the words that might explain this place to her children.

"Yes, this is where the Old Haw stood, where your mother played with her cousins, where she was married. Those teak stumps, those were the foundation. There were more than 200 pillars so strong no earthquake could pull them down."

But she said nothing. Next they visited a hilltop just outside of town.

"See the white pillars and the bit of railing there, that was the veranda of the New Haw. It went all the way round—you could sit there and see the whole valley. There was a piano and chandeliers inside. My bedroom window overlooked the town, and one night long ago I looked out that window and wondered what would become of me."

But again, she said nothing.

On the long journey back to Yawnghwe, she was consumed in thought. It had been marvellous to see her family again. Some of her younger relatives, including her favourite nephew, Saw Ohn, joined the British army and followed them out of Burma on their initial retreat. They told exciting tales of India, the Middle East and Europe, of parachuting behind enemy lines and of leading specially-trained saboteurs through the Shan hills. One of the Hsenwi prince's brothers was captured near Hsenwi and would have been executed, were it not for the family's pleas for his life.

Those who didn't fight, including Sao's mother, hid in the jungle when the bombs fell. They knew the war was over on the day the aeroplanes began to drop food packages instead of bombs. Everyone agreed that the jungle was a great gift to the Tai, a place to shelter and survive during the worst of times.

Sao's brother had no plans to replace their old mansion. He told her he doubted the family would receive compensation for the destruction of the two Haws.

Her brother filled her in on the most recent political developments. The Japanese were gone and the British didn't have any clear plan for the region. Shortly before the war's end, Churchill lost the government in a landslide to Clement Atlee's Labour Party, which favoured an end to the British colonial empire. Commander Mountbatten—who was awarded the title Earl Mountbatten of Burma for recapturing the country—supported British withdrawal from Burma. He was already engaged in talks with Aung San to that end. But Governor Dorman-Smith, who advocated more independence for Burma before the war, now wanted to hang on.

Dorman-Smith had returned to Rangoon with something called the Simla Plan, named for the Indian hill station where he'd waited out the war. Under the plan, he suspended all Burmese government bodies for an indefinite "stabilisation period". He offered Aung San's Thakins'—renamed the Anti-Fascist People's

Freedom League (AFPFL)—just two seats on the administration's Executive Council.

The meagre offer was an insult to the young nationalists. They planned a mass rally for November, at the foot of Shwedagon Pagoda. The battle for Burma's freedom had begun.

Bumping along cratered country roads to Yawnghwe, Sao wondered how the Shan States would fit in with these events. The Saophas had to act before the future was decided for them by others. Maybe they couldn't rebuild the destroyed Haws, but they had to think about rebuilding their homeland.

When she reached Yawnghwe Haw, her husband was pondering whether or not to recall his heir, Prince Sai, from England. The young man had been overseas through all the years of Sao's marriage and cut off from them completely during the war. He was in danger of becoming a stranger to family and homeland.

Sao told the Prince that his eldest son must come back to Yawnghwe and learn how to govern. Then she extended the argument: "It's the same with the people, they must learn how to make big decisions, too. We must bring them together to decide on the future of our country."

It was a good idea. Prince Shwe Thaike issued the invitations personally. For the meeting site he chose a flat patch of market-ground north-east of Taunggyi called Panglong—Great Camp.

The big meeting convened in March, 1946. Sao attended as kitchen boss. On the way, she stopped in Taunggyi and borrowed an Indian sari from a friend, so she would have something decent to wear. Good clothes were still hard to come by.

It was hard work feeding the men. The Kachins and their cousins, the Chins, came down from the north. The Tai Saophas were all there, too, including the ones who'd had their lands transferred to Thailand during the occupation. An American Baptist missionary, Reverend Harold Young, represented the Lahu and the Wa. Someone whispered in Sao's ear: "The Reverend's as wild as the Wa. He even buries his money in the ground like they do."

The meeting gave Sao her first opportunity to meet the leaders of post-war Burma. Thakin Nu—representing Aung San's new Freedom League—was a smiling cherub of a man, a sun-browned delta farmer. A pious Buddhist, he refused all alcohol and passed up the meat dishes. Legend had it that he'd been a drunken delinquent as a youth, but that upon arriving in Rangoon he took a vow of sobriety at Shwedagon Pagoda. He had kept the vow ever since.

The other Burmese representative was U Saw, the pre-war prime minister who was arrested during his return flight from London. Free and home again, he assumed he would take up where he'd left off. He'd already formed his own party, the Patriotic Party, and had cultivated the patronising smile of an experienced elder, which he employed whenever the younger Thakin Nu spoke.

The ethnic leaders took their main meals together and talked long into the night. Sao could feel their sense of confusion and dislocation. The surest among them was Reverend Young, who reported that the hilltribes he represented had already decided they weren't interested in joining Burma. The Kachins and Chins, on the other hand, had not reached a decision.

Even if they knew which course to take, the men weren't certain with whom they should negotiate, the British or the Burmese. The lone British representative gave no hint as to whether his country planned to quit Burma or not.

In the midst of the talks, the Prince's heir arrived on the back of a salt truck, his worn suit-clothes encrusted with powdery white stains. Sao was eager to meet Prince Sai, having exchanged a few letters with him while he was at college. He wore spectacles and had long, pale hands and stooped shoulders, a gangling, scholarly version of his square-postured, soldierly father.

Prince Sai was gracious and friendly, glad to see Sao and gladder still to be among English-speaking relatives. He'd had a long, nerve-racking journey from England.

It began with a surprise telegram. He had just graduated and taken employment with a British engineering firm. His bags were packed and a train ticket to the job site purchased. Then the message arrived, a thinly-worded request from his father urging him to come home. Instead of catching his train, Prince Sai went to the airport, clambered aboard a converted troop transport plane, and embarked on a long, hop-scotching journey from one war-shattered city to the next. The plane stopped for tea, stopped for dinner, then stopped for the night—then did the same the next day, all the way across Europe and Asia. He lost track of time and had no idea what day it was when he finally arrived in Rangoon, sandwiched between other exhausted, confused-looking returnees.

Recounting the story, he had trouble finding the words to tell Sao how the rush of tropical air and strange babble of languages hit him when he stepped onto the tarmac at Mingaladon International. He and his fellow returnees were allowed two nights' stay at the Strand Hotel, which had somehow escaped the air bombardment. He had no idea how to survive in Burma or how to find his family. He carried in his pocket the dog-eared business card of a Rangoon doctor; it was the only name and address he knew of in the whole city of Rangoon.

The first day he wandered the city on foot for hours, pickling in the damp heat. When he finally came upon the doctor's neighbourhood, he discovered it had been bombed flat. Discouraged, he returned to the Strand for a sleepless night.

The second day he got lucky: while he was watching a parade of soldiers in Maha Bandoola Square, a British man approached him and asked if he were related to Prince Shwe Thaike, for there was a marked resemblance. To Prince Sai, the man was no less than a saviour: he spoke the King's English and knew how to get around the country. It was the Englishman who arranged the salt truck ride.

It rained on the way to Taunggyi, uncharacteristically for the season, and the salt bags leached onto his clothes. Once in Taunggyi, it was an easy matter to find his father and stepmother: everyone in town knew they'd gone on to Panglong for the big meeting.

It was a rare opportunity for the heir to meet all the Shan Saophas at once, but the conference finished inconclusively after eight days of talks. The ethnic leaders decided it was best to wait until matters between London and Rangoon were more certain. They agreed to return to Panglong in one year's time to make a final decision about their future.

Sao and her family flew home by light aircraft, landing at the Heho airstrip. From there, the returned Heir-Apparent enjoyed a ceremonial procession complete with musicians and dancers. Arriving at Yawnghwe Haw, he was delighted to meet his new brothers and sisters who were born while he was away in England.

A few days later, he took to his bed, suffering the first of many illnesses as his body painfully readjusted itself to a world he'd left behind at the age of twelve.

In April, the first Obeisance Ceremony since the Japanese invasion was held at Yawnghwe Haw. Before the formalities began, the Mahadevi and Great Saopha called the ministers to the Middle Hall to receive their orders. It was their first traditional council meeting since before the war. Sao and her husband sat on gilt thrones with elephants carved into the legs. When the ministers had all arrived and seated themselves on the floor before them, her husband spoke.

"When the Japanese were here, there was no high or low. I tolerated everything during the war. There was no sun in the sky. Now the sun has returned to the sky, and there is law and order in the state again. If there is any nonsense, arrests!"

The ministers and officials accepted these words with relief, thinking the troublesome Youth League would be reined in and the old ways restored. Lately, the Shan States had become something of a hot-bed, with at least four distinct political organisations emerging in the post-war vacuum, not all of them favouring a return to feudal ways. Prince Shwe Thaike was no foolish despot, though. He knew the youths had a right to meet and form associations, and he had no desire to stand in their way. By "nonsense" he meant setting off bombs or kidnapping people, a level of political violence that was thankfully still unknown in the Shan States.

Not so in Rangoon, where the transition period grew rockier with each passing day. On April 8, 1946, a village woman, Ma Ahma, presented a petition to British authorities in which she accused Aung San of crucifying her husband on the goalpost at the Thaton sports field, a crime of war that had not been forgotten amid the myriad atrocities and tragedies of the past years. Governor Dorman-Smith was in a quandary, faced with prosecuting the man who was Mountbatten's personal choice to lead post-war Burma. He and Aung San were saved by a technicality: a petition had to be followed by a submission to a court. The widow—assuming the Governor would take responsibility for moving the case forward—made no such submission and, as a result, received no justice for her dead husband.

Dorman-Smith was relieved but still reluctant to hand the country to Aung San as quickly as London wanted. His foot-dragging only led to his recall. He departed for London in May, officially to recover from "a severe attack of amoebic dysentery".

Just before he left, police opened fire on a crowd of pro-independence demonstrators in a working class neighbourhood, killing three and wounding eight. Aung San pulled together a massive public funeral. Organised labour adopted the dead as martyrs. Twenty thousand converged on Insein district to mourn. Dorman-Smith's replacement, Hubert Rance, and his wife, Noel, arrived in Rangoon on August 30 to face a month of planned workers' strikes culminating in a general strike on September 23, in protest against police brutality. The strikes were organised by the Communist Party, the most active element within Aung San's Freedom League coalition.

A Labour appointee, Rance advocated independence without delay. There would be no return to the old empire days, as France was rather badly attempting to do in Indochina, and the Dutch in the East Indies. Already facing an anti-French army of resistance, the French turned to their old hilltribe contacts, stepping up opium purchases in Saigon in return for the raising of 40,000 hill men against the anti-colonialists. Such foreign adventures were not for Britain's Labour government, though. Governor Rance was under orders to close up shop.

As the workers' demonstrations gathered steam, a disturbing incident occurred. On September 21, two days before the planned general strike, U Saw narrowly escaped a drive-by assassination attempt. He received a nasty eye injury in the shooting and flew to Calcutta for treatment.

When the news reached Yawnghwe, Sao and the Prince were deeply disturbed. Burmese politicians had always been ardent mud-slingers, but never before was violence a factor. The assassination attempt hung in the air like an evil omen; the perpetrators remained a mystery.

Some months later, Aung San himself toured the Shan States. He was by now clearly the man of the hour, Britain's golden boy, despite the fact that his Freedom League coalition was wracked with internal bickering. In exchange for seven of eleven Executive Council seats, Aung San brought the workers' strikes to an end. In response, the Communist Party members of the coalition accused Aung San—who had been their founding Secretary-General—of collaboration with the enemy. They attacked him in the pages of their bombastic newspaper, the *Thunderer*. Aung San replied by expelling them from the Freedom League. All the while, U Saw remained in Calcutta, nursing his injured eye, cut off, usurped, ignored.

Such local matters barely registered with the British. In ending the strikes, Aung San had proven himself as the one who could command enough influence to bring the country together. On December 3, Rance spoke to the cream of Burmese society at the Orient Club of Rangoon, founded because the Pegu Club was British-only. He announced "full self-government in what must be a relatively short period". Aung San was invited to London to ink the independence agreement. All that was left for him to do was to define the borders of his new nation.

It was the latter task which hastened him to the Shan States in the weeks before his London trip, seeking the Saophas' signatures on a joint proposal for independence. Instead, he met a cautious, intransigent people who had already made up their minds to wait for their next Panglong conference before signing anything. He urged them to form a state association. The Saophas told him they would be meeting very soon, if only he would wait.

On January 2, 1947 Aung San flew to London anyway, without the signatures. Hearing the news, Sao realised they were about to be presented with a fait accompli: an independent Burma that included the Shan States within its borders. She was relieved when her brother called the Saophas to Hsenwi for an emergency meeting. Her husband roared out the palace gate in his jeep, determined to stop London from signing their land and peoples away.

Farewell Shan State

It took a little more than one month for Prince Shwe Thaike and his colleagues to present the Shan peoples with an anthem and a flag. Giving them a country of their own was another matter. At their emergency meeting in Hsenwi, the Saophas hastily formed a skeleton government. Then they despatched an urgent telegram to London. The telegram stated that the Burmese leader Aung San didn't represent the Shan territory. At the same time, the Youth League members—who now had their own political party, allied with Aung San's Freedom League—met in Taunggyi and declared Aung San did represent them.

Despite the telegram's remarkable journey from the distant Shan hills to the corridors of Whitehall, it was ignored by the British negotiators. There was nothing in it that Prime Minister Atlee could recognise: three signatories he'd never heard of—Prince Shwe Thaike's name among them—representing an unelected, unknown government. Putting the telegram away, he instead placed his initials on Burma's document of independence, the Aung San-Atlee Agreement.

By the time the Shan ethnic leaders made their way toward Panglong in February, Aung San had already returned triumphant from London. The agreement promoted "early unification of the Frontier Areas with Ministerial Burma", pending a commission of inquiry.

The pro-Freedom League youths in Taunggyi began clamouring for Prince Shwe Thaike to invite Aung San to the second Panglong conference.

"Why not? It's an open meeting—anyone can come," the Prince said, noncommittally.

Sao wasn't certain it was a good idea, but her husband shrugged off her suspicious attitude. The youths despatched the invitation themselves.

Once again, Sao attended the conference as kitchen boss. She directed the cooks to keep the rice cauldrons and curry pots steaming from morning till night. The first delegates appeared early on February 3, 1947. Parties large and small continued to arrive all that day and into the next. A tent city assembled on the camp ground. The three major ethnic groups were present and, for the first time in Shan history, people's representatives were invited to share decision-making with the princes.

One year ago, the men around Sao's dining table seemed confused. Now they seemed resigned. Obviously, the British weren't prepared to negotiate separate nationhood with the Shan States. Prince Shwe Thaike led the movement toward conciliation with Aung San. A few were still uncomfortable with the idea, Sao included. She had little place in the discussions, though. Her free time was spent with the other wives of the leaders. In the evenings the women gathered under the stars to talk, laugh, and eat together, while the voices of the men rose and fell in the dining pavilion.

During the day, Sao was busy with the kitchen staff while the future of the Shan States was being decided. If she were allowed to attend the meetings, she probably would have just got into an argument with her own husband. When one of the peoples' representatives spoke out against opening negotiations with Burma, Prince Shwe Thaike glowered so fiercely that the man and his supporters sank into embarrassed voicelessness. Although many of the people's representatives were themselves quite high born, they still weren't ready for a world where men must speak their minds freely, much less openly disagree with the Great Saophas. In the old days, their silence would have been enough to indicate disagreement. In the new world of political debate, silence meant nothing.

Within a few days, the framework for an agreement with Burma was laid: the Shan peoples would co-operate, but under their own autonomous government and within a ten-year trial time period. Sao could hardly believe the news. Despite centuries of mistrustful acrimony between the highlands and the lowlands, her husband had led them into a union with Burma—just like that.

On February 7, the delegates founded the Supreme Council of the United Hill Peoples (SCOUHP). Its task was to choose and guide their state representatives to Rangoon. Prince Shwe Thaike was named president. The appointment eased Sao's misgivings somewhat.

It was an important turning-point in Shan history. That day, a loose collection of feudal princedoms was transformed into a single 62,500 square-mile modern state, stretching from the Chinese frontier to the Burma plain. Instead of "the Shan States", from now on their land was "Shan State", a unified singular that belonged to everyone.

The meeting ended with the assembly gathered around a bamboo flag pole. Sao watched the freshly-stitched banner rise against a rim of mountains into a cloudless sky. It featured a white moon, representing purity of heart, resting on three broad bands of colour: yellow for the races of the Shan plateau, green for the forest, and red for bravery.

Her husband's gaze was fixed on the new flag twisting at the top of the bamboo pole. He looked ready to meet the Burmese.

Not everyone shared his optimism. When Aung San arrived three days later, a few Saophas conspicuously absented themselves from the Burmese leader's major speech. Those who came to listen were impressed, though. An intense young man with cat-like eyes, Aung San talked to the Shan leaders in calm, measured tones. He never reminded them that, as a result of his London meeting, he had the upper hand. He wanted the Saophas to come into his dominion willingly. He proposed they share a national government merely to manage currency, national defence and post-war recovery. Other matters were their own affair, the purview of their own state government.

"If you do not wish to join hands with us, we won't force you to do so," he concluded.

Six men were chosen to negotiate the deal with Aung San, two from each of the ethnic groups present. Wanting to encourage the participation of others, Prince Shwe Thaike bowed out. The chief Tai negotiators were Prince Sam Htun of Mong Pawn, who had taken a lead role in helping organise the conference, and Uncle Kya Bu, the fellow who was cowed into silence when he tried to speak against union.

Sao and her husband could only wait, hoping Aung San would accept the assembly's terms: full autonomy in local affairs and the right of secession. They conversed little with each other during the next few days, allowing their thoughts to wander down opposite paths. Sao eyed the Burmese delegates warily. She noted how they picked at the meals her cooks prepared, as if afraid of some sort of back-country disease.

On February 12, the Panglong Agreement was signed. There were just nine points to it, the first four having to do with the selection of representatives to the national Executive Council. The fifth point guaranteed full internal autonomy for Shan State; the sixth, a promise to hold talks on a separate Kachin state; the seventh, a guarantee of fundamental democratic rights; the eighth, financial autonomy; the ninth, financial assistance to the Kachin and the Chin from the national treasury. That was all.

When the signatories stepped forward, no one mentioned the missing tenth point, which the ethnic leaders had all agreed to a few days earlier: "the right to secede after attainment of freedom from Confederation with Burma if and when we choose."

The negotiators had apparently accepted the Burmese argument: the matter of secession rights was complicated, best discussed in a full meeting of Burma's Constituent Assembly, the post-war body that would direct the country toward its first election. The omission troubled Sao; if it bothered her husband, he never said anything.

A rough-hewn table was set up for the signing ceremony. The various representatives formed a tight semi-circle around it and stepped forward one by one to pledge their names. Prince Shwe Thaike bent over the paper and signed as president of SCOUHP. Then Aung San took the pen, narrow eyes brimming with pride.

Together, the two men had created one country, the Union of Burma. It was the last thing Sao had expected.

Not long after, London sent forth a commission of inquiry to examine Rangoon's relations with the frontier states, even though the matter had already been settled by the parties concerned. The Tai princes were invited to make submissions in Maymyo. Before they set off to the colonial hill station, Sao entertained a large delegation of Kachin and Chin representatives at Yawnghwe Haw.

"We shouldn't hitch our carts to Burma, just for the sake of independence," one Kachin man said. She was gratified to hear them revive the idea of seceding from the Union once independence was gained. Telling this to a lame duck British commission was probably no use, though.

No matter. She was glad of the trip north, for whatever reason. It gave her a chance to visit Hsenwi.

When she arrived, though, she found the situation in her home town so changed that it wasn't like coming home at all. For one thing, her old schoolmate, Princess Van Thip, wasn't there to greet her. She had declared herself divorced from Prince Hom Hpa and gone home to Kengtung. Divorce was a simple matter if you had a supportive family to take you in, an option Sao herself never had.

The pleasant country manor was gone, too, replaced by an unfinished-looking bamboo structure on the mound of the Old Haw, where her brother held his meetings and looked after state administration.

Lately, he was embroiled in a secession war in Kokang district. Old Yang had passed on, leaving the Myosa-ship open. Another Kokang family claimed the seat, saying that years ago Sao's father had promised them the next turn. The local militia didn't want a change. They liked working for the Yangs and wanted Old Yang's son, Eddie, to take over so that their profitable trading could continue undisturbed. One of Sao's nephews was despatched to settle the matter; he returned with a broken nose.

Sao was intrigued by the story, which promised to take an even stranger turn a few days later. While the men of Kokang fought over who would be Myosa, a third element arrived on the scene. Olive Yang was like no woman Sao had ever met before. Arriving at the Saopha's house on horseback, she leapt to the ground in a swirl of dust, flipping the reins to a tough-looking teenager. Flanked by two other young thugs, she strode through the door. Sao was amazed. Olive was wearing pants and a weathered army jacket.

Suddenly, Sao remembered the old joke: "Watch out for that one—she carries a revolver in her schoolbag."

Olive, the fierce, thick-legged little child of Old Yang, was now grown up. And instead of a revolver in her schoolbag, she had a pistol strapped to each hip.

Sao's brother stepped forward to greet the unexpected guest, stern but smiling. "Olive, you know you're not supposed to bear weapons in my Haw," he said calmly.

Olive immediately drew the pistols from their holsters and presented them with open palms. "I only brought them as a gift for you, Great Saopha," she said.

A clever one, thought Sao; she didn't hesitate for a moment, had the answer so quick.

Olive's visit was brief. They made small talk about her brother Jimmy, educated on the Saopha's allowance at the Shan Chief's School in Taunggyi. He now lived in Rangoon, and was likely to become Kokang's representative to the Union. Jimmy was a debonair, westernised fellow, already gaining a reputation as a playboy in a smart suit. Olive was cut from different cloth altogether. Her English was halting, heavily accented with Chinese tones. She attended primary school at the Guardian Angel's Convent in Lashio, but then Old Yang sent her to middle school in Kunming, China, at her own insistence, she explained. Convent education was not for her.

When the war broke out, she was stranded. During all those terrible years, the brave soldiers of Generalissimo Chiang Kai-shek kept the Kunming air base open. They were an island of strength surrounded by a sea of defeat, fighting waves of Japanese. Now she heard the Generalissimo's soldiers were having trouble with the communists. She would liked to have stayed to help them out, but her father recalled her to Kokang before he died. She completed her last few years of schooling at the local convent and was now the education minister for Kokang district; her tough-looking young companions were students she was helping, she explained.

Olive shrugged off being a minister, even though she was a woman and just twenty-one years old. She was clearly restless in the position.

"I went straight from the jungle to the convent," she laughed. "Maybe I should go back to the jungle." With that, she took her leave.

Looking back on the meeting, one observation captured Sao's attention. The young men looked on their mentor not just with respect, but with fear and devotion. Surely this strange and remarkable creature was destined to become a force in Kokang. Olive was as tough and primeval as the hills that raised her.

Meanwhile in Maymyo, the British inquiry heard formal, well-presented submissions on the issues of democracy, governance and nationhood. Under the court house's gently swirling ceiling fans, they were far removed from Olive's world and the wilderness of the jungle.

When the presentations were finished, the commission sent off a report to London noting the Shan leaders' desire for "fullest possible autonomy" and the right to secede. They recommended the frontier areas be awarded forty-five seats in Burma's interim Constituent Assembly. It was a small boost of support for Shan State. Sao was aware, though, that London was no longer very concerned with the outcome in Burma. With its terrible war damage, the country had become a liability. As well, Britain had more consuming problems with the controversial creation of East and West Pakistan from the flanks of India.

It was up to Aung San to heed the commission's recommendations or not. The Saophas trusted him to do so. He seemed sympathetic to their aspirations.

When the hearings ended, Sao and the Prince returned to Yawnghwe Haw, where she soon felt herself descending into stifling boredom. Her children were growing older. They spent more time with their nursemaids and the childless Daw Nyunt May than with their mother. Nang Mya Win, the youngest wife, had a second child now, a cute one-year-old nicknamed Stanley. Sao enjoyed playing with the baby, but he could hardly fill all the hours in her day.

It was apparent her younger co-wife felt the same way, perhaps even more so, having come to the palace at such an early age. Other privileged young girls had fun going to movie houses, meeting boys, planning their futures, while Nang Mya Win was already a mother of two with a middle-aged husband and a future cast in stone.

Sao sympathised, for she, too, had lost her youth to marriage. When the Prince informed her that Nang Mya Win wanted to go to university, she readily agreed, thinking the girl should have a chance at a normal life away from the Haw. In any case, her husband should stop his feudalistic dalliance with a concubine if he intended to pursue a political career. But after giving her consent, Sao had a request of her own.

"I want to go to university, too," she told her husband firmly.

Why not? Nang Mya Win wasn't the only one to have her life interrupted by marriage.

Her husband said nothing. In fact, the idea of either wife attending university was never again raised in the household. When the Heir-Apparent heard this titbit of family gossip, he told Sao, "That was brilliant, Mummy!", thinking it a clever ploy to blockade Nang Mya Win's ambitions. But Sao really, truly wanted to go to university. She found it sad that her husband and his eldest son saw it only as a woman's petty scheme. Now what did she have to look forward to in life? Her role as Mahadevi had become unclear under the new order. There wasn't even a Ceremony of Obeisance to prepare for that year, because the Constituent Assembly elections were scheduled for April 9. It wouldn't do to have such a feudal display in the middle of democratic elections.

The elections themselves didn't require elaborate preparation. This was still the dawn of democracy in the hill country. There were no campaigns, press conferences, speeches, or even ballot boxes. Aung San granted the recommended forty-five frontier seats in the 235-member Assembly. To fill them, the Saophas and other traditional ethnic leaders nominated from among their own ranks, agreeably assigning the most prominent leaders from the princely states. As president of the United Hill Peoples, Sao's husband was assured a seat.

In Rangoon, the campaign ran much hotter. The frustrated U Saw—recovered from his eye injury—made a brief alliance with the Communist Party. Despite their combined attack, though, the Freedom League's popularity appeared insurmountable. In despair, U Saw decided the election was a farce and took his Patriotic Party out of the running, leaving the communists to stand alone against the Freedom League.

Watching these events from their southern borderland, the Karen also decided to boycott. They hadn't gained the same written guarantees of autonomy as Shan State had, and there was a great deal of bad blood between their people and the Burmese. The Burmese called them "ah-yaing-ah-saing", barbarians, and "phaya-ma-shee-taya-ma-thee", meaning people without God and without Dharma, a reference to the ethnic group's traditional unstructured monotheism. The Burmese said, "If wild Karen die, they come back as catfish. If catfish die, they come back as wild Karen." It was ironic, for the Karen hardly lacked religion, being devoutly Christian in the majority and Buddhist in the minority.

There was a more recent, still-raw wound between the two races: the Karen died fighting the rearguard during Britain's retreat from Burma. They watched Aung San's Burma Independence Army pillage their land under the Japanese umbrella. Few Karen believed that taking part in Aung San's election would bring anything but misfortune.

Let Aung San's people vote for Aung San, and then we can set up our own free Karen land, they said.

Thus, despite the sound and fury in Rangoon, there was scant real competition for the Assembly seats, with twenty-four Karen seats left vacant, the Shan seats all claimed, just four Anglo-Burman seats and, for the remainder, Aung San's well-loved Freedom League against a group of abrasive, unpopular communists. No one was surprised, then, when Aung San won in a landslide, taking 117 seats to the Communist Party's seven. He was already being called the Father of Independence long before the votes were counted. The first Constituent Assembly meetings were scheduled for May, in Jubilee Hall near the Rangoon Race Course.

The last few weeks of April were busy ones for Sao, as she supervised the arrangements for an extended stay in Rangoon. Just she and the Prince were going. The two oldest boys, Tiger and Tzang, were enrolled in school in Kalaw, while the younger ones would remain with the other wives at Yawnghwe Haw for now.

They left with a skeleton staff and enough clothing and household goods to last them through the sitting, which was expected to carry on through the entire course of the rainy season. To Sao, it seemed an interminably long time. If she could have seen the future, perhaps she would not have gone at all. At the very least she would have paused to say goodbye to her homeland, knowing this was the end of her life among the wild green hills and graceful palaces of Shan State. Instead, she departed Yawnghwe Haw blissfully unaware of what lay ahead, vowing to return as quickly as possible.

Three

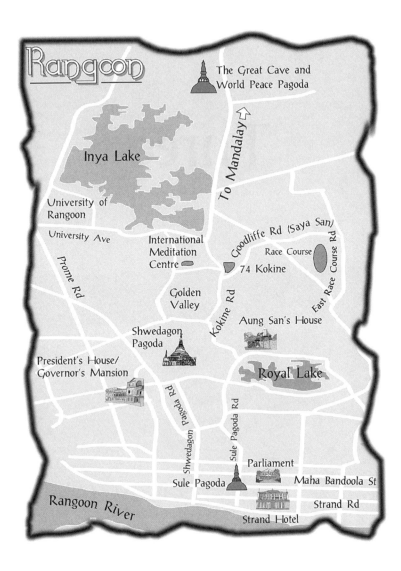

(Right) Aung San and wife Daw Khin Kyi.

(Left) Aung San.

(Below) Painting shows Aung San (left) and Prince Shwe Thaike, (right) signing the Panglong Agreement in 1947.
(Shan State Museum)

Sao entertaining guests at the President's House.

(Above) The President's House.

(Left) The house at 74 Kokine Road.

(Above) Prince Hom Hpa of Hsenwi and his wife Princess Van Thip.

(Above) Sao, during a visit to India, flanked by Indian Prime Minister Jawalharal Nehru and Indira Gandhi, circa 1950.

(Left) General Ne Win. (The Bangkok Post)

Evil Beginnings

Sao and the Prince were assigned a war-abandoned house in Golden Valley, between the city's two lakes. The place was fine, but smaller than what they were used to. It was near Jubilee Hall, site of the Constituent Assembly meetings.

A car and driver ferried Sao's husband to the meeting hall every morning. He was pleased with the progress made in the constitutional talks. The assembly members interacted well with one another; they spoke their minds freely in debate but remained committed to seeking consensus on most issues. It was exactly what he and Aung San had envisioned: a union forged in civilised discussion between men of steady character.

Sao seldom mixed socially with the new Burmese leaders, most of whom spoke no English or Tai. Once in a while there was tea at Aung San's house, which sat on the crest of a steeply-sloping sidestreet, overlooking a lush little garden of palms and peppercorn trees.

Recently, Aung San had resigned from the military, saying the army had no business in politics. He traded his fringed epaulettes and stiff army cap for traditional Burmese dress, as he had worn in his student days. People remarked how relaxed and cheerful he looked, although his aides were worried that he'd given up his armed escort. They didn't think the situation was secure. There were rumours of arms missing from the city garrison. Who might be stockpiling the weapons varied from story-teller to story-teller: sometimes it was said to be Karen who rejected the election's outcome, sometimes it was communists who felt disenfranchised from the political system. But on the pleasant sweep of Aung San's veranda, danger seemed far away. His wife, a former nurse and political activist in her own right, was a gracious hostess. Their children—son Aung San Oo and two-year old daughter Aung San Suu Kyi—scrambled underfoot while gentle talk filled the air.

There were other aspects of Rangoon life less agreeable to Sao and her husband. The rains fell more oppressively than in the hill country. Their tea-water smelled bad, and the household was often hit with stomach ailments.

One day in July, Shwe Thaike took to his bed, looking grey and drawn. It became Sao's duty, then, to meet his political colleagues when they came calling. On July 19 at about 9:30 a.m., Sam Htun of Mong Pawn arrived in her parlour. He was a kindly man who dreamed of retiring to become a farmer. Instead, he'd been drafted onto the negotiating team at Panglong and now, as a result, onto Burma's Executive Council.

Instead of going home to farm, he travelled daily to the Secretariat Building, where the Executive Council met within the halls of the out-going British bureaucracy. The building was much quieter than in the empire's heyday. Most of the old civil service sought retirement or resigned, leaving the country decidedly lacking where once there'd been an overabundance of planners and paper-shufflers.

Prince Sam Htun was on his way to the Secretariat that morning, but something was gnawing so doggedly at his thoughts that he had to stop and talk to someone. When his car neared Sao's house, he told the driver to turn off the road.

Sao greeted him in the parlour. Noting the worried look on his face, she offered a plump chair and tea. Prince Sam Htun sat down heavily and sighed.

"Sao, my horoscope says I'm going to be killed. Do you think it's true?"

Sao considered the question carefully before she answered. "If you came through the Japanese occupation, you're okay. If you think something bad is going to happen, just do some good deeds to improve your Kamma. You'll be fine." Many people felt this way; having survived World War II, there were no troubles worth comparison.

Prince Sam Htun looked relieved. Like many Shan leaders, he had developed great regard for the Mahadevi of Yawnghwe.

"You're right, of course. I was so worried," he admitted, setting down his teacup and glancing at his pocket watch. "I'll pay my respects to your husband, if I may, and be on my way." The Executive Council meeting was set for 10:30, and already it was after ten.

Sao led him to her husband's room. From his bed Prince Shwe Thaike rose onto his elbows, looking hot and uncomfortable.

"What are you doing here? You're supposed to be at the Secretariat," he barked at his visitor.

"Yes, I'm late," Prince Sam Htun agreed.

"Well, you'd better get going," Sao's husband said, then sank back into his rumpled bed.

Aung San looked out over the Executive Council chamber, anxious to get on with the day's business. It was nearly 10:30 and people were still in the corridor. Such small delays were nothing, though, in the swift march toward nationhood. Just over one month ago, on June 9, the Constituent Assembly opened its first session. Five days into the meeting, Aung San moved a resolution that the new constitution would describe an independent, sovereign republic called the Union of Burma.

To ease ethnic concerns, minority rights were assured and guidelines laid out for the establishment of autonomous states. It worked. In the days to follow, Aung San gained from the Shan leaders a constitutional commitment to stay at least ten years within the Union, allowing enough time for the implementation of two five-year national development projects.

One point of contention came with the nomination of Aung San's old school chum, Thakin Nu, as Constituent Assembly chair. Prince Shwe Thaike of Yawnghwe spoke the most plainly on the matter. He described Thakin Nu as a man of "impeccable" moral integrity whose jail-house novel—*Man is to Man a Wolf*—sided with the underdog. Therefore, if Thakin Nu wanted to lead the assembly, he should be prepared to side with the numerically weaker ethnic groups, the Prince reasoned. Their support was conditional, based on that assumption.

"We do not want to be freed from the British yoke only to become the slaves of Burma!" the Prince concluded.

With this caution stated, he then pledged co-operation. The assembly responded by making him vice-chair, second in rank to Thakin Nu.

On June 18, they recessed to let working committees hammer out the constitution's details. A few days later, Thakin Nu left for London to inform Prime Minister Atlee of the assembly's intention to create an independent parliamentary government before the year's end.

During the recess, Aung San carried out daily business through the Executive Council, now expanded to include Shan, Karen and Moslem members. The Shan States were represented by the Saophas of Yawnghwe and Mong Pawn. On the morning of July 19, though, Aung San noted Prince Shwe Thaike's place was empty, while the Mong Pawn Saopha was among the last to enter the room and take a seat.

The lone Shan representative looked ill at ease, jumping at a noise in the corridor as if a demon had called his name. Aung San, on the other hand, looked up calmly when the strange, sudden figure appeared in the doorway. He rose from his seat and lifted his palm outward in a gesture of command before the world exploded in a spray of bullets.

Since moving to Rangoon, Sao and her husband had taken to lunching in what she called the "western way", with a main meat dish, a salad and a single hot sauce on the side. Their staff, however, continued to churn out their own lunches as if they still lived in a grand palace, preparing up to thirteen different curries per meal. The kitchen situation was an ongoing annoyance to Sao; she was engaged in another losing battle over the matter when Prince Sam Htun's driver arrived at the house, breathless and distraught.

Sao emerged from the kitchen just as her husband, up from his bed and dressed for lunch, ushered the man into the hallway.

Caught up in the minutiae of running her household, she had almost forgotten the Mong Pawn Saopha's morning visit.

One look at the driver's face told her that Prince Sam Htun's unlucky horoscope had come to pass, although neither she nor her husband were prepared for the scope of the disaster.

Gulping on his words, the driver told them what he knew. At 10:30 a.m., just as the business of the day started, gunmen burst into the Executive Council chamber. Prince Sam Htun received two bullets to the head; he was alive but not expected to last the night. Six other council members were already dead, including Aung San, the Father of Independence. He was shot thirteen times.

The first thought to flood Sao's mind was that if her husband hadn't been ill, he too would be dead. Then she remembered Prince Sam Htun's visit—how she dismissed his fears and how her husband gruffly ordered him to hurry to the meeting. The realisation was sickening: We sent this man to his death.

The Prince hurried out the door with the driver, to where Sao had no idea. Perhaps the hospital, perhaps the council chamber. She was left alone in whirling silence.

How horrible for Aung San's family—those little children, such a nice wife.

These were her initial thoughts, not matters of state. But in the midst of feeling guilt for Sao Sam Htun's death, relief for her husband's survival, and sorrow for Aung San's family, she saw, too, the yawning political abyss opening up before them all. As the news spreads throughout Burma, an entire nation would ask the same question rising to Sao's mind.

What now?

No one had imagined a future without Aung San.

The President-Elect

A second shock awaited the people of Burma, although in hindsight no one was very surprised. Immediately following Aung San's death, police raided the home of the pre-war Prime Minister, U Saw. He resisted and in a few brief moments of violent confrontation three of his men were killed. The police discovered a large cache of arms and ammunition in the home, revealing the true extent of U Saw's bitterness, a festering anger conceived in a Ugandan jail, nursed in a Calcutta hospital and then unleashed onto a new Burma led by new men.

In a single fit of fury, U Saw destroyed the balance of Burmese politics. Before the assassinations, the top post-war leadership operated as three corners of a carefully-drawn triangle. The mild intellectual Thakin Nu and the fierce military commander Ne Win formed the base. At the apex was Aung San, the charismatic unifying force, the man with the vision. Now there were only two leaders left—Thakin Nu and Ne Win—who were diametrically opposed to one another in character. Neither enjoyed Aung San's ability to craft consensus from disparate viewpoints; neither understood the idea of a multi-ethnic federal state.

In fact, Thakin Nu was growing disinterested in the world of politics altogether. Lately he'd been studying Buddhism more seriously. A sense of cultivated detachment carried his thoughts beyond the concerns of man. Like the would-be farmer Prince Sam Htun, now dead of his wounds, U Nu dreamed of retreating to his own pursuits. He wanted to write more novels and study the Dharma.

The excitement of his university years had not completely left him, though. He remembered the 1930s, when Aung San was expelled and he, Thakin Nu, was left behind to lead the students. Then, he held rallies, burned the Government Act and led the chants. Now a whole nation waited to be led, not just a rag-tag group of students. He would fill Aung San's shoes again if called on, he told himself, because that is what Aung San would want.

Indeed, the call came before the end of the day. On hearing of Aung San's death, Governor Rance immediately appointed Thakin Nu deputy chair of what was left of the Executive Council. Four days later, with the nation still in shock, the Constituent Assembly officially became Burma's interim government and Thakin Nu was raised to the position of provisional prime minister. He said he would take the job for a year, then retire to the monastery.

Thakin Nu's Constituent Assembly chairmanship passed to the vice-chair, Sao's husband, Prince Shwe Thaike of Yawnghwe.

Thus, when the assembly reconvened on June 23, Sao's husband held the country's second-highest position. This was a matter of growing worry to Sao. She had hoped the Prince would untangle himself from the affairs of Burma, not be drawn in deeper. They were needed at home in Shan State, away from this steamy, foreign capital. Instead, he faced several more months of work in Rangoon. The Assembly's second session would look only at a draft of the constitution before its mid-August adjournment. The final document wouldn't be passed until a third session opened in September.

And that wasn't the end of it. The Assembly wanted to present the constitution to the British parliament's autumn session. To meet the deadline, the details of ethnic and state rights would remain incomplete. These points would have to be worked out after the final Constituent Assembly session—or so the ethnic leaders had been promised. More work lay ahead, perhaps stretching into the next year.

Sao hoped such details could be concluded from their home in Shan State. She counted the days to the final Constituent Assembly session.

Time crawled in the little Golden Valley house. Every night the rains poured down with deafening cracks of thunder, leaving the streets mired in sluggish brown pools in the mornings.

Finally, September came and the weather broke.

On September 15, the third assembly session opened. As a provisional government, its first order of business was to elect a provisional president. Aung San was dead; Thakin Nu was already appointed provisional prime minister. Therefore the presidency should go to the next man in line, Prince Shwe Thaike of Yawnghwe.

Hearing the news, Sao said to herself, "Well, it's only provisional." The Burmese would have to find another president when the meetings ended and the Great Saopha returned to Yawnghwe Haw.

It took the assemblymen just nine days to finalise the new constitution. After the shock of the assassinations, the members hadn't much heart to continue arguing over minutiae. No one wanted to miss the autumn session in London and so delay Aung San's dream. They wanted to honour the dead with a new country in the new year. They could fine-tune the document later.

At least the ethnic leaders achieved their main goals. Three constituent states—Shan, Kachin, and Karenni—were named in the constitution. The Chins were given something called a Special Division. Shan State was granted the right of secession by plebiscite after ten years, thus returning the missing tenth point of the Panglong Agreement.

But there were gaping holes. The new states lacked their own constitutions, judiciary and administrative structures. The large Karen territory was left ill-defined, its fate and its borders entrusted to some sort of future referendum. Worse, the document contained no clear demarcation of federal and state powers. Finally, the role of Burma was confusing. The lowland plains region—which the colonialists called Burma Proper—was not listed among the states. "Burma" referred to a mother government, around which revolved the states as satellites. The national government was given a veto over state laws. It was a rather curious arrangement for a federal nation.

On September 24, the constitution was passed despite its shortcomings. Aung San understood the basics of federalism, but his successors did not. The six who died with Aung San were among the country's most experienced politicians, including the Karen leader they'd hoped would bring the Karen people into the Union.

Under the circumstances, their imperfect document faced major obstacles. But when the Constituent Assembly gave its assent, the members cheered and raised their arms in victory. They had met the London deadline. On October 17, Thakin Nu would sign the Nu-Atlee Treaty of Independence, ending British rule in Burma once and for all.

There were points worth cheering. The constitution provided the basic structure of the national government: a bicameral parliament comprised of a 250-seat lower house called the Chamber of Deputies and a 125-seat upper house called the Chamber of Nationalities. Shan State was given twenty-five seats in each house.

The lower house would elect a prime minister to lead them, while a joint session of both chambers would select a president as head of state. The president was given the power to grant pardons and declare an emergency but, beyond that, the position was largely ceremonial.

The assemblymen fully expected that the current provisional president, Prince Shwe Thaike, would become the President of Burma. After all, it was he who called everyone to Panglong and convinced them to join the Union. More importantly, as a well-known ethnic leader, Sao's husband would personify racial harmony. Who better to reward with a prestigious position and the Governor's massive colonial mansion?

Sao tried desperately to argue him out of accepting. "You will leave Shan State in the lurch," she warned him. "There are already some Saophas in the national government—they don't need you, too."

Although she lacked a firm grasp of modern governmental structures, she understood the presidency was a position without power. It would effectively isolate him from Shan politics and the negotiation of states' rights.

She wondered what pressures and promises the Burmese had brought to bear on him. She thought that if she only knew what triggered his decision, she could talk him out of it. But the Prince told her nothing—only that he'd already accepted and she'd better get used to the idea.

Sao wasn't the only one who was upset. One day a small group of Saophas arrived at the Golden Valley house to see her. They begged her to influence her husband to return to the Shan States and continue as SCOUHP president. What could she say? She had already been through the argument with her husband and got nowhere.

"I can do nothing," she told the worried men gathered in her parlour. "You'll have to convince him yourselves."

She never found out whether or not the group dared approach her husband on the matter; the Prince remained a closed book on the subject. If they did confront him, they met no observable success. Prince Shwe Thaike now answered to the title "President-Elect". He informed her that their first state duty was already scheduled, attendance at the November wedding of Britain's Princess Elizabeth.

Sao had no time to adjust to the new facts of her life before a specially-assigned plane arrived from London to collect them. The other Tai wives in Rangoon were thrilled on her behalf; they themselves were just dying to go to England, they told her. What a treat to leave all this post-war scarcity and turmoil, if only for a few weeks! But even though it was Sao's first trip abroad, she had trouble mustering much excitement as the plane lifted away from Mingaladon runway and headed over the soggy delta-lands toward the Bay of Bengal.

The plane flew low and slow. Sao was amazed at how brown India looked compared to the fields of Burma, green even in November. Looking out her window, she was reminded that the assassination of seven men in Rangoon was nothing compared to the bloodshed that rolled over India in the colonial aftermath.

In India, lands were sliced off. In Burma, lands were tacked on. Opposite scenarios, but with the same dangers inherent. Somehow Burma escaped India's fate. Perhaps that's what motivated her husband—the choice between peaceful co-operation and violent deconstruction.

It didn't matter: she was still unreconciled toward their new lives. She didn't want to be trapped in Rangoon.

The hours and days were impossible to separate as they made their long journey west above golden deserts, wide brown rivers, red ripples of ancient mountains and, finally, the startling blue of the Mediterranean. The plane touched down in Cypress and again in Paris, and along the way they got to know the jovial flight captain as if he were an old friend.

Sao was tired and queasy when they finally reached London. She was feeling the effects of another pregnancy.

On arrival, she and the Prince were assigned a hotel and given a handful of ration coupons, needed to purchase necessities. The whole country was on rations, including guests to the royal wedding. Even Princess Elizabeth was expected to use coupons for her dress material, but donations of silk and lace flooded Buckingham Palace.

Sao brought her gold Mandalay sarong, the one she'd worn on her own wedding day. She had her portrait taken in a studio; at thirty-two she still looked pretty in the oufit.

In the days before the wedding, Sao visited a few nearly-empty shops, where she discovered that her ration coupons were not enough to buy a single coat against the cold. She settled on some tiny porcelain pots from a souvenir shop. Out on the street, she passed women in threadbare coats. They clutched worn purses and lines of care bracketed their mouths and eyes. Ahead, she heard a clatter of stone and concrete. A small group of workmen picked through bomb rubble, their shoulders hunched against a cold grey drizzle.

If only her friends could see this place! London, the heart of the great empire that ruled their lives since her father's time, the great capital whose landmarks tantalised them from the pages of school texts: perhaps it was something grand in the last century, when the old Prince of Hsipaw watched the world's armies parade past Queen Victoria. Now it was just a poor, war-worn city, no better or worse than Rangoon.

"We Are Free"

Astrologers chose Sunday, January 4, 1948, 4:20 a.m. as the precise moment of Burma's independence. By the Burmese calendar, it was the Ninth Waning, in the month of Pyatho. Sao was six months pregnant. That morning she awoke in darkness to a scene reminiscent of her wedding day some twenty years earlier: the household was in an excited bustle and her maid stood ready with a glittering silk dress and diamond comb. Once again, Sao felt strangely disassociated, as if these events had nothing to do with her. Really, it was not so different from her marriage. She was about to become First Lady of a country she neither loved nor wanted.

When she and her husband stepped out to meet the car, she was surprised by how chill the air was, almost like a Shan morning. Was this a good omen, or bad? She had little hope for the future of Burma. Already there was too much bad blood, especially between the Karen and the Burmese, whose mutual resentment still simmered from the war. She wondered, does no one else see the shadow that lies on this new country?

The presidential entourage included several cars. Sao and her husband sat in the lead car. Behind them, cars carrying Prince Shwe Thaike's two aides-de-camps, two honorary ADCs, and two colonels of the Burma National Army followed like beads on a string. She was comforted by the fact that one of his ADCs was her own favourite Hsenwi nephew, Saw Ohn. At least she was guaranteed one friend in the capital.

As they passed from dark and leafy suburban lanes to the broad streets of central Rangoon, Sao rubbed the mist from her car window. She saw muted forms moving through the pre-dawn darkness toward the city centre. When the squat form of Sule Pagoda neared, the car slowed and a phalanx of police officers parted a sea of people. The entourage rounded the pagoda and made its way down Maha Bandoola street past City Hall, alive with lights and gay bunting, and entered the Quadrangle of the massive Secretariat, where the flag-raising was to take place.

Inside the wrought iron gates, the airless gravity of British bureaucracy still held. At the Quadrangle's centre, outside the little parliament building, was a platform and a single white flag pole bearing a limp Union Jack. The ceremony was to be simple, dignified and impressive.

Stepping from the car, Sao looked beyond the darkened office windows and saw a faint light in the east and a great arc of stars above. Then there was an explosion of flash bulbs and a rising murmur. For who? For them, Sao realised: "The President and his First Lady arrive at the flag-raising."

Again she noted how chill and clear the air was, so strange, not like Rangoon at all. Nothing seemed right or familiar, least of all her new role as First Lady of Burma. But she smiled, the perfect radiant smile of a politician's wife, and moved forward into the crowd. The baby lay heavy inside her, weighing down her step, but no one noticed. Near the platform was a table of radio technicians and reporters from the Burma Broadcasting Corporation, who breathlessly described their arrival.

Shortly before the appointed hour, the president's guard of honour assembled in the square and Prince Shwe Thaike made his inspection. He had chosen formal Shan dress for the occasion: a long, white satin top-coat with a double row of buttons and embroidered sleeves over wide trousers. A matching satin turban sat on his head, artfully knotted with a small fan of material to one side. So attired, he walked down the ranks with his soldier's step, impressing on the men that he was not only Head of State, but a former army officer, and that the inspection was a real one. Then he mounted the podium and took a place next to Governor Rance and Prime Minister-Elect Thakin Nu, who looked much less imposing in a simple cotton coat and sarong, the ordinary dress of a farmer or workman.

The crowd pressed into the Quadrangle was large. In addition to the president and ministers of the new government, also present were the Chief Justice-Designate, the judges, officers of the defence and civil services, the Executive Council, various foreign envoys, the press, and the 178 Constituent Assembly members. A hush descended as the first red streaks of sunrise lit the sky. At precisely 4:20, they heard the distant, hollow boom of guns fired from the deck of the *HMS Birmingham*, moored on the Rangoon River.

Four white-uniformed guards stepped forward and hauled down the Union Jack. Then the flag of Burma crept up the pole, with no breeze to unfurl its design. Sao knew the flag: a large white Union star centred in a blue canton on a red field, surrounded by five smaller stars representing the five states.

A call to present arms was followed by the precise slap of gloved hands on rifles. Then, after a few seconds of silence, a slow surge of cheers rose from the street outside the compound. Sao shared the sudden, giddy realisation: the British were finished. The cheering grew stronger. Steamers on the river hooted in unison. Factory horns blew, church bells and temple gongs filled the air. Now the sound of the crowd coalesced in a chant: "Lut lat pyi, lut lat pyi, doh-pyi lut lat!—Free we are, we are free, our country is free!" Then, for the first time, the Burmese national anthem rose from the Quadrangle. The tune had enough of a martial beat to suit a military band, but beneath it coursed the melody of an old Thakin folk song, one that Aung San might have sung on his lonely stow-away journey to Amoy.

As our heritage ancestral,
We love our Burma forever.
In this world eternal,
We'll defend our Union forever,

*If need be, to the point of death.
Let us guard our common welfare
And in this great unity our duty share
For this, our golden earth.*

After the anthem faded, the 178 Constituent Assembly members filed into the tiny parliament building tucked between the wings of the Secretariat, ready for their first session as a government. Inside, Sao squeezed into a row of visitor's seats on the Speaker's right, near the new prime minister's wife. Ma Mya Yi was dressed simply, like her husband, although in each of her earlobes was a large diamond stud. Aung San's widow and the minister's wives were also seated in the gallery. The minister's ladies looked so young, some of them surely just teenagers. Their husbands, after all, were still mostly in their thirties.

As they waited for the Speaker to take his chair and announce the President, the baby turned lazy circles in Sao's stomach. She felt tired and hungry and it was still only a little after daybreak.

Thankfully, her husband's speech was short and to the point. He announced simply:

"This morning the Union of Burma attains the status of a sovereign independent republic, the Constituent Assembly has become a parliament and with the approval of this parliament I have appointed and invested the Prime Minister and the other ministers so that they are now the Government of the Union."

Then he sketched the government's main policies: Burma would be a socialist state, private ownership of farm-land would be abolished, but there was to be no unlawful expropriation of property. The main task ahead was reconstruction of property and public works destroyed in the war and the development of a defence force. Friendly relations would be sought with all countries of the world and Burma would apply for membership in the newly-formed United Nations.

"As befits the freedom which Burma has attained today, it is the policy of my Government to suppress all evil practices such as those which oblige one person to fear another or enable one person to oppress another," the Prince continued. In this spirit, he declared that the ancient royal mandates which held grave diggers and temple slaves in bondage were abrogated.

"As laid down by the Constitution of the Union of Burma, let all citizens be accorded equal rights and privileges," he concluded. Then the assemblymen rose and took their Pledge to the Union.

Sao struggled to understand; her grasp of the Burmese language had not improved much during her days in Rangoon.

"We pledge to uphold the equality of status for all peoples living on our land, irrespective of their race, religion, age or sex," the representatives said together.

As the voices rose and fell in unison, Sao gradually lost focus on the words. Who knows what each man really stands for, she wondered, scanning their faces, some familiar, others not. She knew the Thakins began as hard-line leftists, not liberal parliamentarians. She sensed danger ahead for Shan State.

Gaining independence unites us today—but tomorrow is another story, she thought.

When the session ended, a motorcade carried Sao, her husband the President, Governor Rance and Lady Rance into the cheering throng outside the Secretariat grounds. Celebrants lined their route as the cars turned at St. John's Market and followed the flame trees of Prome Road toward Government House.

Entering the mansion's gates, Sao looked upon the familiar, grand old building with new eyes. Never before had it seemed so imposing: three stories of stone colonnades, balustrades, cornices, and black-rimmed windows as tall as church glass, rising behemoth-like from an expansive, well-trimmed lawn. It looked like a parliament building, not a house. But this was her new home, renamed the President's House. The Rances were moving out. She and her husband were moving in.

Within the compound, a white-uniformed brass band waited beside a dais draped in leopard skins. Two flag poles stood side by side near the main entrance. It was still early but the day was warming. In the east, the ancient spire of Shwedagon Pagoda glowed in the morning light.

Governor Rance, dressed in top-hat and tails, looked uncharacteristically stiff when he emerged from his car; Sao remembered him as a nice, friendly fellow who, in the days leading to independence, couldn't hide his own befuddlement over London's intentions. Perhaps he was fighting the urge to walk into his former house, sit down at his former breakfast table, and start the day as usual. He had grown to love Burma. Two days ago, he and his wife visited Shwedagon for the final time.

"Its beauty delights the eye," he wrote in the visitor's book, then added, "This is my last message to Burma: may peace and friendship forever be maintained between Burma and Great Britain."

Beneath his signature—Hubert Elvin Rance, Governor of Burma—his wife penned, simply, "With all my love to Burma Women. Noel Rance." In the end, there was little to say.

His white gloves strangled in one hand, Rance stepped onto the leopard-skin dais. Although he was a head taller than the satin-clad President, the occasion seemed to have lessened his stature. As the band struck up a tinny note, he removed his hat and watched his personal standard descend slowly down the flagpole. Then the tune changed and Prince Shwe Thaike's banner—the flag of Shan State—rose on the pole beside. The transition was complete. It was time for goodbyes.

The Rances left by river, just as King Thibaw had done nearly a century earlier. The *HMS Birmingham* waited for them at the jetty near the Strand Hotel. Next to her sat the warship *Mayu*, a gift to the newly-formed Burma Navy from Britain. Sao guessed the ship was an enticement to join the Commonwealth, a federation created to keep the colonies together as autonomous states under the Crown. Whatever the motive, it was a generous gift.

Indeed, Britain's leave-taking was full of good will and kind words from both sides. When they arrived at the jetty, well-wishers stood hundreds deep. As Hubert and Noel made their way up the gang plank, the crowd broke spontaneously into *Auld Lange Syne*. Streamers filled the air and the *Birmingham*'s guns boomed once more in salute, followed by the guns of the *Mayu*. Then the ship cast off. They all stood on the jetty for a long time, waving at the two diminishing figures on deck, until their arms ached and the ship became a speck in the distance. Then they turned back toward the city. The country was theirs and the day was just beginning.

At Maha Bandoola Square, on a pie-shaped wedge of land in the shadow of City Hall and the Supreme Court, Thakin Nu laid the foundation stone for Independence Monument. The monument was to be a single column in honour of the unity achieved at Panglong. Then Thakin Nu delivered a speech to the throng, pouring all his frustrated writing talents into the address as if he could write this new nation like one of his plays, he taking the role of the actor who delivers the soliloquy.

"This Day of Independence dawns on a people not only free but united," he said, with the unswerving conviction of a faith healer.

"May the unity we have achieved today, like the independence that comes with it, forever endure."

After the stone-laying, they rode by golden barge across Royal Lake—more cheering and waving—and then converged on Jubilee Hall, where the bodies of the assassinated leaders still lay in state. There they paid quiet homage to Aung San, wishing he could have seen this day.

Afterwards, a steady stream of guests made their way to the President's House, formerly the Governor's Mansion. From a throne-like chair under the sweeping ceiling of the Marble Hall, Sao's husband solemnly invested the country's judges. Then he received the foreign ambassadors' credentials, including those of R.J. Bowker, Britain's first ambassador to its former colonial possession. Finally, British Secretary of State Arthur Henderson stepped forward and co-signed a friendship treaty between Britain and Burma.

Sao was grateful dinner that evening was a more relaxed affair. The Prince changed into a western business suit with a crisp pocket hanky. Their guests milled about the lawn, cocktails in hand, chattering happily. Some congregated around a book of goodwill messages sent to Sao's husband from around the world.

"I send you my warmest good wishes for the prosperity of the Union," wrote King George VI.

"May favourable winds attend you," offered Lord Pethick Lawrence, the former Secretary of State for Burma.

President Truman's message was: "We welcome you into the brotherhood of free and democratic nations...We in this country have confidence in the people of Burma and in their leaders." Such words were like a door opening into that special club of free and prosperous nations, where differences were overcome in gentlemanly debate and efficient administrations harnessed the wealth of nations. The milling guests glowed with pride.

Sao soon found herself paired with Mrs. Bowker, the British Ambassador's wife, a remarkably attractive, aquiline-featured woman with an exotic Egyptian accent. When introduced to the new president she addressed him simply as "Thaike."

The Ambassador corrected her, saying, "You must call him 'Your Excellency the President of Burma, Prince Shwe Thaike.'"

Sao's husband, unfazed by the Westernised shortening of his name, laughed off the formalities. At home in cosmopolitan gatherings, he was already used to hearing his name in many mangled forms.

When Secretary of State Henderson arrived, Prince Shwe Thaike greeted him with a cigar. They shook hands, lit each other's stogies, then set off to inspect a new silver Rolls Royce in the drive, a gift from Britain to the President.

There was a black Austin, too, for Prime Minister Thakin Nu, who walked a few steps behind Sao's husband and Henderson, hands firmly tucked behind his back, cigarless, his prim white turban perched above a bashful smile.

When the call to dinner came, Sao watched with interest as everyone took their seats in the Marble Hall. Aung San's widow, she noted, was given a place near the end of the head table, far from the central place of honour occupied by Thakin Nu and his wife. These were the politics at which Sao was most adroit: the politics of the court, where censure was expressed in small discourtesies. She wondered why people were wary of this woman whose husband lay cold in Jubilee Hall; she was no threat to them. Aloud she asked, "Why hasn't Daw Khin Kyi got a place of honour?" No one answered and, in the silence, Sao detected the small daggers of distrust and disunity that would ruin Burma.

First Lady

The long, heavily-scheduled Independence Day celebrations set the tone for life in the President's House. Every day thereafter, visitors drifted through the mansion's imposing doors. Sao organised garden parties, teas, lunches and dinners. Not one meal was eaten in privacy.

Whether the distinguished guest be from Ceylon or Pakistan, she settled on an established model. She and her husband would ceremoniously march down the stairs to the dining hall, accompanied by the President's personal ADCs. To avoid confusion over Burmese customs, the table was set English-style and the menu was western: soup, salad, a meat dish and desert. Shepherding the head table through conversation was like work, not fun at all, she soon discovered. Usually there was a generous helping of government ministers present, but some never uttered a word while others talked only among themselves in Burmese. She was left alone to animate the gathering, sniffing out common interests and safe topics among the foreign guests.

Prime Minister Thakin Nu didn't help her pursuit of a cheerful atmosphere. A strict vegetarian, it was his habit to refuse the main serving and stare moodily at an empty plate. Then the ministers would feel obliged to follow suit, lest they appear comparatively lacking in Buddhist piety.

One day Sao leaned over and said, "Prime Minister, other people here are dying to eat meat, so you'd better be more diplomatic."

After that, he accepted all with thanks, pretending to enjoy the whole meal while eating only the side-dish of vegetables, as Sao had advised. But never once did he touch the whisky and cigars that Prince Shwe Thaike handed out to his guests.

Shortly after Independence Day, Sao's two youngest children, Myee and Ying Sita, moved in, along with their half-sister Haymar and their nursemaids. An upstairs room was made into a nursery. During the day, their shouts filled the corridors, adding a welcome sense of family bustle to the wide, officious hallways. Sao's mother arrived from Hsenwi, too, to take treatment for goitre. Daily tinctures of iodine eased the ageing Lady Gold Diamond's condition.

Despite the additional family members, the house was far too big. There were more than thirty bedrooms, most left empty.

Sao had an office on the second floor, where she planned dinners and other events. Two runners sat outside her door, ready to ferry invitations here and there. Her husband had an office down the hall, also with two runners outside the door. As president, it was his job to represent the country on state occasions and to sign government acts, for which he received a modest salary paid in Burma's new currency, the Kyat. His paycheque was set the same as Governor Rance's had been: 10,000 Kyat, or US$ 2,080, per year.

In addition to the runners, the household staff included an elevator operator, a steward, a cook, a telephone operator and the prince's two Indian butlers. Altogether, the presidential family and staff took up less than one wing of the building. The other wing had a floor of Army ADCs and two rooms for the Navy, with the remaining rooms unoccupied. The secretaries and typists worked in an office building outside the main residence.

Sao and her husband both had private sitting rooms attached to their offices for receiving informal visits. Throughout the day, various MPs climbed the stairs to pay their respects to the President and First Lady. Mostly, Sao guessed, they were just looking for "pocket money"; it was the custom to give freely to poor relations and colleagues. Pocket money was not the same as a bribe, but it conveyed a certain brotherly loyalty between giver and receiver, a loyalty that Sao suspected couldn't be relied on from these politicians and army men.

"They're all a bunch of crooks," she warned her husband.

General Ne Win was a frequent visitor. Unpopular among ethnic war veterans—especially the Karen—he'd been passed over as army Chief of Staff. Instead, he spent his afternoons at the race course. As a Yedaya Chay practitioner, he had a passion for guessing lucky numeric combinations. Sao had no idea if he was a successful bettor; she heard that a well-heeled doctor and fellow race patron commonly slipped the general a little extra pocket money for his hobby.

In one of the bedrooms above Sao's office, Prince Sai, the Heir-Apparent of Yawnghwe State, tossed and groaned. A year after his return from Britain, he was still unable to withstand the local contagions. He caught malaria, then typhoid, then black water fever. Medicines were difficult to find in post-war Burma. The doctor, who confessed he could do little, arrived every day with bottles of purified water. Prince Sai drank six or eight bottles a day. On his good days he studied law and civil administration. Sometimes he played squash with Prime Minister Thakin Nu on a court in the garden. Thakin Nu was glad to find a partner and a court, for squash was an uncommon game which he happened to enjoy. It was a good chance to relax.

A few months into his mandate, the forty-one-year-old PM was already losing control of his government. Within the Freedom League's rank and file, a hard-left minority attacked the coalition's moderately socialist program. For one thing, they disagreed with plans to compensate dispossessed Indian and British landholders under the Land Nationalisation Act. In their minds, the greedy foreign capitalists owed Burma, not the other way round. They were also critical of opening talks to repay London for what the British called "post-war military assistance".

For their part, the moderates wanted to present a friendly face internationally, not pick fights. They believed a modern government should be reasonable and fair—and they were so certain of their path that any opposition struck them as treasonous. Tempers simmered and the fragile peace of Independence Day already seemed destined for disintegration.

The government also suffered from a lack of Karen MPs. Karen activists travelled twice to London to gain separate recognition for their land, but were ignored. Churchill spoke for their cause in the House of Commons but, as he no longer led the government, his fiery speech had no effect.

Old British cronies from the war were happy to meet and commiserate with the Karen over their shabby treatment. The Karen supported the Empire when it counted, the veterans said. They deserved better than to be discarded to Burma like an unwanted playing card. Invariably the meetings ended with braggardly promises of support—even smuggled weapons, if need be.

In the midst of these unsettling political conditions, Lord and Lady Mountbatten came calling. The former Allied Commander and Vice-Regent of India was near the end of his latest appointment, Governor-General of India. Soon he and his loyal wife, Edwina, would sail away from the old jewels of the Crown. But first, a farewell tour of their old haunts was in order.

They arrived on March 11. Sao hosted a garden party to welcome the couple. She made sure Aung San's widow was at the top of the guest list and that her children were invited, too, as playmates for her own children. With the young ones chasing one another between prettily-arranged tables, the party was a cheerful affair. Mountbatten didn't tarry long, though. After a close discussion with Thakin Nu, he disappeared into the Marble Hall to prepare a surprise for the following day.

The next morning the Mountbattens visited Jubilee Hall, where the assassination victims still lay in state. The hall had been decorated in homage to the dead. A freshly-painted, lifelike statue of Aung San stood outside the main doors. Canvas paintings of the ministers hung in the windows. Mountbatten's entourage appeared bemused, as if the decorations were too garish and naive for their tastes.

Inside, flags covered the glass coffins to shield the visitors from the corpses' death-stares. After paying homage, the party returned to the President's House, where Mountbatten, excited as a boy, oversaw the final preparations for his surprise.

At 10:00 a.m., Sao, her husband, and invited guests trooped into the Marble Hall. The place was decorated with strings of Burmese flags, all hanging mistakenly upside-down. A frazzled-looking Englishman grappled with some floodlights, trying to direct their beams around some inconveniently-placed pillars toward a huge curtain stretched from wall to wall. The room was too wide; the curtain sagged wretchedly in the middle, revealing Mounbatten's gift, a towering construction of gilt wood.

When all appeared ready, Mountbatten took the podium. He was a commanding figure, blue-blooded and hawk-featured in a cloud-white uniform. He began with a story about dancing in the Marble Hall in 1928, when he was a young junior officer in the company of the Prince of Wales. Then he spoke of the devastation of war and his meetings with Aung San. Finally, he arrived at his presentation.

"Behind me is the Mandalay Hlutdaw throne, which was last used by King Thibaw of Burma...which used to stand in the Great Hall of Audience in the Palace of Mandalay, now, alas, burnt to the ground," he said.

The audience, having already discerned this, heard little. Their attention was riveted on the precarious curtain, which looked ready to collapse.

Mountbatten pulled a silk cord and waved his hand with a flourish. For a long uncomfortable moment, nothing happened. Then the audience heard shuffling feet as bearers pulled the curtain aside while trying to remain unseen. Mountbatten's men had been unable to devise any sort of mechanical rigging that could haul the huge drape open.

Fully revealed, the twenty-four-foot-high throne of King Thibaw sat with its top nearly touching the vaulted ceiling, grotesquely colossal and carved with a lion, an elephant, and a dancing deva who stilled their battle with a song. During the time Mandalay Palace became Fort Dufferin, then a jail, then a Japanese stronghold, and, now, a mess of ruins, the throne was kept in a Calcutta museum as a souvenir of Britain's conquest. Mountbatten's staff took nearly a month to disassemble, transport and reassemble the throne in Rangoon, a task completed just three days earlier.

Later, at dinner, Sao had no trouble keeping the conversation humming, for Mountbatten was a talkative man with plenty of ideas. Most of his sentences began with, "You should...".

During the meal, Mountbatten accused Prime Minister Thakin Nu of inconsistency, pointing out that Burma's public anti-communist stance was at odds with its nationalisation policy—

a policy which was, in his view, tending toward heavy-handed appropriation. Then he complained that new restrictions on foreign ownership lumped British nationals in with all the others. The British should have most-favoured status, he said.

The robust little prime minister grinned impassively throughout the lecture, as was his manner. Sao smiled, too, the iron-tight smile of a gracious hostess, while inside she fumed.

So easy to say, you should do this, you should do that, she thought.

She knew the British mind-set: Burma had been given a parliament—the rock of civilisation—and only their own stupidity could tear it down. Mountbatten didn't understand the trouble they were in, the dangerous balances which had to be struck, and how quickly the new country could collapse.

Earl Mountbatten of Burma left the next morning, three days before the disintegration began.

On March 12, indignant Socialist Party followers destroyed the printing presses of three far-left newspapers, including the *Oway*, once edited by Aung San himself.

On March 28, the Communist Party of Burma (CPB), expelled from the ruling Freedom League, chose to go underground rather than act as an opposition party within parliament. They were joined by members of a temporary post-war civilian militia, the People's Voluntary Organisation (PVO), which had resisted an earlier government order to disband. A few radical-leaning battalions of the Burma Army followed as well, believing that Thakin Nu had overly softened the hard, clear vision of Aung San's egalitarian state. Thus, within twenty-four hours, the disgruntled leftists became an armed force biding their time in the suburbs and country towns around Rangoon.

On April 9, the remains of Aung San and his slain ministers—dubbed the Martyrs—were interred without incident in a mausoleum on a hill near Shwedagon Pagoda. The man behind their deaths, U Saw, had been convicted in December and would meet the gallows in May. The state funeral was carried off without incident, but the capital was on high alert.

Sao didn't stay for the funeral. Instead she went to Maymyo with her maid, nurses and bodyguard. The new baby's time was nearing.

She was happy to escape the searing plains and distressing political situation. In Maymyo there was a colonial manor set aside as a presidential retreat. It was a large red-brick building nestled in a rambling garden, rather far from the town limit. After the din and bustle of Rangoon, life among the shady pines seemed impossibly quiet.

On April 15—four days after Aung San's funeral—Harn was born. Sao told him, "You went to England and saw a princess get married, although you didn't know it."

Except for her doctor, maid, and nurses, she and the child were alone in the quiet of the manor. Things are so different now, she mused. There was no birthing pavilion in the garden, no crowd gathered to meet the child, no festival. Such things belonged to the distant past, before the war changed everything. This was the modern world.

Four days later, Burma became the fifty-eighth member of the United Nations. All day long the airwaves were filled with proud speeches, briefly reviving the peaceful, progressive vision of Burma.

The reality was more dismal. After the state funeral, the generals of the Burma Army made their way up the hill to Maymyo for a series of meetings at the old British Cantamont. When they descended on the Presidential Retreat for dinners and cocktail parties, tension prevailed. The army was really a collection of smaller armies left over from the war: units that fought with the British, units that fought with the Burma Independence Army, and units from the frontier states. As Inspector-General of Auxiliary Forces, U Tin Tut —newspaper editor, former Rangoon University chancellor and close friend to the PM—was tasked with welding the Burma Army into a modern federal force. A Karen, General Smith Dun, was chosen Chief of Staff, with the idea that such an appointment would placate the Karen separatists.

General Dun was the very image of the British officers who trained him, right down to the pipe planted in the corner of his mouth. So far he had fulfilled his role of appeasing the separatists, but it was now clear that the Karen were not Burma's most immediate problem. The communists and their well-armed supporters posed a more pressing threat.

Since the defections, trust was in short supply. Only the men of General Ne Win seemed solid. As an antidote to army disunity,

Ne Win drilled into his soldiers the old wartime slogan "One blood, one voice, one command", a credo that left no room for ethnic or political diversity. It helped that his 4th Burma Rifles were sent mainly against the Karen, and not against the ultra-leftists, who were fellow Burmese. Ne Win's men fought hard and cruelly. They fired mortars on Karen villages and burned several to the ground, leaving the people without shelter for the monsoon season.

When Sao returned to Rangoon before the rains, the soldiers were forcibly relocating the populations of the city's satellite towns which might harbour rebels. Sad lines of landless workers carried their cooking pots and bundles of belongings along the dusty road. Some hobbled on broken feet; some had faces red with blood. All looked afraid, for banditry was on the rise and they were defenceless. The price of rice was rising, too, and no one knew how they would fill their cooking pots in the days to come. The future was beyond reckoning, so the uprooted families simply walked in silence, heads down, as Sao's private car rumbled toward Rangoon under darkening skies.

Sao and the baby arrived in the capital not a moment too soon; thereafter the road north was too dangerous to travel. The train only went as far north as Thaton, leaving passengers to find their own way through firefights and bandits to Mandalay.

The government accomplished little during these dark days. Much of Burma's planned post-war reconstruction work— the badly-needed bridges, roads and mills—remained undone. Then the Leagues' Socialist Party leader absconded with four million Kyat (US$ 835,000), leaving the governing coalition in a state of public disgrace.

On May 25, Thakin Nu came to the President's House and spent a long time in Prince Shwe Thaike's office. Later that day, he announced his intention to resign the prime ministership so that he could concentrate on rejuvenating his scandal-ridden Freedom League as party president.

The young PM stepped down on July 15, along with his entire cabinet. But instead of dedicating himself to the Freedom League's presidency, as promised, he decided to quit politics altogether. He told the public he had made a religious vow and, although he didn't give the details, many recalled his year-old promise to enter the monastery after independence.

When he brought his official resignation letter to the President's office that day, Sao's husband began the earnest task of talking him out of the decision. Although a lame duck, Thakin Nu was popular with the people, who regarded him as the only honest man in Rangoon. He had no obvious successor. The Prince asked him to remain head of a caretaker government until parliament convened in August. Otherwise, there was no one in charge of the country. Having fought so hard for a government of their own, the people couldn't be abandoned just a half-year into independence.

On July 20, Thakin Nu entered his private prayer room and made a vow of absolute purity, adding sex to his list of taboos, alongside meat-eating and drinking alcohol. Murmuring the words, he wished hard that the insurgency would be confounded if he kept his vow. Eight days later, he returned to Cabinet, agreeing to stay on until elections were held in April, 1949.

The ethnic leaders were greatly relieved. They worried the insurgency would surely find a home in the shelter of their remote hills, if not put down swiftly.

Still, the army defections continued. Then in August the moment came that everyone feared: a company of Karen Union Military Police mutinied in the town of Maubin. Now there were two armed insurrections afoot: a communist-inspired political rebellion and a separatist ethnic revolt.

On August 7, the renegade Karen police broke open the District Treasury and took 3.5 million Kyat cash. Three days later they looted the homes of the local well-to-do. Their rebellion was kindled by a belief that British friends were waiting to come to their aid. Although the promised weapons never materialised, such loose talk provided enough spark to start a civil war.

The rebellion deepened. In mid-August, a platoon of Karen Union Military Police stationed in Insein, just ten miles north of Rangoon, deserted with four truckloads of arms and ammunition from the Insein Police Armoury. Then the First and Third Burma Rifles, veteran defenders of the wartime frontier, joined the mutiny from their stations in Thayetmyo and Mingaladon, where the international airport was located. Rangoon became a shrinking island.

As news of the latest defections spread, the Karen people rose up and overtook the streets of the southern cities of Thaton and Moulmein with help from the break-away military police.

On September 2, Thakin Nu stood in parliament and said, "Burma at present is faced with a rather serious political situation. I take Saya San's rebellion as child's play, compared with the present conflagration."

He must have wondered what had happened to his vow; although he lived a pure life in a small hut in his garden, eschewing his marriage bed and the luxuries of the prime minister's official abode, the rebellion gained in strength every day. When his friend U Tin Tut the army reformer was killed in a mysterious bomb blast in December, it seemed all was lost.

The insurgents' strategy was to occupy police stations and hunker down. By the end of 1948, 13,000 armed leftists and 7,000 Karen stood against 1,000 government troops and a few loyal military police and militiamen.

Then yet another storm broke on Burma's frontier. In December, Chinese refugees poured over the northern border, fleeing the struggle between Mao Zedong's communists and Chiang Kai-shek's nationalists. In a nationwide radio broadcast, Thakin Nu warned that there were communist infiltrators among the refugees.

Strangely, daily life in Rangoon carried on as usual. People went to movies and plays, deaf to the rattle of gunfire outside the city. On January 4, 1949, a mass rally was held outside City Hall to mark the first anniversary of Independence Day. As head of state, Sao's husband addressed the crowd. To his credit, he didn't serve up the previous year's menu of brave words and high purpose. Instead he issued a warning.

"Co-operation and understanding cannot come about so long as the element of violence or threat of violence exits, for violence has no counterpart in freedom, and liberty ends where violence begins," he said.

"The progressive retreat of democracy in the world today is mainly due to the worship by nations of the cult of physical force."

"The deterioration in this direction has been such that the much-vaunted democracies are nowadays hardly distinguishable from totalitarian states," he concluded, making a direct stab at his own country.

Maha Bandoola Square fell silent as people contemplated the sad emptiness of their dreams. A year ago they imagined only one possible future: a just, united, free country. They had forgotten the Dhamma: their sense of control over events was just an illusion, a careless mental mistake. Prince Shwe Thaike's voice echoed tinnily in the sudden quiet, calling on the ancient words of the Buddha to save them from their hubris:

> *Enmity is never ended by enmity.*
> *Enmity is ended only by the absence of enmity:*
> *This has been the truth from all Eternity.*

Mortars and Leeches

As the inferno of rebellion spread, Sao's thoughts turned to her two absent children. In Kalaw, Tiger and Tzang themselves knew nothing of their mother's concern and felt quite alone in the world. Once their father's presidential convoy passed through town en route to a meeting in Taunggyi. They stood on the roadside with their classmates, waving tiny flags as the silver Rolls Royce rumbled by and then disappeared around the bend.

When they contracted typhoid, it was one of the school's senior boys, Prince Sai Leung of Lawksawk, who nursed them. Too ill to continue at school, they returned to Yawnghwe palace. Tiger was eleven years old; Tzang was ten.

Following their recovery, the brothers were sent north to Hsenwi without explanation. Sao had decided to put them in the care of her brother. The boys were unaware of how dangerous the situation had become. Arriving at the bamboo Haw, they knelt before their uncle and touched their small heads to the rough floor three times in respect. Then they were delivered into the arms of Sister Mary (not her real name), a Burmese Christian nun.

"These are the President's children, and his Mahadevi asks you to keep them safe from all harm," Prince Hom Hpa told the Sister, a slender woman of twenty-eight. Sister Mary took the words to heart. Her convent had been established at the Prince's personal invitation; maintaining good relations with the ruling family was important.

The Queen of Peace Convent was a rough collection of bamboo and wood huts at the base of a small foothill past the edge of town. Tiger and Tzang moved into a simple dorm. Mornings they walked through cold mist part way up the hill to a stone school building. As student boarders, they were allowed to speak only English. The only times they heard their native tongue was when the day students—also expected to speak English once they entered the school grounds—accidentally lapsed into Tai.

After lessons, the brothers explored the dense bush around the convent. Sometimes they found Japanese helmets, even whole skeletons. There was a footpath that took them over a small creek to the hilltop. They vaguely remembered climbing to this spot two years earlier, and how their mother looked with sorrow on the ruins of her family's country mansion. The abandoned site was now an arena for children's war games. After school their shouts echoed off crumbled brick walls and fallen pillars until the cold mountain air reddened their cheeks and forced them back down the hill to supper and the heavy warmth of thick blankets on their narrow plank beds, where they dreamed of soldiers—tall, pale airmen who handed out chocolates; men who wore yellow uniforms and tall black boots; and soldiers of their own country dressed in jungle fatigues, with bayoneted rifles slung over their shoulders.

From the school house they could see Chinese refugees dressed in rags trudging down the Burma Road all day long in twos and threes. They passed through Hsenwi and continued south.

The nuns could shed no light on what was happening in Burma, much less in China. Prince Hom Hpa owned the only radio in Hsenwi and there was no newspaper to be had. But something was happening, the boys sensed. Every day, parents came to the school and took their children away, until there were only Tiger, Tzang and a few orphans left. Then one night the boys were awakened by a terrifying screech and bang, followed by another and another, and the nuns came running with lanterns, calling out to the orphans and the President's sons, telling them they must dress quickly and prepare to run.

Throughout the long, dangerous months of 1949, while Tiger and Tzang played games and studied lessons, the insurgency had crept across the country.

At first, there was an attempt at conciliation; Sao met the Karen leader when he arrived in Rangoon for talks. "If I came to Shan State, I would drive into the ditch because I don't know the road. It's the same if you come to Karen land," he told her.

They got on well. Saw Ba U Gyi shared the Yawnghwe family's background: erudite, wealthy and British-influenced. His single biggest task was to convince the Karen separatists to lay down their arms for a promise of statehood, like Shan State's arrangement with Rangoon. All the while, General Ne Win's 4th Burma Rifles attacked and burned their villages. Although World War II had ended, the General still regarded the Karen as pro-British traitors. Hatred burned both ways and reconciliation seemed impossible. Eventually, Saw Ba U Gyi gave up and returned to Karen land.

In January, the Karen received an offer of support from the outlawed communists. At first glance, it was an unlikely alliance. Observers assumed the Karen were anti-communist because of their British ties. But when the anticipated help from their British friends never arrived, the Karen rebels took a long, hard look at their situation. It was too late to back down from the rebellion, they realised. Desperate times called for desperate measures.

On March 13, the Karen and the communists combined their forces and occupied Mandalay, taking control of the trunk road to Rangoon at the same time.

The following day Sao listened to Prime Minister Thakin Nu on the radio.

"Let bygones be bygones," he pleaded. "Nothing in the world can remain unrectified, and to err is only human."

His promise of amnesty only created more fractures: the Buddhist Karen Organisation supported the prime minister's peace appeal, causing a lasting split with the Christian Karen majority. And although the message of peace was largely ignored, the weakness and desperation in U Nu's voice was heard loud and clear. Other ethnic leaders who felt threatened by the Union smelled the blood of a dying government.

When Naw Seng, a Kachin captain in the Burma Army, mutinied, a band of northern Kachin joined the rebellion. At first they hoped Sao's brother, Prince Hom Hpa, would support their cause, renewing the old Kachin-Tai alliance that brought Sao's father to the throne in 1879. Prince Hom Hpa visited the Kachin jungle camp; he returned to Hsenwi two days later claiming he'd been kidnapped and escaped. Sao never learned what transpired during those two days. On his return, her brother raised a levy of loyal Kachin against Captain Naw Seng's band and went to war. The Burma Army came to his aid. The Karen forces came to the aid of the rebels.

It was these events which drew Hsenwi town into the arena of a fierce mortar duel, sending the boys and nuns of Queen of Peace Convent running, lanterns darkened, toward the stone schoolhouse on the hill.

Safe inside, the nuns calmly counted and sorted the breathless, excited children. Sister Mary turned around just in time to see Tiger heading back toward the open door. He'd lost a plastic sandal on the road and wanted to retrieve it. Quickly the young nun bounded over and pulled him back. For the rest of the night she held the two boys in her arms, terrified they would break free and run into the war zone. What would she say to the Mahadevi if any harm came to them?

No one slept that night. The scream of mortars was deafening. Tiger and Tzang were amazed by the sheer loudness of real battle.

In the morning, the shelling gave way to eerie silence. Sister Mary ventured outside to see what was happening.

A voice floated down to her from up the hill. It was the priest from Lashio—he had poorly timed one of his occasional visits to Hsenwi. He hollered down the situation from his vantage point: the Kachin-Karen rebel alliance was in the hills above them; the Burma Army was dug in near the bridge at the entrance to town, next to the market. A third force comprised of Prince Hom Hpa's loyalist Kachin men was also in the area. And down the road was a group of nuns cut off from the convent, without food. Could she help them?

Sister Mary ducked back inside the school and singled out two orphan boys to follow her down the hill. A rescue! Tzang leapt to his feet, begging to be included.

"No," the Sister said firmly, but the boy was already halfway to the door.

In the end, two nuns held him down while Sister Mary made her exit. She marvelled at how fearless and naive the Yawnghwe boys were. Two sons of the President of Burma—they had no idea what valuable prizes they would be to the rebels.

With the more safely anonymous orphans in tow, the young nun hurried down to the convent and collected some chickens and rice. Then she and the orphan boys followed a narrow path through a fallow field, past mounds of gathered leaves and grass. She carried the rice; the boys followed behind with the chickens.

When they neared a small farm house, she saw the nuns running toward her, waving their arms, but their faces were filled with terror, not relief. At the same moment she heard a small noise behind her. Wheeling around, she saw the boys were gone.

They've stolen the chickens, she thought with dismay.

Then the grass moved and her heart nearly stopped. The mounds of leaves rose into the air and suddenly she was surrounded by soldiers. She had walked right through a camouflaged unit of the Burma Army. To her horror, she saw the two orphan boys were on their knees, their arms jerked behind their backs by tight cords. A soldier stood over them, ready to deliver the executioner's bullet to the backs of their necks.

"Those are my students," Sister Mary gasped.

The boys kneeled motionless, unable to speak, not even daring to look at the nun.

"Insurgents. Bandits!" barked the commanding officer. "We caught them stealing chickens from the people."

"No, no," said Sister Mary, and she began to explain, knowing by the dull, angry look in the soldier's eyes that he would never believe her. But in the end, he did believe her. To her surprise, he released both the students and the chickens. They were allowed safe passage to the farmhouse and back.

Sister Mary delivered the food, saw that the nuns there were comfortable enough, then returned to the school house shaking from head to toe with the two terrified boys less than half a step behind her, just as the next round of mortars howled into the air.

The fighting continued all day. Ten-year-old Tzang assessed their situation like a soldier and decided they were in a poor position, too high and in the open. The stone walls were good protection against bullets, but not against stray mortar shells. The nuns prayed. Before evening fell there was a second lull, and they all ran to an old Japanese bomb shelter dug into the hillside. Better, Tzang thought. Sister Mary, on the other hand, felt she would rather take her chances in the school house. More terrifying than mortars, the damp shelter was full of leeches. All night long she fended off the creatures with a bamboo stick.

Next morning, the noise began to move further and further away until there was silence.

They emerged from the shelter and looked down the hill toward town. The Namtu river lay placid and blue-green in the sunshine. Jeeps ground their way up and down the road past the market, and soldiers of the Burma Army walked about openly on the town's single street. They heard the sound of machetes cracking bamboo: townspeople were already rebuilding. The government forces had retaken Hsenwi.

At the edge of destruction, a fragile peace struggled to take hold in Burma.

The Painted Train

During the long days when the country slowly crumbled around them, Sao and her husband received dignitaries and continued the rigorous schedule of dinners and entertainments, woodenly maintaining the facade of peace and democracy. Before the fighting spread to Shan State, she sent her mother home to Hsenwi under the escort of her nephew, Saw Ohn. On his return journey, Saw Ohn made it as only as far as Lashio when the Kachin uprising broke out. He stayed to help lead the 1st Burma Rifles against the rebels. One night his men came upon some suspicious fellows hiding out in a bamboo forest. They opened fire, killing several as they fled. Examining the bodies, they discovered the dead were Burmese, not Kachin. Whether the dead men were from the communist underground or just dacoits—bandits—Saw Ohn never knew.

Back in Rangoon, an April New Year's procession snaked down Sule Pagoda Road, led by a float in the shape of a royal barge. People laughed and danced and splashed water at one another, oblivious to the turmoil beyond the city limits.

April, in fact, was the country's worst month. Dust rose in great yellow clouds from the Burma plain. To the north, the battle to regain Mandalay from the insurgents raged on under a heartless sun. In Rangoon, in the close-packed heat of parliament, the Socialist Party members resigned en masse, leaving a handful of bewildered independents among rows of empty seats.

If nothing else, the defections from democracy helped simplify matters. Thakin Nu took charge of a reduced cabinet. The British-trained Smith Dun was out as army head; the brutally-minded Ne Win was in, as Deputy Prime Minister and Minister for Home and Defence. From this point, the government forces slowly began gaining the upper hand. The warship *Mayu*, donated by Britain for use against foreign invaders, was pressed into action against Karen positions along the river.

By month's end, Sao and her husband felt confident enough to take their family on holiday. The school calendar had changed since Sao's day. The kids had the hot, sunny months of April and May off, returning to class with the June monsoon. It was a more sensible arrangement than following the European school year.

They flew into Lashio, roaring low over fallow paddy fields. Sao was in a familiar state of mind: pregnant again and glad to be free of Rangoon again. In Lashio, they collected Tiger and Tzang at her brother's city house. The reunion was rather stiff. It was hard for the boys to imagine that the First Lady had ever held them in their arms, or that the President once gave horsy-back rides.

Reunited, the family travelled by car within an armed convoy to the Presidential Retreat at Maymyo. They passed by broken dikes and water-filled craters still left from World War II. Many homes stood empty, their rice urns broken open. At Maymyo, though, fragrant blossoms and brick mansions replaced the war-torn rural scene. The clock tower still stood near the market, undamaged by the fighting. The only major difference from Sao's childhood was that there were now as many Willys jeeps as there were ghary-carts on the streets. Their engines growled above the clatter of hooves.

The family enjoyed a few relaxing weeks at the retreat. The weather was pleasantly warm in the afternoons, followed by cool evenings. The children ran around the rambling garden or stayed inside and read comic books. Sao signed up the older ones for water-colour lessons at St. Joseph's Convent. Sometimes the children went on painting excursions to the Botanical Gardens. A few bombs had fallen there during the war, but the place had survived. The gardens' trees, just saplings when Sao was a schoolgirl, were now quite tall.

The kids also took gharies into town to enjoy the cool darkness of the movie house. They saw an old Douglas Fairbanks Sr. version of *Robin Hood* as well as Fred Astare and Judy Garland in *The Easter Parade*, and several Esther Williams films.

Sao herself had little time for relaxation. Some days it seemed like half of Rangoon had followed them to Maymyo. Society ladies came and went, army men popped in between rounds of golf.

She had a chance to become better acquainted with General Ne Win, in whom she discovered confusing contradictions between his personality and his politics. The handsome Lieutenant-General immersed himself in the playboy life, attending parties with a succession of Miss Burma title-holders on his arm. At the same time, he still cleaved to Aung San's original communist-inspired doctrine of an austere, egalitarian state. Sao suspected he dallied in Maymyo to avoid chasing down communist insurgents, especially the ones who had defected from his own army. Rumour had it that Ne Win's men abandoned their weapons too willingly to certain rebels. There was a story that one army chap, on capturing some insurgents, recognised their rifles. "Of course, sir," the rebel leader reminded him. "You gave them to us just last week."

One afternoon Sao came upon Ne Win sitting in the parlour alone. The rest of the men had gone off somewhere, perhaps the golf course. She had him cornered.

"Why haven't you caught up to those communists south of Mong Mit?" she demanded.

"Mahadevi, we don't know where to find them," the General answered.

"Nonsense," snapped Sao. "Everyone knows they stay on one side of the mountain and when your troops go round, they come to the other side."

The General offered something between a laugh and a glower. He didn't know how to take the Mahadevi. Quickly, he set down his teacup and left.

Too soon, the family holiday wound down. A doctor arrived to check on the children before the trip to Rangoon. Prince Shwe Thaike was anxious to find out how the elder boys had fared during their Hsenwi exile.

The boys deserved better than a back-country bamboo convent, the Prince thought. He was eager to send them on to Doon School, in India's Himalayan foothills. The Indian Prime Minister, Jawalharal Nehru, had personally recommended the school to him. Many children of Asian leaders attended Doon in preparation for university in Europe or England. A foreign education was a must, the Prince believed. Sanda and Hseng, the children of his deceased wives, were already enrolled at Cambridge. Sao's husband didn't discriminate among his children, even among the girls, when it came to learning.

The Doon School year began in May. The doctor had bad news, though. Tiger was declared fit to travel, but his younger brother was not. Tzang still had a heart murmur. The doctor forbade flying; a change in air pressure could be dangerous, he warned.

The family set out for Lashio, wondering what to do. Road and rail travel were not fully restored to Rangoon; there were still pockets of rebellion flaring up here and there.

Sao discussed with her husband the idea of bringing Tzang on the plane anyway, with a doctor and oxygen tank at the ready.

Too risky, they decided.

In the end, they left him at Prince Hom Hpa's Lashio home, where he would live while attending the local convent school as a day student. It was at least a little safer than the rough little country school in Hsenwi. Despite the troubles, Lashio had grown into a sizeable town. Its houses and shop-buildings spilled down the hillside, following the dusty road to China like a river.

Until this moment, Tiger and Tzang led shared lives. They swam together in Inle Lake, chased each other over green fields, shared comic books and sweets, sat side-by-side in classrooms, endured typhoid, loneliness and war. Now the plane rose into the sky, carrying one away to a life abroad while the other remained among the Shan hills. Never again would the two brothers see the world through the same eyes.

Tiger went on to India right away, while his brothers and sisters—minus Tzang—settled back into life at the President's House.

Sao resumed work in her office, although she often felt sapped of energy. She flew to India with her personal physician, a British woman, because the specialists there were considered superior. They examined her and said all was fine. While in India, she was the guest of Prime Minister Nehru and his daughter, Indira Gandhi. The Indian PM was anxious to ensure good relations between their two countries. The only contentious issue he faced was treatment of Burma's former Indian landlords, the chettyars. Those who fled during the war had their land taken over by their indebted Burmese tenants, who were subsequently granted legal title by the wartime Adipadi, Dr. Ba Maw. Now the chettyars wanted compensation. Some 2.5 million acres of paddy field were at stake. Sao discerned that Nehru would be flexible on the issue. Jailed nine times by the British, he viewed Burma's new leaders as fellow travellers on the road to freedom. She surmised he wouldn't let the chettyars stand between them, whether their claims were valid or not.

She flew back to Rangoon, still feeling tired, and got back to business. Tai politicians stopped by her office to commiserate about what was happening to the country. One day, she looked out her window and saw Prime Minister Thakin Nu's car drive up to the presidential staff's office building. Her nephew Saw Ohn, who had returned to his duties as the President's ADC, waited to escort the PM inside. Instead of entering the building, though, Thakin Nu took her nephew by the arm and led him into the garden. She watched the tall, angular Saw Ohn bend his head toward the diminutive Prime Minister; for a long time they walked this way, deep in conversation. Then she saw the two men turn back toward the office, no longer arm in arm.

Sao wasn't one for polite discretion. When Saw Ohn stopped by her office, she asked immediately what had passed between him and the PM.

"He asked why I only killed Burmese in the uprising," her nephew answered. "I told him, I don't know who I killed or who I didn't kill. Some got killed and some escaped. You can't tell in battle if they're Burmese."

The exchange troubled her greatly. Despite her husband's appointment to the presidency, the Tai weren't trusted. She had seen this already in the way her nephew was continually passed over for training abroad, despite his long military service. General

Ne Win didn't want non-Burmans rising too high in the military ranks, she guessed. And now Thakin Nu accused Saw Ohn of singling out Burmese during the uprising. The words between the two men sat in her heart like a cold stone, warning her of dangers to come.

The latest news from Shan State was just as disturbing. She learned that rebels had over-run Taunggyi. They were a federation of malcontents: Karen supporters, Peoples' Voluntary Organisation members, pro-communists and disgruntled Pa-O villagers. Train travel was halted, and the only aeroplanes that made the journey were fighters that strafed the hillside, sending rebels and citizens alike running for cover.

Despite the government's recent military gains, peace remained elusive. In the frontier areas the Burma Army was doing its job against ethnic separatists, but in such a rough and cruel manner that many began to wonder who the enemies were—rebels or government troops. Now that the government was winning, it was their soldiers who had the most firepower and inflicted the worst damage. The excesses of the Burma Army men were legendary. They burned, looted, tortured and raped their way from village to village, until the country people learned to walk always in fear, heads down, hearts trembling.

If nothing else could be gained from the past year, the country at least learned a lesson about the price of internal strife. On September 12, in Rangoon's small, plain parliament building, the Finance Minister rose to deliver the national budget. His speech was a litany of the costs of civil war.

Thousands of lives were lost. Villages were deserted. The few roads and rails repaired after the war were destroyed again. Steamers had been sunk, government buildings burnt down. Rice stores intended for export had been seized by rebels and given away. Only 186,000 tons of timber were sold that year, compared to 930,000 tons before the war. Burma's two oil fields at Yenangyaung and Chauk were producing less than a 1,000 barrels a day, compared to the pre-war rate of 15,000 barrels a day. Only five million Kyat in land revenues were collected, far below the initial estimate of 35.2 million. Policing cost ten million more than expected.

The financial plan for 1949-50 contained the saddest legacy of the fighting: defence and police took up 39 per cent of the government's meagre revenues, seven times the amount set aside for education and health, and fourteen times the amount for agriculture, forestry and industry. Across the country, government forces were routing the rebels, but, even in winning, they had created the conditions for continued instability and rebellion. Burma could not even come up with the ten million-Kyat entry fee to join the International Monetary Fund. As Union President, Sao's husband immediately volunteered a fifty percent pay cut, but it was only a drop in the bucket against a 17.1 million-Kyat deficit, equalling more than US$ 3.5 million, at the time a very considerable sum.

In these worrisome days, politicians and the public alike were so focused on internal struggles that few took notice of the great communist-led revolution unfolding on their northern doorstep.

On October 1, 1949, Chairman Mao Zedong stood on the Gate of Heavenly Peace in Beijing and declared the establishment of the People's Republic of China. Like most people, Sao followed the news on radio and in the papers, but its importance failed to impact on her. Even when Communist Party leader Liu Shaoqi condemned Burma's Prime Minister as a imperialist puppet and sent greetings to the communist rebels in Burma, and when the Kachin rebel, Captain Naw Seng, re-surfaced in China as a "special guest" of the new Chinese rulers, it all seemed quite remote.

On November 11, Indonesian Premier Mohamed Hatta and Madame Hatta arrived in Rangoon. Thakin Nu and his wife hosted a state lunch in an elegant dining room at the Strand. As ever, Sao punctuated the meal with witty remarks and laughter. Speeches were made, glasses raised. Later they retired to the President's House, where the men enjoyed whisky and cigars. All the while, outside the high garden walls, past burned-out, empty suburbs and beyond to the troubled frontier, pilots buzzed Taunggyi hill and rained down fire on the people.

Three days later, Sao and her husband stood on a dais in Maha Bandoola Square and watched Ne Win's soldiers march past, rifles shining in the November sun. She remembered Novembers past, nights of fire balloons and lotus flowers and white umbrellas opening in the Great Hall of Audience. Such ancient traditions were now overshadowed by the ceremonies of the modern age. Today was National Day. There was also Independence Day, Union Day, Peasant's Day, May Day—so many days that she lost track of how often she and her husband stood in Maha Bandoola Square to unfurl the flag and take the salute.

When she was a child, the air was filled with the chanting of monks on ceremonial days. Now people listened to boastful speeches on the radio. On this day, General Ne Win took to the airwaves to defend his army's sullied reputation.

"I wish you to constantly bear in mind that the arms and ammunition supplied to us are not meant to be used against the masses but against the enemies of the masses," he said.

"Not everyone in uniform and armed cap-a-pie is a member of the Burma Army, for it is only those who scrupulously act up according to the steel discipline of the Burma Army who can be regarded as the real members of the Burma Army."

The troops were followed by a parade down Sule Pagoda Road in a pale imitation of the processions between temples during the Festival of Lights. A painted wooden mock-up of a steam train, mounted on a truck, led the way. On its side were written the words The Train for the Station of Peace.

Sao didn't walk with the crowd, being nearly nine months pregnant.

A few weeks later, on December 3, she gave birth in her bedroom in the President's House. She was uncharacteristically tired after the labour. Her limbs felt heavy and slow, as if the weight of middle age had descended on her during the pregnancy. She was thirty-four years old. The baby, a girl, was her seventh child, counting the little boy who died of fever. They named her Princess Ying Ratana Hseng Leun, Youngest Lady Light of the Jewels. For short, Sao called her Leun, meaning The Last Born.

A Prayer for Deliverance, Weapons from the Sky

Every morning at 4:30 Prime Minister Thakin Nu awoke in his garden hut, his mind reeling around Burma's unfortunate Kamma. The Dhamma taught him that all the grasping, clawing folly of politics meant nothing. As long as he stayed in the fray, he would never achieve Nibbana. Almost daily he thought of retiring to the monastery. Still, the strings of duty and ambition would not loosen their ties on his heart. Folding his legs into the lotus position before a simple statue of the Lord Buddha, he tried hard to calm his thoughts until gradually his eyes assumed the half-lidded expression of the Buddha and he and the statue became reflections of one another in the half-light. In this manner, for two hours each day Thakin Nu was able to empty his mind and feel something of the Buddha's peace. It was a difficult act, requiring great concentration, but it was possible.

From this, Thakin Nu extrapolated that the whole country could benefit from meditation. If only the masses could calm their souls, there would be peace.

Thakin Nu started at home by lecturing his household staff on the Middle Way to enlightenment. Next, he attempted to convert India's Prime Minister Nehru, who visited Rangoon to discuss compensation for the chettyars. Although Nehru showed no signs of abandoning politics for a life of meditation, the two PMs became good friends and, whether it was discussion of the Dhamma or simple friendship which influenced him, Nehru discouraged the Indian landholders from pressing their claims. In a meeting, he reminded them that they'd sent most of their profits home to India over the years, investing little in Burma.

Thakin Nu decided it was time to expand his evangelical message to the whole population. On December 11, 1949, following his usual morning meditations, he laid the Peace Foundation Stone at Rangoon's Cantonment Gardens and announced the construction of a six million US-dollar World Peace Pagoda and the beginning of a Peace Within One Year campaign.

Although the campaign had a political aim—to end the insurgency—its method was individual transformation. An entire nation must be placed on the path of harmony, Thakin Nu believed.

He declared that all civil servants would be allowed to leave work thirty minutes early to meditate, and all political prisoners who could pass the Buddhist exams would be set free.

He next created a Religious Affairs Ministry to help promote pious acts such as the restoration of war-damaged pagodas. Mindful that Burma's constitution didn't favour a state religion, the ministry also provided funds to translate the Koran into Burmese and to help Catholic priests visit the Vatican. Buddhism remained paramount on the agenda, however.

In early 1950, Thakin Nu borrowed from Sri Lanka a flawless emerald Buddha statue and, even more rare, a tooth of the Buddha. Sri Lankan monks accompanied the holy objects to Burma, where they were worshipped by thousands in Rangoon and Mandalay.

In mid-March, the tooth and statue were flown to Meiktila, then taken by special train to the rural town of Yamethin, just south of Thazi. As the train rumbled by, villagers knelt in the dust.

From the brown western hills of the Pegu Yoma, the high passes of Shan State and the surrounding plains, people of all kinds were drawn to the tooth and the emerald statue. Among them were gaunt-faced insurgents in tattered uniforms. In the past, country folk might have cheered the rebels and pressed a little pocket money into their hands as they walked by, but no more. Both sides had unleashed equal cruelties on the villagers in the year of fighting. The rebels who remained in the field were a spent force, victims of infighting, battle losses and declining popular support. Now they dropped their weapons and prayed before the tooth and the statue, kneeling side by side with soldiers of the Burma Army.

During the two days of veneration not one shot was fired. Thakin Nu was a hero. For the first time in months, peace seemed possible.

In June, the Socialist Party members who resigned en masse from the government returned to the fold. They were eventually awarded three cabinet positions. Later that year, Thakin Nu wrote a play about the insurrection. He called it *The People Win Through*. Following a successful stage debut, the play was made into a movie of the same title.

Thakin Nu, the writer, had made a happy ending for Burma, something Thakin Nu, the politician, could not do. Bright images shimmered on the country's movie screens, but far away, in the darkness of the jungle, beyond the well-lit towns and busy streets, foreign armies were on the move and the troubles of a wider world encircled Burma.

In February, 1950, some four months after its victory in China, the Peoples' Liberation Army (PLA) marched into Yunnan province to sweep up the last remnants of their nationalist enemies. Generalissimo Chiang Kai-shek and the main body of his Kuomingtang soldiers—or KMT, as they were popularly called—had already fled to Taiwan, stranding about 1,500 men and 500 dependants on Burma's northern border. Three generals led them, the most prominent being General Li Mi of the 8th Army.

When the PLA arrived in southern Yunnan to mop up the forces, though, General Li's men had already disappeared beyond the wall of blue hills marking the border with Shan State.

They were not the first KMT to venture into Shan territory. One year earlier, 5,000 KMT troops passed through Kengtung state into Laos, seeking refuge with the Free Laos Movement. The French colonialists promptly disarmed and deported them to Taiwan. Another 200 KMT never made it out of Shan State; they were detained by Kengtung's Great Saopha.

Knowing his army was unwelcome in Shan State, General Li decided the best defence was a strong offence. The KMT wandered at will through the princely states; they took what they needed and burned uncooperative villages to the ground.

At Tachilek, a sleepy riverside town on the Thai border, the General established his first base outside China. Tachilek had trade potential, but it was too southerly to assist their master plan: an attack on China itself. In preparation for the great invasion he set up a second camp as a training centre, near Mong Hsat in southern Kengtung. Like Tachilek, Mong Hsat was closer to Thailand than to China, but it would serve them well enough for now.

General Li dreamed of leading his men into Beijing; he imagined their wonderstruck faces as they passed through the Gate of Heavenly Peace and saw the vermilion walls of the Forbidden City for the first time. But when his men gathered on the parade ground in the cold light of morning, the General had to face reality. The soldiers had few weapons other than the worn-out rifles on their shoulders, and their war record was poor: forced out of Burma by the Japanese in World War II, then forced back into Burma by Mao's PLA. However, they were rapacious and rabidly anti-communist, and they wore their faded cotton-padded uniforms with great pride.

The General's quixotic little army might have faded into history, were it not for one single event. On June 25, 1950, at 4:00 a.m., communist North Korea invaded capitalist South Korea, touching off the Cold War in Asia. Suddenly the lost KMT army began to look interesting to the free world, especially to the Americans and their Taiwanese friends.

Dean Rusk was the U.S. Assistant Secretary of State for Far Eastern Affairs. A wartime veteran of both Burma and China, he hoped to make the U.S. more proactive in the region. With the outbreak of war in Korea, Rusk soon found the way clear for his activist approach, an approach that led the U.S. to Southeast Asia, Red China's southern doorstep.

However small and isolated, the KMT soldiers hiding out in Shan State offered a kernel of an anti-communist force. One day an unmarked C-47 transport plane swooped low over Mong Hsat and dropped several crates bearing the mark of the Sea Supply Company of Bangkok. Inside the crates were weapons, rice, maps and uniforms, supplied by Taiwan with the assistance of the American Central Intelligence Agency (CIA). Thereafter, C-47 and C-46 planes buzzed over Mong Hsat twice weekly. General Li hopped back and forth to Taiwan for strategy sessions. Chinese volunteers from Malaya, Thailand and Burma began arriving via the jungle trails. Soon the general had 4,000 fighting men. The supply flights were increased to five times a week.

In early 1951, just one year after their retreat into the Shan States, General Li and his men took their first steps back toward China.

A place called Mong Yang in northern Kengtung was chosen as the site of the invasion base camp. From there the KMT ranged north on patrols into the wild opium hills of South Hsenwi. On one such journey, they stopped in Loimaw village and confiscated the headman's pack horses, for he was said to be a great horse breeder and trainer. Tears in his eyes, the headman's teenaged grandson showed them which saddle went on which horse.

They encouraged the boy to grow strong and join their fight, for he had a Chinese name—Chang Shi-fu—and he spoke Mandarin well. The boy made no reply, knowing already that when armies passed through a village, silence was survival.

The countryside grew progressively more foreboding as General Li's men crossed the Salween to Kokang district, bordering China, and marched down the crooked, stony streets of Tashwehtang. But it was here that the KMT would finally receive a welcome. They had entered the territory of Olive Yang.

Although Eddie Yang was the Myosa of Kokang, his sister Olive commanded the most respect. Still Education Minister, she had lately expanded her duties to include command of her late father's militia. No one had appointed her military leader. She came to it naturally. Eddie concurred, as did Jimmy, her politician brother in Rangoon.

Jimmy himself had no desire to spend more time than necessary in Kokang; he would die of boredom without evenings at Rangoon's Mayo Marine Club, lunches at the Continental, afternoons at the Race Course. If anyone was to run things back home, it might as well be the tough-talking sister with the pistols on her hips. She belonged in Kokang, wouldn't know what to do with herself in the city.

Jimmy and Edward at least found her a husband, a teenager from Hsenwi. Olive, however, had no desire for men and barely acknowledged the boy's presence. One day her husband was found shot dead. No arrests were made, and no one suggested she should marry again.

Inside the family's large stone house, there was a great deal of business to conduct. Olive divvied up the opium tax for state expenditures and informed the militia which villages were delinquent in their payments. Poor relatives from the countryside sent her their children as servants. Her favourite was seventeen-year-old Chang Shi-fu, the Loimaw headman's grandson; he was always quick to fetch her cigarettes and run important messages. When Chang returned to his village, another favourite, Wey Mong, carried her cigarettes. She liked to think the boys learned something from her: to be hard-headed and fearless, and to rule over men with confidence.

She told them: "An army is like a horse. If you fear it, it will throw you off. But if you have no fear, you can ride."

Her father, Old Yang, had raised his children in the knowledge that Kokang district rightfully belonged to China and that the Yangs would always be Chinese, even after a thousand generations. Olive was grateful for her Chinese schooling, which she felt kept her tough and true to her ethnic roots. She fondly remembered the time spent stranded in China by the war. Her girlhood heroes were the soldiers who kept the airstrip open for the Flying Tigers of Kunming. As Education Minister, she made sure Generalissimo Chiang Kai-shek's sun-emblazoned flag rose every morning outside Kokang's school houses while the children sang the defunct Chinese Republic's anthem.

When General Li Mi's men arrived, Olive met them with mixed feelings. On the one hand, she knew Tashwehtang town would burn if she resisted any of their requests. On the other hand, she was glad to see the familiar uniforms. It was like greeting old friends. She was lonely for people with shared memories of wartime Kunming. In the end, General Li asked only for unhindered passage through her territory. In parting, Olive gave them her serving-boy, Wey Mong. The ten-year-old departed eagerly on the adventure, having heard Auntie Olive's stories about China's great fighting men. Glad to have a pair of young legs to run messages, the soldiers gave him a proper Chinese name: Lo Hsin Han.

A few weeks later, Olive herself rode into Li Mi's Mong Yang camp, wearing a grey uniform and a Belgian pistol strapped on each hip. Three hundred members of the Kokang militia followed behind her. She had renamed them the Kokang Revolutionary Force.

The force was but a small addition to the General's considerable troops. Olive's true contribution amounted to more than men. First, American intelligence officers could now legitimately report that General Li Mi's army had local popular support. As a result, even more weapons poured down from the sky.

The second thing Olive brought was her knowledge of how to make money—plenty of money—from opium. Life in Shan State would never be the same.

Great Expectations

In the lull of Thakin Nu's peace campaign, Prince Sai, the heir, married one of Sao's nieces, a vivacious young woman who went by her English name, "Pat". Sao attended the wedding in Hsenwi. Afterwards, the couple headed south for Yawnghwe, where Prince Sai was to take over administration of Yawnghwe state while his father continued on as Burma's President. They moved into a large apartment overlooking the north courtyard of Yawnghwe Haw.

Although railway service to Mandalay was still disrupted, travellers were beginning to move along the country roads again. One afternoon, Prince Sai and Pat's car came up the sweeping drive of the President's House in Rangoon. They had Tzang with them—the roads were finally safe enough to fetch the boy from Lashio.

For once, almost all of Sao's children were under one roof: Tzang, now twelve; nine-year-old daughter Ying Sita; step-daughter Haymar; the fun-loving little Myee, who was his father's pet; and the two toddlers, Harn and Leun—six children altogether.

From India, her eldest son, Tiger, sent enthusiastic letters about Doon School. The first letter was addressed to Prince Shwe

Thaike; a secretary replied, advising him to correspond with his mother instead, as the President was very busy. After that, his letters were to Sao.

The ivy-covered Doon School offered Tiger a life of adventure and camaraderie unknown in the President's House. He wrote about becoming Swim Captain and a School Prefect. He described how he and some classmates hiked fifty miles to the foot of a Himalayan peak, climbed it, then hiked the fifty miles back, all in one long weekend. Sao read the letters eagerly, but not without a little anxiety. Separation from children was a natural fact of upper-class life, but one still worried. She was grateful to have Tzang at home, his weak heart sheltered from such vigorous regimens.

Tiger's school breaks were in December and June. Back home, a monk instructed him and Tzang to chant Buddhist texts in Pali, so that they could pass their catechism exams when they entered the monastery, as all Buddhist boys must do. They didn't really understand the religious language, but they practised hard. The ordination was conducted in the Marble Hall. With great ceremony, the boys' heads were shorn. They donned novices' robes and correctly recited their texts, successfully fulfilling their monkhood within a few hours.

At the end of his school holidays, Tiger returned to India while Tzang joined his younger siblings at school in Rangoon. Every morning at 7:30 a.m. they left for class with the chauffeur and bodyguards. In the afternoon, the car waited by the school gate to fetch them home. The only time they spent in play with other children was on Sundays, when the presidential staff's children came for weekly examinations by the household doctor.

The children were happy enough on their own, though. The rambling mansion was a magical, spooky place. After school, while their parents worked in their offices, the kids hunted ghosts in the empty rooms or swam in the concrete pool in the garden. If they wanted to talk to an elder, they picked up a phone and chatted with the Karen ladies who worked the switchboard. They also spent long hours in the comptroller's office, playing with the coloured pens and papers he kept in his desk. The comptroller's wife, Daw Daw Bu, entertained them for hours. Gifted with total recall, she recited Great Expectations, Oliver Twist, Jane Eyre and Uncle Tom's Cabin. She could also repeat line-for-line the Hollywood movies that she saw downtown at the President Theatre. The children listened, enthralled. They missed the movie house in Maymyo and their freedom to come and go in a hired horse-cart. Their favourite retold story was the film adaptation of Little Women.

Now and then the children attended state occasions. With everyone else, they stood to attention when their father entered the room. He was a rare and lofty presence in their lives. The elder children never spoke to him unless he asked them a question directly, which was seldom. Only Myee, young and innocent, maintained a childish rapport with the great man. Most evenings, though, the children ate and slept with their nannies in the upstairs rooms while the adults carried on their adult activities below.

Usually, drinks were served in the President's parlour before dinner. One evening Sao noticed how Prime Minister Thakin Nu glowered disapprovingly at the customary glass of whisky in her husband's hand. Thakin Nu's lips hadn't touched alcohol since the day took his vow of sobriety at Shwedagon Pagoda some twenty years earlier. A master of self-denial, he no doubt wondered why the President couldn't follow even the Five Precepts, Buddhism's most basic instructions. The Fifth Precept forbade intoxicants. Prince Shwe Thaike was no drunkard, but he drank, after the manner of the British officers who trained him: a relaxing drink on the veranda at sunset, a cocktail before dinner.

Downstairs in the Marble Hall, there was always someone waiting for them: ambassadors, ministers and foreign dignitaries. On August 28, 1950, they received the first Communist Chinese ambassador. Thakin Nu's round face was bathed in smiles that evening. Burma hoped for good relations with Beijing, despite the enemy KMT troops on Burmese soil. The Freedom League's Socialist Party members viewed the Chinese experiment with great interest. The PM wanted Burma to be a model world citizen, accepting all nations as brothers.

In May 1951 the Soviet ambassador also presented his credentials. Rangoon's embassy district grew steadily. All countries were welcome.

Amid the endless stream of guests, Sao had few friends. There were only a handful of Tai people in Rangoon, some so assimilated that they spoke only Burmese. The one woman she might call friend was Aung San's widow, Daw Khin Kyi. Daw Khin Kyi shared her late husband's interest in politics. She took over his parliamentary seat during the provisional government and headed several social welfare committees.

When the two women got together, the young widow patiently listened to Sao's halting Burmese, amicably correcting the mistakes. A daughter of a Christian pastor, she understood her dead husband's vision of a multi-ethnic, multi-religious state. Unfortunately, her schedule was just as heavy as Sao's. Their meetings were sporadic and usually within a formal setting, such as at a state dinner or around a committee table. It wasn't like a real friendship.

Sao often felt lonely and depressed. Her worst moments came when the youngest Yawnghwe Palace wife, Nang Mya Win, visited Rangoon and prostrated herself at the President's feet.

So much for modern civility, Sao fumed. Her husband was still a Celestial Lord worshipped by a concubine. She heard the younger wife had a boyfriend in the Burma Army. Why didn't she marry him, then? After all, she had no formal marriage tie to the Prince. But still Nang Mya Win came and performed the kadaw, touching her head to the floor three times at her husband's feet. It was beyond Sao's understanding.

Her loneliness was eased when Prince Sai and Pat were in town. The heir's new wife was full of good humour. Within days of arriving in Rangoon, Pat seemed to know everyone who counted and all the most amusing gossip. She and Sao played tennis whenever they had the chance. Sao was quite a good player, having never lived in a home that lacked a tennis court. Their games were competitive and fun. Sao took Pat on occasional doctor's visits to India; Sao still wasn't feeling her old self, although there was nothing seriously wrong, physically. She was sorry when Pat eventually returned to Yawnghwe with Price Sai.

Prince Sai's job as state administrator wouldn't be easy, Sao knew. Shan State didn't receive its full budget allotment from the cash-strapped Union in 1951, leaving many local improvements to the largesse of the Saophas. At the same time, Freedom League members—who established chapters throughout Shan State—resented the Celestial Lords' continued involvement in public life. It was the Saophas who pushed for state autonomy, something the Leaguers understood only as a weakening of the national fabric. To counter the princes' highly visible public works, the local activists spread gossip about gambling, concubines and other debaucheries.

In the southern region of Yawnghwe, the Pa-O hill people listened to the stories. When they brought their tobacco crops to town, they saw with new eyes the largeness of Yawnghwe Palace, with so many apartments for so many bejewelled wives.

It's not fair that the Saophas live in luxury, they thought, while our own leaders have bamboo homes like ordinary people. The Freedom Leaguers told them that loyalty to the Union of Burma—not to Shan State and its Tai princes—would make everyone equal. They helped the Pa-O form their own political organisation. Some Pa-O went underground and were rumoured to be gathering weapons with the help of the Burma Army.

When the news reached Rangoon, Sao was shocked. She couldn't understand why the Pa-O would want to agitate against the palace. Did they not have their own headmen and their own law? Her husband didn't interfere in their business. Clearly, the Pa-O were misled by others, she concluded.

The situation was tense and her cousin, Chief Minister Seng Hpu, wasn't there to guide the heir. Sadly, he had died of suspected cancer just after the war. His replacement, Chief Minister Ko Latt, was a trustworthy man, though, more diplomatic and cool-headed than his fiery predecessor. Still, one worried.

Soon, Sao thought, they would all be back in Yawnghwe to help Prince Sai. After two years of delays, Burma's national elections were finally launched in June, 1951. The polls were to be conducted and tallied over a period of seven months.

By that time, Sao realised with sudden gladness, her husband's presidential term would be complete.

The constitution allowed for two consecutive five-year terms, but Sao doubted he'd be re-appointed. She recalled Thakin Nu's disgusted look at the glass of whisky in her husband's hand. She guessed that the religious PM objected to their whole lifestyle, from their fluent English to the western business suits favoured by the Prince.

The next presidential appointment would doubtless be Thakin Nu's decision: there was no real opposition to the Freedom League. His election victory appeared assured. The people adored their PM's pious, unassuming manner.

Sao took comfort in the thought. Thakin Nu would win, and he would find a replacement for her husband. Then they could move back to Shan State to take care of Shan business. Her apartment at Yawnghwe Haw, once so lonely, now seemed inviting.

Burma could do without them. The country seemed to be emerging from its worst days of rebellion, at least on the surface. By the end of 1951, railway service to Mandalay was restored for the first time since the rebellion broke out in 1948. The Karen uprising seemed on the wane. The previous August, Sao's Karen friend, Saw Ba U Gyi, found himself surrounded by a Burma Army commando unit at his Kawkareik headquarters. "Go ahead and shoot me, if that's what you want," he said. They shot him dead. Of course, Burma no longer had a Karen leader with whom to negotiate statehood, but this weakness had not yet made itself apparent.

In Shan State, the American missionary Dr. Gordon Seagrave —whose Kachin-staffed border hospital reopened after the war— was arrested in January, 1951 and sentenced to six years for aiding the rebels. The sentence was eventually quashed by the Supreme Court, but it consumed nearly an entire year in appeals proceedings. Meantime, the rebel leader Captain Naw Seng remained in China and all seemed quiet on the Kachin front.

But other trouble brewed in Shan State. The KMT continued to mushroom. When Burma asked the U.S. to pressure Taiwan for a KMT withdrawal, Dean Rusk spoke in General Li Mi's defence. Twice that year, in April and again in August, the refugee army attacked China from their Shan bases. They were easily repulsed.

Taiwanese reinforcements marched in from Thailand, carrying American-made weapons. As 1951 came to a close, the KMT had doubled from 4,000 men to 8,000 and had extended their range west of the Salween River, invading towns and taking over roads. Unable to take China alone, they wanted Burma to join the fray. They sniped at both the Chinese and Burmese border-guards, hoping to draw them into an exchange of fire. Shan State was fast becoming a battleground for the wars of superpowers, making a mockery of Thakin Nu's reconciliation campaign. "Peace Within One Year" was a meaningless promise, a prayer answered by still more weapons tumbling down from the sky.

Back to Golden Valley

As predicted, Thakin Nu faced a feeble electoral opposition. A handful of older nationalists led by Dr. Ba Maw ran against his Freedom League candidates, along with members of a new far-left party, the Burma Workers and Peasants Party (BWPP).

The BWPP claimed to be the true inheritors of Aung San's original ideas, before revisionism set in. They were led by Aung San's younger brother, U Aung Than. Even more interesting was their financial backer, a wealthy race-horse breeder who happened to be Thakin Nu's brother. A flambouyant capitalist, he disliked his famous brother's weak-kneed piety to such a degree that he was willing to bed down with the far left.

The politicians were building a quite incestuous little world.

In any case, Thakin Nu's opponents had little impact on the election outcome. Amid the usual boycotts and occasional armed outbreaks, polls were successfully conducted in 217 constituencies. When the final tally was announced on March 16, 1952, only thirty-seven of the 217 seats went to non-League candidates.

Victorious, Thakin Nu announced that he would henceforth be called "U Nu", Uncle Tender. The moniker Thakin—Master—was redundant because the Burmese had truly become masters of their own house, he explained.

The most powerful among the Freedom League's collaberating parties was the Socialist Party, which held eighty of the League's 180 seats. They gained a deciding bloc of eight men within Thakin Nu's twenty-two person cabinet, up from just three socialist members in his previous cabinet. Although Thakin Nu was still Prime Minister and the Freedom League was still the ruling coalition, the composition of the government was different, further to the left.

The Socialist Party influence was defined in the government's major policy initiative announced by Thakin Nu in August. They called their program Pyidawtha—Happy Land—an ambitious, expensive programme of infrastructure reconstruction and social welfare that would form the essence of Burmese policy for years to come.

Sao was partially right about Thakin Nu's presidential choice: it wasn't her husband. He was passed over in favour of a Burmese man, former Chief Justice Dr. Ba U.

She was wrong about their future, though. The Prince told her that his name was being put forward as Speaker of the Chamber of Nationalities, parliament's upper house. They weren't going home.

Sao hadn't contemplated staying in Rangoon. Where would they live? They couldn't stay in the President's House.

In the end, they decided to simply switch places with the incoming President. He had a furnished home in Golden Valley which was plenty large enough for Sao and her family.

Moving day was uncomplicated. Sao and the Prince had few personal possessions in Rangoon. They had never needed their own furniture. There were only some personal papers, clothes, jewellery and books for the staff to pack.

Sao wasn't interested in a more settled arrangement. She still considered their stay in Rangoon to be temporary. Just four more years, she told herself. At least now they had more freedom to move about the country like normal people, although they still kept bodyguards around them.

The newly-elected government was immediately presented with a serious problem: the KMT forces grew like a cancer on the frontier. After his two unsuccessful attempts to invade China, General Li Mi settled into life in Shan State. Olive Yang pointed him in the direction of steady revenue. In early 1952 the KMT built seventy miles of road in Shan State and thirty miles in Thailand. They taxed opium caravans that plied the road and encouraged the cultivation of poppies. The general conducted business in the manner of the warlords of old China, becoming master of a growing swath of Kengtung State.

General Li's budding relationship with the CIA was a worry to Thakin Nu. The Americans were doubtless unhappy about the establishment of Chinese and Soviet embassies in Rangoon, not to mention Burma's recent approval of a Viet Minh office. What if they used the KMT to topple the Socialist-led Freedom League? Another scenario was that China might invade Burma on the pretext of chasing down the KMT. They were caught between both sides of the Cold War, with the freedom of their country at stake. Viewed in this light, the KMT were a greater threat to Burma's government than to China's.

Thus, when China lodged an official protest about the KMT, the Burmese government swiftly responded. On September 23, 1952, the new President declared a State of Emergency in Shan State. In December the Burma Army assumed administration of the state, declaring martial law in twenty-two of the thirty-three Shan principalities.

Burma's retreat from democracy had begun.

Under the declaration, the army entered Shan State like a juggernaut. Sao was immediately suspicious of their motives. Most of the principalities falling under martial law were in the south-west, far from KMT territory. She sensed deceptions within deceptions, just like in the days of the old Mandalay court.

Indeed, with martial law the army gained the power to settle many matters, not just the KMT problem. For example, the Shan habit of carrying a rifle—as common as wearing a hat—had long alarmed and frightened the army men. Now they had greater license to make arrests and confiscate weapons. Villagers were interrogated and tortured for suspected sympathies toward outlaw communists and ethnic organisations—in short, for supporting anyone not allied with the power centre in Rangoon. The Saophas, too, fell under a cloud of suspicion because some were said to have caches of abandoned Japanese weapons inside their Haws. They could easily leak these weapons to the Army's many enemies, a grenade here, a rifle there. Where else could the bandits and insurrectionists be getting their guns?

Sao's nephew Saw Ohn was one of the few Tai officers assigned to the frontier. He was given the job of inspector and told to maintain order on the road north of Loilem, which had recently been the scene of a rash of armed robberies. Bandits and rebellious Pa-O hid out in the surrounding forest. Ironically, they received clandestine support from the army's intelligence men, who were trying to agitate against the Saophas.

One day Saw Ohn's little daughter was caught in an ambush and killed, a bullet piercing her neck. Infuriated, Saw Ohn tracked the ringleader down and had his revenge.

Later, he told Sao that General Ne Win's office phoned him the very next day.

"Why did you kill him? He was our man," the caller said.

"It was night. I shot him in the back. How could I know who it was?" Saw Ohn shrugged.

Of course he knew, thought Sao. In these days, what else could a man do? It's not like he could hire a lawyer. There was no law and order under martial law. Things would be different if the Celestial Lords regained more control, she decided.

Prince Shwe Thaike didn't share his wife's feudal nostalgia. It didn't take a rebellion to show him the truth: inevitably, the rule of the Celestials must come to an end.

"We need to modernise," he told Sao. "Things are moving too slowly."

In 1952 he began talking to the other Shan princes about transferring their powers to the state. There was a lot to sort out: how to survive without tax revenues, whom to assign responsibility for roads and markets, even what to do with the grand Haws.

In leading the power transfer, the Prince had assigned himself a task that would take years to accomplish. The thirty-three celestial lords had hundreds of details to reach consensus on. Then they had to negotiate the agreement with a central government which was in fact in no great hurry to totally abandon feudalism. After all, Rangoon still depended on the Saophas to make up for budget shortfalls.

As one example, U Nu asked the Saophas to raise militias against the KMT out of their own pockets. Every penny would be repaid, the PM promised. Sao's brother—having gained a great deal of respect for military solutions during the Kachin uprising—was among the first to comply.

The transfer of feudal powers provided one of the few political arenas open to Prince Shwe Thaike's involvement. Although the presidency had constrained his voice, being Speaker was even worse. He had to appear neutral on all subjects, even when visitors arrived from Shan State with terrible tales. General Ne Win's "bandit-suppression" campaign had reached maniacal heights. The Burma Army soldiers used villagers as human minesweepers, roping five to a pole like livestock. Women carried supplies by day and endured repeated rapes by night.

Safe in their small Golden Valley sitting room, Sao kept teacups full and listened to the stories. While her husband remained silent, she dispensed warnings against the Burmese—never to be trusted—and openly applauded rebellious attitudes. Fearing no one, she didn't care who overheard. What could they do?

In the meantime, the KMT crisis dominated the newspapers. In January, General Li sent 30,000 men against China, again without success. After three failures, he contented himself with being the eyes and ears of the free world along China's southern flank. There were no more invasion attempts, just occasional skirmishes.

One day in March the newspapers reported that the bodies of three white men turned up among the KMT dead in the aftermath of their last invasion attempt. Editorialists demanded answers: who were these foreigners and what were they up to? The report surfaced just before the March 17 visit of U.S. Vice President Richard Nixon and his wife, Pat.

The Nixons were an appealing couple. To everyone's delight, they appeared on the lawn of the President's House in Burmese dress. Nontheless, such manoeuvres couldn't deflect criticism of the growing U.S. presence in Southeast Asia. Nixon was informed on the spot about the KMT situation. Later that day, Foreign Minister Sao Hkun Hkio told U.S. Ambassador William Sebald that Burma would take its KMT complaint to the United Nations and that, in the meantime, the country no longer wished to receive American foreign aid.

The refusal of aid was a popular decision, but one destined to place great strain on U Nu's ambitious Pyidawtha plan. The country's own resources weren't enough to build the planned roads and port facilities. The price of rice was falling steadily and the oil fields —only recently regained from the rebels—had yet to resume pre-war production levels. The days of Burma's easy self-sufficiency were only a memory.

In the midst of Burma's worldly troubles, the Way of the Buddha was not forgotten. In fact, more people than ever turned to religion. Under a new moon, the International Meditation Centre was founded just south of Inya Lake, next to a new golden pagoda topped with a bejewelled Hti umbrella.

On July 5, 1953 the Meditation Centre hosted a reclusive monk from north of Mandalay. Webu Sayadaw—meaning "the Noble Teacher from Webu"—lived in a bamboo hut at the bottom of Webu hill, near the norther town of Shwebo. He was believed to be an Arahant, one of the few mortal beings to fully understand the Four Noble Truths and attain the end of suffering.

Everyone was surprised when the Arahant accepted the Centre's invitation, he left his remote hut and blithely boarded a plane to Rangoon, as if he did this every day of his life. Arriving at the Meditation Centre, he hopped out the car door, raised his hands in veneration toward the glittering Hti, then climbed the steps to the new pagoda.

Until now, only a few had met Webu Sayadaw in person. The followers who lined the pagoda stairs saw a man with impressive, hawk-like features—high cheekbones, a long, beaked nose and a wide, straight mouth. He circumambulated the pagoda three times, walking with a dignified, ramrod-straight posture. It was said that in all his years as a monk, the Noble Teacher never lay down, being a practitioner of Dhutanga, ascetic practices to combat indulgence. His teachings had reached Rangoon via Burma's Accountant General, who was formerly a humble railway clerk in Shwebo.

The following evening, Sao and her husband arrived among a flock of fellow dignitaries to pay their respects to the venerable monk. They hoped to put in a fast appearance before their next engagement, a dinner party. Time permitting, they would take in some of the Discourse, a lively question-and-answer exchange that had no comparison in other religions. On their way into the Meditation Centre's Dhamma Hall, her husband noted it was already 6:00 p.m. They should try to make a quick exit, her reminded her.

According to custom, the couple presented food and robes and then took their place on the floor for the Discourse, men in front, women behind. Webu Sayadaw faced them from behind a microphone on a slightly raised platform. The Accountant General, whom everyone called Sayagyi, Great Teacher, sat among a row of acolytes.

"The Teachings of the Buddha contained in the Tripitaka—the Three Baskets of our scriptures—have but one object: liberation from suffering," Webu Sayadaw began. His voice was calm and matter of fact.

"Methods vary but the object is the same. Choose one of them, and then put it into practice in a steadfast manner."

Webu Sayadaw's own favourite method was called Anapanasati. The technique involved total awareness of the touch of one's own breath on the upper lip. When one's concentration is complete, he told them, material concerns fall away.

"Wanting, dislike and delusion do not have the opportunity to arise and the fires of greed, anger and delusion will subside," he explained.

Achieving this, one may gain the tranquillity required to understand the three characteristics of nature: Anicca, impermanence, Dukkha, the unsatisfactory nature of impermanent phenomenon, and Anatta, or non-self.

"Such understanding leads to Panna—Wisdom—and Panna leads to Nibbana," he concluded.

The gathering was impressed. The man had the presence of a true Arahant. Sao heard her husband ask if he could learn Anapanasati from Webu Sayadaw's disciple, the Accountant General.

"Oh yes, he uses the same technique. You should study under him," answered Webu Sayadaw.

Addressing the Accountant General, Prince Shwe Thaike said, "Well, Sayagyi, you must teach me some day."

"Why wait?" he replied. "I will take you to a meditation cell right now."

It was an unexpected invitation, impossible to turn down in front of so many people and the great Arahant. As the Prince followed Sayagyi from the room, Sao heard him remind the man in a low voice, "Don't forget, I have a dinner party in an hour."

Her husband gone from the room, Sao listened to the rest of the Discourse with interest. She had never been very religious, but lately she had begun to think about her life. Things that brought her sorrow—a loveless marriage, rankling jealousies, separation from her beloved homeland—were things over which she had no control. Webu Sayadaw's words about Anicca, impermanence, were a comfort. She vowed not to let circumstances upset her so much in future.

"Anicca," she said to herself. "Everything will pass. Nothing is permanent."

Later, during the drive home the Prince told her that Sayagyi led him to a small cell off the main shrine room where the images of Lord Buddha were kept. Imparting a few basic instructions, he left the Prince to his meditations. In darkness, Sao's husband closed his eyes and felt the air pass his upper lip. The next thing he knew, Sayagyi was at the door, saying, "You're late for your party."

Incredibly, two hours had passed. It was nine o'clock. "Never mind, I won't go now," the Prince said.

From that day forward, Prince Shwe Thaike became a religious man. He meditated regularly and formed a society to sponsor Webu Sayadaw's trips to Rangoon. Sao took up meditation, too, finding it calmed her mind and focused her thoughts. She was able to let go of some of the bitterness of her marriage.

Her husband began to talk to her more often about political affairs. In particular, he encouraged her interest in Shan State.

Sao met informally and frequently with the Shan Saophas. She relayed their complaints to the powers-that-be. It was a good role for her, for she never stood on politeness or deferred to military men. She said exactly what was on her mind. Back in Shan State, her fame grew. When people talked about "The Mahadevi", everyone knew they meant the Mahadevi of Yawnghwe.

Meanwhile her husband decided that, as Speaker, the best he could do for his people was to sponsor the translation of the Tripitaka into the Tai language, a huge cultural undertaking. Matters more political could be handled by his wife.

The Cocoon

Some days it seemed like everyone in Rangoon had wrapped themselves in the same cocoon of religiosity and idle social prattle. The paths between the Golden Valley homes were well-worn. People drank tea together, then parted to gossip about one another. Camps and cliques of all types formed among the country's leaders and their families.

One day, Sao went for tea at the Prime Minister's Windemere residence only to find the men all grumbling about her friend, Daw Khin Kyi.

"Well, tell me what's happened," she said, plunking herself down in a parlour chair. The PM's sitting room was austerely decorated with some plain-looking bits of furniture and a few framed photos of state occasions. The PM himself spent most of his time in his garden hut, away from his many children, his devoted wife and his aged mother. His guests that day were mostly army and government men. One of them volunteered an answer for Sao: "Nothing has happened, Madam. That's exactly the problem."

They quickly filled her in about the latest social foofaraw. It seemed the government had hinted at Aung San's widow to move out of her home, which belonged to the state. It was felt the large house could be put to better use. But Daw Khin Kyi and her children were still there, and now the government faced the uncomfortable task of evicting her.

Sao said nothing, but that very evening she went to warn the one woman in Rangoon who was almost like a friend. She could see why Daw Khin Kyi wouldn't want to leave the house she had shared with her husband, with its curving veranda and pleasant garden. And really there was no justice to it. The woman continued to do a great deal for her country. She organised activities for the peace campaign and chaired the National Council on Maternity and Child Welfare, the Social Planning Commission and the Council of Social Service. But it was all women's work—committee meetings, education drives—and therefore invisible to the men in charge.

While they talked, the widow's daughter, Aung San Suu Kyi, appeared on the staircase. She looked at Sao with sleepy-eyed confusion, then asked her mother, "Why does she talk so funny? Is she Chinese?"

"Never mind what she is. Go to bed," her mother said. Sao could see that Suu Kyi was a beautiful girl already, slender with big, beguiling eyes that displayed an open heart. She disappeared up the wide and polished stairs, leaving the two women to the business at hand. Sao went straight to the point. The house was nice, but not worth humiliation at the hands of Rangoon's politicians.

Some time later, Daw Khin Kyi accepted a replacement house on University Avenue. Once fixed up, it was in fact better than the old place, with a large garden compound sloping down to the shore of Inya Lake. Decades later, it would become famous as the scene of Aung San Suu Kyi's house arrest, after the beautiful daughter returned to Burma as a grown woman intent on leading her country to freedom.

Daw Khin Kyi's house problem got Sao thinking about her own life. She didn't like living on the largesse of people she didn't trust. She asked the authorities if their owned borrowed house—also owned by the state—might be for sale. It was not. She put the idea out of her mind. They weren't staying long in Rangoon, anyway.

Before year's end, they were on the move. The opportunity had come unexpectedly during a visit to Taunggyi. Squeezing past market stalls of bright sarongs and bubbling curry pots, Sao met up with an Indian fellow who beamed broadly at the sight of her. She knew him vaguely, a local chap with property in Rangoon, said to be a bit of a tycoon.

"Oh, Madam, I have such a something for you, a so-large house and nine-and-a-half big acres, right in the middle of Rangoon...and very affordable, Madam," he said excitedly.

"We have no intention of staying in Rangoon, so we have no need of a house there," she responded.

To her total surprise, the man plopped to his knees. He looked up at her imploringly.

The Burma Army had commandeered the place after the war, he told her, and there they stayed without paying a Kyat. The house would not sell because no one dared evict the unwanted tenants.

"Only a great high person such as yourself can get rid of them," he begged. "You can bargain as much as you want, please."

For once, Sao was completely speechless. She had to say something, what with the fellow kneeling in the dust at her feet, blocking her path. So she said, "Alright, five thousand."

It was a safe response: 5,000 Kyat was nothing, less than 400 English pounds.

"Thirty thousand and no less," said the man, rising from the dust. Surprising herself, she agreed to look at the place when the family returned to Rangoon.

She followed through on the promise. When they got back to the city, she found the address: 74 Kokine Road. Behind a high hedge sat a large rambling structure and several smaller out-buildings, all in a state of obvious disrepair. But the grounds were huge and the place had potential. It was too good a deal to pass up.

Although Sao swore they didn't need a house in Rangoon, it was she who made the purchase. Hearing who the new owner was, the army moved out without complaint. They left a mess behind. There were still holes left in the walls from wartime looting. But the grounds were every bit as large as the Indian businessman had promised, taking up a nine-and-a-half-acre triangle of land at the corner of Kokine and Goodliffe, north of downtown and south of University Avenue and Inya Lake.

In the midst of the sweeping garden sat a two-storey house with covered portico, a grand old building. King Edward had once stayed there, the former owner told Sao, but now it all looked rather saggy and peeling. Sao had the most obvious damage repaired and they moved in forthwith. The rooms dwarfed their meagre possessions. They had so little furniture that it never looked like more than a temporary camp. The sparse decor suited Sao just fine, though. They weren't staying long.

The new house wasn't too far from the University of Rangoon. It was a good location for Tiger, who returned from Doon in 1954 and enrolled in geology classes at the university. The campus was a lively place, a source of pride for the whole country. Prime Minister U Nu himself had chosen the site for a new Students' Union Building, near the main gate because the Nats would be disturbed by construction near the lake, he thought. He also insisted that Dale Carnegie's *How to Win Friends and Influence People*—the book he'd translated as a student—be required reading. But Tiger was stymied by another requirement: the Burmese language. He knew barely a word, and it was the language of instruction.

Sao hadn't encouraged her children to learn Burmese. In fact, they were forbidden to speak it at home—she worried that they'd become assimilated. Hearing English spoken never bothered her, though.

Her other children chatted easily in Burmese, despite their mother's misgivings. Although they attended English schools, their classmates were mostly Burmese, including General Ne Win's favourite daughter, Sanda; Aung San's children, Aung San Oo and Aung San Suu Kyi; and Prime Minister U Nu's five kids, created before he took his vow of abstinence and retired to the garden.

The move to Kokine Road was a good transition for them all, Sao felt. Students, monks and Shan politicians dropped by freely. The kids had acres of land for their football games. Away from the President's House, they began to function something like a normal family.

Yawnghwe Haw replaced Maymyo's Presidential Retreat as their holiday spot. They went by car under armed guard, following the winding road from dusty Thazi up into the green, timbered hills.

On one such trip, Sao spied some wild orchids near the roadside and ordered the driver to stop. Standing outside on the hot macadam, she heard familiar bird-calls above a rushing stream. She had almost forgotten the sound clear water made when it bounced boulder to boulder down a steep hillside. It was like music. She never heard fast-moving water in Rangoon, where stale green ponds seeped soundlessly into a thousand dull, silt-laden delta tributaries. Before anyone could advise her against it, she followed the sound down a steep roadside embankment. Behind her, the bodyguards leapt from the car, guns ready.

Among dark tree shadows, Sao picked an orchid for her hair and one for each of the girls. They were beautiful flowers, perfectly formed and fragrant. When she returned to the car, she brought the smell of the forest with her. Everyone, even the guards, looked pale and nervous. These days, no one liked to stop long on a Shan State road.

Arriving at Yawnghwe Haw, the youngest ones, who had never known palace life, explored and learned the old traditions. They got to know their half-brother Stanley, and were delighted by the court musicians, who played cymbals and drums at daybreak and sunset. Myee and Stanley took their ordination ceremonies together in the cavernous Hall of Audience, with colourfully-dressed hill people in attendance.

While the children explored, Sao spent her days in the sunny courtyard outside Pat and Prince Sai's apartment. She was delighted to see her fun-loving niece again. The two women enjoyed cold drinks in the courtyard and played tennis on the lawn. There was little work for Sao to do, beyond hosting occasional VIPs who came to enjoy Inle Lake.

She listened to her children's laughter as they played tag in the hall, scrambled out windows, clambered over the rooftops, and clapped their hands at the bottom of the Dragon Stairs to hear the echo. It was as if the old days were reborn.

When the parliamentary houses sat, the family made the long trip back to Rangoon. Budgetary problems still bedevilled the government. The Pyidawtha Plan envisioned new highways, irrigation systems and ports. The problem was how to pay for it, especially with rice prices falling globally and American aid in suspension. As well, Burma had already agreed to repay

London a lump sum of four million pounds for the "post-war military assistance".

There were a few positive developments, though. Burma finally lifted its old official war declaration against Japan, clearing the way for a US$ 250 million war reparations package. The government's complaint to the UN about the KMT troops was partially successful: 5,700 troops and about 1,000 of their dependents were evacuated to Taiwan. General Li Mi announced an end to his command on May 30. Although some 3,000 armed KMT remained in the area, it signalled enough progress for Prime Minister U Nu to include the United States in his western tour the following year.

In the U.S. he informed American officials about the benefits of Buddhism and donated US$ 5,000 to help children of American soldiers who died in the Burma campaign. Then he asked for a resumption of financial assistance.

His tour took him to Italy and the Holy Land, as well. Returning to Rangoon, he presented Burma's Catholic community with 1,112 crucifixes and eighty-five bottles of water from the River Jordan. He also brought back a 150 million US-dollar American aid package.

On the international scene, U Nu courted the communist camp, too. Burma had been the first non-communist country to recognise the People's Republic of China, and Chinese Premier Zhou Enlai visited Rangoon twice in two years. During a reciprocal visit to Beijing, U Nu promised Premier Zhou that Burma would never become a "cat's paw" for China's enemies. Enroute to Beijing, he stopped in Hanoi and dined with North Vietnamese leader Ho Chi Minh. Then, in November 1955, Premier Nikolai Bulgannan and Soviet First Communist Party Secretary Nikita S. Krushchev visited Burma.

None of these encounters pleased Burma's American aid benefactors. U Nu was determined, though, to show the world that in politics, as in religion, the Middle Path was best.

Within the United Nations, Burma became a leader of the growing non-aligned movement. At the Bandung Conference of April 1955—sponsored by Burma—the emerging nations of Africa and Asia revelled in their growing international importance. They were a new power to be reckoned with, a "Third World".

None knew yet the narrow and treacherous path between Cold War superpowers, nor of the associated wars and coups d'état waiting to shatter their dreams.

Back home, Rangoon was a beehive of religious activity. On May 17, 1954, the Sixth Buddhist Synod was convened in the capital. It was a great event in the history of Buddhism, only the sixth such meeting in the two-and-a-half millennia since Lord Buddha's passing. Monks and scholars from around the globe came to develop a common interpretation of the Teachings. The meetings, scheduled to last two years, were held near U Nu's World Peace Pagoda in a massive, specially-built artificial cavern called Maha Pasan Guha—the Great Cave.

The fast-rising religious tide created pressure to declare Buddhism the state religion. U Nu waffled and experimented unsuccessfully with religious instruction in government schools. Buddhism was introduced to the classroom while a committee was struck to study non-Buddhist instruction. In essence, the half-baked move gave Buddhism alone official sanction.

It was not what U Nu hoped to achieve in his multi-religious country. He blamed his religious problems on other politicians and had them arrested.

U Nu himself was untouched by the controversy. It was his idea to host the Synod, and he who gained parliament's support for the undertaking. The people loved him for it. Proud of their country's contribution to Buddhist thought, thousands volunteered to cook meals for the monks.

It mattered not what transpired in parliament or in the finance office. In the peaceful enclave of the Great Cave, people felt their country was on the right track.

There was little to occupy Sao during these times. In 1955 they hosted Yugoslavia's Marshal Tito at the Inle Lake retreat. For the most part, though, the entertainment of foreign visitors was no longer her responsibility. She attended dinners at the Marble Hall like any other guest.

Her husband was kept busy with his Speaker's duties and the transfer of feudal powers. On October 20, 1954, the Celestial Lords finally entered formal negotiations with the government. They wanted seats in the Chamber of Nationalities, the right to keep arms for self-protection, free government education for their children, and the right to hold elected positions in the lower house. They also wanted to retain their royal titles and nine-gun salutes.

The government negotiators indicated acceptance. Many members of the public, on the other hand, were incensed.

A few days later, Sao picked up one of the daily papers, the *Nation*, and was startled by the front page story. Anti-feudalists had held a protest meeting in Taunggyi, right in their home state, within a few miles of Yawnghwe Haw. She read on, shocked by the protesters' reported description of the Saophas:

"They have collected many forms of taxes to enrich themselves, to enable them to stay in palatial residences, to keep an unlimited number of wives, to travel abroad and generally to live in the lap of luxury."

Sao had never looked at her life that way. She thought she and her husband worked hard for the people. She was completely bewildered. The protesters ended their meeting with a demand that the Saophas refund their "ill-gotten gains", rather than receiving compensation.

"Without the Saopha's school allowances, they'd still be pulling ploughs like oxen," she seethed, not for the first time, and folded the newspaper shut. She could only surmise that the Burmese were manipulating the young people to stir up trouble.

There were others stirring the pot, too. Novelists wrote stories about lecherous Saophas who kept fair maidens prisoner behind their stout-walled Haws. Sao never related her own youthful anguish to the cliché. It was all nonsense, she thought, but the books were best-sellers. Worse than words, in protest against the "ill-gotten gains", a young man tried to lob a home-made bomb into the crowd at Yawnghwe's annual gambling poy. The bomb went off in his hands and he was the only one injured. Lucky for him, it was not a well-made explosive.

The anti-Saopha campaign brought on a backlash. It turned out that Sao's views were not so isolated and anachronistic as the rebellious students may have hoped. The majority of Shan citizens were conservative-minded farmers and small traders bound to their ancient traditions. To them, an attack on the Saophas was an attack on Shan State autonomy and culture. The chief author of the damaging novels, Bo Ni, was denounced as an army intelligence agent. Racial tensions increased between Burmese and Tai. At the markets and poys, one never knew when a fist fight might break out.

To help ease the tension, the government ended its unpopular martial law in Shan State, returning power to the civilian government in Taunggyi. But the Burma Army troops remained in place, just in case.

Sao chafed. Something should be done about the rising violence in Shan State, but she felt constrained. She perceived that her once all-powerful family had been diminished in subtle ways: her husband silenced by his political appointment, their children raised outside their homeland and she, suffocating in the cramped circle of Rangoon high society. They needed to regain themselves and it was up to her to find the way.

Four

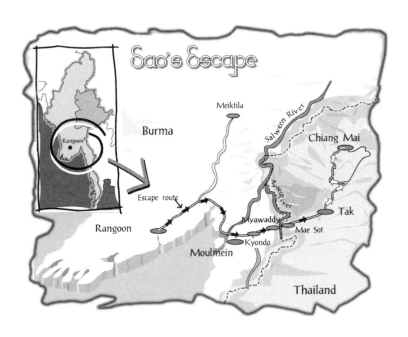

Prince Hom Hpa of Hsenwi.

Aung San's widow, Daw Khin Kyi being appointed as Burmese Ambassador to India and Nepal. (The Bangkok Post)

Aung San's house, typical of Rangoon's colonial mansions. (Don Jedlic)

A devout Buddhist, Prime Minister U Nu. (The Bangkok Post)

(Right) General Ne Win shaking hands with UN Secretary-General U Thant. (AP)

(Below) Lo Hsin Han (centre) with leaders of the Shan State Army (on the right) and Lo's KKY men (on the left). The picture was taken near Mae Hong Son in 1974. (The Bangkok Post)

Aung San Suu Kyi, leader of the National League for Democracy, during one of her public addresses at her house in Rangoon. (The Bangkok Post)

Jimmy Yang of Kokang State, a former Member of Parliament, held on charges of illegal entry to Thailand in 1974. (The Bangkok Post)

Member of Parliament

From the moment Sao decided to run for Parliament, the family's Rangoon home became a magnet for pro-Shan activists. Everyone thought the idea was a good one, especially her husband.

"We need MPs who aren't afraid to open their mouths," he said.

Ironically, the opportunity to run came from Sao's nemesis: her elder brother offered her Hsenwi's parliamentary seat.

The last time Sao and her brother had met, she'd complained long and loud about the arrangement between Shan State and the Union government. Shan villages paid an indemnity tax to Rangoon, she pointed out, only to be continually short-changed by the national budget. Where was all the tax money going, she wanted to know, and why didn't Shan representatives raise this question more often?

"Our people approach the government like beggars," she griped.

In answer, Prince Hom Hpa invited her to run in his constituency.

Sao's brother wasn't one for open rebellion. In fact, he'd grown rather close to the generals and government types stationed in Lashio. He reasoned, though, that it couldn't hurt to raise a few issues in parliament. If the instigator was his own little sister, he could exercise some brotherly control. In any case, he thought she couldn't do worse than the other Shan MPs, many of whom were chosen simply because they had university degrees, not because they had any political skills.

This election, the Freedom League couldn't expect their usual cakewalk. The opposition was beefed up somewhat when a new centrist group, the Justice Party, joined Aung Than's left-leaning BWPP. Their combined forces took the name National Unity Front.

In Shan State things were more straightforward. Sao travelled to Hsenwi in early 1956, leaving behind the political clamour of the lowlands. Twenty-five Shan constituency seats were set aside in the lower-house Chamber of Deputies. The Hsenwi constituency was more or less filled by appointment.

Sao made no speeches, distributed no leaflets. The village headman and Myosas came to her brother's bamboo Haw to meet her. Arriving by ones and twos over the next several weeks, they sat round her on bamboo mats, sipped tea and ate salty snacks. And they talked. Sao was a good listener. During those long afternoons, she heard enough cruel stories to make her blood hot.

One story made a particular impression. When an important country funeral was held, it was the practice for the village headman to carry packets of tea to the headmen of neighbouring villages. On presenting the tea-gift, the whole village would be invited to the funeral. Usually a small group would tag along with the headman, for it was a good opportunity to visit relatives.

One day some villagers from the Mong Yaw area set out on such a journey, but were stopped on the trail by a Burma Army patrol. None of the villagers knew enough Burmese to explain where they were going. In horror, the villagers watched the soldiers throw their headman to the ground. The army believed that only bandits and troublemakers travelled in gangs. The torture was hideous: the soldiers forced a mixture of water and sand down the headman's throat, then stamped on his belly until he regurgitated the water. They repeated the procedure several times, meaning to fill the poor man's stomach entirely with sand.

"Funeral, funeral!" the headman sputtered in Tai, until suddenly one of the soldiers made sense of the word. They stopped the torture, but there were no apologies.

The villagers who related this story to Sao told her that everyone was afraid to lodge a complaint with the local police. In fact, only one witness ever spoke about the incident. The witness, a woman, was so afraid the army would come and kill her that she ran away from Mong Yaw.

The rural people were in despair. How could they fight back against such cruelties?

Some asked Sao about a rumoured cache of old Japanese weapons kept at Hsenwi. They begged her to open her brother's storehouse.

"You're too late," she told them. "My brother gave the guns up to the army."

It was true. Prince Hom Hpa handed over his weapons to set a good example for the other Saophas, the same motivation he'd had for being the first to raise a levy against the KMT. He ordered several of his nephews to join the Burma Army, too, and married some nieces to army officers. Maybe it had something to do with the fact that he'd been raised a soldier by the British. Maybe it was because the Burma Army helped save Hsenwi from the Kachin uprising. Who knew? Sao could hardly believe he was the same man who'd once travelled all the way to England to argue for Shan sovereignty. How people change!

For her part, Sao wouldn't give the Burma Army one grain of rice, and she couldn't understand why anyone would do their bidding. She noted that her brother hadn't received a single Kyat for fighting the KMT, despite the Prime Ministers's promise to repay expenses.

When Sao railed against the Burma Army, the headmen listened and nodded their heads in agreement. She chastised villagers who complained about the army, then sold their daughters into marriage with the soldiers. Their downcast eyes told her they agreed but were too afraid to refuse such marriage proposals.

The Mahadevi, as they called her, was just as bold and brassy now as when she was a young princess who didn't want to get married. Physically, she was a bit heavier in the bone and the tiny gap between her teeth had widened a little, but she was still youthful-looking, vivacious and energetic. She knew the political scene in far-away Rangoon. She hobnobbed with the highest of the high as an equal and seemed capable of defending their interests.

Just one man struck up an argument with Sao. He was a young Kachin university student, home for a holiday. The student lectured her about the Saophas' riches, which he said were taken from the poor through taxation.

Sao answered back that the Saophas worked out budgets every year to pay for this project and that. "They don't just spend the money however they want. There's never enough money to pay for everything," she said.

Sao was proud of her knowledge, for not many women knew about budgets. The young student apologised, saying he never knew the Saophas paid for public works. They parted with friendly words. There was no telling if he was convinced, or if he simply realised it was futile to argue with the Mahadevi. Likewise, there was no telling if the headmen supported her—she felt certain they did—or if they simply agreed politely with whomever her brother chose. Anyway, they didn't object, so the polling was as good as done. Sao returned to Rangoon a full-fledged Member of Parliament.

On June 13 Sao joined a stream of new faces entering the parliament building. She sat as an independent. Forty-eight of the new members belonged to the National Unity Front, the largest single opposition the government had ever faced.

The Freedom League and its allies still filled up an entire side of the parliament and more, with 182 seats altogether. Used to almost no opposition at all, though, they were in a deep stew about their future. U Nu had already stepped down, saying he would take one year away from the prime ministership to "clean up" the League. It was the second time he'd made such a promise.

The first day of parliament was given over to procedure and ceremony. Sao and the other new members sat quietly, not knowing what to say. U Nu's Deputy Prime Minister, Ba Shwe, was made Prime Minister. He was leader of the Socialist Party, the League's strongest member. The Socialist Party had come a long way from the days when they'd all resigned; now, they held the most power within the Freedom League coalition. When the twenty-eight cabinet members were introduced that day, eleven were socialists.

In its opening address, the new government stated its dedication to "independent neutrality" in world affairs. Meanwhile, in the upper house Chamber of Nationalities, Sao's husband was elected Speaker for a second term.

Parliament's main order of business that session was presentation of the financial estimates. Sao's lap became a nesting-place for sheets of paper, down which marched long columns of revenues and expenditures. She bent her head over the papers while the finance minister droned a dismal, all too familiar speech about the country's poor financial prospects.

From morning till afternoon Sao listened gravely to the ministers, slowly bubbling with ideas, complaints and arguments that remained unspoken. She attended every session, for which she earned a daily allowance of twenty Kyat—about one English pound and fifty pence. She also received a monthly salary of three hundred Kyat, or twenty-three pounds.

As an MP, Sao was automatically a member of the Shan State Council, which held regular meetings in Taunggyi. The small city was no longer a rugged frontier town. The road from Rangoon was surfaced all the way, and the train now reached its terminus there. Fine gated homes clung to the hill-crest and a new state capital building sat near the old British Residency. It was here that the men of Shan State took their places along rows of wooded bench-desks to debate their future. Sao took a seat among them, no longer just a kitchen boss in a borrowed sari.

The constitution and how to deal with Rangoon was uppermost in their discussions. Sao quickly realised they'd been too naive in the initial negotiations. They'd been told not to sweat the details, that problems could be fixed after the document was approved. Then the rebellion broke out and the constitution was set aside while the government dealt with the emergency. They never did get to tinker with the fine points. The one major change was the inclusion of a Karen State in 1955, but the new state was brought in under the same old faulty framework. With too much power centred in Rangoon, many Karen people remained unhappy with joining the Union and continued their underground agitation.

Constitutional jargon befuddled Sao as much as anyone. She suspected they were being short-changed. She thought the Shan politicians' major failing was that they were too agreeable.

She suggested they hire some lawyers and even offered to pay the costs herself. No one took her up on the idea.

Returning to Rangoon, the lively debate continued in her parlour. Tzang had graduated from the English Methodist High School and joined his brother on campus. Their classmates made themselves at home at 74 Kokine Road, engaging in fiery discussions with the monks, scholars and politicians who dropped by. All kinds of topics were raised but the talk always made its way back to the constitution.

Most of Shan State's promised jurisdictional powers remained under Rangoon's control. Burma should be a state just like the other states, the students argued. Luckily, the constitution provided the right to separate after ten years. Amazingly, eight of those years had already passed. In two years' time, they could consider leaving the Union.

Sao revelled in the heady parlour atmosphere. Her new house was becoming a small hot-bed. Good, she thought. We've all been too quiet for too long. It's time to make noise.

An Invitation

Sao's activism didn't come easily. Seated among tight-packed rows of parliamentarians, she was acutely aware that she had entered a man's world. There were only a handful of other women members, all Freedom League supporters. They sat across from Sao among a sea of male faces and never said a word.

Her fellow Shan State politicians weren't very vocal, either. Of the twenty-five honourable Shan members, just two belonged to opposition parties, while thirteen were allied with the ruling Freedom League through the Hill People's Union. Ten members, including Sao, were independents, many of whom looked unsure of themselves in their new surroundings.

There were a few more experienced types among them, like Jimmy Yang from Kokang. Sao observed, though, that if Jimmy put his Rangoon experience to work, it wasn't in the cause of promoting political debate. He arrived every day wearing a confident smile and a stylish suit jacket, but once seated he seldom rose again to speak.

Sao, on the other hand, couldn't bear to remain silent. When an Arakanese member complained about the Saophas, she simmered: What do they know about Shan State? When a Freedom Leaguer complained about a robber baron who attacked government forces near Ton-huung village, she boiled over.

"Why not? The Burmese have been robbing us for years," she snapped.

The house came down: ethnic members erupted in laughter and some broke into spontaneous cheers and applause. Until now, their bitterness had been politely hidden.

Afterwards, though, not one Shan MP congratulated Sao. She learned it wasn't fitting for a man to agree openly with a woman even if she was an MP. They treated her politely but never as an equal. She didn't care. If they agreed with her in private, that was good enough. She didn't need public praise.

There were some advantages to being a mere woman from the hills, though. She could safely mask sharp criticisms behind feigned ignorance. "Excuse my poor Burmese. Did I understand the Honourable Member correctly?" she would ask sweetly, before launching into a devastating summary of his remarks. If she perceived an injustice, she spoke, never fearing consequences. She believed herself immune from the charges of "sedition" and "treason" that landed others in jail. Many of the growing population of political prisoners were former Freedom League insiders who had a falling out with their own people. Sao reasoned that such arrests were the result of squabbles among the Burmese that had nothing to do with her. They wouldn't dare go after a Tai Mahadevi.

Indeed, since independence, the jail cells remained just as busy as under the British, perhaps more so. The jailers had changed but activities deemed seditious remained a crime.

Among the incarcerated were a good number of soldiers and politicians associated with the past, a situation brought to light when the Mountbattens visited that year.

Sao was seated near Lady Edwina at the state dinner. The Mountbattens were both in bubbling high spirits. Lord Louis had just been invested with the country's noblest title: Agga Maha Thiri Thu Dhamma—Highest and Most Glorious Commander of the Exalted Order of Truth. It was just the sort of "native" honour that tickled him pink. Glad to be back in their old stomping grounds, the couple glowed with excitement.

Sao liked Edwina Mountbatten better than Lord Louis. Although just as talkative as her husband, she refrained from dispensing advice and opinions. Instead she asked about various war veterans the couple had known.

Impressed by the Lady's memory and kindness, Sao answered truthfully: "Most of them are in prison."

She felt a sudden silence around them, forks and glasses paused half way to mouths. Lady Mountbatten flushed slightly, but hardly missed a beat. "I should go visit them," she said firmly.

For a moment, Sao considered taking up the challenge. She would love to take Lady Mountbatten to see the missing men. But such things were impossible, she knew.

"It wouldn't do. They won't even admit they are there," she said quietly.

She noticed U Nu staring at them. He'd overheard. What did she care? The man was in temporary retirement. Nobody frightened her, not even General Ne Win—he was just a young fellow who used to cadge pocket money at the Race Course, pleasant in a good-looking-but-vacuous sort of way, not really a threat.

Thus Sao carried on her political life, blithely speaking the truth and attacking perceived injustices. In doing so, she tapped into a sea change of political opinion. The days of tightly-controlled diplomacy were fading.

In December, 1956, 150 Saophas and peoples' representatives came together for a meeting of the Shan State Organisation. It was held in Mong Yai, where the British had first convened the Celestial Lords—including Sao's father—after the conquest of 1887.

At the modern-day meeting, people spoke bitterly about the unfairness of the Union government. They were tired of budget cuts and wanted a share of the Japanese war reparations money. After all, Shan State had suffered the greatest damage during the air campaign.

They also wanted to know what happened to the Namtu-Badwin Mine revenues. Since independence, the portion paid to Shan State had disappeared. In colonial times, the British took Shan minerals but at least they handed over a set portion of the profits. Under the Union, the region's natural prosperity was in freefall. The delegates also raised rumours about a Rangoon-hatched plan to donate Shan land for the settlement of displaced European Jews. Not Burmese land, mind you—Shan land.

It wasn't the donation itself that rankled people, it was Burma's assumption of sovereignty over their territory.

The talk swirled onward like a monsoon-filled river. Grievances burst open in thunder-clouds. The meeting closed with a call for secession from the Union of Burma at the end of the constitution's ten-year grace period, just two years hence. Suddenly, the Union of Burma was close to breaking up.

By year's end, Sao could look back on a time of surprising personal change. In the past she felt stifled, lacking any useful role beyond managing the household servants and hosting gossipy tea parties. Now she had a new home and a political career. Best of all, her querulous, traditionalist politics seemed to have found great resonance with the ordinary folk of her home state.

It was as if they had all emerged from the same cocoon together.

On February 7—the anniversary of the Panglong Agreement's signing—a mass rally was held in support of the Celestial Lords' hereditary rights. At the rally, speakers decried the abolishment of princely powers as an interference in Shan affairs.

A committed modernist, Prince Shwe Thaike ignored the protests and continued his efforts to transfer the Saopha's royal powers to the state. Sao felt the people were right and her husband was wrong. Changing the deep traditions of the hill country would create social chaos, she believed.

"Only the Saophas know how to run things properly," she told her husband.

He listened, but had different ideas about what the pro-Saopha movement was all about. He told her the protesters were really concerned about autonomy, not about who sat on the golden divan. The Saophas were just symbols.

For the most part, though, Prince Shwe Thaike tried to remain disengaged from the political dialogue. While people rallied in Shan State, he busied himself with arrangements for the monk Webu Sayadaw's annual visit to Rangoon. He also engaged scholars and linguists for his scriptures translation project.

But people in the know about Burmese politics recognised that Sao's husband maintained an underlying political currency. He was the one who brought the hill people into the Union and he was the one who could take them out.

In particular, the Chinese embassy officials never discounted Prince Shwe Thaike's importance. They always made sure the Prince and his Mahadevi were on the guest list when Premier Zhou came to Rangoon. The Chinese premier's visits had become an annual affair. By the third visit, in December 1956, Sao felt she knew him perhaps the best among Asia's leaders.

When Sao and the Prince arrived at the Marble Hall for the ubiquitous state dinner, Premier Zhou greeted them like old friends. As always, he was dressed in a silver-grey Mao suit, simple but impeccably fitted. One could hardly imagine him as a guerrilla fighter in the People's Army. He was an elegant figure, tall and square-shouldered, with a thick shock of dark hair combed neatly back from his forehead.

The speeches and toasts were as comradely as ever. Premier Zhou promised China would never engage in "big power chauvinism". Underneath the good will, though, a chill was developing between the two countries. There were frequent reports of Burmese communist rebels crossing into China for refuge and support. As well, three northern Kachin villages had been annexed by China; Kachin students at Rangoon University staged a silent protest during the Premier's visit.

Shortly after Zhou's visit, the Prince received an official invitation from Premier Zhou and Chairman Mao Zedong to tour the new China as their personal guests. The whole family was invited. Sao and her husband pondered the invitation at length.

What did it mean? They were being courted, obviously, but the reason remained unclear. Maybe it was just a public relations gesture. Or perhaps if Burma's political state worsened, China hoped to gain a prominent exile in the prince.

"The Americans won't be happy. They already say we're too friendly with the Chinese," Sao said. She was trying to be prudent.

Her husband frowned briefly. Then his face brightened.

"Let's show them how communist we are. Let's go!" he said, and they both laughed.

The children, especially the older ones, could hardly believe their luck when they heard the news. Tzang was especially excited, having fallen head over heels for politics in his first year of university. He had read a few Marxist books and Edgar Snow's Red Star Over China. His classmates talked about communes and barefoot doctors but none of them had seen such things first hand. He would be the envy of the other student radicals.

He had medical clearance to fly, too. A doctor had finally diagnosed his heart problem as something called patent ductus arteriousus, PDA, an anomalous connection between the "in" vein and "out" artery of his heart which allowed the blood to mix. It was a worrisome condition, but, unlike a hole in the heart, not one affected by air pressure.

Sao was as excited as Tzang. The closest she'd been to China was when she went to see the bomb crater before the war. She remembered looking across the valley toward a spine of hills. Beyond a winding river was the other half of the Tai world. She could name the towns and villages on the Chinese side from a lifetime of hearing stories about aunties, uncles and cousins thrice-removed who lived there. Now she was about to see the hidden land with her own eyes. They started packing.

Two Emperors

Less than an hour after take-off from Mingaladon Airport, the Yawnghwe family soared over the north-eastern peaks of Shan State. Below them the broad river valleys of Kengtung state gradually folded into a tight knot of thickly forested hills. There was neither town nor road, only scattered plumes of smoke from tribal villages and jungle encampments, and the scar of a KMT airstrip on a steep hillside. When the hills gave way to a broad plain of paddy fields, Sao realised they had passed into China's Yunnan province. The green table-top landscape was the fabled Tai enclave, Sip Song Panna, cut off from the world by a circle of sub-tropical mountains.

The plane droned north above the narrow ribbon of the Burma Road, then banked over West Lake toward the city of Kunming. Sao felt a thrill of recognition. Kunming was the ancient Tai capital, named Talifu in the old palm-leaf documents tucked away in Hsenwi's monastery. Here the Tai king distributed his royal seals to his princes and gave them leave to establish southern kingdoms. That is why the formal title for Mahadevi contained the words "Lady of the Seal". The Hsenwi seal was so old that for a time Sao's family had forgotten what it was, until some relatives from Yunnan identified it. In those days, Sao remembered, Yunnan still seemed part of their world, even though the British had given it away to China. Had she made this trip in her mother's time, they would have travelled leisurely on horseback from one village to the next, stopping to meet scattered relatives and swap family stories over salads of pickled tea and banana flowers.

If she imagined such a homecoming on this trip, Sao was far wrong. At the airport a flock of Chinese guides and translators awaited them. A man who identified himself as Chairman Mao's personal secretary stepped forward.

"You may go anywhere you like, see anything you wish," he promised. "You don't have to ask our permission."

This being said, the family was immediately whisked away by car, not toward the city but into the countryside. On the way they passed by large red banners with Chinese characters.

"Let a hundred flowers blossom, let a hundred schools of thought contend," the secretary translated. China had just launched a campaign to encourage free criticism of wrong-headed policies, he explained. In China, no one had to fear speaking freely.

The guest mansion was a beautiful old place at the edge of a small town, some distance from Kunming itself and set in a walled garden with a heavy wooden gate. On the first day, Tiger, Tzang and Ying Sita watched over the younger children as they played idly in the garden. Then they found a small side gate that opened onto a road leading into the town. So far the children had seen almost nothing of China, just an airport, the inside of a car and a garden. Together they set off down the road to explore the town. They walked almost a half mile before a gang of interpreters and guides caught up to them.

"Oh, it would be better for you to come back," they said in a chorus, herding the kids back toward the walled villa.

That was the last of the family's free time in China. There were banquets and tours, followed by more banquets and tours. In Chengdu they met farm families and saw the small plots they'd been given through land reform. The farmers they met had clean clothes, kettles, pigs, and rice to eat. It wasn't much, the guides said, but it was better than before. Sao couldn't dispute this. China had moved beyond the old newsreel images of stick-thin landless peasants, driven to the cities to beg and sell their daughters. Collective farming hadn't reached these parts yet and there was no visible warning of 1957's coming agricultural disaster.

In Chongching the family boarded a river steamer which was to take them down the great Yangtze River from the highlands of central China to the coastal plain. For the next several days, being stuck on a boat, they enjoyed the tour's only relaxing moments. The Chinese landscape slowly unrolled before them like a silk scroll painting as they floated past grey-silted riverbanks that gradually rose into tall, misty crags. Entering the first of the Three Gorges, the steamer passed between jagged, copper-coloured cliffs that soared 3,000 feet into thick mist, until the sky became just a pale sliver of light between the cloud-topped summits. Gnarled pines clung to the cliff-sides and the river's roar filled the family's astonished ears.

After the Gorges, the river carried them more sedately toward Wuhan, where they toured a tea plantation and watched large machines clear silt from the water. Then they re-boarded the steamer and travelled on to Nanjing, the war-time capital. At a former millionaire's mansion transformed into a Children's Palace, Chinese youngsters knotted Young Pioneer scarves around the necks of Sao's children. "Welcome," they chimed. In a Chinese jacket and red scarf, little Harn looked just like one of the local youngsters. Afterwards, one of the family's interpreter-guards mistakenly tried to shoo him away from the car. He burst into tears.

From Nanjing they carried on to Suzhou and Shanghai, then turned north to Xian, finally arriving in Beijing after a journey of many thousands of miles. Here the banquets and meetings intensified. Over the next several days, Premier Zhou introduced them to all the top leaders, including Marshal Zhu De, First Vice-Chairman Liu Xiaoqi and Defence Minister Marshal Peng Dehuai. These days the three Chinese leaders were engaged in a delicate stand-off with their unpredictable, left-leaning Party Chairman, Mao Zedong, who was pushing China towards the disastrous Great Leap Forward. At the banquet table, though, the rigours of internal battles were kept well hidden from Sao and her husband.

Finally the day came when a gleaming Red Flag limousine arrived to take them to an audience with Chairman Mao himself. He met them in a pavilion of the Summer Palace, at the foot of

Longevity Hill far from Beijing's centre. Sao could hardly believe that the simple-looking middle-aged man was China's leader. His clothes were rumpled and he seemed unaware who they were. Only the deferential, anxious looks of his entourage revealed the man's status. After a few words with the interpreter, the Chairman took a seat with the family and pronounced, "You look just like Chinese." Then, to Sao's surprise, he began to talk informatively about Tai history. The Chinese are like that, she thought to herself. They don't tell the world, but they know a lot.

The Chairman smoked incessantly and drank dark-coloured tea throughout the hour-long meeting. His smile revealed a row of blackened teeth.

"Think of this visit as a homecoming," he said. "There are 200 million Tai people in China." Sao was amazed, for they numbered just 1.5 million in all of Shan State in 1957. She had seen with her own eyes China's vastness; was it was conceivable that so many could be tucked away in mountain pockets throughout the land? It also occurred to her that Mao regarded the Tai as essentially Chinese, sharing the same ancestors despite some 1,900 years of separation. He saw one big pan-Asian family, not separate peoples. He told them they must visit Mongolia, to see where the Tai were said to have begun their centuries-long southward migration.

Sao said little during the meeting, leaving her husband to voice the appropriate words. The Prince told Chairman Mao he was impressed by the factories and farms they'd seen, given the terrible conditions from which the country had risen.

"You've accomplished a great deal in a short time, with so little suffering," he said.

The Chairman smiled, looked down, and, attempting humility, answered, "Oh, no, it wasn't so easy. We had to kill about five or six million people to get this far." Then he signed autographs for the children and took his leave.

The family remained in Beijing for the annual May Day celebrations. From a VIP enclosure they watched phalanxes of soldiers, schoolchildren, and workers' representatives fill Tiananmen Square. The marchers waved banners and saluted Chairman Mao. He looked like a tiny, remote god standing above the gate of the Forbidden City, nothing like the rumpled, friendly figure they'd met in the pavilion.

Afterwards, the family continued north because even before their conversation with the Chairman had ended, arrangements were being made for a trip to Inner Mongolia. Once again Chairman Mao's secretary told them they could see anything they liked along the way. This time, Prince Shwe Thaike decided to test the promise. He asked to visit the last Emperor of China, Pu Yi, in prison. The secretary, not batting an eye, said the arrangements would be made.

They left Beijing by train, travelling beyond the Great Wall into the harsh Manchurian landscape. The first stop was the Port Arthur naval base, on a narrow point of land jutting into the Bohai Sea. Amazingly, they were given a tour of a new top-secret submarine.

Back on the train, their guide reiterated the sentiment that they were all friends, with nothing to hide from one another.

At Mukden they disembarked and travelled by car the short distance to Fushun prison, where Emperor Pu Yi was held. The place had high walls and watch-towers but inside there were decent-looking buildings and a large exercise yard where smiling guards mingled with the prisoners, mostly men associated with the wartime Japanese occupiers. They were there to be "re-educated".

In the prison's sparsely-furnished reception room, a delicate, bespectacled man with doe-like eyes awaited them. The Emperor Pu Yi looked rather nervous. For their part, Sao and her husband were unsure what to ask or say in the presence of Pu Yi's guards. Their meeting was brief and awkward, amounting to no more than an exchange of respectful pleasantries. Pu Yi said he was being reformed and would soon be taken on a tour of the "new" China. Small-talk exhausted, they smiled at one another some more, and then Sao and her family said goodbye.

From Manchuria they crossed into Mongolia's eastern mountains, where they were introduced to some people said to be members of the original Tai clans. Sao was disappointed. She tried a few simple sentences in her native tongue but it was clear their languages were mutually unintelligible. The only phrase they understood was "ride horse", and that only because it was pronounced the same in Tai as in Mandarin Chinese, which they also spoke.

After nearly one month of frenetic travel, the family backtracked to Beijing and boarded a plane for Rangoon. They had seen a tremendous amount of China in a short time. On the journey home, Sao thought about Emperor Pu Yi, about to embark on his own guided tour. What would he think of the new world beyond his prison walls? She guessed the last Emperor's life in jail wasn't so different from his days inside the Forbidden City, where Chairman Mao now lived. In her musings, though, she never once considered that Pu Yi's fate might mirror her own future, as Asia passed from feudal god-kings to the rule of ideology. In fact years later when someone raised this question, she was insulted and surprised.

"That was China," she said. "It had nothing to do with us."

The Big Split

Although poor, China appeared stable, Sao thought; the people seemed to share a common purpose. In contrast Burma was foundering, its far-flung states at constant loggerheads with the central government. They arrived home in mid-May just as a second Mong Yai conference was getting under way. Delegates to the meeting resolved that "Shan State people must [be] united in blood and soul." From now on, only Shan people would lead Shan affairs, they vowed. A short time later, a group of university students held a seminar at Rangoon City Hall to discuss a thesis titled *Shan State Grievances*.

The Shan State Council convened in Taunggyi for the latter part of 1957 and into the new year. For their extended stays in the Shan capital, Sao and her husband purchased a modest wooden house, painted green, on a quiet sidestreet.

The 1957-58 Council session concentrated on finalising the transfer of feudal powers. In the end, the Saophas decided to make a clever end-run around the Union government: they conferred their powers on Shan State, not Rangoon. Under the proposed agreement the Saophas would give up their nine-gun salutes—which always rankled the Burmese, Sao's husband noted—but would keep their Haws and royal titles. Over the next year, public properties such as schools and hospitals were to be inventoried and handed over to the Shan government. In exchange for taxation rights, also given over to Taunggyi, the Saophas asked for a compensation package and pension fixed according to their previous incomes. In Prince Shwe Thaike's case, the amount included lost land and forest revenue. The buy-out packages for the Saophas would total, in the end, two million British pounds, paid from the federal budget.

In the midst of the hand-over discussions, Burma's tenth anniversary passed. There was little for Unionist politicians to celebrate. As of January 4, Chapter Ten of the Union Constitution—"The Right to Secede"—allowed every state to hold a separation plebiscite if it so chose. Burma's survival had never been so tenuous.

Before any serious discussion on the matter was undertaken, the Shan State Council session came to an end. Thus the 1958 deadline arrived on a tide of general unrest with no plan of action.

In the meantime, U Nu returned from his hiatus to resume leadership of a swiftly unravelling government. His campaign to "clean up" the Freedom League had been hugely unsuccessful. The leaders of Burma had simply been too long together in the fight. Young no more, their idealism and patience for one another had worn down to nothing. Minor disagreements regularly blossomed into major catastrophes. Even their wives, who sat on various committees together, were constantly at one another's throats. Years ago, under the spell of nation-building, petty disagreements meant little. Now they meant everything.

U Nu was desperate. In February he had the opportunity to address 100,000 members at a League National Congress. He spoke for four hours without pause, dedicating the party to the principles of democratic socialism, Buddhism and anti-communism. In a world torn between left and right, he preached the Middle Way.

The delegates endorsed his speech. It looked like he had helped them all turn a corner. U Nu prayed that the ill will had been healed and the League would hold together. But by April the party was officially split, almost exactly down the middle. The Deputy PM, U Ba Shwe, declared his leftist camp in opposition, leaving U Nu within a few votes of losing his government. True to form, the final straw was a relatively minor matter, a petty conflict over the appointment of a party secretary.

After the split neither faction was willing to give up the Anti-Fascist People's Freedom League (AFPFL) moniker. Instead they chose adjectives to distinguish themselves from each other. U Nu's faction became the "Clean" AFPFL. The other half called themselves the "Stable" AFPFL.

Neither side warranted the nicknames. Over the next several months the newspapers overflowed with charges and countercharges of corruption and scandal. The names "Clean" and "Stable" became a farce. Eager to find out which imploding faction would survive, people began counting the days to an early election, scheduled in November.

Under the circumstances, no one was very focused on the lingering constitutional problems, including the Shan Saophas, who were engrossed in negotiations for their compensation packages.

Into the vacuum stepped a young orator named Saw Yanda, claiming to be the illegitimate son of a Yunnan prince. If politicians were unwilling to act, he said, then a separation plebiscite must be brought about through force of arms.

Like Teacher San of the 1930s, Saw Yanda made a camp in the jungle. Tucked between the Salween River and the Thai border in the remote township of Mong Ton, it wasn't easy to reach. Nonetheless, a few hundred patriotic young Tai made the journey, drawn by Saw Yanda's charisma and tales of American-supplied weapons. They heard there were crates of brand-new carbines and machine guns waiting to be opened, and that tanks and aeroplanes were kept across the Thai border in secret warehouses. Following such rumours might have seemed naive, but the Tai still couldn't accept that the outside world had abandoned Shan State to the Burmese. The alliances made with British and American forces during World War II constituted a pact of loyalty, they thought. It seemed absolutely plausible, indeed expected, that help had arrived.

On May 21—thereafter knows as Shan Resistance Day—Saw Yanda announced the foundation of the Noom Suk Harn, the Brave Young Warriors. He had a flag, an eight-pointed star above a crossed sword and spear, but there were no new carbines or tanks.

Undaunted, the young men marched north through a range of steep ridges, carrying a variety of weapons cobbled together from here and there. Just south of Kengtung they attacked some Burma Army units. As news of the fighting spread, people across Shan State formed small bands to attack local army units. No one led the village bands; they each acted independently, carving out small territories in the mountains and forests.

From her home in Rangoon, Sao watched the development of armed rebellion in Shan State with great interest. Her husband and the other Saophas vowed to stand back from the events, neither encouraging nor discouraging the Warriors. After all, they said, they had no power to intervene. They had given up their feudal powers in spirit, even if the document wasn't signed yet.

The household at 74 Kokine Road was also in a state of flux that year. To begin with, fourteen-year-old Haymar was sent to Yawnghwe Haw to live with her biological mother and younger brother, Stanley. Shortly after, a beautiful Yunnan refugee arrived at the house and threw herself on their mercy. She was the daughter of a distant cousin, married to a Chinese general who had disappeared to Taiwan, leaving her destitute with two daughters to feed. At first Sao feared her husband would take the woman as a minor wife. Instead, he agreed to adopt one of her children. There was no formal procedure. Htilar simply moved in and began calling the other children brother and sister. Sao accepted the arrangement gladly thinking: better the daughter than the mother.

There were changes in store for Tiger, as well. Like his mother, Tiger had no talent for the Burmese language. He was on the verge of flunking out of Rangoon University. Sao and the Prince agreed he should continue his studies abroad. He enrolled in the Bell School of Languages at Cambridge for the fall term. His classmates would include many other prominent foreigners who hoped to gain a foothold in England's elite colleges, including a Laotian princess and Kaiser Wilhelm II's grandsons, Michael and Frederick of Prussia. Tiger wouldn't be alone in England: his two elder half-siblings, Hseng and Sanda, attended Pembrook and Girton.

The shifting of children here and there was an established pattern of family life, a way to maintain harmony between wives and equal opportunities among the children. The kids themselves adjusted quickly to whatever arrangements were set. To them, the large, scattered family was a single unit—one dad, three moms, eleven kids, now twelve counting Htilar—not at all complicated.

On June 8, parliament convened and Sao returned to her familiar seat among the Shan State members. Looking around the room, she saw that the Freedom League faces were the same but now they were divided into two opposing camps. Prime Minister U Nu held the majority by just eight votes.

To keep its majority intact, U Nu's Clean AFPFL faction now kowtowed to the Burma Workers and Peasants Party members, who wanted amnesty for the some 10,000-15,000 communist rebels who remained underground. To maintain power the PM had to deliver the amnesty despite opposition from General Ne Win and the Burma Army. From the army's standpoint, amnesty would give the rebels the balance of power within a badly split parliament.

When Sao and her fellow parliamentarians studied the budgetary estimates that June, the future looked bleak. Drought and floods had reduced potential rice exports, world mineral prices were depressed and, with the PM and his top general squared off over the amnesty issue, political uncertainties had triggered a general economic malaise.

On August 1, U Nu pushed through the amnesty order. Two weeks later, on August 15, rebels connected with the old post-war People's Voluntary Organisation established an above-ground political party, the People's Comrades Party. Rebels under the Communist Party of Burma elected to stay underground and continue their armed insurrection.

General Ne Win's movie-star smile disappeared overnight. This was his worst-case scenario: rebels in parliament and rebels still in the field.

Sao found the whole business a confusing, distasteful mess. Whether they called themselves the Workers and Peasants, the People's Comrades, the Communist Party or, for that matter, the Burma Army, they were all communists of one stripe or another, she decided. Their bickering was pointless.

She carried on blithely, speaking as she pleased, consequences be damned. She kept on talking even when the Kengtung Saopha's brother, a prominent war veteran, was arrested for criticising the government. Lately, though, her second son Tzang had begun questioning her hitherto-unchallenged pronouncements. With a year of university under his belt, he liked to apply "political analysis" to the bumpy situation. Unbidden, he began speaking up during discussions in the parlour and around the dinner table. "Exercise some strategy," he said. "Play the factions to your advantage."

"Why not exercise some respect for your elders," Sao responded sharply.

Then Sao's own body sounded a warning not so easily brushed off. One day she noticed a milky fluid oozing from her breast. A few days later her doctor found a lump. Proper diagnosis and treatment could not be had in Rangoon. However, a referral abroad was no simple matter. A panel of experts had to meet and review the case.

Sao pushed the worry from her mind. There was nothing to do but wait and trust in fate.

At the end of August, Tiger left for England. In September, Prime Minister U Nu travelled north to Mandalay, where he was welcomed by a large pro-Clean contingent of the Union Military Police. Their leader vowed to protect the prime ministership no matter what happened. General Ne Win and the Burma Army—now solidly behind the opposition Stable faction—watched the developments with rising concern.

Near September's end, U Nu announced he would return to Rangoon not to lead, but to dissolve the government and retire to a life of meditation once and for all. But when he left Mandalay on September 22, his supporters, the pro-Clean police units, also began moving toward the capital.

Inside the city, people carried on their daily lives. Parlour discussions focused on the communist insurgency in the north. The circling of General Ne Win's troops around Rangoon was hardly noticed. Everyone expected the problems between the PM and the General to blow over, or to be settled at the ballot box.

Thus, when Sao received word that the medical panel had granted a referral to a London specialist, her husband decided to accompany her; it was a good opportunity to check on the older children and visit their growing colony of relatives in England. As their plane lifted from the runway at Mingaladon International with a roar, Sao peered down at her breast and thought about the lump. When she finally looked out the window they were already well away from Burma, over the open sea.

"Let Us Wash Our City with Our Sweat"

Thankfully, the lump was pronounced benign. Sao could now admit to herself how truly worried she'd been. At age forty-three, she finally felt as vulnerable as the next person. The impact was profound; for the rest of her days she imagined cancerous lumps inside her body and made frequent trips to the doctor.

Released from hospital, she found London much improved from her previous visit. Its streets were crammed with cars. People carried full shopping bags; bright smiles replaced the pinched, hungry look of eleven years past. At Cambridge they found Tiger in his element, speaking clipped, fluent English with his high-toned classmates. His studies were going well and he was looking forward to choosing a college and a major, perhaps political studies. His father suggested geological engineering. Shan State needed mining experts to manage the considerable mineral resources which still lay beneath the soil.

Sao felt relaxed in England. If there was one thing she missed, it was news of home. She felt like a wall had closed behind them when they flew out of Rangoon. When they had time to listen to the radio or read newspapers, there was no mention of home. Then one day Sao saw the word "Burma" in the headline of a socialist newspaper. She picked up the thin, crinkly paper and greedily read the story. That is how she learned about the coup d'état.

According to further news reports, the transfer of power to General Ne Win was peaceful. No bloodshed. Without a sense of urgency, Sao and her husband made their way home slowly, via Moscow and Beijing.

Within days of their return to Rangoon, the Kokine Road house was full of guests eager to talk about the coup. Sao listened, astounded by how swiftly the political landscape had deteriorated as she and her husband flew toward London.

Their Rangoon friends were astounded, too. They'd had no hint of the behind-the-scenes drama. The day U Nu arrived from Mandalay, the newspapers described him as "radiant and elated", ready to contest the election after a "triumphant" northern tour.

Then a few days later he made a radio broadcast to the nation. The November elections were postponed till April, he said. In the meantime, he was turning the government over to General Ne Win.

Everyone was stunned. He hadn't even discussed the matter with his cabinet. He just did it.

Why? It seemed that while people carried on their daily lives, a serious situation had developed right outside the capital. General Ne Win's men formed a circle around Rangoon, and they were in turn encircled by the pro-U Nu police units arriving from Mandalay. At the same time, the Karen rebels—who continued their fight, despite statehood—moved their headquarters to within nine miles of the capital.

Refugees began filtering in from the surrounding countryside, but their numbers were small. Few city-dwellers took alarm.

In the end, the situation was diffused behind closed doors. For now, General Ne Win would act as prime minister of a "caretaker" government.

No one was sure of Prime Minister U Nu's motives. Perhaps he wanted the army to save them from a potential communist victory at the ballot box. Perhaps the General threatened him with an armed takeover. The following morning people asked each other: Was it a coup or not? During the broadcast the ex-PM's voice sounded weary and defeated. Using this as a basis, the Rangoon press announced it was indeed a coup d'état.

On October 28, a special parliamentary session was convened to make the handover official. U Nu stated he would give up all his personal belongings so that he might leave office as poor as when he entered.

"Well, his wife is rich, so he won't suffer long," Sao snorted. The parlour denizens laughed. In the brightness of the sitting room, the coup, if one could call it that, seemed not very serious. General Ne Win had already stated the army had no interest in politics. Life would return to normal with the April election.

There was one last piece of news: General Ne Win had placed Sao's brother, Prince Hom Hpa, in charge of all of Shan State. A reward for loyalty, Sao guessed.

She seemed fated to be under her brother's thumb: ruled over in childhood, sold in marriage to his friend, and now, just as she was coming into her own, made his political subordinate.

In the first month of the caretaker government, General Ne Win concentrated on "cleaning up" Rangoon. On November 28, he replaced the Mayor with Colonel Tun Sein, who vowed he would personally sweep the streets if Ne Win asked. Then the Colonel fired 3,000 city workers, prompting people to wonder if he would have to make good his promise.

Instead, Colonel Tun Sein ordered an army of volunteers—citizens, soldiers and civil servants—to haul garbage, sweep streets and clean sewers every Sunday. He even came up with a slogan to inspire their labours: "Let us wash our city with our sweat."

Everything unsightly was ordered eliminated: stray dogs, cats, crows, betel stands, pony carts, street stalls, and, finally, entire neighbourhoods. As the army moved in on their impoverished shacks, 160,000 slum dwellers—nearly a third of the population—were forced to the outskirts of town. The new "suburbs" set aside for them, North and South Okkalapa, were little more than empty, unserviced fields. There the slum dwellers were left to rebuild their lives without tools, materials or sufficient funds. Their new constructions were as poor and ramshackle as the old, but now they were hidden from public view.

The Colonel then went after small business owners. Property owners were forced to make costly renovations. The police launched a series of raids on warehouses and shops, demanding proof of ownership of the contents. Those found guilty of "improprieties" were mainly Chinese and Indian merchants, many of whom were summarily deported.

For the first time since the war, the streets of Rangoon were noticeably clean and free of squatters and refugees, but the army's fervour was alarming. There was a rumour that lipstick and short-sleeve blouses were next on the banning list.

Political deviants were also high on the roster of undesirable elements. General Ne Win rounded up student radicals and sent them to a detention centre on Cocos Island. Sao and the Prince began to worry about Tzang's campus politicking, especially after several of his classmates disappeared into the jungle to join the Brave Young Warriors. Tzang, now twenty years old, began staying on campus late into the evening. Sao seldom saw him and when she did, there was no talking to the young hot-head. Lately, all their conversations ended in argument.

Tzang told Sao he was trying to unite all the ethnic student associations into one organisation. He warned that the army presented a great danger to civil society. Its reach extended into all areas of Burmese life, he said.

Indeed, in the past few months it had become readily apparent that the General had spent his years quietly building a web of institutions: the Defence Services Institute, which had far-ranging business investments; the politically-motivated National Solidarity Association, with numerous local branches; the dreaded information-gathering Military Intelligence Service; the Psychological Warfare Department, the General's pet project and; his latest progeny, the National Defence College. The various military institutions were united under the old slogan "One Blood, One Voice, One Command". The slogan didn't bode well for ethnic federalists, Tzang pointed out.

Sao disagreed with her son's alarmist tone. Parliament was still in control, she maintained. The constitution allowed Ne Win, as a non-MP, to serve as Prime Minister no more than six months. She had no fear of a mere playboy and race course rail-bird. She doubted he had any ambition at all, never mind political ambition. If they could use him, fine.

She held to this opinion even in February, when a special session was called to extend the General's six-month term.

Both the lower and upper houses were called to the meeting. In a room filled to overflowing, the General made his arguments. The country was not yet secure. He could not under the circumstances recommend an election, at least for another year. He needed more time to set things right. The ruling Clean faction supported his request, he noted. Now he needed both houses to approve the appropriate constitutional amendment, allowing an extension of the six-month term.

Sao could only guess why U Nu's people went along with the General. If they agreed to postpone the election, they must fear the results. Perhaps it wasn't communists they worried about, but General Ne Win himself. He could run the Stable faction against them and win the balance of power legitimately.

As for the other members, many no doubt considered it a dangerous act to defeat the government with a vote against Ne Win. They would then have to dissolve parliament and, at the moment, parliament was the only thing standing between democracy and a military junta.

Sao's reasoning was more elementary. "Somebody's got to bell the cat," she said to herself, before casting her vote for Ne Win.

Everyone but the most ardent ultra-left members did the same. That very evening, February 27, 1959, the General was sworn in for the second time, with the proviso that elections be held no later than April, 1960.

Power secured, General Ne Win extended his "clean-up" beyond Rangoon into the country's farthest reaches, launching full-scale military offensives throughout the country. The main targets of the "Bandit Suppression Campaign", as he dubbed it, were 4,000 communist insurgents, 4,000 Karen rebels, some 1,400 to 1,500 KMT and no less than 6,000 to 7,000 civilian "sympathisers". He recruited paid informants called Peoples' Reporters to find the sympathisers.

Despite their comparatively small number, the few hundred Tai rebels didn't escape the full wrath of the General's campaign. When the Brave Young Warriors crossed the Salween and captured Tangyan town, airforce jets strafed their positions. The young rebels' week-long defence became legend, touching off more small rebellions throughout the state. Even Prince Hom Hpa's driver ran away and became commander of a rebel band.

In parliament, Sao no longer spent her days peering at budget estimates and discussing rice exports. Instead, the parliamentarians were presented with harsh new laws.

One such law stated that anyone bearing arms would be tried as a traitor. Sao was first to rise to her feet.

"I want to ask...Mr. Speaker, please forgive me, I don't understand Burmese very well, so I don't understand this new law."

"Now as far as I know, all the Saophas have given up their arms and moved into the city where it's safer. And none of the traders and merchants have arms. Also, we politicians have no arms. No one gives arms to anyone, they're so frightened of the military."

"The only people who have arms and can rob the people are the military. So I don't understand this law."

The other side of the house remained silent. Even the opposition benches went quiet.

Days later, when Sao was still among them and not in prison, someone asked her, "How did you get away with it?" She replied with characteristic good humour, "I voted for Ne Win, remember." But she was starting to doubt at her luck so far.

The Caretaker

On April 26, Sao and her husband travelled to Taunggyi for a grand ceremony marking the end of feudal power. General Ne Win also attended, adding to the long line of heavily-guarded cars that glided end to end down Taunggyi's main street. The ceremony should have been a triumph: the civilian government of Shan State had come into its own, inheriting from the Saophas, new jurisdiction over taxation, education, justice and public works. Sao couldn't help feeling vexed by the whole scene, though. At the right hand of the General was her own brother, Prince Hom Hpa, smiling broadly under his bristly crew cut. As the new head of Shan State, it was he, of all people, who accepted their surrender of royal power.

After the handover, Sao and her husband studied the household accounts. They were to receive a lump sum pension of just over 1.2 million Kyat—about 96,000 pounds sterling—based on fifteen years of projected land and forest revenue. Beyond that, they had only their small parliamentary allowances, some investments and their jewels.

From now on the family would have to watch its budget more closely. Although they no longer paid for local public works, they still had the upkeep of the palace and its staff to worry about, including the pensions of retired retainers. They also had a host of dependent relatives. Then there were school fees for the children, three of whom were studying abroad. Finally, they had houses in Taunggyi and Rangoon to maintain. To continue his scholarship programme for poor students, the Prince sold his gold regalia. He no longer had occasion to wear it.

The family continued to live much better than ordinary citizens, though, and Sao and her husband were still addressed as Mahadevi and Great Prince. To outsiders, the change in their lifestyle was subtle at best.

During the school break, Tzang boarded a rickety country bus with a knapsack slung over his shoulder. He wanted to discover Shan State on his own. Sao wondered if he would ever return, or if he was going to join the Brave Young Warriors. The Prince was furious. Sometimes he felt he'd had no luck with the Mahadevi's eldest sons. Tiger was too proud and Anglified, Tzang too impulsive and combative—traits of the mother, Prince Shwe Thaike thought. Luckily the next-eldest, Myee, was more agreeable. At fourteen, Myee was charming and outgoing. He got along easily with people, more like his father than his mother. Of all his children, Myee was the one to whom Prince Shwe Thaike felt closest.

Tzang reappeared in time for the next school term. He was tanned and fit after two months of tramping about on foot and hitching rides in bullock carts. For the first time he'd seen the outside world with his own eyes, unprotected by bodyguards and palace walls. The countryside was in the throes of the worst excesses of General Ne Win's Bandit Suppression Campaign. In the villages he heard how the Burma Army soldiers raped women, tortured headmen and looted the meagre possessions of farmers and merchants. The rural people were so angry that they formed small gangs and fought back, although they knew the army would abuse them all the more for it. They even rioted when a Burmese-made movie depicted a beloved 11th Century Tai princess as an evil sorceress.

One afternoon in Mong Kung town, just north of Loilem, Tzang came upon a group of elderly men resting in the shelter of a monastery pavilion. The old men talked about the troubles that beset Shan State, speaking in the fast, colloquial Tai of rural villagers. Tzang listened closely, straining to follow the conversation. He heard them grumble about how the Celestial Lords had sold them out to the Burmese. The Great Saopha of Yawnghwe was especially to blame, the old men agreed.

Tzang wanted desperately to explain the whole complex story: how the British abandoned the frontier areas, how Aung San promised them equality, how they were tricked into giving up the Right of Secession for ten years and, especially, how his father had done his best to protect Shan State. Instead, he stewed in frustrated silence. After years at private boarding schools and a Burmese university, he could no longer speak Tai well enough to join the conversation.

Back on campus Tzang found a ready audience for his stories of life in the Shan rural areas. Far from his image at home as an insufferable upstart, at university he was well known and well liked. At first he was shy, but he was coming out of his shell. His fellow students regarded him as humorous, intelligent and easy going, quite suited for the role of bringing together factious student associations. He got involved in the Tai Literary Society and began to pen romantic stories about dying for Shan freedom.

The remainder of 1959 passed uneventfully, with the kids in school and Sao back to parliament in August. After the initial shock of the coup, the MPs conducted business as usual. Studying the government accounts, Sao discovered that the economy had improved under the caretaker government. Parliament passed a budget and carried out other routine business until its dissolution in December. True to his word, General Ne Win announced that an election would be held on February 6, 1960.

"Let the country make its own choice. It will get the government it deserves," he said.

As for himself, he had accomplished his goals. Two thousand rebels were dead, 2,000 were wounded, and 3,600 had surrendered. His intelligence reports told him there were just 5,000 left in the field. Before leaving office, though, he had one final decree: the northern Kachin territory bordering China was transferred to direct Rangoon control. Similar measures would be taken in Shan State as soon as possible.

Western governments praised the General for his decisive action, which stood in marked contrast to the bickering civilian government of U Nu.

For all his military sweeps, though, the atmosphere of violence and lawlessness in the frontier was growing, not abating. While General Ne Win chased communists and ethnic rebels down, the opium barons flourished. Farmers found they could sell as much as they could produce. With their newly-constructed roads and donated cargo planes, the renegade KMT provided access to a ready international market. Their storehouses in Thailand bulged.

Pistol-packing Olive Yang of Kokang ran opium, too. She transported it by truck through Tachilek on the Thai border. Her protégés prospered. Ten received special training under the KMT, including Lo Hsin Han and Chang Shi-fu.

Lo Hsin Han, who used to carry her cigarettes, was now a second lieutenant in her Kokang Revolutionary Force. He collected a toll for her on the road leading to Hsenwi. He also set up his own consortium of young Kokang traders. In Rangoon, Olive's brother, Jimmy Yang, revealed his true talent in politics. Putting his political connections to work, he made sure Lo's consortium obtained a special opium exporter's licence. Then to help Lo ferry his crop from Kokang to Lashio, Jimmy finagled an aeroplane from the Communications Ministry, too.

Olive's other favourite, Chang Shi-fu, had a good year as well. He was now headman of his grandfather's village, Loimaw. In January, 1960, his private militia received official status under the Burma Army's Eastern Command. Tasked with fighting Communist Party insurgents and the KMT, Chang instead contacted his old friends and got into the booming drug trade.

With Lo's license, Chang's officially-sanctioned "volunteer army" and Olive's KMT connections, the trio were untouchable. The only ones they need answer to were the KMT themselves, who by now controlled the roads and border crossings in a full third of Shan State.

While the General ran parliament and the opium barons took over the hills, U Nu spent 45 days in a religious retreat, emerging to deliver a lecture series on Buddhism and socialism.

Burma was essentially a Buddhist nation, he said. Democratic socialism was the political expression of Buddhist selflessness.

A good Buddhist was a good socialist, and vice versa. U Nu was not content to merely theorise, though. 1960 had arrived. His ideas would form the basis of an electoral crusade in the February contest. He chose yellow, the colour of Buddhism, as his campaign signature. He wasn't ready to retire to the monastery yet.

Neither was Sao ready to retire from politics, even after she received word that her brother had withdrawn his support. The message came via Prince Hom Hpa's private secretary, who was called into the Hsenwi prince's office one day and simply told: "The Mahadevi will no longer be our MP."

The secretary was surprised. "Why shouldn't she represent us? She's doing very well."

But Sao's brother wouldn't hear any arguments. He had already chosen someone else: his younger brother and heir-designate, Prince Munn Pha. He had saved the younger prince's life during the war, brazenly pleading with his Japanese captors to let him go. After the war, he appointed him state administrator. Prince Munn Pha was a man close to him in blood and in duty. Sao, on the other hand, was far too difficult to control. And the army didn't like her.

Unfazed, Sao let her name stand. Why not? She didn't trust her brother and his heir to keep the army out of Shan State. Prince Munn Pha would have to defeat her if he wanted to represent Hsenwi.

A total of 934 candidates filed for the 250 Chamber of Deputies seats. It was a far cry from Burma's very first post-war election, when only a handful of unpopular communists ran against the Freedom League. For once, the contest meant something. Even Hsenwi had a choice of candidates. Despite the previous year's setback, Burma was starting to look like a real democracy.

Welcome to the Underground

U Nu dove straight into the fray. His competition was the Stable faction of his own shattered party, which had close ties to the military. Clean and Stable went after one another like mongoose and snake. They dug dirt, slung accusations and called each other names.

"U Nu will sit in a pagoda for ten hours if he thinks it will help him politically," Stable leader U Ba Shwe charged.

U Nu responded by embracing Buddhism all the more. He publicly called on his party members to practice metta, love. They should do so, he instructed, by paying homage to their parents, their wives, their children and the Nats. At the height of the mud-slinging, he donned monks' robes and promised to make Buddhism the official religion, forsaking the long held goal of a multi-religious country.

Having secured the Buddhist vote, he next went after the ethnic vote, promising to finally amend the constitution to enhance states' rights.

The combination of piety and promises carried U Nu straight to victory. He took no less than 168 seats, a resounding majority.

For all his political weaknesses, the common people loved and trusted him. They called him a Buddha-in-Progress.

Before parliament convened, U Nu gave his Clean AFPFL faction a real name: Pyidaungzu, the Union League, a name he thought befitting of Burma's natural governing party. On April 1, they filed into parliament to hear the Prime Minister's opening day address. Across from the government members, the sparse opposition benches held 45 Stable members and a cluster of ethnic and state leaders. The National Unity Front, powerful in the last election, had been completely annihilated at the polls, and the feared communist take-over had never occurred.

One familiar face was missing. Sao had lost the Hsenwi vote. Prince Munn Pha sat in her place while she squeezed into the visitor's gallery. She didn't take the loss personally. She heard there'd been some confusion over the ballot; the villagers weren't sure who they were voting for. Many put their mark beside Prince Munn Pha's royal symbol, thinking it represented Sao.

She wasn't overly disappointed. What was done was done. Her brother had his man in place. He sat there looking rather lost and confused. Prince Munn Hpa was an able administrator, but he had no political experience.

Sao listened intently to U Nu's address. The speech, "Crusade for Democracy", was characteristically long and prosaic. Finally U Nu arrived at what they were all waiting to hear: the campaign promises would be honoured, including constitutional renewal. Shan State had the chance to renegotiate its place in the Union.

Another ousted onlooker listened very carefully to U Nu. General Ne Win had kept his promise to stay out of the elections. In public, he was the picture of restraint. Before stepping down he retired several colonels and generals who were prominent in his caretaker government, a signal that the army was finished with politics. It was a gracious, noble exit.

In his heart, though, General Ne Win felt a sting of hurt and resentment. U Nu's campaign slogan, "Democracy Against Fascism", was a direct dig against him. Such shabby treatment after he had handed U Nu a healthy economy, labour peace and reduced insurgency. Burma was on the upswing for the first time since World War II. Before the election, General Ne Win felt something like a hero. Some people called him the Constitutional Soldier.

Now they called him a fascist.

On the General's last day in power, U Nu offered him an opportunity to "make merit" by reinstating an old ban on the slaughter of cattle. It would improve his Kamma, U Nu suggested. Ne Win flatly refused, thinking the law an unnecessary vexation to non-Buddhists.

"Go ahead, make your own merit," he said.

Two hours after being sworn in, U Nu saved the nation's cattle from the butcher's knife while Ne Win sat on the sidelines.

The following month, the General left for the U.S. on an unspecified medical leave. The Burma embassy staff hosted him, including Sao's nephew, Saw Ohn, who had been posted to Washington as a military attaché. It wasn't easy to arrange meetings with the higher-ups. Rumour had it that Ne Win was disappointed by the weak reception he received during his visit. A few months ago the Americans sang his praises. Now he was a nobody, hardly worth a cocktail party.

On his return to Burma, the General took up golf. Day after day he swatted at the tiny white ball until finally it began to do his bidding. Marching down the rough fairways of Maymyo and Kalaw, he had time to think. Bodyguards, umbrella bearers and caddies fanned out behind him, none daring to interrupt the General's reveries. Mostly, Ne Win thought about how good his caretaker government had been and how unfairly maligned it was now. Taking club in hand, he swung with all his might.

The civilian government in Rangoon made little difference to Shan State, where the army continued to lord over the populace. Tzang had seen enough during his tour. He decided to return to the countryside next school break, only this time he would do something to help the rebels. He was particularly interested in a group called the Shan State Independence Army (SSIA), a new offshoot of the Brave Young Warriors. Unlike the Warriors, the SSIA had a modern constitution and a political programme, and was led mostly by students.

Talk of the underground was all part of the allure of campus life. The Tai students were having a great time. There were any number of home-town clubs to join, along with the Tai Literary Society and the Shan State Students' Association. They presented cultural performances and held social events. Tzang busied himself trying to unite all the ethnic students under the Nationalities Student United Front. Ying Sita arrived on campus as a freshman and was soon as involved as her older brother.

One of the Yang sisters, Judy, was their classmate. In the evenings her brother Jimmy Yang threw his University Avenue house open to the students. They played tennis, swam and sampled expensive liquor. Boys and girls alike competed with one another in revolutionary fervour. Tzang struck up a romance with a pretty undergraduate named Nu Nu Myint, "Nang Nu" for short.

When the hot season arrived the Yawnghwe family travelled up to the Haw for holidays. Once again, Tzang disappeared into the countryside. Near Laikaw he met some of the SSIA leaders, young men with long unkempt hair, mostly from the Hsipaw area.

Tzang was eager to prove himself. Remembering the fabled weapons cache in Hsenwi he headed north with one of his school chums, a shy, thin fellow who called himself "Robert". When they arrived in Hsenwi, though, Prince Hom Hpa was unwelcoming. He offered neither weapons nor even shelter.

Empty-handed, the boys followed the dusty track out of town, wondering what to do next.

"I know a monk nearby. He'll put us up," said Robert. But when they arrived at the monastery they found the walls were covered in Burma Army graffiti and the monks were nowhere to be seen.

Tzang recalled an old house belonging to his sister-in-law Pat's family. As night fell, they located the abandoned building and broke into its attic storeroom. Inside they found a bottle of brandy, dusty but still sealed. Deep into the night the boys drank, talked and slapped mosquitoes. Robert bitterly remembered a professor who encouraged students to go underground while he himself continued his comfortable professor's life in Rangoon. Tzang pined for his girlfriend, Nang Nu. Melancholy overtook them, until finally they drained the bottle and slept.

Next morning they found a truck going west to Kokang. After a long, uncomfortable journey they arrived at the Yang family's big stone house in Tashwehtang. Olive wasn't in. The famous bandit queen was either in the jungle or in Rangoon, where she'd struck up a scandalously open love affair with a Burmese actress, Wa Wa Win Shwe. Instead, her brother Eddie the Myosa met them at the gate. He too gave them the bum's rush.

If Tzang had any romantic notions about becoming an underground hero, they were fading fast. He'd assumed his family's powerful connections would leap to his aid. Instead the boys wandered south again, weaponless. But Tzang was persistent. He wasn't going to give up.

Tzang and Robert's next assignment was to help a young sympathiser organise the Loimaw area, in the heart of Chang Shifu's opium territory. They were so dirty and mosquito-bitten when they arrived that the townspeople shunned them, thinking they had smallpox. Worse, the man they were assigned to help was busy planning his wedding. He had no time for political activities.

The trip was not a total loss, though. Tzang wandered into the market looking for a new shirt, and there discovered a few weapons for sale, including some pistols and a sten gun. If no one would give them guns, at least they could buy some.

They went back to Yawnghwe to gather some money and a vehicle. Ying Sita and one of her friends were invited to come along on the trip as cover. With a small bundle of Kyat and a borrowed jeep, they set out on the northern road in high spirits. At the military checkpoint outside Taunggyi, Robert told the guard they were going to the waterfalls, a local lover's hang-out. Then for good measure he slipped the soldier a bottle of brandy. With a broad wink, the guard raised the bamboo-pole barrier.

Luckily, the guns were still at the market. They turned back for home, Tzang at the wheel, Robert beside him, the girls in the back and the pistols under the seat. Just in case, Robert set the sten gun on the seat beside him. Now they were real revolutionaries.

It was a long journey. They sang songs and told jokes until around a bend in the road they came suddenly upon the checkpoint. Alarmed, Tzang took his foot off the accelerator. The same guard was there, only now he was hastily jamming bullets into his rifle chamber. Robert reached for the sten gun and a magazine of ammo.

"What are you doing? The girls are in the back!" cried Tzang.

"Girls or no girls, if he shoots, we have to shoot back," said Robert.

He fumbled the magazine into place just as the soldier pulled his bolt back. But instead of aiming at the jeep, the guard turned his back to the road and fired at some paddy birds.

The birds rose into the air. Robert crammed the sten under the seat, next to the pistols. They pulled up to the checkpoint, trying to look calm. The guard smiled, remembering them, and waved them through.

The young students had just completed their first clandestine assignment. The feeling was exhilarating. They were ready for more.

Season of Rain

The rains of 1961 came early and fell harder than anyone could remember. Lowland rivers spread over their banks, turning the Burma plain into a churning brown lake. Two hundred thousand homes and 300,000 acres of rice paddy were lost. Prime Minister U Nu disappeared as well, on a 45-day religious retreat.

U Nu had spent the past year immersed in the nation's perceived spiritual needs. At his first Cabinet meeting, he established a State Religion Advisory Committee. The nation's Moslems, Christians and Hindus were greatly alarmed. When members of the Religion Committee travelled up-country on a tour of inquiry, protesters threw stones at them. Despite U Nu's election victory, there was no national consensus on the matter of a state religion.

Throughout 1960, the Saophas of Shan State continued to converge on 74 Kokine Road to bend Sao's ear. Their complaints were growing. For one thing, they still hadn't received compensation for raising levies against the KMT. The Shan State government was covering several federal public expenses. They were angry, too, about the exploitation of Shan State's gems and minerals.

"Those hills are old, older than the Himalayas, and full of rubies and sapphires," one fellow told Sao. "When Shan people want to open a mine, the Burma Army says, 'we can't guarantee your safety'."

"So they back off and then the Burmese come in and take over. The local people end up as workers, breaking their backs for a few Kyat."

Burmese-led state enterprises had also set up a cement factory and tin mine near Taunggyi, with profits funnelled to Rangoon. Still, Sao had little sympathy for the complainers.

"You're stupid. You say yes to everything. No wonder the Burmese are running Shan State," she told them bluntly.

"Look at that cement factory: the government advisor was a Shan girl who married a Burman. What do you expect?"

One day U Nu himself appeared in the parlour. He looked tired. "What exactly do you want from us?" he asked Sao and the Prince.

Prince Shwe Thaike made no answer so Sao, as usual, forged ahead: "Look Prime Minister, when Shan State came into the Union, we didn't come empty-handed. We didn't come a-begging. So what do you say to that?"

U Nu gulped down his tea and rose to his feet without answering.

This was one of the last times her husband remained silent. After the election, the Prince wasn't re-appointed Speaker of the Upper House. Instead, he became an ordinary member. It was a fateful miscalculation on the part of the Rangoon establishment. For the first time in the twelve years since independence, Sao's husband was free to speak his mind.

Almost immediately he resumed his nominal leadership of the Shan politicians, and one of his first acts was to devise an answer to U Nu's parlour-room question.

In December he handed U Nu a "bill of particulars": Shan State wanted financial settlement on a number of outstanding items. The Prince also threw in a criticism of the Burma Army for its continued hegemony in Shan State. It was the state government's right to recruit soldiers and station units, not Rangoon's, he wrote.

The document was quoted in the *Guardian* on December 23, raising an alarm among Burmese elites. They responded in the press themselves, accusing "a person as prominent as the sun and moon" of fomenting secession.

Sao found herself taking a back seat to her husband in politics. While she held forth in the parlour, railing against intermarriage and Shan "stupidity", the Prince dove headfirst into more decisive action. At the beginning of 1961 he took the helm of a newly-formed National Religious Minorities Alliance (NRMA)—a group of Baptists, Moslems, animists and Buddhists united against U Nu's state religion plans. Prince Shwe Thaike was a good choice for leader: well known as a devout Buddhist, he nonetheless favoured religious freedom. The Buddhists of Shan State balked at state religion as much as any other group because their Buddhist practices were culturally distinct. They feared state religion would bring Shan monasteries under the more strict and culturally different Burmese Sangha.

U Nu hardly noticed the Alliance, though. New projects consumed his mind, such as the construction of a modern dog pound in Rangoon. And he wanted to build shrines to the Nats on Mount Popa, a sacred hill east of Meiktila.

Meantime, his Union League followers fell to bickering among themselves. Conflicts flowered between the old Thakin members and political newcomers. All the while, General Ne Win looked on with growing consternation.

The New Year of 1961 brought some hope. Chinese Premier Chou Enlai visited, and on Independence Day he announced a thirty million pound interest-free loan to Burma. Shortly after, Insein and Maubin-area communists surrendered with a large quantity of arms. Then on January 26, 20,000 Chinese People's Liberation Army troops poured across the border into Burma. They were joined by 5,000 Burma Army men in a joint offensive against the lost KMT army of General Li Mi.

The peaceful Shan hills echoed with the sound of rocket launchers and strafing fighter planes. Taken by surprise, 42,000 KMT soldiers sought refuge in Thailand. There, tens of thousands agreed to be airlifted to Taiwan. On April 11 a joint Taiwan-U.S. communiqué was issued:

"The 6,000 KMT soldiers remaining in Burma's Shan State are not in any way concerned with the U.S. or Taiwan government."

The severance of American ties was only within official circles, though. Within months of the communiqué, a large group of

KMT remainders were hired on by the CIA to carry out clandestine operations in north-western Laos. Other KMT soldiers, cut loose from the past, decided to concentrate on illicit black market activities. During the January confrontation, the joint forces shot down an American plane and captured a large amount of U.S.-made military hardware. When the weapons were brought to Rangoon for public display, people exploded in anger. How dare the Americans arm the KMT interlopers? On February 21, angry students converged outside the gates of the American Embassy on Merchant Street, near Sule Pagoda and the city centre. The demonstration soon escalated into a full-scale riot. Police moved in, killing 2 and wounding 53.

Being a student radical was no lark. There were serious consequences, including arrest and death. Few were deterred, though, least of all Sao's second son, Tzang. Tzang was starting to know the jungle and the people who hid out there. His Shan and Karen contacts expanded. On campus, he became an important connection to the underground. He helped a radical monk named U Gondra go underground, and helped smuggle an SSIA leader into Rangoon.

Tzang still believed the powers-that-be in Shan State might help them. He approached the Hsipaw Saopha—a young, American-educated man—and offered to set up a meeting with the smuggled-in SSIA leader. In answer, Prince Kya Seng handed Tzang a copy of the Union constitution and said, "Please read the oath we have sworn as MPs." The Saophas still had faith in the system.

When Tzang slipped into the jungle to attend a secret conference of ethnic minority groups, his father sent a monk to fetch him back. The monk sat him down and talked to him about democracy and the rule of law. Tzang agreed to return to school. Maybe reform could be pushed through the system.

He attended the Interstates Convention on Amending the Constitution, convened in Taunggyi on June 8, 1961. His father was there, too, working on the inside with 330 delegates from all the frontier states. During the week they studied a proposed Federal Bill, modelled after the American system. The Bill would clearly define areas of federal responsibility, make Burma Proper a constituent state, and give equal power to the two houses of parliament.

Outside the state building, Tzang cobbled together a few hundred highschool students and monks to march around town in support of the Bill. Mindful of the monk's advice, he was willing to give parliamentary democracy its due.

His mother, on the other hand, held no hope in constitutional talks. She stayed in Rangoon.

"Take us out of this wretched Union," she advised the Prince before he left for the meeting.

Her husband paid no attention. Instead, he concentrated on securing Shan State's rights within Burma's constitution. Others felt the same way. The convention closed on June 16 with unanimous support for the Federal Bill and a call to extend statehood to the Mons, Chins and Arakanese.

Father and son returned to Rangoon through the driving rain. Thunder crashed and the flood-waters kept rising. Inside the Kokine Road house, the atmosphere grew claustrophobic.

Prince Shwe Thaike decreed that the entire family must come together at supper to discuss the day's events. He didn't care where they went before or after, as long as they were seated at the table when the evening meal was served.

The meals often descended into long and fruitless arguments. To Sao's surprise, her radical son proved in some ways more conservative than either she or her husband. He begged them to temper their constitutional demands. Parliament, he warned, was not in control of the military. General Ne Win disliked federalism, especially the idea of statehood for the Mon and Arakanese. They had to be careful, he said.

In fact, Tzang argued, maybe they should just forget the whole thing. They could sell their property, cash in their investments and move to China or Thailand.

Sao could hardly believe such talk. What was he afraid of? General Ne Win was relegated to the background and U Nu was eager to talk. The PM had called a Federal Seminar to meet in Rangoon on February 24, 1962. He said he wanted to solve the ethnic issue once and for all. Sao's husband was optimistic: this was their chance to make a new Union.

Personally, Sao disagreed. There's no use making more deals with the Burmese, not in my books, she thought. She couldn't help saying so aloud at the dinner table, even though she knew it would lead to endless bickering between her and the Prince while the children picked at their food in silence. Of course they were bored with the constant arguing. Even she was bored. She was tired, too.

One day Sao noticed fluid leaking from her breast again. Once more, arrangements for treatment in Britain were made. This time, though, her husband said he would stay behind to attend U Nu's Federal Seminar.

Despite her worries about her health, Sao looked forward to England and the chance to visit son Tiger and his half-sister, Sanda. She needed a break from Rangoon, her husband, and their arguments. She wouldn't miss much—Burma's problems would be there just the same when she got back. She'd thought the same thing when she left Rangoon in 1958, just before General Ne Win's coup. It never occurred to her that the same scenario could happen twice.

Night of Guns

As Sao flew to England, the planets entered the most inauspicious alignment calculated to occur in the next 5,000 years. Prime Minister U Nu chose to ignore the astrological warning. On February 24, 1962, he went ahead and opened the Federal Seminar. All of the country's minority and state leaders came to Rangoon for the meetings, ready to give up talk of secession in favour of a re-composed political structure.

Prince Shwe Thaike attended the seminar daily. He worked behind the scenes, too, seeking a middle position that would hold the Union together and appease the secessionists.

Despite everything, the democratic process was bumping along fairly well. In fact, Burma was developing an international reputation for moderation and fairness, highlighted by the 1961 appointment of one of their own, U Thant, as the United Nations Secretary-General. The election and the UN connection gave people a sense that they were making progress, and that somehow they would work through their problems in a reasonable manner.

On March 1, the Prince joined a small group of Shan and Kayah leaders at U Nu's Windermere residence to discuss compromise proposals. He had something else on his mind, though. After years of work, his Tripitaka scriptures translation project was complete. Earlier that day, the printer delivered the texts to 74 Kokine Road. The only room large enough to hold them was the grand entrance hall. They were stacked almost to the lofty ceiling.

At St. George's Hospital in London's toney Belgravia district, Sao rested in bed, awaiting test results. She read to pass the time, or visited with relatives and well-wishers. In addition to her stepdaugher, she had several nieces and friends in the city.

Her eldest son, Tiger, stayed in Cambridge. He planned to attend a ball in a few days, but was caught between two girls who both expected an invitation. To escape the problem, he decided to take a shift as a bartender in a campus pub on the night of the ball. That way he could tell the girls he had to work.

It was a nice time to be in England. The trees were greening, the days warming.

With Sao away, the dinner-time combat at Kokine Road abated. Tzang noticed that he and his father were finally starting to have real conversations. Lately, the Prince talked to him like an equal.

Tzang had no time to chat on the evening of March 1, though. He had taken a teaching assistant's position at university, a job which carried a small amount of prestige and a large amount of work. After dinner, he retired to his bedroom with a stack of exam papers. The Prince wandered into the hallway to have another look at his Tripitika editions. Later, Tzang heard Myee climb the stairs to his second-floor bedroom.

At the Prime Minister's residence, U Nu counted the Buddhist rosary before bed.

Across town, General Ne Win enjoyed a ballet performance by a troupe from China. When the curtain fell he shook hands with the prima ballerina, then left.

Darkness fell on the city.

At 2:00 a.m. Tzang marked his last exam paper for the night. Exhausted, he threw himself on his bed. Within moments, he was in deep sleep.

It was still dark when Tzang awoke. He looked at his clock: 4:00 a.m. Something had wakened him. Then he heard it again, in the distance. Gunfire. There was no mistaking the sound. He lay listening, eyes still closed, unable to put his tired mind in gear. The sound drifted in and out. Then two short, sharp cracks jolted him to consciousness. What was happening? He heard voices in the garden, feet running, someone shouting in Burmese.

Heart pounding, Tzang bounded to his feet and ran out into the hallway. The rest of the family was already awake and gathered in the large entrance hall. They looked at each other in confusion but there was no time to talk. The men outside opened fire.

Window panes shattered and bullets thudded into the walls. Prince Shwe Thaike herded them all behind the Tripitika texts, still piled several editions thick to the ceiling. Ying Sita was pale and grim-faced. Harn looked completely terrified. The younger ones sat in a huddle, hands over their ears. Myee was missing. Bullets whizzed above the books and ricocheted off the walls. It went on for a very long time.

When the shooting stopped, they heard heavy boots outside the door. Prince Shwe Thaike stepped out from behind the books.

Tzang followed his father outside under the portico, where the air smelled of cordite. From the darkness, two men dressed in Burma Army uniforms stepped forward and levelled their bayonets at the Prince. Then they marched him across the garden, Tzang hurrying behind them.

Amazed, Tzang saw the soldiers had cut a large hole in the surrounding hedge. He wondered why they didn't just use the front gate, and how he could have slept through the initial commotion. Helpless, he watched the soldiers march his father out through the hedge and into the back of a waiting van.

Next, the soldiers searched the house. Tzang led them from room to room. All they found was a pistol in a fancy case, a gift to his father when he was President. It had never been used.

Outside, a grey dawn streaked the sky. As the soldiers made their exit, Tzang saw a figure lying in the grass beside the portico. It was his younger brother Myee, face down with a Naga lance— another souvenir gift—in one outstretched hand. The family kept the lance in the main hall for decoration; Myee must have grabbed it for protection before going outside to investigate the first furtive noises.

Tzang leaned over the boy. He saw a small rifle wound in his ankle. It was just a tiny hole, but there was blood everywhere and Myee wasn't moving. Then Tzang saw the large, execution-style bullet wound in the back of Myee's head. His little brother was dead.

At his Windermere home, Prime Minister U Nu awoke looking down the barrel of a revolver. Like Prince Shwe Thaike, he was arrested on the spot.

Many others were taken from their beds that morning: five cabinet ministers, the Chief Justice and thirty-six Shan and Kayah leaders. The Prince of Kengtung, a sickly man, was roused from his hospital bed at Rangoon General. Sao's brother, Prince Hom Hpa, was one of the few Shan Saophas who remained free. Vans rumbled out of the city under a rising sun, delivering the arrested politicians to a nearby army camp.

At 8:50 a.m. General Ne Win made a radio broadcast. "I have to inform you, citizens of the Union, that the armed forces have taken over responsibility and the task of keeping the country's safety, owing to the greatly deteriorating conditions of the Union."

"I urge the education authorities and the students who are in the midst of their examinations to carry on their work."

Tzang listened, outraged. His father was gone, his brother dead, and General Ne Win wanted him to carry on marking exam papers. Instead, the young man went to the police station the next day and laid a charge of murder against the army.

At Cambridge, Tiger was enjoying himself. Being a bartender was fun. It gave him a chance to say hello to everyone. Seeing a classmate from the geology department, he smiled broadly and measured out a drink.

"Did you hear there's been a coup in Burma?" the classmate asked. Tiger looked up, surprised.

"Oh, nothing serious, though," the fellow added quickly. "Only one dead, a son of the first president."

Tiger turned pale. He set the drink down slowly in front of the fellow.

"Did I say something wrong?" his classmate asked, looking embarrassed. Tiger was too dumbstruck to answer. The student picked up his glass and hastened away.

In her hospital room, Sao was sheltered from the worst of the news. Her relatives arrived in a pack the next day. They told her about the coup and her husband's arrest, but not to worry. Everyone from U Nu on down was arrested, not just Prince Shwe Thaike. They would soon be released. The army could hardly run the country with all the leaders in jail. The *Times* reported that the army had acted to resolve factional disputes, and that General Ne Win's policies were "likely to be sensible and moderate".

"It happened again, and I'm in England again," Sao marvelled aloud. For the second time her body had taken her out of harm's way when her mind refused to see danger.

Whether or not the visitors explained exactly what happened to Myee, Sao could never remember later. For a long time she had the impression that her son was only wounded.

Twenty-four hours after the coup, General Ne Win took the chairmanship of a hand-picked eight-member Revolutionary Council. The Council gave Ne Win full executive, judicial and legislative power. He immediately dissolved parliament and suspended the constitution.

Two days later, the Revolutionary Council was introduced to the public in a press conference. They were not the same bunch of democratic parliamentarians who got behind Ne Win during the caretaker government. The new leaders were mostly army men, all of them known as committed, radical leftists. Seated in the middle, General Ne Win explained the Revolutionary Council was interested in "healthy politics". He noted that the internal problems of Vietnam and Laos led to foreign domination. The Revolutionary Council would not allow this to happen in Burma.

He also explained that there would be no more state governments to bicker over constitutional power. Instead, the Council planned to set up its own five State Supreme Councils.

Flashbulbs popped and reporters scribbled in their notepads. It was a confusing moment. Was this the Constitutional Soldier talking, the same man who said the army had no interest in politics?

Ne Win was no dictator. Surely, this was temporary.

Weeks passed, though, and the civilian leaders remained locked up. The grapevine reported that U Nu's first question on being arrested was whether or not General Ne Win was okay; he didn't understand it was the General who arrested him.

There were a few other arrests around the country in the wake of the coup. The retired Chief Minister of Yawnghwe, Ko Latt, was briefly detained in Taunggyi. The young, U.S.-educated Prince Kya Seng of Hsipaw dined with Prince Sai and Pat one evening, then disappeared. He was last seen in a bamboo army hut.

Just outside Rangoon, Prince Shwe Thaike shared a cell with Khun Bya Nu, the people's representative who stood up at Panglong and spoke against union with Burma so many years ago. Back then, he was intimidated by the Great Saopha. Now they were jail-mates. They talked for hours and, for the first time, the Prince agreed joining Burma was a mistake. It was a discouraging moment. The two men waited for their release, wondering what was happening in the world outside. They were allowed no visitors.

Tzang and Ying Sita took charge of the family. They closed up the Kokine Road house and moved in with their elder step-brother, Hseng. A recent Cambridge graduate, Hseng had his own house now and a position with a Rangoon chemical company.

Fourteen-year-old Harn grew up overnight. He helped Tzang and Ying Sita watch over Leun, the youngest. There were only four of them now, with no father or mother. Their adopted sister Htilar was reclaimed by her mother, who no longer seemed so alone and destitute compared to the shattered Yawnghwe clan.

Myee's body was cremated without ceremony; the monastery held his ashes for safe-keeping. He was seventeen when he died.

After a while, Tzang returned to campus. It was the only home he had left. The student body was in an excited buzz. No one knew what to make of General Ne Win. The General was said to be well-read, an expert in the history and philosophy of China's old Confucian courts. Still, most people saw him as a lightweight playboy, more concerned with beauty queens than politics.

On March 15 the *Guardian* reported that horseracing was to be banned within the year. Two days later, beauty contests and gambling in Shan State were also named on the to-be-banned list.

Surely this had to be a joke, Tzang's classmates said. How could the King of the Race Course, the man who dated every Miss Burma, be responsible for such laws? This is crazy! they howled. Ne Win didn't have the brains to run a country.

Home

Once again no malignancy was detected, but Sao remained a day patient for some time after her hospital release. The doctor advised her to remain in London until he was sure she was in the clear. She stayed with a Tai friend for a while, then moved in with step-daughter Sanda and her husband, an Englishman, Peter.

Sao wasn't entirely happy with the situation—she didn't like being dependent on others—but she felt she could do little else. Best to stay, get better, and wait things out, she thought. The coup would soon blow over like the last one and she could return home safely.

Her friends and family in Burma felt the same way: it would all blow over. But the country was being transformed.

On April 30, General Ne Win called a conference of Burma Army commanding officers. At the meeting, he outlined Burma's new political program. He called it "The Burmese Way to Socialism".

Democracy, he explained, was a defective system. It was full of weaknesses and loopholes, open to abuse by devious men. Politicians did whatever they wanted because the population wasn't mature enough to control them. Democracy created exploitation. Socialism needed a more solid foundation. His expert advisors, including a well-known Marxist economist, had come up with a more stable "Burmese Way" of doing things. It was time to revolutionise the political and economic system, and to purge Burma of cultural impurities.

The General announced a number of immediate measures. True to the *Guardian*'s earlier reports, horse-racing and beauty contests were outlawed. The Race Course would be converted into a parade and meeting ground. Dance competitions were also banned.

There was more: the Ford Foundation, Rockefeller Museum Project, Asia Foundation and Fulbright Scholars Program were ordered to quit the country. The British Council, the United States Information Services Library and the American Consulate in Mandalay must close. Henceforth, the media would be overseen by a Press Council. The Revolutionary Council would form a single political party to advise the government. Civilians were welcome to join. Parliamentary democracy, with its arguments and scandals, was finished in Burma.

If Sao knew such details, she wouldn't have believed them. In London she only heard the basics: no post-coup violence was reported and her children were in the care of close relatives. They would be okay. She felt confident enough to take a side trip to Denmark to visit some relations. It was a welcome diversion.

Back in Burma, though, the country was becoming progressively more dangerous, especially for Tzang. In May, the Revolutionary Council assumed direct control of the universities.

On July 4, the Council unveiled plans to form the Burma Socialist Programme Party (BSPP), now Burma's single allowable political organisation. It was to be a vanguard party made up only of Revolutionary Council members. They would expand later, General Ne Win promised. The party's ideology was neither left nor right, because left-right thinking was an imperialist import. Instead, they followed the Middle Path. Or so he said: in reality the party never materialised until 1970s.

Hearing the news, the students at Rangoon University decided the General had gone far enough. The situation was no longer laughable. This was getting serious. There were police wandering around campus, spying on them and breaking up meetings. One student was shot and wounded in a scuffle.

On the morning of July 7, the students banded together and surrounded the police. They chanted, shouted and threatened the outnumbered policemen, who backed slowly out the campus gate and onto University Avenue. Cheering in victory, the students pulled the gate shut and declared the campus a fortress of democracy.

When Tzang arrived later that day, he found the students in a jubilant mood. They milled in and out of the Students Union building, laughing, talking and feeling on top of the world. The historic building, with its ties to the Thakin movement and U Nu, gave them a sense of purpose. The country was founded by student protesters. It was up to the new student generation to save the day. Their leader was a fiery fellow named Aung Win, a cousin to Tzang's girlfriend, Nang Nu.

No one attended classes that day. Instead, the students listened to speeches. Tzang drifted off to the judo gym for a workout.

When he decided to head home for the day, evening was falling and a sizeable crowd of students remained at the University Avenue gate. Spying two of his English tutorial students among the crowd, he stopped for an update on events of the past hour. Soldiers were now deployed along the avenue, he learned. They were armed with new West German G-3 assault rifles.

As Tzang and his students chatted, the sound of boos and whistles filled the air. Tzang looked toward the gate. At that moment, the army opened fire.

General Ne Win's regime was only a few months old, and already Tzang faced his second barrage of gunfire. He dropped into a ditch by the lane. Other students lay huddled beside him. The volley seemed to last forever. When it stopped, some of the students broke and ran. As soon as they were on their feet, the firing started again.

Tzang waited in the ditch, listening to the bullets whiz overhead. When the second volley ended, he, too, ran. It was a terrifying scramble. He tripped over a body, grabbed a fallen red flag of the Students Union, and stumbled forward just as a third volley of shots filled the air.

Miraculously, he reached the relative safety of the campus hostel. Inside, the survivors lay on the floor, eyes wide. The sound of breaking glass and bullets slamming into the walls filled their ears. Finally there was silence.

Looking out the shattered windows, Tzang saw bodies littered across the campus grounds. It looked like hundreds were dead and dying, although when the official body count was released days later, it numbered just 15 dead and 27 wounded.

The next morning, Tzang awoke at his step-brother's house to the sound of an exploding dynamite charge. It was the Students Union Building being levelled by the army. Throughout the city, people were stunned. The Students Union Building was Rangoon's symbol of free-thinking modern Burma.

More dismaying news came before the day's end: all the country's universities and colleges were closed until further notice.

Martyr's Day, the anniversary of the 1947 assassinations, was commemorated two weeks later. Among the official remembrance party was a son of the Mong Pawn Saopha, the man whose unlucky horoscope foretold his death. His son was brought out of jail for the public ceremony, then returned to his cell at day's end.

The English summer turned into autumn. Sao learned to cook her own meals; none of her London relatives had servants. Her nieces, in-laws and step-daughter fawned over her but she remained wary of their affections. She was the "rich auntie" in their eyes, she suspected. She wondered when she might get back to Burma, where she wasn't so reliant on others.

She continued her daily trips to the hospital's out-patient clinic, travelling by herself on the tube to Knightsbridge Station. It was a different experience from travelling with chauffeurs and bodyguards. Emerging from the station, the first thing she always saw was a brightly-lit advertisement for something called the Spiritual Society. She often paused to peer at the mysterious sign. Someday, she decided, she would see what it was all about.

The opportunity came unexpectedly in late November, when she met a woman who'd lost a son in the war. The woman confided to Sao that she kept in touch with her late son through the Spiritual Society. Would Sao like to come along?

Sao was happy of the chance to unveil a mystery and partake in a little adventure. Together they set out for the Society's address, off Belgrave Square, a short walk from her usual underground station stop.

Someone was selling entry tickets outside the door. Sao bought one and followed her companion inside. As they took their seats, the medium, a woman, entered the room. The small assembly rose to its feet, said a prayer, then sat down again. The woman preceded to pick a few people out of the crowd, delivering their loved one's messages from beyond.

Suddenly the clairvoyant pointed at Sao and said, "You!"

"Me?"

"Yes, you. There is a message for you."

Sao rose to her feet.

"The man who is talking to me is dressed like a bishop. Do you know any bishop?" the medium asked.

"I know a bishop in Rangoon, but he isn't dead. He's very much alive," answered Sao.

"Well, this man is dressed all in white robes, and he's telling you to go home," the medium declared. Then for good measure, she added: "You look like your mother, but you have your father's spirit."

Sao sat down, not knowing what to think. It was true: people always said she looked like her mother, but was a fighter like her father.

As for the man in white, she had no idea. She never pictured her husband in his formal Shan tunic and trousers, flowing like white robes.

Tzang picked up the ringing telephone at his step-brother's house. It was November 21, eight months and twenty days since his father disappeared.

The voice at the other end of the line introduced himself as Major Thein Shwe, an old classmate of Tzang's step-sister Sanda. Could they meet? Curious, Tzang agreed. He hoped the Major had news of his father.

There was no time to talk when they met later that day, though. A car whisked them immediately to Dagon House, a reception centre for the army brass.

Tzang followed the Major into a lushly furnished sitting room, where a uniformed, beribboned soldier stepped forward to greet them. Surprised, Tzang recognised the man instantly: Colonel Lwin, head of the dreaded Military Intelligence Service (MIS). The Colonel shook his hand congenially and broke the news: Prince Shwe Thaike was dead. He handed Tzang a Scotch with soda and a Benson and Hedges cigarette.

Tzang sank into an overstuffed chair, drink in hand, numbed. Colonel Lwin offered no further explanation. Instead he, too, took a chair and, on making himself comfortable, launched into small talk about the China-India border war. Tzang dragged heavily on the cigarette and gulped his Scotch, rattling the ice cubes in the glass, hardly hearing a word. His mind screamed with questions. Dead, how? Torture, execution?

The Colonel smiled and prattled on as if it were a typical cocktail hour at Dagon House.

When Sao received the news, she too was completely stunned. Things were far more serious than she or her London relatives ever imagined. We were so innocent, she realised.

She decided to return to Rangoon immediately. Tiger tried to dissuade her. She would end up dead or in prison, too, he warned. But Sao would hear nothing of her eldest son's advice. She was going, and he was welcome to come or stay as he pleased. In the end Tiger gave his blessing to the journey, not that Sao needed it. He himself would stay behind as an overseas anchor, should the family need to escape Burma.

"You never know what's waiting for you. You need someone on the outside, just in case," he said.

Sao agreed this was wise and so she said goodbye, never suspecting how many years it would be until they met again.

Arriving in Rangoon a few days later, she was greeted by her children and step-children, along with the Prince's old Chief Minister and an orange-robed monk who presented her with an urn containing the ashes of her most precious son, Myee. It hit her again—how innocent she'd been until now.

The Funeral

Sao gathered up the kids and moved back into 74 Kokine Road. The official word was that Prince Shwe Thaike died of heart failure, and Myee of an unfortunate "mistake". She didn't want to guess what might have really happened to her husband. It was true he had high blood pressure, but he wasn't sick enough to die, at least not under normal circumstances. She only hoped that his mind was calm at the time of death so that he could pass to a higher plane. She trusted his meditative training carried him through the last moments without fear or anger.

She was more certain of the circumstances surrounding Myee's death: it was cold-blooded murder.

A Tai soldier told her they'd been given information that there were armed Karen rebels inside the house, when in fact there were only the sleeping family members and the maids. He described how the soldiers advanced stealthily in two battle lines, one line on each side of the house. When Myee appeared holding a lance, nervous troops opened fire. Soldiers on the opposite side of the house answered back. Myee dropped to the ground, wounded, and the mêlée of bullets continued until the soldiers realised they were shooting at each other. The man couldn't explain why Myee was also shot in the back of the head at close range with a pistol, though.

Although her husband's death was unexpected, Sao adjusted to the news. It wasn't unusual for a wife to attend her husband's funeral. But losing a child was another matter. She never imagined that Myee, so lively and full of fun, could die. The army's excuses only made her mood darker. She was angry with everyone, even her own family.

She sniped at her two step-sons, Prince Sai and Hseng, who were in the midst of planning the funeral when she arrived. The authorities were present, too. They wanted a list of invitees to the funeral and their identification numbers.

The ceremony was no simple matter. The Prince's older sons favoured a relatively modest burial. The Buddhist clergy refused. A Celestial Lord should have a worthy funeral, they ruled: after a period of public homage at Yawnghwe Haw, the body must be cremated and entombed with due ceremony. Ko Latt, the retired Chief Minister, set about making the arrangements, which were considerable. The sons asked him to ship the body by train to Yawnghwe. Sao was appalled by the idea, for the weather was hot and the journey would take at least two days. The Prince deserved an aeroplane. She would pay the cost herself, she declared, if the sons were too cheap.

The heir apparent and his brother had considerations other than money, though. There was the question of whether an old-style feudal funeral was in keeping with the times. Then there were the authority's suspicions to worry about, especially if the family had to withdraw a large sum of money all at once. Sao didn't care. She took 200,000 Kyat in cash from her own bank account.

"If they think I'm using the money to arm people, they're stupid," she said. "Two hundred thousand is nothing to an army."

At least if she footed the bill herself, the sons couldn't scrimp, she thought. There would also be donations, she reminded them, for it was the custom for people to leave offerings when they viewed the body. They could expect contributions of about 40,000 Kyat, she guessed.

"Don't worry, we won't spend your inheritance," she groused. From that moment, she was in charge.

The Prince travelled by plane, as Sao wanted. The family accompanied his body. They were all dressed in royal white mourning clothes. Landing at Heho, they peered out the aeroplane window in wonder. The surrounding fields overflowed with mourners. Given the atmosphere of fear, the family hadn't really expected anyone to come. Yet here were thousands of ordinary people who had walked from their mountain villages and valley farms. As the funeral cortège wound its way down the mountainside to Yawnghwe valley, the people followed silently, creating a dramatic picture of defiance against the military rulers.

Slowly they made their way to the Haw, where a spontaneously gathered multitude was already camped on the palace grounds. The Prince's body was carried into the Great Hall of Audience and laid on a golden divan. Sao took her place beside him for the last time. She sat there for the next seven days while thousands of people came and knelt before the last Great Saopha of Yawnghwe.

While her husband lay in state, every bit of empty space in the town filled up with people. They kept coming, walking days over mountain ranges to make their final obeisance to the Prince. To feed them all, the palace cooks tended huge pots of rice and curry over open-air fires. Their sheer numbers defied the military's request for names and ID numbers.

Sao arrived at the Hall each morning before daybreak, so that she would be there when the monks came to pray. After the monks received their alms, the ordinary folk filed in. Pa-O hill folk and Intha fisherman knelt on the polished floor. Long-necked Paduang women prostrated themselves with painful grace. School children brought flower wreathes. A university graduate looked at the body and said, "What I am today, I owe to this man."

Two Burma Army men in gold-braided uniforms made an appearance. They came empty-handed, paid their respects and left quietly. General Ne Win stayed away.

On the seventh day, Sao and the family followed Prince Shwe Thaike's body to the pyre. His old royal umbrella bearers came out of retirement to carry the white umbrellas of state over his canopied bier. A seemingly endless procession walked behind them. The music of horns and drums filled the air. Everyone agreed the Prince led a good life but there was no atmosphere of celebration.

People watched sombrely as the pyre was lit. When it was over, Prince Shwe Thaike's ashes were placed in a tomb near the canal, beside two smaller tombs containing the ashes of his first wife and his son, Myee.

The mourners soon departed for their towns and villages. It was the last traditional royal funeral they would ever see in Shan State, and the last time they would pay homage to a Celestial Lord.

After the funeral the family returned to Rangoon, where life seemed oddly normal in some respects. The universities were open again, so the kids went back to their classes. Tzang resumed tutoring. All the while, though, men loitered on the street outside their home, watching their every move.

One day Tzang bumped into another car with his Land Rover. Sao sent their driver to view the other car. Finding the damage to be minor, he offered to make the necessary repairs. Instead, the other driver demanded a huge compensation settlement. When no money was forthcoming he called Sao's driver a "pro-feudalist", spitting out the word like the worst insult imaginable. Lately, anti-feudal propaganda filled the airwaves. It was having its effect on people.

In April they closed up the house for the hot season and escaped back to Yawnghwe. For Tzang, the sense of entrapment remained. One night he told Sao, "There are only two ways out of this Haw. Either I wait from them to arrest me in the night, or I go into the jungle."

"In the jungle there are hundreds of escape routes. Here, the only path leads straight to prison."

What he said was true, Sao knew. They could arrest him at any time. She couldn't ask him to stay.

The next morning he was gone. She could only wonder how he slipped past the spies and where he went. Perhaps he was dead or imprisoned already.

Harn and Ying Sita knew more than their mother. They met up with one of Tzang's classmates, who told them Tzang was very near and badly in need of weapons. Tzang had spoken to his comrades about a cache of Japanese weapons in a storeroom underneath the Dragon Stairs at Yawnghwe Haw.

The fellow showed up in his jeep later that evening, when darkness had fallen and everyone was inside their rooms. Harn and

Ying Sita helped him find the storeroom. Inside, they discovered a pile of rusty grenades and some rounds of ammunition, never handed in to the government because they were dangerously unstable to move.

Quickly, they loaded the jeep. Ying Sita suggested they put one particularly rusty-looking grenade in the tool box. Tzang's friend laughed and said, "If it blows, a tool box isn't going to save us."

He put the grenade in his pocket and got behind the wheel. Ying Sita took the seat beside him; Harn climbed into the back with the rest of the grenades.

They pulled onto the tarmac leading from town, spirits high. They knew the danger but didn't care. They were thankful for a chance to help the rebels.

Just past Taunggyi they pulled off the road. A dark shape emerged from behind a tree to collect the weapons. It wasn't Tzang.

Harn and Ying Sita were back at Yawnghwe Haw before they knew it. They never found out if the rebels made use of the aged weapons.

The family returned to Rangoon with the June rains. The big old house at Kokine Road seemed empty—just Sao, Harn, Ying Sita and their little sister, Leun. Tiger was far away in England, Myee and his father were dead, Tzang had disappeared into the jungle.

We used to be such a big family, Sao mused sadly.

She didn't want the military to think they'd defeated her. She travelled around the city freely, visiting friends and going to market. There were still social events where everyone put on a stoic face. At one such gathering she ran into the old wartime Chief Justice, who said he wanted to come to live in Shan State again, as he'd done in the first years of Japanese occupation. Sao had to shush him; there were military men in the room.

When she drove out the gates of Kokine Road, soldiers on the street watched to see which direction she took. "Ask them if they want a ride," she joked with the driver.

When the men outside came too close to the house, she said to her staff, "Tell them to come in for tea." She didn't want anyone to think she was afraid.

The other politicians' wives were just as closely watched and, like Sao, refused to be intimidated. The Mong Mit Saopha's wife picketed the Defence Ministry daily, carrying a sign demanding the release of all political prisoners. She was an Englishwoman who had come to Burma just before the coup; the authorities confiscated her passport so she couldn't go home.

The Hsipaw prince's Austrian wife assailed the authorities with requests for information about her missing husband. They wouldn't even admit he'd been arrested. His disappearance was never explained.

U Nu's wife descended on the jailers in a fury. It was the first time Ma Mya Yi was separated from her husband since the British jailed him, before the war. She cursed and hollered and threatened to slap the guard's face. The army men had to hold her back. After several of Ma Mya Yi's dramatic visits, they finally brought out the ex-prime minister.

"You musn't lose your temper like that," was all U Nu said to her.

Sao continued to welcome Tai politicians into her home. All their leaders were gone; she was the only one they could turn to. Sometimes they asked for her intercession, as if she were still able to corner General Ne Win and give him a dressing-down like she used to do.

She had to answer: "What can I do? I'm in deep trouble, too." Ne Win, she knew, was only waiting for a good excuse to arrest her.

In the meantime she went about her business, daring his henchmen to come and get her. She even travelled outside the city from time to time. She and Prince Sai visited Webu Sayadaw, who assured them that her husband had passed to a higher plane.

She went up to Hsenwi, although people warned her it was too dangerous. She wanted to see her mother.

She found the old woman in poor health and despondent. Lady Gold Diamond understood little about what was going on in Rangoon, but she knew things were amiss in Hsenwi. She told Sao that a soldier tried to rape one of the nuns from Queen of Peace Convent. She'd seen a lot of warfare in her eighty-eight years, but never such despicable behaviour as that.

Sao didn't see her brother during the visit. Suffering terrible stomach pains, Prince Hom Hpa had gone to England for medical treatment. The army doctor told him not to worry, he'd just eaten too much sticky rice over the years. Everyone save Sao's brother himself knew it was cancer. By the time he left, he was unable to keep food down.

Saying goodbye, Sao wondered if she would ever see her Hsenwi family again. It was a sad journey back to Rangoon.

At 74 Kokine Road, the days melted one into the other. The army left her alone, but she wasn't free. The rains beat down and the house grew dark. The city was changing. Overnight, familiar companies and banks disappeared from the central district. General Ne Win nationalised them all, beginning with the Burma Oil Company. It was a highly symbolic act: the company was 49 per cent British-owned, and had been the lynchpin of Britain's colonial interests before the war.

The oil company take-over was only the beginning. In February the country's 24 banks—10 Burmese and 14 foreign—were nationalised. Then the junta commandeered all commodities production and export industries. A law was passed stating no new private businesses could be created. One of General Ne Win's closest colleagues on the Revolutionary Council, Aung Gyi, resigned in protest, saying the policy was too extreme. A black market—people called it the shadow market—sprang into existence. Ousted from parliament, Jimmy Yang hungrily eyed up his sister's opium army, knowing that those who were strong and crafty could make money from the situation.

Sao wasn't part of the shadow world, though. She wondered how she and the kids and all the staff and relatives who depended on them would survive. For the first time, she wished her husband had invested abroad. He'd always taken special pride in supporting local companies. Now those companies no longer existed. She thought wryly that the junta might even come to take the milk cows they kept in the garden, because she sold their excess milk to a few English families who were still about. When the milk delivery man arrived at the door looking highly excited one July morning, she was prepared to hear that the cows were gone.

The Warning

In the forest between Mong Mit and Hsenwi, Tzang found the 4th Battalion of the Shan State Independence Army. The rebel soldiers were huddled under two makeshift lean-tos roofed with leaves and multi-coloured scraps of plastic sheeting. A former police sergeant and a World War II veteran were in charge of basic training. They taught Tzang how to handle a rusting Japanese .303 and to move men through the jungle. When the training was over, he was appointed political officer of the Northern Command.

Shortly after, he requested a transfer to the SSIA's southern headquarters. Permission granted, he set out through southern Kengtung State almost to the Thai border. At the Salween ferry crossing, he remembered the last time he'd travelled this far and how his father sent a monk to fetch him back. What would Prince Shwe Thaike say now? Democracy was finished.

He disembarked on the other side, in no-man's land. Turning back was no longer an option.

At the SSIA headquarters, the acting Chief-of-Staff greeted him warmly. Officer Khun Kya Nu was the son of Prince Shwe Thaike's cellmate. He'd been underground since 1959, starting out with the Brave Young Warriors. In his young life he had already led several guerrilla attacks against Burma Army convoys.

Although Tzang was younger and still combat-green, the SSIA leaders were impressed by his political acumen and inside knowledge of the Rangoon scene. He was immediately pulled into discussions about how to deal with General Ne Win. The General had sent word that all rebel organisations were welcome to join his proposed Burma Socialist Programme Party. Peace talks were scheduled for July in Rangoon. A cease-fire was declared to allow rebels time to consider the offer and make their way to the capital.

The young rebels looked at the peace offering from all angles. General Ne Win primarily wanted to win over the underground Communist Party, they guessed. After all, many of the communist outlaws were in fact Burma Army defectors. Ne Win hoped they would return to the fold now that the army was in power.

As for Tzang and his student friends, they were mere fleas nibbling the elephant's hide. Expecting to gain little, they hoped at least to drag out the cease-fire as long as possible. That way, they'd have time to gather more men and weapons.

The only problem, Khun Kya Nu noted, was if the General was laying a trap. The delegation shouldn't include too many senior leaders, in case they never returned from Rangoon.

This is how Tzang ended up back in Rangoon in July, 1963, as team leader of the Peace Talks delegation. The negotiators consisted of himself and two fellow SSIA officers. At a pre-arranged village on the road near Taunggyi, they met up with a representative of the army brass. He was an old-style army officer, well-educated and gentlemanly, courteous and non-threatening. So far so good.

While waiting for a plane to fetch them at Heho, the peace team heard a radio report that a fourth Shan rebel had arrived from Thailand to represent exiled students. It was an unexpected development. They requested the new arrival be made part of their delegation.

In Rangoon, they were met by a contingent of MIS officers and taken to a comfortable old house inside the Turf Club grounds. The exiled student representative, Sai Pan, was already there waiting for them. When evening fell, the young men walked the abandoned Race Course to discuss strategy away from listening ears.

Sai Pan wanted to lay their demands squarely on the table, but Tzang was under orders to move slowly, play for time. They argued inconclusively while a hollow wind blew through the bleachers, where Ne Win used to cheer on his favourite steeds.

Next morning, they awoke and gathered on the veranda. That's when Sao's milkman happened by, saw Tzang, and hurried the few blocks back to 74 Kokine Road with the news.

Sao was elated and terrified in the same moment. Her son was alive but he had walked straight back into danger. They exchanged messages and made arrangements for a brief family reunion at the Turf Club house. Their contact was minimal during the talks though. Mother and son were mindful of the need to protect one another from trouble with the authorities.

Not that they weren't already in deep enough trouble. Tzang was having difficulty with the negotiations. The talks were held in a sprawling mansion that formerly belonged to a Chinese tycoon. The first meeting was a disaster.

General Ne Win opened with the words: "We are giving you a chance to live. If you don't co-operate, we'll dig you out, root and all."

The exiles' representative, Sai Pan, responded by plunking a paper down on the table. Tzang knew it contained a demand for an immediate return to civilian federal government, no compromises. The paper made its way around the table, finally coming to General Ne Win. Judging by the scowl on the General's face, Tzang considered it lucky they weren't arrested on the spot.

In the weeks to come he had to work hard to keep the talks open and the cease-fire in place. It wasn't easy to instil discipline among team members older and more experienced than he. Patience, he counselled. No sudden moves. They were gaining excellent publicity from the talks. The press was fascinated by the young Shan State rebels, especially the late President's son. Tzang's picture appeared regularly in the papers. He had grown a sparse beard. Curling locks tumbled across his forehead and touched his thin shoulders.

The strategy was paying off in the field, where the Burma Army had orders to assist the Shan rebels as long as the talks were ongoing. Back at rebel headquarters, Khun Kya Nu asked for a helicopter to Thailand. He was amazed when the army provided one, flying him into Chiang Mai for supplies.

What did General Ne Win care? The Shan rebels were nothing to him. He was really interested in the Karen, who were a formidable force, and the communists. The top Karen leader capitulated and received an ambassadorship to Israel. The communists, on the other hand, refused to submit to Ne Win's political party. The problem was both sides insisted there was only one true party, and they were it.

The first round of talks ended and Tzang returned to the field. A second round was scheduled for September in Taunggyi.

Following events in the newspaper, Sao began to worry that the authorities could get to her son through his family. They could be arrested at any time, a threat that might be used to pressure him.

For the first time, she thought seriously about leaving Burma.

The few politicians and Rangoon society types that visited her home began imagining escape routes. A loose plan took shape: head north, then double back and make for the border. Sao asked the kids to pack small suitcases and keep them under their beds. She didn't feel like they would actually follow through on the precautions, though. For now, it was just something to talk about.

As it turned out, Sao needn't have worried about upsetting Tzang's negotiations. He bowed out to more senior leaders for the second round. In any case, the Taunggyi talks were off. Unable to pull the Communist Party onside, General Ne Win saw no point in meeting again with the Shan rebels. He never really cared if the long-haired students were part of his government or not. Their inclusion in the peace process was purely window-dressing. He would just as soon "dig them out, root and all", as he'd promised at their first meeting.

When the SSIA delegates arrived in Taunggyi, Ne Win's Revolutionary Council demanded immediate surrender. The rebels melted back into the jungle.

Thus Tzang disappeared from Sao's life again, pushed even deeper into the underground. She spent lonely days at the Kokine Road house, wondering what would become of them all. Pat and Prince Sai sent parcels of fruit from Yawnghwe. A sympathetic local businessman—Mr. X, she called him—stopped by occasionally to see how the family was faring. He had access to occasional bits of inside information, through connections with Burma Army men secretly unhappy with Ne Win's regime.

One October day he brought a warning: he'd heard there was a cell being prepared for the Mahadevi at the women's prison.

Sao sat back in her chair, mind whirling. She believed the rumour but had no idea what to do about it. Her thoughts raced back and forth between arrest and flight. Then she remembered how meditation had always helped her focus. The monk Webu Sayadaw was in Meiktila. She would go see him, and maybe the answers would come.

She packed nothing, just walked out the door in an old sarong and jacket. She left the children with the household servants, didn't even take her own maid. No entourage, no car, no bodyguard—it wasn't like the old days. Mr. X was her only escort.

They took the train. She arrived in Meiktila rumpled, dusty and completely unrecognisable as the former First Lady. Even Webu Sayadaw didn't notice her among the crowd until Mr. X introduced her.

"Child, come here," he said, beckoning her forward. "Your family has helped me many times in Rangoon. Now what can I do for you?"

"I only came here to meditate," said Sao. The monk smiled, an ocean of calmness. Sao was immediately glad she'd come. Two of the arahant's followers led her to a meditation cell.

She spent the whole day in the cell but worry kept crowding her mind. She couldn't concentrate, couldn't achieve the blissful letting-go of daily cares. In the evening two women came to join her.

"We came to keep you company," they said.

"If you came to meditate, stay. Otherwise, go," answered Sao. She wasn't ready to give up yet.

One of the women offered some advice. "If you have any questions in your mind, ask them while you are meditating," she said.

There was only one question in Sao's mind: Should she leave Burma? If arrested, her children would have no parents. But if she fled, the Tai would have no leaders left, for everyone else was in prison. She herself had only escaped jail by fate, but for what purpose? She closed her eyes and thought hard on the question.

"He will answer you tomorrow," the women said and left her to her meditation.

At dawn Sao joined the crowd gathered for Webu Sayadaw's discourse. The monk sat on a raised platform before them, legs folded in the lotus position. "In general, times are very bad," he began. "Seek prayer and universal love."

"Someone wants to go abroad and get some help. Let us all pray for that person."

That was all he said. Sao wondered, "Is this my answer?" The assembly began to pray. I suppose he means me, she thought. I guess I have to go. Then she felt great relief, for the decision was made.

She borrowed a jeep and headed for Mandalay with a small group of acquaintances and a tail of MIS spies. Taking their time, the travellers stopped at monasteries and made donations, like any party on pilgrimage. Then late one night Sao and Mr. X doubled back to Rangoon, as planned. They drove all night long, pulling up to the gates of 74 Kokine Road before sunrise. Sao noticed in an instant that the watchers were not yet at their usual places. It was now or never.

Mr. X headed to the railway station for tickets, pondering a logistical dilemma along the way. First class tickets would put them in the same carriage as army officers, too close for comfort. Yet if any soldiers recognised them travelling third class, suspicions would arise; it wasn't a usual way for the Mahadevi to travel. Incredible luck was on his side that morning, though. As he stood outside the platform wicket wondering what to do, an old colleague hailed him. He was a senior railway official, happy to assist his friend gain tickets for a pilgrimage tour to the south. The men made arrangements to add an old-style private carriage for eight onto the morning train. It was perfect.

It was still dark when Sao roused the kids from their beds. She was wearing the dust of the road. They decided to leave their suitcases behind. Harn gathered a few Kyat and his father's pocket watch. Sao had her sapphire ring and the jewelled buttons from her good aingyi. Her maid was awake, knowing the moment had come. Once Sao asked her if she wanted to escape, too, but she said no. Now Sao whispered, "Send a message to Thailand, if you change your mind."

She packed no clothes, made no trip to the bank: it wasn't open yet. She handed the house key to Mr. X, who promised to take care of the place in her absence. The jeep was waiting outside. A young guide, a "Mr. Y", would meet them at the station to accompany them on the journey. That was it. They were going, not next week, not tomorrow, but now. Sao walked out the door without looking back.

Flight

They travelled all day and night, following the long curve of the Gulf of Martaban to where the River Salween meets the sea. The air grew humid and tropical. In the early morning they reached the rail terminus at Martaban town, 187 miles south of Rangoon. Leaving the station, the family followed a stream of traders across a bridge made of lashed-together pontoon boats. Ocean-going ships and kattu sailboats crowded the Salween's mouth. On the opposite bank, the small port city of Moulmein lay between steep pagoda-crowned ridges and the gulf.

Mr. Y told them he had a friend in Moulmein who would put them up for the night. He led them through streets lined with mango trees and old stone houses with wrought-iron balconies, the legacy of Portuguese teak traders.

Sao was impressed by their guide's efficiency. Shortly they came to his friend's house, and there he left them to make arrangements for the following morning.

Her children—twenty-one-year old Ying Sita, Harn, fifteen and Leun, almost fourteen seemed ready for the adventure. They slept, then rose before sunrise. Mr. Y explained they were to take the public ferry inland to Kyondo, on the Huangtharaw River. It was risky travelling so openly but there was no other way. At this point, "going on pilgrimage" no longer held as an excuse. They were heading off the beaten path, moving toward Thailand.

They ate a little rice and then hurried through the dark streets to the landing. The ferry was crowded. After finding seats together, Mr. Y went off to buy drinks. He returned with steaming coffee in condensed milk tins. He also had some good news. While buying the coffee, he met a cargo boat captain who was willing to take on passengers. It would be a more secretive way to make the trip.

Presently a fully-laden timber boat chugged out of the morning mist. When it sidled near, Sao and the kids jumped from one deck to the next. Mr. Y stayed behind on the ferry, promising to meet up with them at their next destination.

The timber boat turned upstream. They were away. Sao and the kids relaxed and watched the riverbanks slide by. It was a peaceful interlude, over too soon. Just twenty miles upstream they came to a southward bend in the river. They had reached Kyondo where a jeep waited by the dock to take them to Kawkareik, the next town inland.

Mr. Y had arranged everything. The jeep driver took them to a house on the edge of Kawkareik town, where a kindly Burmese woman was happy to hide them from the hated army. Her place was quiet and pretty, shaded by tropical trees. Sao felt relaxed. They were in real jungle now, in the foothills of the Dawmna mountain range. Thailand was forty miles away, just behind the green peaks. Fear never entered her mind. They had moved so far, so fast that reality hadn't time to sink in.

Mr. Y caught up with them later in the day. Their reunion was happy. Everything was going according to plan. Assured that the family was settled comfortably, he left them again, saying he had some business to do.

He returned a few hours later, smile gone. The word was out that "some prominent people" were trying to flee the country and must be stopped.

"They're checking cars on the road. We have to be careful on our way out," he said.

By next morning, Mr. Y had a plan. To fool the police, the family must split up. The kids would ride in the jeep through the roadside checkpoint while Sao took a trishaw through the jungle by herself.

Her Burmese hostess gave her some old clothes and a basket for market. Then, to complete the disguise, she handed Sao a thick cheroot to smoke, as country women do. Although she'd never smoked before, Sao puffed gamely on the tobacco roll while the trishaw wallah pulled her down a narrow jungle track.

Safely past the police, the trishaw wallah turned off the road and deposited her in a farmyard. Suddenly alone, Sao looked around. The morning sun was high and steam rose from the jungle hills. In a moment the farm couple, seeing a stranger in their yard, stopped their work and offered her a dipper of cool water and a seat in the shade. The whole family gathered around, glad for some conversation and a rest. Sao asked after the crops. The couple answered that farming was too much trouble because there was no profit selling only to the government, as the new policy dictated. The family had no idea who Sao might be, just a lady who made small talk and waited in the shade for her friends.

Nearly two hours passed before Mr. Y arrived with the kids and jeep. They'd encountered no trouble at the checkpoint. The guards looked inside the vehicle but saw only some youngsters. They didn't look "prominent". Without asking for ID, they waved the jeep through.

Reunited, the party spent the rest of the morning on the road, grinding slowly through the mountains. They passed two more checkpoints but no higher-up army officers were present and the local guards lazily waved them past. Word of the "prominent persons" hadn't reached this far yet.

Fearing stricter checks ahead, when they neared the border Sao and the kids decided to get down from the jeep and cut through the jungle on foot while Mr. Y drove ahead. Leaving the jeep, they slipped into the trees. It wasn't a long walk, but it was hot. Harn took off his jacket. Unnoticed, his father's watch slipped to the ground. It was the only thing he'd brought with him from Rangoon.

Under the hot afternoon sun they soon came to a village on the Moei River, a green ribbon cutting through the bush. Thailand was on the other side. Mr. Y was waiting with a young student sympathiser sent to aid them. The student, Sai Nyan Win, would drive the jeep through the crossing at nearby Myawaddy. Getting Sao and the kids across was a trickier matter.

Mr. Y found them a resting spot under a bush near the river's edge, then disappeared into the jungle. Sao listened to his steps in the underbrush fade gradually into the distance. She gazed up into the jungle canopy, spread over their heads like a roof. They would be okay, she was certain. For some reason, she still didn't feel afraid.

It wasn't long before Mr. Y returned and led them downstream to where a simple raft was tied to a tree-branch. He'd purchased it from a villager. The family clambered on board.

Having safely guided them as far as he could, Mr. Y slipped the rope-end and tossed it onto the raft's slick timbers. He wished them luck. Sao took up the raft-pole, dug it into the river bed and, without further ceremony, pushed her family toward freedom.

Three hours later, the Burma Army arrived and sealed the border.

They spent several weeks within a few miles of the border, waiting for permission from the Thai authorities to move inland. The first day, they took a bullock cart from the river's edge to a poor farm house outside Mae Sot, the border-town. The farmer had only a little rice and fish paste to share.

A Thai official stopped by in the afternoon but he didn't seem to understand who Sao was or why she wanted to stay in Thailand. He told her there were many people to pay off, including the Burmese border patrols. She gave him the stone from her sapphire ring and the name of a prominent Thai banker who would send more money if needed. The man was impressed and didn't bother her again.

Word spread quickly that a woman of some importance was in town. The next day the family was invited to move into the house of a former Forestry Department official who worked the teak forests around Mae Sot. He was a wealthy man who kept armed guards outside the gates of his home.

Sao was not the only border-crosser about. Hundreds passed over, mostly Chinese and Indian traders and a few Tai. The Tai stopped in to pay their respects to the Mahadevi and exchange news, creating a constant flow of people which made the timberman anxious. Some he chased away from the house because they had the look of spies.

One Tai woman arrived at the house with a frightening story. Travelling with her children, she'd been mistaken for Sao and chased across the border by gun-wielding Burma Army men. She had to swim for her life. Hearing this, the timberman began to truly fret. He had a wife and daughter to protect. He worried that Burma's MIS would send a team of hunter-killers across the border. Such things were not unheard-of.

They were all getting jumpy. A few days after Sao's arrival, the local police informed the timberman that they'd captured a suspicious person who was asking after the Mahadevi. He seemed to know too much about the family and their movements. What should they do?

The timberman put the question to Sao.

"Throw him in the river," she suggested.

"No, wait, he might be one of us!" her son Harn said, for the timberman said the man was tattooed and was named "Win", or something like that. Tattooing was an old Tai tradition.

Harn went to the police station to investigate. The captured man was Sai Nyan Win, the young student who had driven the jeep across the border for them. They had almost caused him to be deported. Released, he joined them at the house.

Within a few days, the local police captain arrived to interview Sao. She was happy for the chance to explain events in Burma and why they were forced to flee.

The conversation took a completely different tack, though. Speaking through a translator in the Central Thai dialect—not the familiar border lingo—the policeman's comments left Sao speechless. In the awkward silence, the translator said softly: "Perhaps you don't understand the police chief, madam. He thinks you've come here to trade in opium."

"Why should I trade opium?" Sao asked weakly. It seemed like a completely bizarre accusation. Opium, she thought, was for outlaws like the KMT and Olive Yang. Respectable people didn't make their living that way.

"You know very well who sells opium," she told the police chief, anger rising.

"Yes, but they are only small fry," he answered.

"And you think I'm their ringleader?" Sao shot back. "I don't even know what opium looks like, if it's black or white. Go to Bangkok and ask everyone, from the King on down, if I'm the kind to trade in opium."

She felt deeply let down. This was their welcome to Thailand. When the timberman asked the Mahadevi how long she planned to stay, she had no answer. He wrote a letter on her behalf to Thailand's Prime Minister, Sarit Thanarat. The PM and Sao knew each other, so surely he could hurry the situation along. But Sarit was on his deathbed and could make no reply.

By the time the local Governor arrived from the district capital, Sao had lost all sense of self-importance. They were just a family of refugees, fleeing for their lives. She was honoured that the official and his aides wore full military dress for their meeting.

The Governor explained that they needed permission from the Interior Ministry to settle in Thailand. With the PM gravely ill, however, everything was in flux. His words were not very encouraging: without permission to remain in Thailand, the family faced deportation back to Burma.

Days passed. No permission arrived from Bangkok. A man claiming to be looking for ice for sale tried to get into the house. After spotting Sao inside, he took off. The police were called in for a hasty conference with the timberman and his wife. The wife put her foot down.

"That woman has to go, right now, before we're all killed," she declared.

That evening the police placed a special patrol outside the house. The timberman loaded his gun and sat on the stairway till dawn.

Next morning, an ambulance with blacked-out windows came to collect the family and their student companion. A plane to Tak, the district capital, was waiting for them at the airstrip with orders not to lift off until they were all aboard.

Sao was happy to be on the move, even though Tak was only about forty miles east. It took just minutes to reach their destination. Then the waiting began anew.

The Governor greeted them. Prime Minister Sarit was dead, he informed them. It would take time for the new regime to hear their case. In the meantime, they could go no further into Thailand.

He found them an apartment on the second floor of the town bank. The bank guards would double as their bodyguards. He

paid a nearby restaurant to cook them meals three times a day. They entered a new limbo.
    Finally, news of Sao's plight reached her Thai banker friend. A wealthy and influential man, the banker took special interest in promoting cultural ties between the Tai people settled throughout Southeast Asia. Knowing that Thai and Tai shared the same blood, he was ready to help. He despatched the editor of a Chiang Mai newspapers he owned. A senior Tai monk and the SSIA rebel leader Khun Kya Nu went along, too, to help make the introductions.
    Welcoming the party, Sao poured out her story. At last, here were people who nodded their heads sympathetically.The editor marched down to the post office and sent a wire to the Interior Ministry in Bangkok. The reply was swift: due to diplomatic links between Thailand and Burma, Sao could not be accepted as a refugee. However, she was welcome as a visiting member of the Tai royalty.
    No one stood in their way. They climbed into the editor's van and set off for Chiang Mai, Thailand's second-largest city, 165 miles straight north. On the way, they stopped for a tour of Bhumibol Dam, the pride of modern Thailand. There a Thai health officer inoculated the kids, a small but significant symbol of sanction.
    They arrived in Chiang Mai in February 1964, three months after leaving Rangoon. It had been a long and unsettling journey with more starts and stops than Sao had ever imagined.
    At first it seemed she would face familiar problems in Chiang Mai. Low-level bureaucrats sought bribes and made veiled threats to send the family back to Burma. But things were different now. She was surrounded by a supportive community.
    The banker turned over his summer house to her and the children. The city had its own resident royals, who accepted her with respect. She met up with people from Kengtung, too. The Kengtung Saopha's brother—arrested during U Nu's time—lived in Chiang Mai, as did descendants of the fellow who was exiled to Thailand in 1939 for assassinating his uncle; Sao remembered his trail in Taunggyi. Their Chiang Mai-born children married well and had good connections in Thai political circles. Sao had a small circle of friends and protectors. The bribe-seekers soon gave up their threats.
    Within weeks of her arrival, Tai students began arriving from the border areas. They came in ones and twos, drawn

by news that the Mahadevi of Yawnghwe had escaped the clutches of General Ne Win. They hoped she could help their resistance movement.

Sao was dismayed by the students' apparent disunity. When she asked who their captain was, the students offered a variety of names. They belonged to any number of little armies, and none of them had much in the way of weapons. The situation seemed quite hopeless but Sao was never prone to despair.

"You'd better get organised," she told the students.

Already the wheels turned in her mind. She must win Shan State back, but how? There had to be a way to make a real army out of the poorly-equipped youngsters. Then one March day, Tzang appeared in her doorway. After nearly a year in the jungle, Sao's second son looked like a battle-hardened guerrilla fighter. He said he'd been in Laos buying guns. From that moment, Sao knew they had a chance.

Five

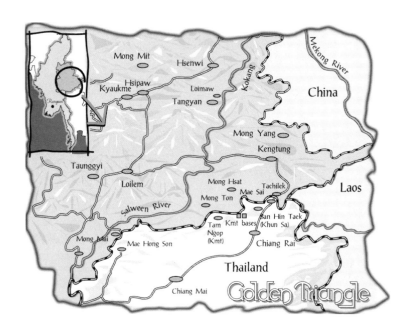

(Above) Tzang as a Shan State Army (SSA) officer, addressing a village meeting in 1967.

(Above) Lo Hsin Han. (The Bangkok Post)

(Left) Li Wen-huan on the left. (The Bangkok Post)

(Above) Well guarded by armed troops, Khun Sa with his senior officers. (The Bangkok Post)

(Left) Chang Shi-fu aka Khun Sa. (The Bangkok Post)

(Below) A mule caravan approaching Thailand, opposite Mae Hong Son. (Patricia Elliott)

U Nu and his wife, Ma Mya Yi, during their visit to Thailand in August 1969. (The Bangkok Post)

Shan State Army recruits, 1990. (Patricia Elliott)

Khun Sa giving an interview at his base. The author is on the far left. (The Bangkok Post)

The tomb of Prince Shwe Thaike. (Don Jedlic)

Mandalay Palace's walls, now used as both a jail and a tourist attraction. The sign says: "Tatmadaw (the army) and the people eternal unity. Anyone attempting to divide them is our enemy." (Don Jedlic)

The Shan State Army

Sao soon had her army. The first to join up were the Shan State Independence Army and the Shan Nationalities United Front. They combined their forces on April 22, 1964, just a few months after her arrival in Chiang Mai.

"Who will you fight?" Sao asked.

"The Burma Army," the students replied.

"Well, then, you can call yourselves the Shan State Army," she said.

The Shan State Army (SSA) made her chairperson of their War Council, which would set policy and garner outside support. A Thai intelligence officer was assigned to work with them. He was a sympathetic fellow related by marriage to the Kengtung clan.

Sao told her young soldiers not to waste too many bullets on the Burmese. "One bullet, one man," she advised. Tzang agreed, and restricted his men to fifty rounds each when they went into battle.

The rebel army began its fight short of men and guns. Then hope sprang from an unexpected source. The word spread that

Jimmy Yang was back in Kokang raising the banner of revolt. Tzang led a high-level delegation to win him over to the SSA. His men had to fight three battles with the Burma Army just to get to Kokang.

Jimmy's tale of the past year was a twisted one. First of all, his sister Olive was in jail. He himself had tipped off the police. Olive had become an embarrassment to the family, twice requesting a judge to allow her to marry her girlfriend. Meantime, the Yang family was losing its hold on the cross-border trade to Olive's own protégé, Lo Hsin Han. A clever businessman, Lo brought in chemists to create liquid morphine from the sticky opium sap. Easier to transport than opium bricks, the refined drug accounted for 15 per cent of his profits, a portion he hoped to expand. His wealth bought him popularity with the people of Kokang, for he was generous in his business dealings.

Olive had time only to give her cash and jewels over to her actress friend before the police led her away. Her jail cell was not so bad. She was fed decently—rice, vegetables and tea—and allowed to visit with others in the same cell block. They threw notes back and forth to women in the neighbouring block. Olive was tough. She'd seen worse deprivation in the jungle.

Jimmy headed up into the hills to reclaim his family's army. Since the coup ended his political career, there was no point staying in Rangoon. His brother Eddie the Myosa was in jail, too, arrested at the same time as Olive. No one stood between him and the Kokang Revolutionary Force. When he arrived, he made the crafty Lo Hsin Han his top captain. It would prove to be a near-fatal mistake.

Lo and Jimmy worked on raising money, and they were successful. General Ne Win's national economic program was a boon to black marketeers. Its essence was nationalisation. Nearly every store, co-op and warehouse in the country was taken over. By May, 1964, 3,000 firms were nationalised and 1,000 were declared superfluous. All of Burma's once-vibrant trade was hammered into twenty-two state corporations.

To save foreign exchange, General Ne Win restricted imports. Each household was given a ration booklet issued by the Security Administrative Committee. Nails, petrol, coffee, cooking oil and other daily goods became scarce. The busy markets where Sao used to shop all but dried up. People instead joined long queues outside the state corporations. They tended to buy up large amounts of things when they got the chance, in case the item never went on sale again. Then they turned around and sold the excess. They nicknamed the resulting black market "Trade Corporation No. 23".

Trade Corporation No. 23 was a going concern in Kokang. Jimmy had access to opium and good connections with Chinese merchants in Thailand. Burma needed a lot of things: razor blades, playing cards, watches, you name it.

Many small traders and ordinary citizens were financially wiped out when General Ne Win—alarmed by the black market—suddenly demonitised all fifty and one hundred Kyat notes on May 17, 1964. But the big guns like Jimmy and Lo survived and prospered all the more.

When Tzang arrived in Kokang, he saw impressive fortifications and well-armed troops. The talks went well. Jimmy told him to come back later and they would make the SSA membership official.

Tzang crossed back over the Salween to SSA land, where his 1st Brigade ranged the wild hills between Hsenwi and Mong Mit. In the rebel army's first year, Burma Army patrols swept their territory. Tzang led sniper attacks on foot columns and ambushed convoys. They made a lightening strike on the Namtu-Badwin mining town. It wasn't easy work. He organised some mountain tribespeople to ambush a train but at the crucial moment they ran away in fear —they'd never seen a train before. Another time he narrowly saved some recruits from blowing themselves up with a landmine they'd just planted: one of the soldiers, driven by curiosity, was about to poke it with a stick.

However inexperienced, the rural people were at least enthusiastic about the cause of Shan independence. Tzang held meetings to organise the villages. The SSA provided food and clothes to village boys who joined up. The recruits had to bring their own shoes. The girls were trained to work as barefoot doctors and given a few medicines and vaccines to carry in their bags. At regular meetings, the youngsters sang the Shan anthem and studied the freedom movement's history. Their parents, meanwhile, paid taxes to the rebel army, as they had always done to whomever was currently in control of their lives and their farmland.

The system Tzang and his friends organised was very much like the traditional Saopha's tax. They charged just one pound of rice and twenty Kyat per household per year, with exemptions for poor households and a ten per cent return for village administration. More money was raised through road tolls and the licensing of local industries, such as mills and slaughterhouses. The SSA's profits financed 217 schools. There was never enough money to arm all their recruits, though.

It so happened that some people began to pay their taxes in opium, which was easier to come by than cash. By the end of 1964 the SSA found itself in possession of 160 kilograms and faced with the dilemma of how to get rid of it. When some Chinese merchants connected with the KMT expressed interest, the SSA put a mule caravan together and embarked on their first trade trip across the border, under heavy guard. They wound down a narrow mountain path through dripping vegetation, ears straining for enemy footsteps, rifles at the ready. Anyone could attack the prize caravan—bandits, rival armies, government forces, the KMT themselves.

Crossing the border to one of the KMT's Thai-based villages was just as nerve-wracking. It was a rough-looking town of wooden shacks with a deeply rutted main street cut into a steep hillside. Technically they were enemies. Only recently Khun Kya Nu had hijacked a KMT salt shipment, telling them in harsh words to go back to China.

The Chinese traders greeted them with open arms, though. When it came time to trade, there was no sense harbouring old grudges. Tzang and his colleagues discovered that the profit margin was astounding. A viss of opium valued at 350 Thai Baht in the villages sold for 1,100 Baht on the border.

In the KMT villages of Tam Ngop and Mae Sa Long, drug refineries disguised as rice-whisky breweries and lumber mills sat within spitting distance of the local police stations. There the merchants turned the sticky sap bricks into morphine and heroin, selling it for even more astronomical profits. The European heroin price was US$ 600,000 a kilo that year, and rising.

The SSA's gain from the trade was far more modest, but no less important to them. It was guns they needed, and guns they got. Their trading partners were in an unusual position: the KMT-CIA connection created a weapons surplus. They were happy to exchange excess CIA arms for the raw opium.

By the time Tzang and his army leaders returned to Kokang in early 1965, they knew something about the tools of survival. They soon learned a quick lesson on how suddenly balances and alliances could shift.

Just as talks with Jimmy got re-started, his lead captain, Lo, shamelessly announced that he'd just been bought off by the Burma Army. The Burmese forces had captured a twenty-one ton consignment of opium about seventy miles away from the Tachilek crossing. They told Lo he could have the opium back if he agreed to be deputised as a Home Guard leader. He accepted. His first assignment: attack his boss, Jimmy Yang.

The Burmese didn't trust Jimmy, who was smart and political. The moon-faced, money-motivated Lo seemed a safer bet. To his credit, though, Lo gave Jimmy ample warning time to flee for Thailand.

The well-constructed little empire of Jimmy Yang fell into chaos. The place emptied out as his men ran to the river crossing. Tzang and his men joined the fleeing horde.

Shortly after, Jimmy showed up at Sao's Chiang Mai house. He still looked the same, a broad-shouldered man with a hint of the devil in his eyes. Even as a refugee, he wasn't lost. His still had his army and his family's long-time connection to the powerful KMT.

When Sao told him about her encounter with the police chief in Mae Sot, he laughed.

"Jeez, madam, don't say that next time—that you don't know if opium is black or white. Opium is both!"

The white he referred to was high-grade heroin, the ultimate refined product of the poppy plant. So far, the KMT's border-based refineries made only a low-grade smokeable brown heroin called No. 3. Their dream was to produce No. 4, the whitish powder that foreigners injected directly into their veins.

Looking around Sao's borrowed house, Jimmy said, "I hate to see you living in poverty, madam. Put 40,000 Baht with me, and we'll trade in opium. At the very least, you'll make another 40,000."

Sao refused politely. The stars were her excuse. "Jimmy, my horoscope says I can do anything, but no opium. If I do opium, I will lose."

Sao's real worry was that the Shan State Army would get into trouble with the Thai government if they were pulled into the drug trade. The Thai intelligence officer had warned her bluntly: "No drugs, or we'll send you packing." She suspected he was merely trying to protect the interests of Thai traders, who kept the military greased.

Still, she was happy to have Jimmy join the SSA. His men were disciplined and well-armed. As for Jimmy's shady KMT friends, she was fast losing her initial snobbery towards the drug trade. A blind eye was the best policy. In meetings of the War Council, she stressed her credo:

"If there's opium, I don't want to know about it. And for god's sake, don't bring it across the border. Sell it on the other side!"

The caravan trips continued, once or twice a year. The SSA officers encouraged the villagers to grow more poppies. But the territory they controlled was not like the hills of Kokang. The lowland rice farmers looked down on opium farming. Only a few braved the social stigma that came with poppy cultivation. As a result, the SSA shipments never amounted to much.

There were other ways to make an income, including controlling the border routes. The Thai-Burma border was 1,250 miles long, but almost all the crossings were spoken for by competing groups. Through a clever misinformation campaign, the SSA managed to steal a crossing from the KMT. They paid villagers to spread rumours of a large approaching force and stationed men on hilltops, clearly visible, as if they were sentries for a hidden army. The KMT fell for the ruse and gave up the crossing without a fight. It was a quite profitable enterprise: the SSA levied a five per cent tax on all goods passing through.

After a few skirmishes and some unsuccessful assassination attempts on the SSA leadership, the Burma Army withdrew from the volatile border region. In its place, they instructed their paramilitary Home Guards to keep order. The Home Guards were hardly on the clean side of the law. The most important Home Guard force belonged to Olive Yang's other wiley protégé, Chang Shi-fu.

After losing out in the de-monitisation, Chang Shi-fu flirted briefly with rebellion, then returned to official sanction. It was easier to operate with the Burma Army's blessing. He held the land between the SSA's territory and the Salween. The rebels often flitted through the edges of his domain but he didn't really want to fight them. It was better to make a deal.

He had an uncle who knew Tzang. Through the uncle, the two armies—one official, one underground—developed a line of communication. They agreed to leave each other alone. Such symbiotic relationships were born of the necessity to keep trade routes open.

About that time the region where the borders of Shan State, Laos and Thailand converged acquired a nickname: the Golden Triangle. It was a shady, violent world where all kinds of balances were struck and deals made in the interests of survival. Sao's small army had landed right in the thick of it. All they wanted out of the whole morass was to get their country back.

Survival of the Fittest

The SSA's income helped expand the Chiang Mai headquarters. They obtained a walled compound for training recruits. Sao's house became the War Council's information centre. All day long, people trooped in and out to exchange news and discuss strategy. Teenaged Harn kept up the SSA's paperwork and coded and decoded messages over the wireless. The messages told of battles and casualty counts from hit-and-run fighting in the field.

Their Thai intelligence contact stopped by occasionally to see how they were doing. If there was any hint of danger, he stationed plain-clothes men outside their gates. Deaths were appallingly easy to arrange in Chiang Mai. Assassins charged just five Baht to stab someone in the back, ten Baht to stab them face to face. The officer gave Harn a small pistol to carry in his pocket, and told him to make sure he stuck by his mother's side whenever she went out.

"If there's any trouble, shoot first and we'll clear it up later," he said.

Sao chaired regular meetings of the War Council. The army leaders were a varied bunch, from grizzled veterans to fresh-faced students. Jimmy Yang was made a member. Sao's job was to find the support they needed to go into battle. She met with U.S., British and Thai officials, but the meetings left her frustrated and empty-handed. There were larger, more sinister games afoot in the Golden Triangle. The SSA was left to its own devices while weapons poured in for the two main Cold War rivals—the KMT and the Communist Party of Burma.

Li Wen Huan—everybody called him Lao Li, "Old Li"—was lord of the Golden Triangle. A minor functionary before the revolution, he crossed over to Burma with General Li Mi when the KMT lost in China. He'd been through the failed invasion attempts and had learned to focus his efforts on trade. Jade, tusks, hides and cattle flowed down his caravan routes to Thailand. When General Li Mi resigned his position, Old Li stepped into his place. He shifted the focus to the Triangle's most valuable commodities: drugs, guns and intelligence. Soon he had control of a full 90 per cent of the cross-border trade.

He had none of his former boss's ambitions to free China, but the Americans didn't know that. As far as they were concerned, Old Li was their anti-communist warrior. They kept the weapons support flowing. Aware of the CIA's special interest in Old Li, the Thai authorities turned a blind eye to his two growing bases in Thai territory. The Americans put him in charge of watching China and keeping the communist rebels in check.

The Communist Party of Burma experienced its own small windfall as China's revolution deepened into Chairman Mao's Great Proletarian Cultural Revolution. Well armed and fully indoctrinated with Marxist theory, the communist underground introduced collective agriculture and endless political meetings to the villages under their control. In the mornings they faced the sun, copies of Chairman Mao's quotations held over their hearts. Disillusioned apathy overtook the farmers, and the villages soon began to dry up.

Although the communists were their own worst enemy, their very presence nonetheless struck fear in the hearts of the Americans, who believed in dominoes.

The fear led the Americans onward; their embroilment in Southeast Asia spread from the southern coast of Vietnam to the foreboding hills of Laos, Thailand and Burma. They worried that Burma would become China's back door to the region, along a route familiar to foreign invaders: the Burma Road, which cut through the heart of Shan State.

Every now and then, Sao had tea with William Young, an American missionary who spoke the languages of several hilltribes. He was the third generation of Youngs to tramp the wild hills since the turn of the century. His grandfather, William Sr., carried out 4,919 baptisms in 1905-06, a record his descendants had yet to surpass. It was William Sr.'s son, Harold, who came to Panglong in 1946 to represent the Wa and Lahu. "As wild as a Wa," Sao remembered.

William Jr. wasn't interested in converting Sao over tea; he just wanted to talk politics. He had carried on the family's mission among the hilltribes and he was determined to see the region remain part of the free world. In 1965, the Burmese junta took over Dr. Gordon Seagrave's missionary hospital at Nam Hkam. It was a sobering development, but nothing compared to what the Chinese or Russians might do if they had their way in Southeast Asia, Young thought.

Young became a valuable asset to the Americans. Through his hilltribe contacts, he helped the CIA establish three radio listening posts in Shan State. He also organised intelligence-gathering forays into Yunnan province. Then he busied himself in Laos, making sure support for communism didn't spread among Laotian hilltribes. To help build loyalty, the Americans agreed to help Laotian opium growers ferry their crop to Thailand. They set up an air cargo run under the name Air America. When things got really busy, they seconded their own soldiers from Vietnam to help Air America load the shipments.

Young thought he could build an anti-communist fighting force among the Lao hill folk, but Sao was sceptical. She'd seen how difficult it was to instil discipline among her own foot soldiers. The SSA officers were well-bred young men and good fighters, but she had to admit that the volunteers were uneducated and unruly. If they captured a consignment of whisky they were apt to drink it up on the spot and get up to all kinds of nonsense.

"Bill, you're going to be disappointed," she warned. "The Lao are just as easy-going as the Tai. I don't think you can do anything to help them."

But William Young wasn't ready to give up without trying.

Sao wouldn't give up, either, even after her six-member War

Council descended into bickering. In the absence of any reliable means of outside support, they fought about how best to survive: who to make alliances with, how to get help from abroad.

Her most heated arguments were with Jimmy Yang. The two constantly picked at each other. Sao didn't trust Jimmy's friendship with the KMT. He kept his men camped next to Old Li's village. She worried that he might be sharing information with them, a dangerous move because the KMT maintained links with the Burma Army.

"You have to decide who you're with," Sao said crossly one day, "Old Li or us."

Her bluntness didn't help matters. She griped about Jimmy in front of the wrong people. Word got back to him, making things worse.

By 1966, Jimmy was out of the game altogether. The Burma Army let it be known that if his men surrendered, they would receive Home Guard status. Jimmy's soldiers wavered. Home Guard militias were profitable and safe. They would gain the protection of the Burma Army. The other Kokang boys, Lo and Chang, were doing very well with their Home Guards.

A large group of Jimmy's men were staying in Chiang Mai at the time. Jimmy alerted Sao: "Don't let them leave the city." But one day they disappeared.

It seemed the Yang family were doomed to continually undercut one another. Jimmy had a brother, Francis, who took charge of the troops in Kokang and surrendered them to the Burmese.

Jimmy declared himself retired from the revolution and took a job managing a Chiang Mai hotel.

Developments within the Golden Triangle continued at a bewildering pace. The Communist Party began actively courting Sao. Their chairman, Than Tun, sent her a letter that talked about "the fighting unity of all Shan peoples." She ignored it, knowing contact with the Communist Party would scuttle all hope of American aid.

Other War Council members were less dismissive: maybe the communists could help them, if the Americans would not. They should at least consider it. The young men began to grumble that the Mahadevi was imperious and feudalistic, too much of a spoiled princess, used to giving orders instead of consulting with others.

Sao didn't live like a princess, though. To help make ends meet, Ying Sita took a job teaching English. She earned 800 Baht a month. Sao was happy the girl had a job; she wanted to keep her daughter out of politics.

One day, Sao received a letter post-marked Canada. It was from Tiger, her eldest son. He was working for a mining company in a place with the improbable name of Flin Flon, in the pine forests of northern Manitoba. He knew through the Tai grapevine that his family had crossed the border but it took some time to track them down. After that, they maintained sporadic contact. Tiger's work kept him on the move. Sao could hardly hop on a plane to go see him, being a woman without a passport, but it was a comfort to know he was out there somewhere, still an anchor.

She worried about all her children. Harn and his little sister Leun went to school so they could learn Thai. Luckily, supportive friends paid their tuition. Sao herself could barely afford the basics for her family. She sold the jewelled buttons she'd brought from Burma and was surprised to discover that inexpensive Burmese stones were quite valuable in Thailand. For a while she tried her hand at trading a few gemstones, but she didn't earn much.

There were others in Chiang Mai who prospered well from the anarchic border situation. Walled villas with swimming pools were under construction. Addicts appeared on the streets. Ethnic refugees from Burma became easy scapegoats. When the various ethnic armies feuded among themselves, the occasional violence didn't help their reputations. Complaints began to appear in the newspapers.

Sao still had benefactors and supporters to help keep her family afloat. When Harn was accepted to Bangkok's Chulalongkorn University in 1966, the Thai authorities overlooked his lack of resident's papers. Then they suggested Sao and the girls move to the capital with him. Friends would loan them a comfortable house with modern appliances.

Sao got the message that she was wearing out her welcome in Chiang Mai. She didn't care. In fact, the move might work in her favour. In Bangkok, she'd be closer to the American embassy. It didn't matter where she lived—she would still be chair of the SSA's War Council.

So Sao moved to Bangkok, while in the jungle her army continued its struggle to survive in a lawless netherworld of spies and insurgents. Tzang did his best to hold things together. Some days it seemed an impossible task.

His men faced constant temptation to defect. The Burma Army extended its offer of Home Guard status to all armed rebels, having learned that a policy of co-option worked best. Everyone knew life was easier as a government-sanctioned unit than as a outlawed rebel band. Home Guard caravans snaked along the border trails, teams of eighty mules led by a half-dozen trucks. The trucks returned to Burma stuffed with consumer goods. When Lo Hsin's Han's 1967 caravan crossed the river at Tachilek, he made US$ 500,000 in the blink of an eye.

Olive's boys made money only as long as the balance was maintained. If one army stepped into the wrong territory, bloody chaos ensued.

In early July, 1967, Chang Shi-fu prepared to transport the largest opium shipment ever seen in the Golden Triangle. He'd been gaining strength in the past few years, gradually rising to challenge the KMT's hegemony over the trade. By 1969, Old Li had lost 40 per cent of the market to Chang. The two forces were now nearly equal in influence, and Chang was ready to push himself over the top.

The consignment weighed in at just over 13,000 kilos, compared to the biggest SSA shipment of 1,600 kilos. His customer was Laotian Supreme Commander General Ouane Rattikone, the man the U.S. depended on to keep the communists from overrunning Laos. General Oaune placed his order through Chang's broker in Chiang Mai.

Chang needed 300 mules to carry the shipment and 500 men to guard it. They set out on the shortest possible route to Laos, straight through Old Li's KMT territory.

In a small Laotian village on the banks of the Mekong River, the caravan was overtaken by 1,000 KMT. Chang's men dug in for battle in the monsoon mud, right next to General Oaune's lumber mill and opium refinery. But their firefight came to an abrupt end when General Ouane himself stepped in and attacked both sides indiscriminately from the air. He sent five T-28 bombers and two infantry battalions at the warring opium traders and then, for good measure, sailed two gun boats up the Mekong. Both sides fled the scene, leaving most of the opium behind. Years later, General Ouane told the press he processed the abandoned opium in his refinery, then sent it to Hong Kong.

With 100 men dead, Chang Shi-fu sustained twice the KMT's casualties and lost an entire year's harvest.

As a result of the Opium War, Old Li tightened his grip on the drug trade. He could no longer allow upstarts—any upstarts, including the SSA—to run goods across the border.

Thus, Chang was not the only loser in the Opium War fallout. After 1967, the SSA only managed to get one caravan into Thailand. They became an army without revenue, relying on the meagre handouts of Sao's Thai and American contacts.

Later that year, the Thai military brought Tzang and a number of his men to Bangkok for specialised training. There he found that the situation with the War Council was as bad or worse as the situation in the field. Sao and her co-councillors fought constantly.

The major point of contention was how to get by. While Sao hadn't brought them any help through her American contacts, the Communist Party's overtures were still on the table. Within the War Council, a camp formed in favour of an alliance.

Compared to the tight-fisted, bumbling Americans, the communists were beginning to look rather brilliant. They were winning not only in Vietnam, but in Laos and Cambodia, too. Communism appeared to be the wave of the future.

They were making stunning advances in Burma, too, where the old Kachin leader Captain Naw Seng suddenly resurfaced. He hadn't been seen in the eighteen years since he overran Hsenwi and sent Tiger and Tzang scurrying for cover in the old stone school house. He spent the time as a "special guest" in Beijing. Now the Chinese returned him to his homeland at the head of a new force of ethnic fighters borrowed from China's People's Liberation Army (PLA).

His ranks received an immediate boost when anti-Chinese riots broke out in Burma, sparked by a failing economy and accusations of political interference. There were more than 350,000 Chinese in Burma. Thousands fled the cities into the waiting embrace of the Communist Party of Burma. Naw Seng's forces blossomed.

With the support of Marshall Lin Biao and Madame Jiang Qing, he brutally purged the old CPB leadership. Than Tun, the man who wrote to Sao in 1966, was shot dead by his own bodyguard.

More single-minded and deadly than ever before, the communists began advancing through Shan State, taking one village after another. They had everything the SSA desired: rifles, mortars, rocket launchers.

Sao wasn't swayed an inch.

"Since when did communists care anything about Shan freedom?" she asked.

So far, the majority of the War Council agreed with her. She had Tzang to back her up, perhaps the toughest and most respected SSA commander.

But some of the students started whispering: "The Mahadevi and her children are feudalist reactionaries, lackeys of the Americans, just like Naw Seng says."

After his training in Bangkok, Tzang prepared to return to the field. There was trouble at his back, he knew, and God knew what lay ahead. He told Sao of his plan to make a new general headquarters that would report directly to her, so they could circumvent her fractured War Council as necessary.

Sao found such plans and counter-plans maddening. She only wanted to do what was right. She didn't want to fight the communists or the KMT or her own War Council members or who-knows-who-else. She wanted to fight General Ne Win, the man who killed her son and husband and stole her country. After Tzang said goodbye, she felt at sea, unsure what to do with herself. Neither of them knew it would be years before they met again.

Voices in the Wilderness

In 1969 Sao boarded a passenger jet bound for Toronto, Canada with a vague plan to seek overseas support for Shan State. There was no sense going to Britain—she no longer knew anyone important there. Harn, Leun and Ying Sita had gone on before her and were already reunited with their long-lost brother, Tiger. She herself was delayed. It wasn't easy for her to gain an exit permit from Thailand. The military didn't want her to go; they relied on her for information. The Thai authorities hinted she might not be allowed back in the country if she left. She decided it was worth the risk. Maybe from Canada she could work on the Americans and gain some help for the Tai people.

Unsure when she might return, she closed up her house in Bangkok. She tucked a small antique statue of the Lord Buddha in her bag. It was a gift from the abbot of the Marble Temple.

In 1969, Bangkok was still a pleasant city, not yet congested. She had friends and a nice modern house. The stress of dealing with the Shan State Army was too much, though. The War Council members barely spoke to one another. She couldn't remember the last meeting when they'd actually accomplished anything. On the frontline, there had been a dizzying array of developments in the past year. Sao could hardly keep it all straight. It was frustrating being so far from the action. She could barely keep up with troop movements, much less provide any sort of leadership. She needed a break.

1968 had begun badly enough when her son Tzang returned to the front. The War Council gave him the task of consolidating 24,000 square miles of northern territory. As was often the case in those days, he found himself fighting not the Burma Army, but rival insurgents: this time, the Kachins.

In the midst of an operation to take the Hsenwi area, 200 of his SSA men defected to the opium trade. The following months were chaotic. The SSA 1st Brigade ended up fighting a band of fellow Tai who were allied with the Brave Young Warriors. The demoralised Shan fighters began to sneak off in twos and threes. Whole squads began asking Tzang if they could go home. The rebellion was disintegrating.

In desperation, Tzang met secretly with Sao's old helper and nephew, Saw Ohn, who had returned from his Washington post. He was now manager of the Namtu-Badwin mine. Although retired from the military, he still had some influence. However, he only made the same tired offer: give up your fight against Rangoon and join the battle against the communists as a Home Guard unit. He said this because he believed the Communist Party was their one true enemy. For the same reason, he managed to hold the Burma Army off from attacking the SSA for a time.

The Shan State Army was not the only force experiencing set-backs. Having lost the Opium War, Chang Shi-fu no longer found much profit in being a Home Guard leader. He contacted Tzang to sound out the idea of defecting to the rebels.

Somehow, the Burmese authorities got wind of Chang's potential defection. On October 17, 1969, they lured him to Taunggyi for an urgent military conference. On his arrival he was taken to military headquarters and sentenced to five years. The military police transported him to jail inside the walls of the former Mandalay Palace.

Suddenly leaderless and outlawed, Chang Shi-fu's men came to join the SSA. It was a welcome morale boost. The SSA needed the extra help. The two forces didn't get along well, though.

Chang's men were brutal and lacked empathy with the common people. They were a warlord's army and they acted like one. Meanwhile, their jailed leader Chang was placed in a special enclosure away from Mandalay jail's main cell block, where his greatest torture, apart from boredom, must have been the knowledge that the Golden Triangle was enjoying its richest year ever without him.

The trade explosion of 1969 began when Old Li managed to recruit some Hong Kong chemists to his refineries. For the first time, his labs produced No. 4, the high-grade injectable heroin favoured by foreign users. They used bicycles pumps for vacuums and bamboo for tubes but the quality was good. The brokers found a ready market among the thousands of American GIs who poured into Vietnam that year.

Through the veins of young, traumatised soldiers, the heroin spread to the U.S., where it was called China White. Groups of servicemen got into the trade; they used military freight parcels to transport the drugs to American shores. One gang sewed heroin packets into their comrades' dead bodies. It was a sad and ironic outcome to the CIA's clandestine opium flights out of the Triangle.

The beast fed itself. Old Li's No. 4 labs increased the demand for raw opium from the hill country while the farmers, displaced from their lowland fields by the endless fighting, turned increasingly to the poppy as their only means of survival.

When Tzang travelled the hill country, he saw poppies everywhere. In a few short years, annual production had risen from 60 tons to 200.

While other armies busied themselves with the border trade, Tzang and his recruits fought on alone for Shan freedom. They got into a dust-up with the KMT, who tried to establish a CIA-sponsored listening post in the middle of SSA country. Then three Burma Army divisions swept Shan State.

Tzang was on the run much of the time, attacking and then falling back in the classic pattern of guerrilla warfare. They marched 150 kilometres a month on average. It was a very tough life.

Somehow, in the midst of this, he managed to track down his old college sweetheart, Nang Nu. She was working as a schoolteacher in the south. Tzang despatched a friend to fetch her. It took some convincing, but Nang Nu agreed to meet Tzang at a jungle camp. Once she arrived, she realised it was impossible to ever go back. They were constantly on the move. At first she was wracked with homesickness but, as she became more involved with the army's political programme, she grew to love the people of the remote mountain villages, who were so trusting and eager to help the rebels. For them, they must keep fighting.

Sao never guessed that she was on a one-way journey. At first sight, she wasn't particularly impressed with Canada. She'd travelled a lot already; it was just another place on the map.

Her reunion with Tiger was delayed; he was at a mining camp in northern Quebec. The rest of the kids were at Tiger's rented townhouse in Willowdale, a Toronto suburb. He'd arranged for a neighbour and mining colleague to take care of them.

When Tiger finally arrived, Sao could hardly believe her eyes. He was thirty-one years old, a grown man. Since they parted in England, he'd been all over the world. He worked his way through university by taking summer jobs as a farm hand in Denmark. In 1964, he received his bachelor's degree from the University of Keale, with a double major in geology and political institutions. Then he took a diamond exploration job in the Ivory Coast. In 1966, he was given the choice of an assignment in Australia or Canada. Thinking the cool Canadian climate would be a nice change, he signed on with the Hudson Bay Smelting and Mining Company in Flin Flon.

Through all the years and all his travels, he'd waited for word from his family, ready to help if they needed to escape.

His family connection restored, Tiger was eager to help the cause. He and Sao drafted letters to newspaper editors and politicians about the sorry situation in Burma. Ying Sita helped with the letter-writing, too. Nothing came of their efforts. They waited, then tried again. Still nothing.

To pass the days Sao enrolled in some art classes at George Brown College, finally fulfilling her girlhood dream to continue her education.

Until now, Sao's life had been bombarded by one dramatic event after another. Tragedies, joys and adventures unfolded in rapid, continuous sequence. If she looked back on any given year, sometimes any given month, it always seemed like a life-time had passed. But in the peace and quiet of Canada, time moved at a different pace altogether. Things stayed the same, days melted into weeks, weeks into months and, inevitably, months into years. She hardly noticed.

Ying Sita took a job in New York. The rest of them moved west to Edmonton, where Tiger had a new mining assignment.

No one told Sao that she was no longer chairperson of the Shan State War Council back in Thailand. They didn't have to. She knew her place at the head of the decades-long battle for Tai freedom was coming to an end. She could only marvel that she had survived.

Back in Shan State, Tzang managed to hold the SSA together against all odds, and even to turn the tide in their favour for a while. Joining with Chang Shi-fu's army of outlaws, they ambushed military trains and launched a grenade attack on an Independence Day parade right in the middle of Lashio, the Burma Army's northern outpost.

From this point, things progressed. In the first six months of 1971, Tzang's 1st Brigade took 600 government troops out of action between Hsenwi and Lashio. Once again they were fighting the Burma Army, not the KMT or the Kachins or the Brave Young Warriors. The successful campaign restored the SSA's battered credibility. Recruits started filtering in again.

In the villages, Tzang set up self-help organisations and youth associations. His army built roads and wells and introduced basic health and hygiene programmes. They wanted to set themselves apart from the warlord armies.

A leadership school was established to train officers in military tactics, intelligence-gathering and international politics. Tzang also worked hard at reform, bringing an end to some of their cruder practices, such as executing suspected spies on the spot. During a lull in the battlefield action, he concentrated on drafting a constitution and forming a political wing, the Shan State Progress Party (SSPP). When the fighting resumed, the party held its first convention on the run, protected by a force of 600 men.

In December, Nang Nu gave birth to their first child, a boy, on a jungle riverbank. She hardly had time to recover before they were on the move again.

The SSA's situation was vastly improved. They now had 3,000 men under arms, another 9,000 volunteers in reserve, and four bases strung between the northern hills around Hsipaw and the border country south-east of Taunggyi. Their headquarters were near Kyaukme, just south of Hsipaw.

They were a well-respected and well-organised force, generally considered "clean" in comparison to the opium warlord bands. Since the Opium War, their involvement in the drug trade was comparitively minimal.

None of this helped them in their fight to regain Shan State, though. They had enough arms for only half of their volunteers, and little outside support. Weapons were expensive: US$100 to US$150 for an M16, US$ 200 to US$ 250 for a grenade launcher. They had to feed their soldiers, too, and provide medicine.

They weren't big enough or important enough to hold the attention of foreign benefactors. Their cause—Shan independence—stood outside Cold War geopolitics. To the world's military advisors, it was just a meaningless local squabble.

Meanwhile, the Communist Party of Burma continued its stunning advance through northern Burma. Under Naw Seng, they gained 15,000 square miles of territory and inflicted 20,000 Burma Army casualties. The actions of the various ethnic armies paled in comparison.

Over the years, Tzang had lost his college-student attraction to Maoism. Dogma didn't work in the villages, he observed. Ethnic movements that adopted communism quickly became subservient to Beijing or Moscow. As well, the inner workings of the CPB featured a constant cycle of purges and counter-purges. Even the great Captain Naw Seng wasn't safe. In 1971, he died of gunshot wounds sustained in a "hunting accident". But despite all the internal upheavals, Chinese sponsorship remained constant and the communist army grew in strength.

Tzang wasn't worried so much about the Communist Party's military strength, though. It was their skill in making propaganda that presented the greatest challenge. They placed relentless pressure on the SSA, cajoling and making promises to bring them to their side, using relatives and old classmates to make connections.

When Nang Nu's cousin Aung Win—leader of the ill-fated 1962 student demonstration—emerged as a top communist leader, Tzang found himself caught in an awkward position. He politely refused his new in-law's offers to help the SSA.

Partly to get away from the communists' insidious overtures, he moved the army HQ south to Mong Mai in southern Kengtung, very near the Thai border.

The geographical separation led to an ideological separation. The men who stayed at the northern base began to openly disagree with Tzang's anti-alliance line.

They thought, why not take the offered weapons? The Americans were too tight-fisted; they only gave freely to their KMT friends and didn't care about Shan State. And they were weak. They were losing in Vietnam. Communism was the future.

In the meantime, the financial pressures remained. It cost 20,000 Baht a month just for food and medicine for the Mong Mai camp. Tzang was faced with a difficult problem.

Finally, he had an idea.

The Americans were under growing public pressure to curtail the illegal drug trade. They weren't interested in the SSA as a political force. Maybe they would back them as an anti-drug force, instead.

The Last Adventure

It just might work. The U.S. was up to its eyebrows in the opium problem and anxious for a way out.

Too many of their GIs were coming home as addicts. In October, 1972, the U.S. Defence Department's chief medical officer identified 52,000 servicemen as hard drug users. In November, the Bureau of Narcotics discovered that 30 per cent of heroin entering the U.S. now came from Southeast Asia, gradually overtaking traditional Near Eastern sources. Previously, they had estimated only five to 15 per cent of the drugs originated from the Golden Triangle.

At the same time, media reports were beginning to surface about Air America's opium shipments out of the Golden Triangle. It was an embarrassment.

As a token gesture for his American friends, Old Li burned twenty-four tons of opium and declared a fresh start for the KMT under a new name, the Chinese Irregular Forces. The ploy worked. His army's status as the region's main anti-communist force was preserved.

Old Li's face-saving gesture did nothing to stop the drug trade, however. His refineries and warehouses remained open for business. He had 3,000 soldiers, 2,500 mules, two bases and thirteen settlements in northern Thailand, four bases inside Burma and annual opium sales of 200 tons.

American anti-narcotics officials could hardly go after their own government's client army. They cast around for an alternate villain and found one of Olive's boys, the moon-faced Lo Hsin Han.

Lo had done well for himself. He'd started his career with 150 men. Now he had 1,300, not a huge force but just big enough to be noticeable.

Being noticeable was his undoing: the U.S. Narcotics Bureau christened him the Opium King of the Golden Triangle. Overnight, Lo became internationally famous. Narcotics officials pushed the Thai border police for an arrest.

At the SSA headquarters, Tzang watched the developments with growing interest. He got to thinking: if the U.S. was suddenly so concerned about drug trafficking, what if the SSA promised to end the trade? Could they gain U.S. aid? The SSA just needed a dramatic gesture, like Old Li had done. But, unlike Old Li, the SSA didn't have twenty-four tons of opium to burn.

Tzang hit on an alternative. If the Americans wanted to believe that Lo Hsin Han owned all the opium in the Golden Triangle, fine. They could use Lo to reel in U.S. aid.

Tzang guessed Lo might be interested in making a deal. The so-called Opium King was backed into a very tight corner. In February, 1973, the Burmese government decided to disband the Home Guards. He was ordered to give up his men and weapons. He refused. Then he heard that his old comrade, Chang Shi-fu, was about to be released from jail. The price of his release, rumour had it, was to take down Lo. Targeted by the Americans, abandoned by the Burma Army, about to be attacked by his friend, he was doomed.

Tzang was in deep trouble, too. On April 4, he was shot at while driving his motorcycle down a Chiang Mai street. The bullet killed his chief-of-staff, who was sitting behind him. The next morning the *Bangkok Post* reported that Tzang was the real target, and that "the reason for the assassination was opium and the money it represents for Shan armies to continue their revolution." Thailand's patience with the violence-prone refugees was waning.

Thus, in a fateful convergence of mutual desperation, Tzang and Lo Hsin Han, the Opium King of the Golden Triangle, came together for one final adventure.

After a series of battles and misadventures, Lo Hsin Han and 400 followers reached the SSA's Mong Mai camp on June 29. He'd lost half of his opium, a gold bullion payment, and several men along the way. But he still had 1.5 tons of opium and five tons of morphine valued at US$ 1 billion. He was ready to give it all up if the SSA would help him gain asylum in Thailand as an anti-communist fighter.

Tzang's plan was to use Lo's name and his drugs to prove to the Americans that the SSA could eradicate the drug trade. To help gain some publicity, two British television journalists were invited to film the whole operation.

The timing was perfect. U.S. Congressman Lester Wolff was scheduled to visit in August. Congress was reportedly unhappy with Thailand's role as drug conduit; there was a possibility U.S. aid to Thailand might be cut back as a result. There was also a Senate investigation committee looking into trafficking problems in the U.S., on the heels of a scandal in which a CIA operative was caught smuggling fifty-nine pounds of opium into Chicago.

Thus, both the Thai enforcement officials and the CIA needed some public redemption, which the SSA promised to deliver.

Barely literate but not sure what else to do with himself, Lo signed the SSA's five-point proposal to the U.S.

"The SSA and its allies will attack all opium convoys which will not subject to an agreement based on these proposals," it stated.

"Because the opium trade can only flourish in a state of anarchy, and since this anarchy will never cease until the people of Shan State are allowed to have democratic elections and political self-determination, foreign organisations interested in an end to the opium trade will be expected to use their influence to persuade the Government of Burma to return to the legal Constitution of Burma," the proposal continued.

"Once Shan State has a democratically-elected government, those countries which will gain from an end to the opium trade will be expected to provide financial help for an economic and agricultural campaign to assist the people of Shan State to replace opium with other crops."

Lo's drugs were offered up at US$ 12 million, a fire-sale price. One of the TV journalists, Adrian Cowell, agreed to carry the document, along with a letter to U.S. President Richard M. Nixon, to the embassy in Bangkok.

Tzang held his breath. All of his ideals and struggles boiled down to one desperate measure: he would buy Shan State's freedom with drugs.

Everything went wrong. While they awaited an answer, the Burma Army attacked the SSA's Mong Mai camp. To escape the fighting, Lo took seventy of his men and crossed over to a Thai village near Mae Hong Son. It was his understanding that the SSA had negotiated at least temporary asylum for him.

They had—but with the wrong people.

In response to the Congress-driven clean-up, the Thai Border Patrol was under orders to stop unauthorised crossings. A few weeks earlier, a crack unit arrived in Mae Hong Son aboard four turbo-props, three belonging to the border police, the fourth to Air America. They knew nothing of asylum deals being brokered.

During a sweep of the countryside, they accidentally stumbled on Lo. The opium warlord boarded one of their helicopters willingly, believing he was being taken to a meeting with Thai officials. Instead the border patrol whisked him to their camp just north of Chiang Mai.

High-level Thai officials were surprised and embarrassed. They had no intention of prosecuting Lo, who, the Deputy-Director-General of Police noted, was not carrying any narcotics when he was arrested.

On August 3, they gave him a limousine ride to Bangkok's Don Muang International Airport, where he was handed over to Burmese authorities. With handcuffs on his wrists and a nervous smile plastered on his round face, he joined forty-one other passengers on the 6:55 a.m. Union of Burma Airways flight to Rangoon.

On September 16, journalist Adrian Cowell delivered the SSA proposal into the hands of Congressman Wolff, who dutifully reported its contents to his House Sub-committee on Narcotics, then handed the text over to the U.S. State Department. There was no response.

It no longer mattered. Tzang had lost his trump card. Accusing the SSA of betrayal, Lo's men left Mong Mai, taking the drugs with them. The SSA was left with nothing to deliver to the Americans in exchange for democracy.

Almost immediately, Lo's followers started a small war with the SSA that lasted seven months. Watching from the sidelines, Old Li was reportedly delighted, for now his ex-KMT forces had a secure monopoly on the drug trade.

Tzang had risked every ounce of his credibility and lost. His rivals within the SSA seized on the incident as proof that the "capitalist world", represented by the Americans, couldn't be trusted.

Following the disasterous Lo Hsin Han affair, the SSA accepted as a gift from the Communist Party of Burma a small 200-piece arsenal, including AK-47s, light machine guns, 60-mm mortars, B-40 rockets, recoilless rifles, ammunition, mines, explosives and grenades.

With the new weapons, they took 900 Burma Army soldiers out of action. The men needed no better proof that a communist alliance was the way to go.

Tzang hung in long enough to deliver a second opium-suppression offer to Congressman Wolff in 1975. The SSA promised to gather six tons of opium from the various ethnic armies, which would be burned in exchange for help. Wolff appeared on the American TV news magazine *60 Minutes* to talk about the deal, but that's as far as it went.

By now, Tzang was physically ill as well as politically damaged. His life-long heart condition was catching up on him. He wasn't strong enough to hold off fevers and viruses. Eventually, he ended up in hospital in Thailand, where a surgeon repaired his malformed vein and artery.

Meanwhile the SSA's political wing, the Shan State Progress Party, officially acknowledged the Communist Party as Burma's "sole proletarian party", and accepted "Marxism-Leninism and Mao Zedong Thought as its basic and guiding ideology". They were rewarded with uniforms, medicine and 1,000 additional military pieces.

In 1976, they asked Tzang to take a medical leave. As he was already on leave because of the surgery, he knew it was a message to resign. It could have been worse: later, he found out there'd been a motion to court-martial and execute him. Luckily, the motion failed.

Tzang had begun his fight full of hope and idealism. The world around him bore no resemblance to his youthful dreams. Children as young as ten begged for drug money in the streets of Chiang Mai, while opium brokers roared past in their limousines. Caravans flowed over the border, bringing 400 tons of drugs into the world that year, with more expected the following year. Thousands of poor villagers crowded the borderlands, refugees from the constant internecine warfare. After thirteen years of civil war, 25,000 ethnic rebels and 10,000 Burmese government men were dead. Ten of Tzang's colleagues had already been assassinated, and he himself could be gunned down at any moment. They were no closer to democracy in Burma, which had slid from being one of the wealthiest countries of Asia to one of the poorest and most politically isolated.

He wasn't bitter. The time had come to do something else with his life. He took a job as a loans officer in a Chiang Mai financial company. His family settled in. Nang Nu gave birth to a second child, a daughter.

One day in 1978, Tzang received a message from the would-be top dog of the Golden Triangle, Chang Shi-fu. He had been released from jail less than a month after Lo Hsin Han's arrest. One opium lord came in the front door of Mandalay jail, one went out the back. Suddenly a free man, Chang bided his time in Rangoon for a while, then made his way back to the Golden Triangle where he hoped to begin life anew as a political rebel, with Tzang's help. He'd gathered some men, christened them the Shan United Army and adopted a Tai name for himself: Khun Sa, Lord Prosperity.

Curious to meet the man in the flesh for the first time, Tzang travelled to his camp at Ban Hin Taek in northern Thailand. The obscure eight-hut Thai village was in the midst of being transformed into a comfortable villa with swimming pool, brothel and a 100-bed hospital. Tzang wasn't overly impressed. He'd seen enough petty warlords and opium money in his lifetime. He told Chang Shi-fu, aka Khun Sa, he wasn't interested in joining his revolution. He returned to his job in Chiang Mai and was still working there quietly in 1985, when his mother returned to her old stomping grounds.

Bitter Melon

Sao was accepted as a Canadian citizen. The judge, an Italian, said, "You speak English better than I do." With a passport, she was safe. She could travel abroad.

In 1980 she insisted on going to India over her family's objections. She wanted to see the old Prime Minister, U Nu, released from jail and a fellow refugee since 1968. General Ne Win had recently offered all the prominent exiles amnesty. She thought they should discuss what to do, develop a common response.

"You'll get sick," her children warned. She thought she could handle it. She was sixty-five years old, but she wasn't an invalid.

She found U Nu living with his wife, Ma Mya Yi, in Bhopal. His experiences of the past years were legion. Out of prison, he was allowed to go abroad for medical treatment. As soon as he got outside, he declared himself the true elected leader of Burma.

Dr. Gordon Seagrave's son, Stirling, and retired CIA agent William Young helped pave his way to Thailand, where he set up a government-in-exile in 1970. He was given a big compound in Bangkok with a tall radio tower. A Lebanese-American named Ahmed

Kabal funnelled US$ ten million to him through a Canadian company, Asmara Oil, promising more when U Nu reached Rangoon. U Nu thought he could do the job in one month's time. SSA rebels like Tzang, who had been in the field for a decade, thought the claim ludicrous. They chose to keep their revolutions separate.

The doubters were right. Three years later, U Nu left, beaten. Suspicious of his shadowy financiers, the Thai government burned down his field camp. He took a job teaching Buddhism at New York State University.

Now he lived as a guest of the Indian government. They gave him a house and staff, but no income. He was rather destitute when Sao arrived. He talked about travelling overland to Europe.

As predicted, Sao fell ill. She lay in bed, wracked with stomach cramps. U Nu and Ma Mya Yi took turns at her side. As a treatment, they knelt and chanted the Buddhist rosary around the clock. After several days of this, Sao rose from her bed and said goodbye. U Nu could do what he wanted.

He chose to accept the amnesty. He flew to Burma in August.

Sao went back to Canada but remained drawn to her old life. In 1985, at the age of seventy, she got on a plane bound for Thailand.

From the moment of her arrival in Chiang Mai, memories came flooding back. She walked through the markets, breathing in the familiar smells of frangipani, incense and frying chilli paste. After the dullness of Canada, the colours assaulted her senses. But nothing was truly the same.

Her old Shan State War Council colleagues were scattered here and there. Some of them had become quite rich. Jimmy Yang was nowhere to be seen. He was arrested for illegal entry to Thailand in 1974, then allowed to emigrate to France; later, he accepted the 1980 amnesty and returned to Burma.

The KMT leader Old Li was dead, and even the meddling communists had faded into the woodwork.

She stayed with Tzang, where she learned one thing hadn't changed. They were still closely watched. One day an intelligence officer came to ask her about a broad-shouldered man observed making a visit. He thought it might be Jimmy, come back to see his old crony. "No, you didn't like Jimmy, so he went back to Burma," Sao said. In fact, the visitor was one of U Nu's sons, also a strongly-built man.

As for the American agents, they had a new Opium King to chase. This time it was Khun Sa, the man she had known as Chang Shi-fu.

She was dismissive of the Tai name he'd adopted. Khun was a title of the lowest royal rank. She supposed he'd taken it because his grandfather was the Loimaw headman. The anti-communist faction of the SSA had gone over to him, because they had nowhere else to go. He had quite a lot of men and access to a healthy market: the 1985 international price for unrefined opium was US$ 500,000 a kilo. He promised to buy their cherished freedom with the drug. Always the same bargain, freedom for opium. Everything changed, everything stayed the same.

After she got back to Canada, Khun Sa sent a message asking her to join his army. She didn't give the proposition any more thought than she'd given Ne Win's amnesty offer.

One year later, Tzang joined the family in Canada, where they all did what they could to keep their cause alive.

Tiger, full of enthusiasm and high purpose, wanted to march back to the border and reclaim his family's revolution. Tzang, on the other hand, had seen a lot in the jungle, enough to conclude that politics were never so easy. They traded barbs: Tiger was "naive"; Tzang was "cynical".

Circumstances had thrown the brothers into completely different worlds: the clearly-expressed moralism of western democracy versus the dark, complicated world of the Golden Triangle. Robbed of their childhood closeness, the brothers argued a lot, but they also kept looking for ways to aid the freedom movement, never forgetting the land they'd been exiled from.

Sao never forgot, either, despite the frustrations. In Canada she was just another face in the pool of political refugees from around the world. They all had one thing in common: the belief that justice would be done if people only knew what was going on in their respective countries.

Some people helped, some people listened, but most didn't know or care where Burma was. In Canada, she had no army and no name. But at least she was her own person—not Khun Sa's, not General Ne Win's.

She had a few friends, ladies she played cards with in the senior citizen's highrise. They thought she was Chinese. It wasn't worth trying to explain differently.

Inside her little room, she lit three incense sticks daily and placed them before the black stone Buddha image. Then she would sit back and try to make sense of her life.

She wanted nothing more than to go back to Shan State. The people left behind crowded her thoughts. She wished she could find her old household staff and give them some money, not that she had any to give. She would love to slip something to the timberman who helped them on the border, as well.

She wondered about the Yawnghwe shopkeeper, Mr. Nine Paise. His sons all left for India, but he stayed behind. She heard the Italian nuns at Kalaw were ordered out of the convent. They left weeping, for they never intended to leave Shan State.

What was Yawnghwe like now? Returned travellers told her the Haw was still standing, that it was even a tourist attraction. The attendants never swept the floor, though, and they weren't allowed to say anything about her husband. The fancy court dresses they left behind were in a glass display case at the state building in Taunggyi. The state building was a museum now, too, for there was no longer a Shan government. Taunggyi hill was denuded of its thick forest.

She thought about her husband. He seemed to exist in another time. She would never know how he died. She had never wanted to marry again.

It was her destiny to leave Shan State, of this she was certain. She remembered how during the war she thought life was horrible, hardly worth living, but they got through it.

Now I know what the Buddha taught about impermanence, about Anatta, she thought.

She realised suddenly that she couldn't hate the Burmese anymore. They lived according to Anatta, too. Everyone was human, full of success one minute, down the next. They were all mortal, and even Ne Win must die one day. She wondered what would happen when he became ill. No country would take him in.

If Ne Win dies, still there are no answers, she mused. Even if he went to hell, his mind was gone. He would be punished, but he wouldn't know why.

She wondered if any punishment awaited her. She had tried all her life to do good, to help people. But she knew she had at times been petty and selfish, especially when she was young. She remembered how she and Mary Josephine gave the cold shoulder to their schoolmate, Louise. In her mind, she begged for forgiveness, even though she knew Louise was long dead. Her other school chum, Princess Van Thip, was dead, too. Sao heard she'd passed away in a meditation hut in Kengtung. Her brother Prince Hom Hpa was killed by his cancer. Lucky man, thought Sao. He never lived to see what misery was inflicted on Shan State.

She wondered, How did I manage to outlive them all—me, who took so many chances?

She wondered, too, if she ever really believed her rebel army could win back Shan State. At least we could make some trouble, she decided. Maybe that was enough.

They're good fighters, the Tai, once they make up their minds, she thought. The funny thing is, they can never make up their minds. Maybe her children would have better luck, although they often made the same mistakes as she did in her younger days: sometimes too impatient, sometimes too imperious. They had trouble getting along with each other, never mind re-forging a political movement. But maybe, as they got older, things would be easier for them.

When the winter sun slanted in through her window, beginning the long northern dusk, she rose easily, for she was still quite limber, and stepped into her tiny kitchen. There were dishes in the sink, charred pots on the burner. She'd learned to cook a little but was no housemaid. Tonight she wanted bitter melon; you could buy it in the Canadian supermarkets these days.

While she prepared the dish, she repeated the recipe in her mind, just as Uncle Ong the cook had explained it to her back in the days of Yawnghwe Haw. "When you cook bitter melon, don't stir it," he said. "Onion, garlic, eggplant, a little pork, if you like, soy sauce, oil and salt. Not too much salt. Mix it all up, put it in water and boil. But don't stir. The more your stir, the more bitter it gets."

She watched the pot boil, resisting the urge to stir.

Epiloque

In 1988, thousands of students, workers and monks throughout Burma took to the streets in sheer frustration with the regime of General Ne Win, precipitating the dictator's surprise resignation. The General had achieved the dubious distinction of being the world's longest-serving ruler. During his reign, his lifestyle and obsession with black magic became increasingly bizarre. His inner circle of sorcerers advised him, among other things, to switch the country's roads from left-hand to right-hand drive, to achieve greater political balance. His 1987 decision to de-monetise several denominations of Kyat and replace them with forty-five and ninety Kyat notes—corresponding to his personal lucky number—led to the 1988 riots.

Upon his resignation, he left his military protégés to run the country under the name State Law and Order Restoration Council (SLORC). SLORC launched a crackdown on the civilian population. Some 10,000 citizens are estimated to have been killed.

During this time, Daw Khin Kyi, the widow of slain independence leader Aung San, grew gravely ill. Her son Aung San Oo, who lived in exile in England, was not allowed to attend her bedside for fear he would create political trouble. Instead, a visa was granted to her daughter, Aung San Suu Kyi. She arrived in April, 1988, and witnessed the hopeful days of uprising and the horrible aftermath. She decided to stay on after her mother died.

Despite the crackdown, SLORC announced that a democratic election would be held May 27, 1990. Aung San Suu Kyi led the National League for Democracy (NLD) to resounding victory in the elections, even though SLORC kept her under house arrest throughout the campaign. The election was declared null and void, and Aung San Suu Kyi remained under house arrest. For her efforts she was awarded a Nobel Peace Prize. Today she continues her democratic quest under the close watch of the military regime.

Olive Yang was released from jail in 1968, but was unable to regain her former status. Her actress lover's family forbade any further contact between the two, which meant Olive never re-covered the cash and jewels she'd left in the woman's care. Today she spends her time sending petitions to the military junta, asking for Kokang statehood within their promised renewed constitution.

Her brother, Jimmy Yang, returned to Burma a year after the 1980 amnesty was declared. He died during an all-night game of Mah Jong in 1984.

Although sentenced to death by Burma's People's Court, Olive's protégé, Lo Hsin Han, was released in 1981. He returned to Kokang to start a tea plantation. He also received a timber cutting concession from the government in return for convincing some of his men to return from Thailand. He is now a wealthy businessman, with houses in Rangoon, Taunggyi and Lashio.

The alliance between the Communist Party of Burma and the Shan State Army's northern wing lasted only a few years. In August 1981 they officially broke ties, amid a CPB campaign in which people were executed for crimes such as owning a corrugated zinc roof, or owning more than one bullock cart. "They treated us like slaves in our own country," a senior SSA officer observed.

The Communist Party officially disbanded in 1989. In a development which defied all past ideologies, they then joined forces with the remnants of the anti-communist KMT, under the name United Wa State Party. The combined forces made a peace pact with the Burmese junta and, working in concert with the Burma Army, gained control of the lucrative Burma Road trade route to China.

Khun Sa, alias Chang Shi-fu, took control of the rebel Shan armies through most of the 1980s and early 1990s. Under his leadership, heroin production tripled and the opium yield rose from 750 metric tons in 1986 to more than 2,000 metric tons in 1990, sparking a worldwide resurgence in the availability and popularity of heroin. A New York grand jury indicted him on March 10, 1990, on charges of smuggling US$ 350 million of heroin into the United States. He was never arrested though, and in early 1996 he retired to a mansion on Inya Lake near the home of General Ne Win. In exchange for his "surrender" he received the right to run a private bus line between Rangoon and Taunggyi.

Sai Nyan Win, the student who helped Sao escape, was killed at a meeting at his home in 1983.

Prime Minister U Nu became a monk at the International Meditation Centre in Rangoon. He died of old age on February 14, 1995, an auspicious full-moon day.

The great monk Webu Sayadaw died on June 26, 1977 in his native village near Swebo. It is unrecorded if he finally laid down when he died.

The house at 74 Kokine Road was taken over by the military junta after one of Sao's relatives tried to donate it to a monastery. In the early 1970s, it burned to the ground, reportedly because of faulty wiring. It has been replaced by a housing complex for foreign embassy staff; most of it remains vacant due to shoddy construction.

The President's House was destroyed by the junta. It was said General Ne Win ordered the destruction because the place was bad luck.

Sao Hearn Hkam, the subject of this book, now lives with close family members on Canada's west coast. She still dreams of someday returning to Shan State, if democracy is restored.

In 1964, the Prince's other wives and children were ordered to vacate Yawnghwe Haw within twenty-four hours. The place is now a rather derelict museum. Sao's photo is noticeably absent from the display; the Prince's first wife is instead identified as the last Mahadevi of Yawnghwe. Most of their royal regalia and other family heirlooms were "lost" by the authorities.

The Prince's other wives, Daw Nyunt May and Daw Mya Win, are still living. His heir, Prince Sai, died peacefully of old age in 1998.

Sao's surviving children remain active leaders of the Shan freedom movement. Tiger Yawnghwe leads a Canadian-based support group, Burma Watch International. Tzang Yawnghwe, now a doctor of political studies, regularly writes and lectures about the situation in Burma. He also travels to the border to help refugees study democratic political systems. Harn Yawnghwe staffs the foreign liaison office of the National Coalition Government of the Union of Burma—Burma's government-in-exile—in Brussels, Belgium. Ying Sita and Leun are also active democracy supporters.

The military junta remains in power in Burma. In late 1997, they renamed themselves the State Peace and Development Council.

Thousands of refugees from Shan State remain on the Thai border amid appalling conditions of political violence, poverty and disease, but also amid continuing hope and a vibrant culture of resistance. Readers wishing to assist them may make donations to:

The Shan Human Rights Foundation
PO Box 201
Phrasing PO
Chiang Mai 50200
Thailand
http://www.shanland.org/shrf

As for Burma, someday it will be free.

Author's Notes

I was vastly unprepared for my first encounter with the people of Shan State, Burma. On a July afternoon in 1990, my husband Don and I were in the midst of packing up our one-room Bangkok apartment. We had just finished our work in Thailand: he at a refugee camp, me at the *Bangkok Post*, where I interned under the sponsorship of Ottawa's International Development Research Centre (IDRC). We both loved our jobs; it was an exciting time in our lives. But as we sorted through our belongings, which amounted to a few clothes and books and a lot of files, I assumed the adventure was over. When the phone rang, our apartment already had the echo of an empty room.

It was Sornchai Nokeplub, my morning news editor, a great guy to work for and a fantastic reporter. On my last week at the *Post*, I noticed his desk was empty. "He's gone to see Khun Sa," someone told me.

I was impressed. General Khun Sa was a Golden Triangle drug lord, the biggest and toughest of all of them, the one the American drug enforcement officials called the Prince of Death.

But a skirmish broke out between Khun Sa's men and another armed group (there were many in the area), so Sornchai returned to Bangkok empty-handed.

Now it was my turn. That morning, he'd received a message from the border: "The way is clear." But as luck would have it, all hands were needed in Bangkok, where the Thai government was about to face a non-confidence motion. So could I do the interview with Khun Sa? It took me a minute to realise what he was asking. I paused, looking around my apartment: half-packed bags, plane tickets on the dresser, husband happily sorting through papers. I asked if I could think about it and let him know.

"Okay, two minutes," Sornchai said.

I took less than two minutes. I phoned back: Okay, I'll do it.

The sum total of what I knew about General Khun Sa: he was reportedly top dog in the opium trade, a U.S. prosecutor indicted him for drug trafficking that May, and many Thais regarded him with a little admiration, a sort of modern-day Robin Hood, an attitude I found somewhat baffling.

On the heels of the indictment, Khun Sa wanted to tell his side of the story, and not for the first time. The general was a bit of a media hound. Over the years, at least a dozen reporters made their way into his territory. It was a kind of rite of passage for journalists in the region. Each one wrote as if only he had found the opium lord's secret lair, after enduring many hair-raising experiences. Like climbing a mountain, you needed the right preparation, the proper boots, a pharmacy of snake-bite remedies, the local contacts to pave your way—and you had to be especially intrepid and fearless. Interviewing the Prince of Death was quite a macho undertaking.

As for myself, I stumbled into it. The plane left at 5:00 p.m. I had to go immediately to the *Bangkok Post* office to collect the ticket, and from there to the airport. There was barely enough time. I grabbed a plastic shopping bag and stuffed it with the following items: my tape recorder, some batteries, two notebooks, two pens, a toothbrush (no toothpaste, I realised, after it was much too late), a skirt for the interview, and a rumpled windbreaker. Then I dug out a pair of broken-down leather loafers, thinking they were somehow more sturdy than my sandals, and ran out the door.

In those days, the *Bangkok Post* was housed on a re-made main floor of a parking garage. The walls and cement pillars had a coat of white paint, but it still looked like a parking garage, a big, open, messy space of ringing phones and overflowing desks. I was always worried the several storeys of cars parked above our heads would fall down on us. One night there was a horrible crash and I was certain we were all dead, but it was just a sub-editor going berserk. Working there was never dull.

The person who held us all together was Pichai Chuensuksawadi, then the newsroom boss but nowadays, editor of the entire paper. When I arrived, he was sitting in his spot at the head of a U of desks, grinning. It was he who suggested to Sornchai that I be the replacement reporter, after my last official day of work, just like it was he who sent me off to a press conference before my first official day of work, when the paper's Managing Editor wanted me to learn about copy-editing instead.

Later, I learned that after I'd been gone a few days and no one had heard from me, Pichai and Sornchai began to think they'd made a big mistake: they'd sent a green intern, carrying a plastic shopping bag, off to sneak illegally across a border which featured landmines, warring armies and bandits. Whoops.

At the time, though, it all seemed easy. I was to meet up with *Post* photographer-reporter Subin Kheunkaew in Chiang Mai, then fly to Mae Hong Son, near the Burma border. Then, Pichai explained, we would join a Japanese TV crew and take a truck down one of Khun Sa's well-built roads. Simple, not really dangerous at all.

When we arrived at the little border village, though, there was no Japanese TV crew, no truck and, more significantly, no road. We sat alone in the courtyard of someone's house watching peppers dry in the sun until finally, around 4:00 p.m., two teenage boys showed up with a string of pack mules and two saddled ponies—our guides.

We left too late. Darkness fell before we climbed the first hill. Then the rain set in. The ponies bogged down to their knees. My old loafers turned into sodden pancakes; I was afraid to move my feet at all in the stirrups in case they fell off into the darkness—and it was really dark. As the hours passed, my legs ossified. I thought forlornly about the windbreaker in my shopping bag, which was trussed to a pack mule underneath god-knew-what contraband. At some point in the night, one of the teenagers cut a head-hole in a garbage bag with his long knife and handed it to me. The knives were the only weapons they had, just enough to kill us, not enough to stave off a bandit attack.

We arrived safely and the interview with Khun Sa went well, perhaps precisely because I was so unprepared. I asked him questions out of sheer curiosity. What was it like to be an opium lord? What did he do with his days? I also asked him a lot about the Burmese elections, conducted two months earlier, on May 27, in response to the mass protests of 1988. On polling day, photos flooded the newsroom: people smiling, waving at the camera, arms raised in victory. It was a Burma we'd never seen before. Aung San Suu Kyi's National League for Democracy (NLD) won a brilliant victory.

Khun Sa, as it turned out, didn't much care. Burma was for the Burmese, he said. His land, Shan State, was different. They were fighting for Shan freedom. Opium merely paid the way. He added that there were Shan refugees around the world, including some in Canada—members of the old royal families. I should talk to them someday, if I wanted the whole story.

I did, I did, not because of opium poppies and rocket launchers and private militias and all that other macho stuff, but because I wanted to find out more about the people of this land, who drifted through Khun Sa's base camp, ill, impoverished, beaten down, scared, seeking refuge. Children joined his army; women waited for their men to return from the front. They could be attacked at any time; Khun Sa's enemies wouldn't care who got in the way.

How did they end up in such a mess? Why did they turn to a warlord with a vicious reputation for deliverance? They seemed willing to cut a deal with any devil to get their country back.

When I got back to Canada, after a while—not right away —I did an article for Saturday Night magazine about Khun Sa and the drugs trade. There was a Canadian angle: a sudden explosion of cheap, high grade heroin on the streets of Vancouver. I was fortunate that my editor at the time, Anne Collins, understood and indeed encouraged my way of thinking: a butterfly flaps its wings in Burma, an addict dies in Vancouver. She gave me free rein to relate the drug problem to conditions in the source country, conditions which, I discovered, had been steadily worsening since a military coup of 1962.

There was hope for Burma, though, in the person of Aung San Suu Kyi, who was under house arrest in Rangoon. After she received the 1991 Nobel Prize for Peace, Canadian radio host Peter Gzowski interviewed a dissident living in Canada. While driving to an appointment, I caught the tail end of the interview on my car radio. During the conversation, Gzowski mentioned that his guest was a Shan prince. I remembered Khun Sa's mention of Shan royalty living in Canada. I still have the envelope I scribbled the man's name on: "Tiger Yonway", spelled wrong.

When I found Tiger, one of the first things he said to me was, "You have to meet my mother."

We went for ice-cream together, even though it was a cold afternoon. Sao Yawnghwe had recently suffered a stroke and her speech was laboured. It was hard work following what she had to say, especially with the unfamiliar names and places she talked about. But I began to pull together the threads of a story, her story, which was also the story of Burma, Shan State, the Golden Triangle, colonialism, Southeast Asia in the turbulent Sixties, nationalism, feudalism, you name it. She skipped through the names of history as if they were casual acquaintances (which they were) from the halls of power—Nehru, Gandhi, Mao, Mountbatten—to the hills of the Golden Triangle—Jimmy Yang, Lo Hsin Han, Khun Sa.

The resulting story, "A Life in the Drug Trade", appeared in *Saturday Night*'s December, 1993 issue. It was about Khun Sa, but Sao, as she asked me to call her, took centre stage. Readers seemed interested in the arcane, mysterious world of the Golden Triangle. That spring, the article was nominated for awards from the Canadian Association of Journalists and from the National Magazine Awards Foundation.

It was Anne Collins, my mentor and teacher, who said, "Where's the book? I'm dying to read it."

Some days I thanked her for the suggestion, but most days I cursed her. It wasn't an easy topic to tackle for a first book. I spent many hours in Sao's apartment slowly absorbing the essence of Burma: the names, places and events that at first seemed completely incomprehensible. Luckily, her speech and memory recovered well from the stroke. I marvelled at the designs of fate. In the middle of the Canadian prairie—as far removed as one could be from the scene of the action—a woman who wants to tell her story meets a writer who has, by fluke, visited her far-distant, off-limits homeland. I often thought about the things that brought us together: a phone ringing, a radio conversation overheard, that's it.

I was fortunate to receive the support of the Canada Council and the Saskatchewan Arts Board, even though writing about another country is considered a radical act in Canada. We usually let our American neighbours interpret the outside world for us. In my home province, both a back-bench opposition legislator and a newspaper columnist very publicly condemned my project: a book about Burma? How ridiculous! It was a disappointing reaction, especially because just fifty years ago many Canadian pilots and soldiers died fighting for Burma's freedom. Their bodies rest in Burmese soil, and that alone provides us with an intimate connection to Burma and an interest in its future well-being. I was angry, too, because despite Sao's Canadian citizenship, she was still apparently seen as one of those "other" Canadians whose story wasn't worth telling. If she'd been, say, a Scottish pioneer named Mary McSomething, the reaction would no doubt have been completely accepting.

Thankfully, the infamously insular Canadian viewpoint is a dying institution, and many others with broader vision offered words of encouragement. In particular, Myrna Kostash, who looks toward Eastern Europe in her excellent books, convinced me the story had value and must be told. Khun Priyarat Ma-in of the books department of the *Bangkok Post* came to the fore, too, with an offer to publish. My husband, of course, was a constant help. He spent hours combing through libraries and archives, transcribing tapes, copying photos and sticking to my side along the mountainous tracks of Shan State.

Sao's story led me back to her homeland. There, many people aided me and gifted me with their memories. It is my dream that someday, when Burma is free, I will be able to thank them publicly, too.

Somehow, in the middle of this, Don and I had a beautiful baby boy. As I work, he shows me his toys and tells me new words, a sweet reminder that writing a book is not such a great accomplishment.

List of Sources

Culture, Geography and Early History

Anonymous. *Yawnghwe*. Unpublished manuscript. circa 1940.

Aung, Pearl and P. Aung Khin. *Pearl of the East: A Guide to Burma and its People*. Rangoon. Pearl Publishers. 1961.

Bischoff, Roger, translator. *Selected Discourses of Webu Sayadaw*. Dhamma Text Series 3. Trowbridge, UK. Roger Bischoff. 1992.

Brant, Charles S. "Annex A. The Shans." Subcontractor's Monograph HRAF-37. NYU-2. *Burma*. Vol. II. New Haven. Human Relations Area Files Inc. 1956.

Leach, E.R. *Political Systems of Highland Burma: A Study of Kachin Social Structure*. Boston. Beacon Press. 1954.

Lebar, Frank M., et. al. *Ethnic Groups of Mainland Southeast Asia*. New Haven. Human Relations Area Files Press. 1964.

Mi Mi Khaing. *Burmese Family.* Bloomington. Indiana University Press. 1962.

Nath, Dewan Mohinder. "Botanical Survey of the Southern Shan States. With a note on the vegetation of Inle Lake". *Burma Research Society Fiftieth Anniversary Publications No.1*, some of the papers presented at the Fiftieth Anniversary Conference, Rangoon, 1961. Rangoon. Burma Research Society. 1961.

Spate, O.H.K. *Burma Setting.* Burma Pamphlets No.2. London. Longmans, Green and Co., Ltd. 1943.

Stevens, H.N.C. *The Hill Peoples of Burma.* Burma Pamphlets No.6. London, Longmans, Green and Co., Ltd. 1944.

Yawnghwe, Tiger. *Shan (Tai Ahom) Kings of Assam (Asom, Ahom) 1228-1821 C.E.* Unpublished manuscript. 1998.

Yape Hpa, Sao. *Hsenwi Chronicle*, Translation and compilation. Unpublished manuscript. nd.

Colonial Period

Collis, Maurice. *Lords of the Sunset: A Tour in the Shan States.* London. Faber and Faber. 1938.

Crosthwaite, Charles, Sir. *The Pacification of Burma.* 2nd ed. London. Frank Cass and Co., Ltd. 1968. First edition published 1912.

Damrong Rajanubhab, H.R.H. Prince. *Journey Through Burma in 1936.* English ed. Bangkok. River Books. 1991.

Enriquez, C.M., Cpt. *A Burmese Loneliness: A Tale of Travel in Burma, the Southern Shan States and Kengtung.* Calcutta. Thacker, Spink and Co. 1918.

Greary, Grattan. *Burma, After the Conquest, Viewed in its Political, Social and Commercial Aspects from Mandalay.* London. Sampson, Low, Marston, Searle and Rivington. 1886.

Harvey, G.E. *British Rule in Burma: 1824-1942.* London. Faber and Faber. 1946.

Hendershot, Clarence. *Pacification and Administration of the Shan States by the British, 1896-1897.* Typed manuscript, 272 p. Library of Congress Microfilm 11002.

Ireland, Alleyne. *The Province of Burma. A Report Prepared on Behalf of the University of Chicago.* Vols. I and II. Boston and New York. Houghton, Mifflin and Co. 1907.

Khin Gyi, Saw. *History of the Cis-Salween Shan States (1886-1900),* Ph.D. Thesis. University of Wisconsin. 1962.

Nisbet, John. *Burma Under British Rule—And Before.* Vols I and II. Westminster. Archibald Constable and Co., Ltd. 1901.

Saimong Mangrai, Sao. *The Shan States and the British Annexation.* Ithaca, NY. Cornell University. Southeast Asia Program. Data Paper No. 57. July 1965.

Scott, James George, Sir. *Burma and Beyond.* London, Grayson and Grayson. 1932.

World War II

Allen, Louis. *Burma: The Longest War 1941-45.* London. J.M. Dent and Sons. 1984.

Beldon, Jack. *Retreat With Stilwell.* Garden City, NY. Blue Ribbon Books. 1944.

Chan, Won-loy. *Burma: The Untold Story.* Novato CA. Presidio Press. 1986.

Churchill, Winston S. *The Second World War: Closing the Ring.* Cambridge. Riverside Press. 1951.

———*The Second World War: Triumph and Tragedy.* ibid. 1953.

Khin, U. (recorded by). *U Hla Pe's Narrative of the Japanese Occupation of Burma*. Cornell University. Southeast Asia Program. Data Paper No.41. March 1961.

Matsumura, Kihei. "Suffer, Suffer, Then Die". *Cries for Peace: Experiences of Japanese Victims of World War II*. Tokyo. Japan Times Ltd. 1978.

Mercer, Derrick, ed. *Chronicle of the Second World War*. UK. Longman Group UK Ltd. 1990.

Milberry, Larry and Hugh A. Halliday. *The Royal Canadian Air Force at War 1939-1945*. Toronto, CANAV Books, 1990.

Toland, John. *The Rising Sun: The Decline and Fall of the Japanese Empire, 1936-1945*. NY. Random House. 1970.

Weinberg, Gerhard L. *A World at Arms: A Global History of World War II*. Cambridge. Cambridge Univ. Press. 1994.

Post-War

Furnivall, J.S. *The Governance of Modern Burma*. 2nd. ed. Reprint, 1961. NY. Institute of Pacific Relations. 1960.

Maung Maung. *A Trial in Burma: The Assassination of Aung San*. The Hague. Martinus Nijhoff. 1962.

Maung Maung Gyi. *Burmese Political Values: The Socio-Political Roots of Authoritarianism*. NY. Praeger Publishers. 1983.

———"Foreign Policy of Burma since 1962: Nagative Nationalism for Group Survival". *Military Rule in Burma Since 1962*. F.K. Lehman, ed. Hong Kong. Maruzen Asia. 1981. pp. 9-28.

McEnery, John H. *Epilogue in Burma 1945-48: the Military Dimension of British Withdrawal*. Turnbridge Wells, Kent. Spellmount Ltd. 1990.

O'Brien, Harriet. *Forgotten Land: A Rediscovery of Burma*. London. Michael Joseph Ltd. 1991.

Pye, Lucien W. *Politics, Personality and Nation Building: Burma's Search for Indentity*. Mass. MIT. 1962.

Sesser, Stan. *The Lands of Charm and Cruelty: Travels in Southeast Asia*. New York. Alfred A. Knopf. 1993.

Silverstein, Joseph. *Independent Burma at Forty Years: Six Assessments*. Ithaca, NY. Cornell University. Southeast Asia Program. 1989.

———— "Minority Problems in Burma since 1962". *Military Rule in Burma since 1962*. F.K. Lehman, ed. Hong Kong. Maruzen Asia. 1981. pp. 51-58.

Singh, Balawant. *Independence and Democracy in Burma, 1945-1952: The Turbulent Years*. Mich. University of Michigan Centre for Southeast Asian Studies. 1993.

Smith, R.B. and A.J. Stockwell, eds. *British Policy and the Transfer of Power in Asia: Documentary Perspectives*. Papers from a Symposium at the India Office, Library and Records Division of the British Library, September 1985. London. University of London. 1985.

Somit, Albert and Jane Welsh. "Annex A. The Constitution and Government of Burma". Subcontractor's Monograph HRAF-37, NYU-2. *Burma*. Vol II. New Haven. Human Relations Area Files Inc. 1956.

Taylor, Robert H. *Foreign and Domestic Consequences of the KMT Intervention in Burma*. Ithaca, NY. Cornell University. Southeast Asia Program. Data Paper No. 93. 1973.

————*The State in Burma*. London. C. Hurst and Co. (Publishers) Ltd. 1987.

Thompson, John Seabury. "A Second Chance for Burma: The Interim Government and the 1960 Elections". Supplement. *The Governance of Modern Burma*. 2nd ed. reprint 1961. J.S. Furnivall. NY. Institute of Pacific Relations. 1960.

Tinker, Hugh. *The Union of Burma: A study of the First Years of Independence*. 4th. ed. London. Oxford University Press. 1967.

Yawnghwe, Chao-Tzang. "*Burma's Aborted Transition: Rethinking the State-Society Paradigm*". Unpublished paper. November 1993.

Toomey, Rowena Yukiko Leilehua. "*A comparitive study of the coup d' état by General Sarit of Thailand and General Ne Win of Burma*". M.A. Thesis. The American University. 1969.

Political Movements

Drake, B.K. *Burma: Nationalist Movements and Independence*. Kuala Lumpur. Longman Malaysia Sdn. Herhad. 1979.

Fleischmann, Klaus, ed. *Documents on Communism in Burma 1945-1977*. Hamburg. Institut fur Asienkunde. 1989.

Kasem Sirisumpundh. *Emergence of the Modern National State in Burma and Thailand*. Ph.D. thesis. University of Wisconsin. 1962.

Lintner, Bertil. *Land of Jade: A Journey Through Insurgent Burma*. Edinburgh. Kiscadale Publications. 1990.

————*Outrage: Burma's Struggle for Democracy*. Hong Kong. Review Publishing Co. 1989.

People Action Committee. *An Appeal of the Mong Tai People to the World Concerning Inhumane Actions Against Them*. People Action Committee. March 13, 1987.

Shan State. Department of Information. *Historical Facts About Shan State*. Shan State Department of Information, 1986.

Smith, Martin. *Burma: Insurgency and the Politics of Ethnicity*. London. Zed Books. 1991.

Tai Revolutionary Council. *Flags and Emblems of Shan State*. Shan State. TRC. nd.

―――――*General Khun Sa: His Life and Speeches*. Shan State. TRC. Dept. of Information. August 1989.

Opium Trade

Delaney, William P. "On Capturing an Opium King: The Politics of Law Sik Han's Arrest." *Drugs and Politics*. Paul E. Rock, ed. New Brunswick, NJ. Transaction Books. 1977.

Elliott, Patricia. "How Prince of Death Sees Bright Future for Shan." *Bangkok Post*. July 29, 1990.

―――――"A Life in the Drug Trade." *Saturday Night*. December 1993.

Freemantle, Brian. *The Fix*. London. Michael Joseph. 1985.

Landon, Kenneth P. "The Politics of Opium in Thailand". *Drugs, Politics and Diplomacy: The International Connection*. Vol. II International Yearbooks of Drug Addiction and Society. Luiz R.S. Simmons and Abdul A. Said, eds. Beverly Hills. Sage Publications, Inc. 1974.

McCoy, Alfred W. *The Politics of Heroin in Southeast Asia*. New York. Harper and Row. 1972.

Schroeder, Richard C. *The Politics of Drugs: From Marijuana to Mainlining*. Washington. Congressional Quarterly Inc. 1975.

Singh, A.J. "Bumper Crop Bolsters the Prince of Death". Gemini News Service. 1990.

Tailand Revolutionary Council and Shan State United Patriotic Council. *Shan State and the Narcotic Drug Problem: A Report Presented to the Public and World Organizations on Human Rights*. Shan State. TRC and SSUP. Dept. of Information. Oct. 1986.

Yang, Bo. *Golden Triangle: Frontier and Wilderness*. Hong Kong. Joint Publishing Co. 1987.

Biography and Memoir

Aye Saung. *Burman in the Back Row: Autobiography of a Burmese Rebel.* Hong Kong. Asia 2000 Ltd. 1989.

Ba Maw. *Breakthrough in Burma: Memoirs of a Revolution, 1939-1946.* New Haven and London. Yale University Press. 1968.

Baird-Murray, Maureen. *A World Overturned: A Burmese Childhood, 1933-1947.* New York. Interlink Books. 1998.

Butwell, Richard, *U Nu of Burma.* Stanford. Stanford University Press. 1969.

Campbell-Johnson, Alan. *Mission with Mountbatten.* 2nd. Ed. London. Robert Hale Ltd. 1952.

Churchill, Winston S. *Memoirs of the Second World War.* Cambridge. Riverside Press. 1959.

Dun, Smith. *Memoirs of The Four-Foot Colonel.* Ithaca. Cornell University. Southeast Asia Program. Data Paper No. 113. May 1980.

Gundevia, Y.D. *Outside the Archives.* Hyderabad: Orient Longman. 1984.

Mountbatten, Louis. *Time Only to Look Forward.* Speeches of Rear Admiral the Earl Mountbatten of Burma as Viceroy of India and Governor-General of the Dominion of India 1947-48. London. Nicholas Kay. 1949.

Nu, Thakin (U Nu). *Burma Under the Japanese: Pictures and Portraits.* London. MacMillan and Co., Ltd. 1954.

Sargent, Inge. *Twighlight over Burma; My Life as a Shan Princess.* Chiang Mai. Silkworm Books. 1994. c. University of Hawaii Press. 1994.

Ziegler, Philp. Ed. *The Diaries of Lord Louis Mountbatten 1920-1922: Tours with the Prince of Wales.* London. Collins. 1987.

———Ed. *From Shore to Shore: The Tour Diaries of Earl Mountbatten of Burma 1953-1979*. London. Collins. 1989.
———*Mountbatten: The Official Biography*. London. Collins. 1985.

Yawnghwe, Chao-Tzang. *The Shan of Burma: Memoirs of a Shan Exile*. Singapore. Institute for Southeast Asian Studies. 1987.

Yawnghwe, Harn. *Yawnghwe Family Tree, with Notes*. Unpublished manuscript. nd.

Yawnghwe, Tiger. *Who's Who in Alberta Biographical Submission*. Unpublished manuscript. nd.

Burma—General

Aung Chin Win. *Burma: From Monarchy to Dictatorship*. Bloomington. Eastern Press. 1994.

Bixler, Norma. *Burma: A Profile*. New York. Praeger Publishers. 1971.

Hall, D.G.E. Burma. 3rd. ed. London. Hutchison and Co. 1960.

Maung Htin Aung. *A History of Burma*. NY. Columbia Univeristy Press. 1967.

Woodman, Dorothy. *The Making of Burma*. London. The Cresset Press. 1962.

Trager, Frank N. *Burma: From Kingdom to Republic: A Historical and Political Analysis*. NY. Frederick A. Praeger Inc. 1966.

Southeast Asia

Allen, Richard. *A Short Introduction to the History and Politics of Southeast Asia*. NY. Oxford University Press. 1970.

Cady, John F. *Southeast Asia: Its Historical Development*. Toronto. McGraw Hill. 1964.

Dobby, E.H.G. *Southeast Asia*. 11th ed. London. University of London Press. 1973.

Fifield, Russel H. *The Diplomacy of Southeast Asia: 1945-1958*. New York. Harper and Brothers, 1958.

Fisher, Charles A. *South-East Asia: A Social, Economic and Political Geography*. London. 1964.

Mayerchuk, Patrick M. *East Asia and the Western Pacific 1993*. 26th. annual ed. Washington. Stryker-Post Publications. 1993.

Related and General Histories

Akbar, M.J. *Nehru: the Making of India*. London. Viking. 1968.

Fairbank, John K. and Albert Feuerwerker, eds. *Republican China 1912-1949*. Part 2. The Cambridge History of China Vol. 13. Cambridge. Cambridge University Press. 1986.

Fraser, Robert, ed. *Keesing's Contemporary Archives*. London. Keesing's Publications (Longman Group Ltd.). Vol. XXII, 1976. Vol. XXVI, 1980.

Macadam, Ivison, ed. *The Annual Register of World Events*. (serial) 1954, 1958, 1959, 1961, 1962, 1972.

Government Documents and Publications

Allied Forces

Combined Chiefs of Staff. Reports of Conclusions Reached by Combined Chiefs of Staff, Quebec. August 24, 1943. In *World War II Policy and Strategy, Selected Documents with Commentary*. Hans-Adolf Jacobsen and Arthur L. Smith, Jr. Oxford. Clio Books. 1979.

Burma

Director of Information. *Burma Handbook*. Rangoon. Director of Information. 1959.

Government of the Union of Burma. Dept. of Information and Broadcasting. *Burma Independence Celebrations*. Burma Information Independence Celebration Number. Burma. The Superintendent, Government Printing and Stationary. 1948.

Burma Secretariat, the. *The Shan States Manual (corrected up to the 1s.t August 1925)*. Rangoon. Government Printing and Stationary. 1925.

Military Administration, the . Doc.52. The Military Administration Order, No.3 re. The Shan States. In *Burma: Japanese Military Administration, Selected Documents, 1941-1945*. Frank N. Trager. Philadelphia. University of Pennsylvania Press. 1971.

State Law and Order Restoration Council (SLORC). *The Conspiracy of Treasonous Minions Within the Myanmar Naing-Ngan and Traitorous Coherts Abroad*. Rangoon. SLORC. 1989.

Union of Burma, the. The Directorate of Information. *Burma's Freedom: Second Anniversary*. Rangoon. Directorate of Information. 1950.

<u>Great Britain</u>
Parliament. Burma Frontier Areas Committee of Enquiry, 1947. *Report Submitted to His Majesty's Government in the United Kingdom and to the Government of Burma*. London. His Majesty's Stationery Office. June 1947.

Parliament. Government of Burma Act 1935. *Report by Sir Laurie Hammond, K.C.S.I., C.B.E. on the Delineation of Constituencies in Burma and Connected Matters*. London. His Majesty's Stationery Office. 1936.

<u>Japan</u>
Foreign Ministry. "General outline for hastening the conclusion of war against the United States, Great Britain, Netherlands, and the Chungking Regime". Nov. 12, 1941. In *World War II Policy and Strategy, Selected Documents with Commentary*. Hans-Adolf Jacobsen and Arthur L. Smith, Jr. Oxford. Clio Books. 1979.

Liaison Conference Division. "Japan's policies for November 1941". Nov. 13, 1941. in Jacobsen and Smith. *ibid*.

<u>United States</u>
Bunge, Frederica M. *Burma: A Country Study*. The American University, Foreign Area Studies. Research completed March 1983. U.S. Government as represented by the Army. 1983.

Department of State. Bureau of Public Affairs. "Background Notes: Burma, February 1989". Washington. Bureau of Public Affairs Office of Public Communication. Feb. 1989.

Memorandum by General Stilwell's Political Advisor (Davies), Cairo, November 1943. "The China and South East Asian Theatres: Some Political Considerations". In *World War II Policy and Strategy, Selected Documents with Commentary*. Hans-Adolf Jacobsen and Arthur L. Smith, Jr. Oxford. Clio Books. 1979. pp. 288-9.

"United States note to Japan, Nov.26, 1941. Oral". *ibid*. p. 171.

White House. Press communiqué. Dec.1,1943. *ibid*. p. 289.

Periodicals
The Bangkok Post. 1969-1995.
The Bangkok Post. Sunday Magazine. 1973.
The Bangkok World. 1969-1975.
Burma Alert. 1996-1998.
Burma Links. 1996-1998.
The Irrawady. 1996.
The New York Times. 1930.

READ MORE IN POST BOOKS

For complete information about books available from Post Books and how to order them, write to us or visit our website at the following address:
Post Books, The Post Publishing Plc. 136 Na Ranong Road,
off Sunthorn Kosa Road, Klong Toey, Bangkok 10110, Thailand.
Tel: (662) 240-3700 ext. 1691-2 Fax: (662) 671-9698
e-mail: postbooks@bangkokpost.co.th
http: //www.bangkokpost.net/postbooks

Softcover:

One Step at a Time: Buddhist Meditation for Absolute Beginners
Phra Perter Pannapadipo
5" x 7" — 178 pp. — 1998
Written with an objective of making meditation more accessible to those who do not have easy access to a guide or an instructor, this book presents Buddhist meditation in a very straightforward and practical way while offering basic guidance frequently overlooked by even very knowledgeable instructors or authors. A good start for those who are looking for nothing more than peace of mind.

Phra Farang: An English Monk in Thailand   Phra Peter Pannapadipo
5" x 7" — 242 pp. — 1999 — 3rd printing
An English Buddhist monk describes his experiences in an unfamiliar culture in a lively and gripping style. Readers will find the author's treatment of Dhamma easy-to-understand, his soul-searching moments touching and thought-provoking. But it is the author's remarkable sense of humour that sets this book apart from most others on similar subject.

Thai Ways   Denis Segaller
5" x 7" — 248 pp. — 1998 — 6th printing
An informative and enjoyable book which articulates very succinctly much that is Thai in custom and tradition. It plays a significant part in encouraging the non-Thai as well as Thai readers to better understand and appreciate the intricacies that comprise Thailand.

More Thai Ways   Denis Segaller
5" x 7" — 248 pp. — 1998 — 4th printing
A sequel to the best-selling Thai Ways. The book covers a host of subjects from ceremonies, customs, to Thai language, legendary animals, sheding light into the fascinating background of the Thai ways of life.

Three Decades of Asian Travel and Adventure Harold Stephens
5" x 8" — 232 pp. — 1991
A collection of stories by a tenacious adventure and well-known author who scoured the roughest mountain peaks, trekked the densest jungles and explored the most dangerous deep in Asian waters and related his unique experiences in pages of insightful prose that gives a vivid idea of how it was to travel off the beaten track in Asia way back then.

The Vanishing Face of Thailand: Folk Arts and Folk Culture Suthon Sukphisit
5" x 8" — 168 pp. — 1997
Published in the Bangkok Post's Outlook, this collection of feature articles shed light into Thailand's intriguing yet fast disappearing folk art and culture. It also reveals the difficult life of Thai artisans which often go unnoticed. The book is a footnote in Thailand's history of change.

Vietnam: The Ascending Dragon Allen W. Hopkins and John Hoskin
7" x 10" — 144 pp. — Fully-illus. — 1995
An ideal souvenir for travelers to Vietnam. It unveils the mystic beauty of a country hidden from the outside world for decades because of war and civil strife.

Vietnam: Reforming the State Enterprises Nguyen Tien Hung
8" x 11" — 88 pp. — 1996
Vietnam's state enterprise sector is said to have become a major road-block to the country's economic and social development. In order to sustain the success of stabilisation and to position the economy for economic take off, the author propose a change in the reform policy that is from corporatisation to privatisation.

Hardcover:

Bangkok By Design: Architectural Diversity in the City of Angels
Allen Hopkins and John Hoskin
9" x 11" — 216 pp. — Fully-illus. — 1995
Bangkok is a visually unique capital city with diverse styles of architecture. With emphasis on contemporary styles, this book traces the evolution of Bangkok's prominent buildings and captures the architectural wonders in over 100 colour plates. It also offers interesting architectural dimensions of individual buildings along with viewpoints and personal choices of Thailand's top architects.

The Mekong: A River and Its People Allen W. Hopkins and John Hoskin
9" x 12" — 232 pp. — Fully-illus. — 1995 — 2nd printing
The first book to trace the awesome journey of the mighty Mekong River from its source in the Tibetan mountains to the nine mouths of the Vietnamese Delta on the South China Sea, a distance of 4,200 km.

Menam Chao Phraya: River of Life & Legend Jock Montgomery and William Warren
12" x 13" — 252 pp. — Fully-illus. — 1999 — 2nd printing
A coffee-table book that provides vivid proof of the historical and cultural significance of the Chao Phraya River while capturing the vibrancy of contemporary life along the banks of this important waterway.

The Royal Palace of Phnom Penh and Cambodian Royal Life Julio Jeldres and Somkid Chaijitvanit
9 1/2" x 10 5/8" — 132 pp. — Fully-illus. — 1999
While Angkor Wat is famous the world over, little is known about Phnom Penh's Royal Palace. After two years of painstaking research, the author who is King Sihanouk's official biographer finally shed light into the King's ancestral home and offered glimpses into court life. The book is the first of its kind with a wealth of rare prints of royals, buildings and artefacts, some of which are from the King's private albums.

Thailand's Guiding Light (Book and CD) Bangkok Post senior journalists
9" x 12" — 180 pp. — Fully-illus. — 1996
A comprehensive account of King Bhumibol Adulyadej's roles and achievements in different areas of development. In addition to materials derived from the book, the CD features excerpts of the Royal Speeches on self-sufficiency, slide shows, video footage and Virtual Reality presentation of the Golden Jubilee Pavilion.

Thai Silk Jennifer Sharples
9" x 12" — 160 pp. — Fully-illus. — 1994
A book that weaves together the history, production and myriad of uses of Thailand's most sought-after cloth. An answer to all one may want to know about the world-renowned Thai Silk.